Magic in the Middle Ages

Third edition

How was magic practiced in medieval times? How did it relate to the diverse beliefs and practices that characterized this fascinating period? This much revised and expanded new edition of *Magic in the Middle Ages* surveys the growth and development of magic in medieval Europe. It takes into account the extensive new developments in the history of medieval magic in recent years, featuring new material on angel magic, the archaeology of magic, and the magical efficacy of words and imagination. Richard Kieckhefer shows how magic represents a crossroads in medieval life and culture, examining its relationship and relevance to religion, science, philosophy, art, literature, and politics. In surveying the different types of magic that were used, the kinds of people who practiced magic, and the reasoning behind their beliefs, Kieckhefer shows how magic served as a point of contact between the popular and elite classes, how the reality of magical beliefs is reflected in the fiction of medieval literature, and how the persecution of magic and witchcraft led to changes in the law.

Richard Kieckhefer has taught in Religious Studies and History, and is now Emeritus Professor at Northwestern University, where his work focuses on the history of late medieval religious culture and the history of magic and witchcraft, with particular focus on the late Middle Ages. His published books include *European Witch Trials: Their Foundations in Popular and Learned Culture, 1300–1500* (1976), *Repression of Heresy in Medieval Germany* (1979), *Unquiet Souls: Fourteenth-Century Saints and their Religious Milieu* (1984), *Forbidden Rites: A Necromancer's Manual of the Fifteenth Century* (1997), *Theology in Stone: Church Architecture from Byzantium to Berkeley* (2004), and *Hazards of the Dark Arts: Advice for Medieval Princes on Witchcraft and Magic* (2017).

Magic in the Middle Ages

Third edition

Richard Kieckhefer

Northwestern University, Illinois

CAMBRIDGE
UNIVERSITY PRESS

CAMBRIDGE
UNIVERSITY PRESS

University Printing House, Cambridge CB2 8BS, United Kingdom

One Liberty Plaza, 20th Floor, New York, NY 10006, USA

477 Williamstown Road, Port Melbourne, VIC 3207, Australia

314–321, 3rd Floor, Plot 3, Splendor Forum, Jasola District Centre, New Delhi – 110025, India

103 Penang Road, #05–06/07, Visioncrest Commercial, Singapore 238467

Cambridge University Press is part of the University of Cambridge.

It furthers the University's mission by disseminating knowledge in the pursuit of education, learning, and research at the highest international levels of excellence.

www.cambridge.org
Information on this title: www.cambridge.org/9781108494717
DOI: 10.1017/9781108859721

Previous editions © Cambridge University Press 1989, 2000, 2014

Third edition © Richard Kieckhefer 2022

First published 1989
Reprinted 1990, 1991, 1992, 1993, 1995, 1997
Canto edition 2000
10th printing 2010
Canto Classics edition 2014
7th printing 2019

Third edition 2022

Printed in the United Kingdom by TJ Books Limited, Padstow Cornwall

A catalogue record for this publication is available from the British Library.

ISBN 978-1-108-49471-7 Hardback
ISBN 978-1-108-79689-7 Paperback

Contents

Illustrations

Preface to the Third Edition

Since this book was first published three decades ago, our understanding of medieval magic has broadened and deepened dramatically. Numerous studies and editions have appeared. The Magic in History Series that began in 1997 and the Micrologus Library, initiated in 1998, have both contributed much new material on medieval magic. The journal *Magic, Ritual, and Witchcraft* was inaugurated in 2006. Since the mid-1990s, the University of Lausanne has been a leading center in the study of early trials for witchcraft. International conferences on medieval magic and cognate fields have occurred regularly, strengthening a sense of community among scholars from several disciplines working on magic, witchcraft, and related fields. The scholarly Societas Magica has played a role in this exchange since its founding in 1995. So far as possible, this new edition of *Magic in the Middle Ages*, while remaining recognizably the same book, tries to take into account the proliferation of material and the multiplicity of perspectives that did not yet exist in the late 1980s.

There are subfields in the history of medieval magic that give new understanding of the subject. One could list many such areas of inquiry, but they would include magic and material culture, the archaeology of magic, magic and visual culture, and the psychology of magical illusion and delusion. The connection between Christian magic and Muslim magic was already well-known thirty years ago, but recent scholarship has begun to explore more fully the links between Christian and Jewish magic. And areas of Europe that had been peripheralized – Ireland, Scandinavia, and eastern Europe – now count as part of a broader mainstream.

Surely the most important development, however, has been the rise of interest in angelic magic, and the publication of fundamentally important editions and studies on the invocation and conjuring of angels. The rise of this subfield is particularly significant because it challenges the very definition of magic. Medieval people who spoke of magic often distinguished between demonic magic (which calls on the powers of demons to achieve magical effects) and natural magic (which exploits occult or hidden powers within nature). But how does one classify angelic magic? Must one assume that angelic magic was actually demonic? Or must the conjuring of angels be excluded from the field of magic on principle, even when it closely resembles other activities that would be included? We may wish to take account of medieval definitions of magic (or anything else), because the ways our historical subjects mapped their world of experience is an important part of our historical understanding. But if their definitions do not recognize one of the most important forms of magic practiced at the time, what use were those definitions? Are we forced to recognize that their conceptual map was not fully adequate to the terrain of experience on which they traveled, because it did not recognize the territory of angelic magic? If so, are we licensed to substitute our own definitions for those of our historical subjects?

Anthropologists once gave us definitions of "magic," "religion," and "science" as distinct phenomena. Few today would persist in drawing sharp conceptual lines between magic and religion, or between magic and science. Recent work on angelic magic, however, points helpfully in a different direction, suggesting that what is at stake are two different approaches to religion. On the one hand there is religion which may delight in paradox but has little use for ambiguity: it prefers certainty and clarity about its theological and philosophical teachings, its distinction between the forces of good and those of evil, the moral principles it upholds, and the power structures with which it is allied. On the other hand there is religion that has considerable tolerance for ambiguity: such religion admits a wider range of spiritual beings, not all clearly good or manifestly evil; it may be used for harm, but then even the Psalms call down the wrath of God upon enemies; it may be used to uphold power structures, or to challenge them, or both. At times, adherents of one religion may claim that theirs is unambiguously good, while the religion of their enemies or of the people they have subjected is messy and ambiguous. But even within the same religion – certainly within medieval Christianity – both tendencies can be seen side by side. What gets called magic is often religious ritual that seems to have a strong tolerance for all these ambiguities. They can be seen with special clarity in the case of angelic magic, but once they come into focus there, they become more apparent in other forms of magic as well.

Similarly, there are different approaches to science. Some medieval sciences worked with principles and forces that could be clearly discerned and accounted for, while other sciences talked about the "occult virtues" or hidden powers in nature. But what exactly were these, and how could they be discerned? They might arise from "sympathies" or "antipathies" between one object and another, from a kind of radiation streaming down from the heavenly bodies and captured by plants and stones and talismans, or from the power of the soul itself mediated by language. Somewhat as religion could be less or more tolerant of ambiguity, so too could science, and the science that spoke about occult virtues in nature tended in the thirteenth and following centuries to be called "natural magic."

The study of medieval magic may have been a complex area of historical inquiry three decades ago, but in the meantime it has become far more so, partly because there is so much more material to take into account, but also because all these ambiguities make it as challenging a subject of inquiry now as it was then.

In view of these shifts in the field, this new edition adds an entirely new chapter (Chapter 7) on angelic magic, a new section (in Chapter 1) on the magical efficacy of words and of illusion, a new section (in Chapter 4) on the archaeology of magic, and reference to numerous recent studies and editions, which are reflected in larger or smaller revisions to the text. The original edition of the book was meant to have light annotation and to acknowledge sources partly in footnotes and partly in the list of further reading. As much as possible, this arrangement has been preserved, although the state of the field has required considerable expansion of both notes and bibliography. When I have added notes without altering the text, I have usually introduced the insertion with "See now." At several points this edition calls attention to recently published collections of articles meant as general guides to the study of magic. Of particular importance is Sophie Page and Catherine Rider's *Routledge History of Medieval Magic*, which brings together work by leading scholars from many countries and provides up-to-date introductions to texts, traditions, and themes in the history of medieval magic. Valuable in themselves, these books also serve as pointers to recent literature, and they thus provide indirect access to bibliography far beyond what can be listed here.

For this edition it is a special pleasure to acknowledge the help I have received from friends and former students, which are very much overlapping categories. As doctoral adviser or as outside examiner, I have learned as much as I have taught. Michael Bailey's work on witchcraft has led him to become our main expert on the theme of superstition. Maeve Callan has expanded our notions of how heresy and witchcraft were pursued even where they did not exist. David Collins, S.J., has brought new sophistication to the study of magic and scholasticism. Claire Fanger has worked with me as co-editor of a book series and a journal and has impressed me constantly with her judgment and dedication. Frank Klaassen is known particularly for his work on magical books, but is no less expert in the study and reproduction of magical objects. Benedek Láng's study of magical texts in central European libraries testifies well to the scholarship fostered at the Central European University. Katelyn Mesler's remarkable powers of analysis and synthesis have given her unparalleled expertise in the relationship between Jewish and Christian magic. Sophie Page has developed several new areas of study and shown how they can be brought before a broader public. She provided invaluable help for preparation of this new edition.

I am further indebted to the publisher's readers and Alison Tickner for providing invaluable feedback as I prepared this revised edition. Stephanie Pentz, too, has performed the invaluable service of double-checking the text of this book. Barbara Newman has borne with me through both the writing and the rewriting of this book. To all of them, to William Paden and Elizabeth Wade, and to others too numerous to name, I owe deep gratitude.

Preface (1989)

Some years ago I wrote a book about notions of witchcraft in late medieval Europe. My own greatest reservation about that book, after I had written it, was that it seemed artificial to discuss witchcraft in isolation from the broader context of magic in general. I thus accepted the invitation to write this present book partly as an opportunity to do what I did not do earlier: examine the full range of medieval magical beliefs and practices. In the process of research and writing I have come to realize more fully the complexity of this topic, and the need to see each of its parts in the light of the whole.

I have written for an undergraduate audience, although I hope others as well may find the book useful. In attempting to do a rounded survey I have had to synthesize a wealth of secondary literature in some areas, while for other topics there is such a dearth of usable material that I have turned mainly to manuscripts. The result is in some ways a new interpretation. I have tried, first of all, to rethink the fundamental distinction between demonic magic and natural magic. Secondly, I have tried to locate the cultural setting of the magicians (as members of various social groups) and of magic (as a cultural phenomenon related to religion and science). Especially in my presentation of necromancy I have had to tread on uncharted ground.

Nonetheless, I have of course stood on the shoulders of Lynn Thorndike and other giants. While I have provided only a minimum of notes, I trust that the notes and bibliography taken together will sufficiently indicate my indebtedness to these scholars.

My personal debts of gratitude are many. My colleague Robert Lerner and my wife and colleague Barbara Newman read the book as it progressed, provided numerous valuable suggestions about matters of detail, and helped in repeated conversation to clarify the focus of my presentation; their aid has been invaluable. I am grateful also to Robert Bartlett, Charles Burnett, Amelia J. Carr, John Leland, Virginia Leland, and Steven Williams for reading one or another version of the typescript, making helpful comments, and correcting errors. David d'Avray,

Timothy McFarland, W. F. Ryan, and students in my classes were useful sounding-boards for my ideas and sources of further insight and information. Dr. Rosemary Morris and the staff of Cambridge University Press provided expert assistance. Christine E. E. Jones of the Museum of London gave me important references, and Margaret Kieckhefer helped by providing valuable bibliography.

Librarians at several institutions aided my efforts patiently. Without listing them all, I must at least thank those at Northwestern University and the University of Chicago, the Warburg Institute, the Bodleian Library, and the libraries of Trinity College and St. John's College, Cambridge. My debt to both the British Library and the British Museum goes well beyond what the notes and the list of illustrations might suggest.

I am indebted also to the National Endowment for the Humanities, whose support for an unrelated project allowed me the opportunity to gather materials and carry out revision of this book.

Finally, I must thank T. William Heyck, without whom this book could have been written, but might not have been.

Richard Kieckhefer

Note. Translations in Chapter 2 are from the sources cited. Elsewhere translations are my own except where noted. Biblical quotations are from the Revised Standard Version, but are consistent with the Vulgate text.

1   Introduction: Magic as a Crossroads

This book will approach magic as a kind of crossroads where different pathways in medieval culture converge. First of all, it is a point of intersection between religion and science. Demonic magic invokes evil spirits and rests upon a network of religious beliefs and practices, while natural magic exploits "occult" powers within nature and is essentially a branch of medieval science. Yet demonic and natural magic are not always as distinct in fact as they seem in principle. Even when magic is clearly nondemonic it sometimes mingles elements of religion and science: a magical cure, for example, may embody both herbal lore from folk medicine and phrases of prayer from Christian ritual. Secondly, magic is an area where popular culture meets with learned culture. Popular notions of magic were taken up and interpreted by "intellectuals" – a term used here for those with philosophical or theological education – and their ideas about magic, demons, and kindred topics were in turn spread throughout the land by preachers. One of the most important tasks in cultural history is working out these lines of transmission. Thirdly, magic represents a particularly interesting crossroads between fiction and reality. The fictional literature of medieval Europe sometimes reflected the realities of medieval life, sometimes distorted them, sometimes provided escapist release from them, and sometimes held up ideals for reality to imitate. When this literature featured sorcerers, fairies, and other workers of magic, it may not have been meant or taken as totally realistic. Even so, the magic of medieval literature did resemble the magical practices of medieval life in ways that are difficult but interesting to disentangle.

In short, magic is a crossing-point where religion converges with science, popular beliefs intersect with those of the educated classes, and the conventions of fiction meet with the realities of daily life. If we stand at this crossroads we may proceed outward in any of various directions, to explore the theology, the social realities, the literature, or the politics of medieval Europe. We may pursue other paths as well, such as medieval art or music, since art sometimes depicted magical themes and music was seen as having magical powers. Because magic was condemned by both Church and state, its history leads into the thickets of legal development. Indeed, magic is worth studying largely because it serves as a starting-point for excursions into so many areas of medieval culture. Exploration of this sort can reveal the complexity and interrelatedness of different strands in that culture.

Humor and seriousness also converge in the magic of medieval Europe. Many of the recipes for magic that we will encounter in this book may strike a modern reader as amusing or frivolous, and may indeed have been written in a playful spirit, but it is seldom easy to know for sure whether a medieval audience would have been amused or shocked by such material. Some of the magic that medieval people actually employed may now seem merely inane, but the judges who sentenced magicians to death did not take it lightly.

In a further and rather different sense, magic represents a crossroads. The ideas about magic that flourished in medieval Europe came from various sources. Magical beliefs and practices from the classical culture of the Mediterranean regions mingled with beliefs and practices of Germanic and Celtic peoples from northern Europe. Later on, medieval Christians borrowed notions about magic from the Jews in their midst or from Muslims abroad. It is sometimes hard to distinguish precisely where a specific belief first arose, but to understand the overall patterns of medieval magic we must be aware of these borrowings from diverse cultures. The study of magic thus becomes an avenue toward understanding how different cultures relate to one another.

Two Case Studies

What all of this means can perhaps best be clarified by looking at two fifteenth-century manuscripts in which magic plays an important role: a book of household management from Wolfsthurn Castle in the Tyrol, and a manual of demonic magic now kept in the Bavarian State Library in Munich.

The Wolfsthurn handbook shows the place magic might hold in everyday life.[1] Its compiler was an anonymous woman or man involved in running a large estate. Perhaps he or she lived at Wolfsthurn, or came from nearby. At any rate, the book is in the vernacular language, German, rather than in Latin, and the compiler was probably a layperson rather than a priest or monk. The work reflects all the practical concerns

---

[1] Oswald von Zingerle, "Segen und Heilmittel aus einer Wolfsthurner Handschrift des xv. Jahrhunderts," *Zeitschrift für Volkskunde*, 1 (1891), 172–7, 315–24.

of a household. People on the estate were constantly prey to illness. The fields needed cultivation and protection from the elements. Rats had to be driven from the cellar. Much of the knowledge required for these tasks could be kept in one's head, but a literate householder might usefully write down some of the details to ensure that they remained fresh, and the book was a convenient place to record such information. It contains instructions for almost every aspect of running a household. It tells how to prepare leather, make soap or ink, wash clothes, and catch fish. Intermingled with such advice are medical prescriptions for human and animal disease. Claiming the authority of Aristotle and other learned men of antiquity, the compiler tells how to diagnose and treat fevers, ailments of the eyes, and other medical problems. Further added to this potpourri are prayers, blessings, and conjurations.

Medieval people who assembled this and other such manuals would never have thought of themselves as magicians, but the book at hand contains elements of what we can call magic. It recommends taking the leaves of a particular plant as a remedy for "fever of all sorts;" this in itself would count as science or as folk medicine, rather than magic. Before using these leaves, one is supposed to write certain Latin words on them to invoke the power of the Holy Trinity, and then one is to say the Lord's Prayer and other prayers over them; this in itself would count as religion. There is no scientific or religious reason, however, for repeating this procedure before sunrise on three consecutive mornings. By adding this requirement, the author enhances the power of science and religion with that of magic. Religion and magic support each other again in the treatment suggested in this book for a speck in the eye. The prescription begins with a story from the legends of the saints, and then gives an adjuration addressed to the speck itself:

[Legend:] Saint Nicasius, the holy martyr of God, had a speck in his eye, and besought that God would relieve him of it, and the Lord cured him. He prayed [again] to the Lord, that whoever bore his name upon his person would be cured of all specks, and the Lord heard him. [Adjuration:] Thus I adjure you, O speck, by the living God and the holy God, to disappear from the eyes of the servant of God N., whether you are black, red, or white. May Christ make you go away. Amen. In the name of the Father, and of the Son, and of the Holy Spirit. Amen.

The legend itself is religious, and the formula has some of the trappings of a prayer, but magic enters in with the notion that the disease itself has a kind of personality and can respond to a command. Similar to this is a cure for toothache that starts with a legend of St. Peter. The saint is suffering from a worm in his tooth. Christ sees him sitting on a rock and holding his hand to his cheek, and cures him by adjuring the worm to depart, "in the name of the Father and of the Son and of the Holy Spirit."

This healing act of Christ becomes an archetype, whose power can be invoked to heal one's own dental afflictions. In the Wolfsthurn book, however, the concrete healing procedure is not explicit. Rather, the legend is followed by a few snippets of religious vocabulary ("Ayos, ayos, ayos tetragrammaton"), and then by the unrelated counsel that a person suffering this affliction should write a mixture of Latin and nonsense ("rex, pax, nax in Cristo filio suo") on his cheek.[2]

At times, the liturgical formulas in this handbook are put to patently magical uses. For a woman with menstrual problems, the book recommends writing out the words from the mass, "By Him, and with Him, and in Him," then laying the slip of paper on the afflicted woman's head. Even more clearly magical is a remedy for epilepsy: first one puts a deerskin strap around the patient's neck while he is suffering a seizure, then one "binds" the sickness to the strap, "in the name of the Father and of the Son and of the Holy Spirit," and finally one buries the strap along with a dead man. The sickness is thus transferred from the patient to the strap, then relegated safely to the realm of the dead so it can cause no further harm in the world of the living.

The Wolfsthurn book recommends not only Christian prayers, but also apparently meaningless combinations of words or letters for their medical value. At one point it says to copy out the letters "p. N. B. C. P. X. A. O. P. I. L.," followed by the Latin for "in the name of the Father and of the Son and of the Holy Spirit." For demonic possession, the book recommends that a priest should speak into the afflicted person's ear the following jumble of Latin, garbled Greek, and gibberish:

Amara Tonta Tyra post hos firabis ficaliri Elypolis starras poly polyque lique linarras buccabor uel barton vel Titram celi massis Metumbor o priczoni Jordan Ciriacus Valentinus.

As an alternative remedy for possession, the book suggests taking three sprigs of juniper, dousing them three times with wine in honor of the Trinity, boiling them, and placing them on the possessed person's head without his knowledge.

Prescriptions containing verbal formulas usually come from Christian liturgy, but other prescriptions contain no spoken words at all and have nothing religious in them. To ward off all forms of sorcery, for example, one should carry the plant artemisia on one's person. Or to ensure keen

---

[2] *Hagios* (given here in corrupt form) is Greek for "holy;" Christian liturgy often uses it (or the Latin *sanctus*) in threefold repetition. The Tetragrammaton is the sacred Hebrew name for God, which would have been written in Hebrew without vowels: "YHWH." *Rex* means "king," *pax* means "peace," *in Cristo filio suo* means "in Christ his son," and *nax* does not mean anything.

eyesight by night as well as by day, one should anoint one's eyes with bat's blood, which presumably imparts that animal's remarkable ability to "see," even in the dark. The appeal to ancient authority might indeed seem plausible in such cases: classical writers like Pliny often referred to cures similar if not identical to what we have here. Tracing exactly where the compiler found any particular recipe, however, would be a hopeless task, leading down labyrinthine byways.

Indeed, little if anything in this compilation is altogether original; much of its material echoes ancient formulas or at least those of other medieval compilations. The cure for toothache beginning with the legend of St. Peter, for example, is a commonplace. Essentially the same formula occurs in many different manuscripts, from early medieval England and elsewhere in medieval Europe.

Not surprisingly, material of this sort could raise eyebrows. Marginal comments added to the Wolfsthurn manual in slightly later handwriting indicate that the manuscript came before disapproving eyes. One passage that gave offense was the above-mentioned cure for menstrual problems. A later reader wrote beside this prescription, "This is utterly false, superstitious, and practically heretical." Indeed, certain pages were excised from the compilation, perhaps by this same reader. Because of this censorship, some of the author's formulas are badly mutilated, such as the instructions for making oneself invisible, while others have been lost altogether. At another point, however, the book evoked skepticism rather than disapproval: a reader commented beside a particularly dubious passage, "This would be good – if it were true!"

In short, the Wolfsthurn handbook raises a series of questions regarding the history of magic: how does it relate to religion? How does it relate to science and to folk medicine? What role does the tradition of classical antiquity play in medieval magic? How and why did Christian liturgical formulas get used in magic? To what extent was magic an activity of the laypeople? To what degree did it involve the clergy, such as the priest whose aid is invoked for exorcism? How would a philosopher or theologian such as Thomas Aquinas have reacted to the magic in this book? All these questions will recur in later chapters. The point for now is merely to see how the magic of the Wolfsthurn handbook could serve as a starting-point for exploration in various directions, or as a crossroads in medieval culture.

The second manuscript raises a somewhat different set of questions.[3] Unlike the Wolfsthurn book, the Munich handbook involves

---

[3] The manuscript in question is Clm 849 (Bayerische Staatsbibliothek, Munich), fols. 3^r–108^v. For brief discussion, see Lynn Thorndike, "Imagination and magic: Force of imagination on the human body and of magic on the human mind," in *Mélanges Eugène*

straightforwardly demonic magic, or what came to be known as necromancy. Also unlike the Wolfsthurn book, the Munich manual is in Latin (though some vernacular material is appended to it), and the author and owner probably belonged to the clergy. On practically every page, this handbook gives instructions for conjuring demons with magic circles and other devices, commanding the spirits once they have appeared, or compelling them to return after they have been dismissed. The purposes served by this magic are many. It can allegedly be used to drive a person mad, to arouse passionate love, to gain favor at court, to create the illusion of a mighty castle, to obtain a horse that can carry the magician anywhere he wants to go, or to reveal future and secret things. The magic of this handbook involves elaborate paraphernalia. Apart from the magic circles, the magician needs wax images of the people he wishes to afflict, or rings, swords, and other objects. In some cases, the handbook requires that he sacrifice a hoopoe to the evil spirits,[4] or burn certain herbs so that the smoke can serve as a magical fumigation. Like the Wolfsthurn book, the Munich handbook draws from the riches of Christian liturgy, but it does so much more fully. Rather than merely borrowing short fragments and familiar prayers, the Munich handbook takes over lengthy passages from the Church's ritual, and in other cases uses new formulas clearly modeled on Christian precedent.

Other elements in the work resemble Jewish or Muslim magic. Some formulas involve magical incantation of names for God, as in Jewish magical practice, while the recitation of names for Christ is, in effect, a Christian version of the same thing. Indeed, a great deal of Jewish and Muslim magic seems to have revolved about the basic notion that by magical formulas one can compel the demons to come and do one's bidding. An important Arabic magical text, well-known in the later medieval West under the title *Picatrix*, also contains formulas similar to some in the Munich handbook. Furthermore, certain passages in the Munich manuscript presuppose at least a crude knowledge of that astrology which later medieval Western culture had taken over from Arabic sources.

The magic in this Munich handbook is often quite complex. One section, for example, tells how to obtain the love of a woman. While

Tisscrant, 7 (Vatican City: Biblioteca Vaticana, 1964), 356–8; for a full account, see Richard Kieckhefer, *Forbidden Rites: A Necromancer's Manual of the Fifteenth Century* (Stroud: Sutton, 1997; University Park: Pennsylvania State University Press, 1998).

[4] The hoopoe is an extraordinary crested bird that figures prominently in magic and in folklore generally. Ulysse Aldrovandi, in his *Ornithologia*, vol. 2 (Bologna: Nicolaus Tebaldinus, 1634), 709, exclaims that he will not record the superstitions that have arisen regarding this bird, but then he does so anyway.

reciting incantations, the magician takes the blood of a dove and uses it to draw a naked woman on the skin of a female dog. He writes the names of demons on various parts of this image, and as he does so he commands the demons to afflict those parts of the actual woman's body, so that she will be inflamed with love of him. He fumigates the image with the smoke of myrrh and saffron, all the time conjuring the demons to afflict her so that day and night she will think of nothing but him. He hangs the image around his neck, goes out to a secret place either alone or with three trustworthy companions, and with his sword traces a circle on the ground, with the names of demons all around its edge. Then he stands inside the circle and conjures the demons. They come (the handbook promises) in the form of six servants, ready to do his will. He tells them to go and fetch the woman for him without doing her any harm, and they do so. On arriving she is a bit perplexed, but willing to do as the magician wishes. As long as she is there, one of the demons takes on her form and carries on for her back at home, so that her strange departure will not be noticed.

The compiler of this manual had further mischief up his sleeve. He tells, for example, how to arouse hatred between two friends by using a complex ritual in which two stones are buried beneath the friends' thresholds, then unearthed and cast into a fire, then fumigated with sulphur, left three days in water, and smashed together. As the magician fumigates them he conjures forth "all hateful demons, malignant, invidious, and contentious," by the power of God. He demands that these demons arouse between the friends as much hatred as exists among the demons, or as much as existed between Cain and Abel. While striking the stones against each other he says, "I do not strike these stones together, but I strike X. and Y., whose names are carved here." Finally, he buries the stones separately. The handbook warns that the details of this ceremony must be kept secret because of its ineffable power. In case the magician should wish later to undo his damage, he should dig up the stones, heat them, crush them, and cast the fragments into a river.

Another section of the book tells how to become invisible. The magician goes to a field outside of town and traces a circle on the ground. He fumigates the circle, and sprinkles it and himself with holy water while reciting Psalm 51:7. He kneels down and conjures various spirits, compelling them in the name of God to come and do his bidding. The spirits suddenly appear within the circle and ask what he wants. He requests a "cloak of invisibility." One of them goes and procures such a garment, and gives it to him in exchange for his white robe. The ritual is not without its hazards: if the magician does not return to the same place three days later, retrieve his robe, and burn it, he will die within seven days.

The author of this book is not squeamish about conjuring "demons" or "evil spirits." Sometimes he invokes them by name, as Satan, Lucifer, Berich, and so forth. Even when the ceremonies do not explicitly identify the spirits who come as demonic, the intent is usually clear, and certainly no inquisitor would have thought about the question for more than a moment.

The materials in the Munich handbook, like those in the Wolfsthurn manuscript, are not entirely original. Parallels can be found in other manuscripts, from other parts of Europe, as well as in Arabic and Jewish traditions. Medieval European examples are rare, since whenever possible the inquisitors and other authorities consigned such stuff to the flames. Enough manuscripts escaped this fate, however, to give an idea of the genre.

This handbook, like the first one, raises a series of important questions: how does this magic relate to religion? (Very differently from that of the Wolfsthurn manual!) Precisely how does this material resemble that found in Jewish and Muslim magic, and how does it differ? What historical links can be established between this magic and Jewish or Muslim precedent? What sort of person was likely to own such a book? Did the owners really practice these rituals, or was it all an elaborate game or fantasy? If the owners did actually carry out such magic, how did they resemble the magicians depicted in medieval sermons, or the sorcerers in medieval romances? Once again, these are questions that will arise later in this book, and for now the point is simply to show how magic can lead to such wide-ranging inquiry.

Definitions of Magic

The most fundamental question for present purposes is how to define "magic." If a person rubs bat's blood into his eyes, is that magic, or is it a kind of primitive medical science? How can we define the border between magic and science? Even if we want to say that there are instances that lie near or on the border, it seems that we must be able to define the border itself. So too, we must be able to indicate how "magic" relates in principle to "religion," even if we want to acknowledge many cases where they resemble each other closely. Still further complications arise. Some people, for instance, would want to say that conjuring a demon merely to foretell the future is not magic, since magic involves practical manipulation of things in the world – making people ill, gaining favor at court, and so forth – rather than simply learning about predetermined states of affairs.

What would medieval Europeans have said about these questions? Most of them, perhaps, would have given them little thought. There were people who tried to use knowledge such as that in the Wolfsthurn or Munich handbooks, others who worried about it being used against them, and still others who made it their business to keep it from being used; but few of these people would have asked themselves whether the term "magic" applied to these practices. They might have said that the Wolfsthurn book contained "charms," "blessings," "adjurations," or simply "cures," without calling them specifically "magical." They might have called the Munich handbook a book of "necromancy" or "sorcery" rather than of "magic." Only the theologically and philosophically sophisticated elite bothered greatly about questions of definition. When the intellectuals attended to such matters, however, they were reflecting on contemporary practices, and often they were articulating explicitly what other people merely took for granted. By looking at theological and philosophical notions about magic, we can at least take an important step toward understanding how medieval people thought about the subject.

Broadly speaking, intellectuals in medieval Europe recognized two forms of magic: natural and demonic. Natural magic was not distinct from science, but rather a branch of science. It was the science that dealt with "occult virtues" (or hidden powers) within nature. Demonic magic was not distinct from religion, but rather a perversion of religion. It was religion that turned away from God and toward demons for their help in human affairs.

The key question was the source of power employed: demonic magic, virtually everyone in medieval Europe agreed, could work because it invoked demons; if a practitioner or observer recognized angelic magic as distinct from demonic, that person saw angels as the sources for a particular kind of magic power; officially approved religion could be effective for material as well as spiritual ends by appealing to God and other beneficent spirits; natural magic, for those who recognized that category, worked because it exploited "occult virtues" or hidden powers within nature; and ordinary science made use of manifest powers in the natural order. To be sure, not everyone recognized all these distinctions, and the boundaries may have been more often murky than clear. A manuscript might juxtapose Latin liturgical formulas and prayers with Old English charms to aid in beekeeping and to counteract theft, making no clear distinction between religious and magical, clerical and lay,

Christian and pagan or folkloric material.[5] A practitioner might be unsure in practice whether the use of a herb, along with recitation of a particular charm, was natural or demonic magic, or whether the charm was actually a kind of prayer. If the question arose what sources of power lay behind the healing efficacy of a herb or a verbal formula, people might disagree. Still, there were conceptual categories available that could be invoked: it was possible to assert and perhaps persuade others that wondrous effects could be ascribed to God (in which case, the category "religion" might seem to everyone appropriate), to demons (which would lead many to speak of "magic," or perhaps "sorcery" or "bewitchment"), or to mysterious powers within nature (which some, but not all observers would call "natural magic").

One might quickly conclude that the magic of the Wolfsthurn handbook exemplifies natural magic, and that of the Munich manuscript represents demonic magic. From the viewpoint of the practitioners, this conclusion might be essentially correct. But from the vantage point of medieval theologians, philosophers, preachers, and inquisitors, matters were not so simple. Many of these observers would have suspected demonic magic even in the Wolfsthurn book. The unintelligible words that it prescribed might contain names for demons. The use of a deerskin strap to remove a case of epilepsy might be seen as a signal or sacrifice to the demons. If artemisia had power to ward off sorcery, the knowledge of that occult power might have been imparted by demons. Whether knowingly or unknowingly, the person who used the Wolfsthurn handbook might be engaged in demonic magic. The people who went out to gather apparently innocent herbs, or the midwife who seemed blameless and helpful might turn out to be in league with demons (Fig. 1). Indeed, for many writers in medieval Europe, all magic was by definition demonic; not everyone agreed that there was such a thing as natural magic. For such writers, the material in the Wolfsthurn handbook could be called magical only because it seemed likely to rely on the aid of demons. But the term "magic" has a history, and understanding what it meant at a given time requires some knowledge of that history.

In classical antiquity, the word "magic" applied first of all to the arts of the magi, those Zoroastrian priests of Persia who were known to the Greeks at least by the fifth century B.C. Some of them seem to have migrated to the Mediterranean world. What, precisely, did these magi

---

[5] Karen Jolly, "On the margins of orthodoxy: Devotional formulas and protective prayers in Cambridge, Corpus Christi College 41," in Sarah Larratt Keefer and Rolf H. Bremmer, Jr., eds., *Signs on the Edge: Space, Text and Margins in Medieval Manuscripts* (Leuven: Peeters, 2007), 135–83.

Fig. 1. Group of woman magicians with demons, from Lydgate, *The Pilgrimage of the Life of Man*

do? Greeks and Romans generally had imprecise notions of their activities: they practiced astrology, they claimed to cure people by using elaborate but bogus ceremonies, and in general they pursued knowledge of the occult. Whatever they did, however, was by definition "the arts of the magi," or "the magical arts," or simply "magic." From the outset, the term thus had an imprecise meaning. Because the magi were foreigners with exotic skills that aroused apprehension, the term "magic" was a deeply emotional one, rich with dark connotations. Magic was something sinister, something threatening. When native Greeks and Romans engaged in practices similar to those of the magi, they too were feared for their involvement in magic. The term was extended to cover the sinister activities of occultists, whether foreign or domestic.

Early Christian writers who used the term played on these undertones. If the Greek and Roman pagans could foretell the future, or heal diseases, that was because they had help from their gods. But the gods of the pagans were no real gods; from a Christian viewpoint, they were in fact demons. Thus the thaumaturgy of Graeco-Roman paganism was unmasked as demonic magic. Even if the pagans did not realize they were using the aid of evil spirits – indeed, even if they were merely using curative herbs and amulets made from precious stones – a Christian writer such as Augustine of Hippo (A.D. 354–430) was quick to see demonic involvement. The demons took these objects as signs or tokens calling them to do their work. It was demons who had founded the magical arts and taught them to human practitioners, and it was demons who actually carried out the will of the magicians. Divination (or fortune-telling) was also possible only with the aid of demons. These are dominant themes in Augustine's classic book *On the City of God*, and Augustine's authority in medieval culture was so great that on this issue, as on many others, his outlook prevailed.

Up through the twelfth century, if you asked a theologian what magic was, you were likely to hear that demons began it and were always involved in it. You would also be likely to get a catalogue of different forms of magic, and most of the varieties would be species of divination.[6] Isidore of Seville (ca. 560–636), borrowing from classical authors such as Varro (ca. 116–ca. 27 B.C.), listed geomancy, hydromancy, aeromancy, and pyromancy (divination by earth, water, air, and fire) under the heading "magic," and then went on under the same heading to discuss divinatory observation of the flight and cries of birds, the entrails of sacrificial animals, and the positions of stars and planets (i.e. astrology). Only after cataloging these and other species of divination did he include enchantment (magical use of words), ligatures (medical use of magical objects bound to the patient), and various other phenomena in his discussion of magic. All these practices, he said, involve the art of demons, passed along to magicians by a "pestiferous alliance of humans and evil angels."[7] For centuries, writers repeated and adapted these categories in their discussion of magic. At least into the twelfth century, these categories remained standard, and writers repeated and adapted them in their discussion of magic, although no one in the high Middle Ages was still foretelling the future by inspecting the entrails of sacrificial animals. Not everyone followed Isidore to the letter: in the mid-thirteenth century, the theologian Alexander of Hales (ca. 1185–1245) used "divination" as a generic term under which he distinguished various species of occult art, including sorcery and illusion. In one way or

---

[6] Lynn Thorndike, "Some medieval conceptions of magic," *The Monist*, 25 (1915), 107–39.

[7] *The Etymologies of Isidore of Seville*, bk. 8, ch. 9, ed. and trans. Stephen A. Barney, W. J. Lewis, J. A. Beach, and Oliver Berghof (Cambridge University Press, 2006), 181–3. See now William E. Klingshirn, "Isidore of Seville's taxonomy of magicians and diviners," *Traditio*, 58 (2003), 59–90.

another, however, medieval writers tended to see magic and divination as closely related.[8]

Two major changes began to occur around the thirteenth century. First, there were writers who began to see natural magic as an alternative to the demonic form. Secondly, the term came to be used for operative functions such as healing as much as for divination. William of Auvergne (ca. 1180–1249), an influential theologian and then bishop at Paris, recognized the distinction between demonic and natural magic and devoted considerable attention to the latter sort. Albert the Great (ca. 1200–80) also acknowledged the possibility of natural magic in his scientific writings, though in his theological work he was cautious about distinguishing it from the demonic kind.[9]

Many people, to be sure, persisted in thinking of all magic as demonic and in seeing divination as a central purpose of magic. Even those who referred explicitly to occult powers (*virtutes occultae*) in nature did not always use the term "magic" in reference to them. Thomas Aquinas (ca. 1225–74) believed in occult phenomena caused by the influence of stars and planets, but tended to follow Augustine in reserving "magic" for processes involving demons. Roger Bacon (ca. 1214–ca. 1292) also believed in mysterious and awesome powers within nature, but typically used the word "magic" for various kinds of fraud and deception. During the fourteenth and fifteenth centuries, however, the notion of natural magic took firm hold in European culture, even if it was still not universally recognized or uniformly described.

When writers spoke of natural magic as dealing with the occult powers in nature, what precisely did they mean? How did occult powers differ from ordinary, manifest powers? In some cases it seems that the distinction was a subjective one: a power in nature that is little known and arouses awe is occult, unlike those well-known powers that people take for granted. *Picatrix*, for example, remarks at one point that it is dealing with matters which are "hidden from the senses, so that most people do not grasp how they happen or from what causes they arise."[10] The term had a technical sense, however, that referred not to the subjective

---

[8] This was not always true of ecclesiastical legislation, which often mentioned them separately, without giving precise definitions.

[9] Steven P. Marrone, *A History of Science, Magic and Belief: From Medieval to Early Modern Europe* (London: Palgrave, 2015), 82–126; William of Auvergne, *Universe of Creatures*, trans. Roland J. Teske (Milwaukee: Marquette University Press, 2007); Thomas B. de Mayo, *The Demonology of William of Auvergne: By Fire and Sword* (Lewiston, New York: Edwin Mellen Press, 2007).

[10] *Picatrix: The Latin Version of the* Ghāyat Al-Hakim, ed. David Pingree (London: Warburg Institute, 1986), 5.

response of the beholder, but to the objective status of the power in question. Most properties of herbs, stones, or animals can be explained in terms of their physical structure. A herb that is "cold" or "moist" can treat an illness caused by excess of "heat" or "dryness." (These are standard Aristotelian categories; a plant might be classed as "hot" or "cold" by nature, regardless of its actual temperature at a given moment.) Other properties, however, cannot be explained in these terms. The power of a plant to cure certain ailments, or the power of a gem to ward off certain kinds of misfortune, may derive not from the internal structure of the object, but from an external source: emanations coming from the stars and planets. These latter powers were technically known as occult, and natural magic was the science of such powers. The properties in question were strictly within the realm of nature, but the natural world that could account for them was a broad one: instead of examining the inner structure of a plant to determine its effects, one had to posit influences that flowed from the distant reaches of the cosmos.

Another way of thinking about the magical properties within nature was grounded in Avicenna's notion that each medical compound has a "specific form" over and above what its constitutive elements contribute. Later writers developed this notion into that of a "whole substance" which again goes beyond the powers of the individual elements in the compound. The working of the compound might still be unexplained and indeed occult, but the notion of the "whole substance" provided a way of thinking about magical effects that did not have to appeal to the influence of heavenly bodies. It was a way of thinking and talking about mysterious effects that were inherent in the material compound, but not reducible to the qualities of its constituent parts. There was something inherent in a particular stone or plant or other object that gave it magical virtues, without its needing to absorb and transmit the influence of the planets.[11]

By extension, a power might qualify as occult if it was grounded in some symbolic feature of the powerful object, rather than its internal structure alone. Plants with liver-shaped leaves might thus promote the health of the liver; or the keen sight of the vulture might cure eye ailments if it was wrapped in the skin of a wolf and hung around the patient's neck. What we have in these instances is "sympathetic magic," as James G. Frazer called it: magic that works by a "secret sympathy" or symbolic

---

[11] Isabelle Draelants, "The notion of properties: Tensions between *scientia* and *ars* in medieval natural philosophy and magic," in Sophie Page and Catherine Rider, eds., *The Routledge History of Medieval Magic* (London and New York: Routledge, 2019), 169–86.

likeness between the cause and the effect.[12] A medical scroll from around 1100 advises that the herb dracontium, so called because its leaves resemble dragons, can counteract snakebite and internal worms.[13] The reverse principle, also important for magic, is that of "antipathy." The wolf is antipathetic toward the sheep, and its antipathy is such that even a drumhead made of wolf's hide will drown out the sound made from a drumhead of sheepskin. For most writers of antiquity and the Middle Ages, sympathy and antipathy were principles of ordinary science, not magic, but writers in the later Middle Ages who worked out the concept of natural magic often included in it phenomena of this sort.

In other cases, the effect of the magical object rests on "animistic" principles: the notion that things throughout nature have spirits or personalities dwelling within them. One plant seen as having powerful magical effect was mandrake, the root of which vaguely resembles a human being planted upside-down in the ground. Because this root was thought to have a sort of personality, those who uprooted it to make use of its power feared that it would take vengeance on them. To avoid this fate, they would extract it from the ground by tying a rope around it and affixing the other end to a hungry dog, then throwing meat to the dog. The animal would pull the mandrake from the ground and would thus suffer its vengeance (Fig. 2). Symbolic thought of this sort lay behind many of the phenomena we will be dealing with in this book.

Even when such symbolic principles underlie magic, however, the intellectuals seeking to explain the occult powers in question were likely to posit stellar or planetary influence rather than principles of sympathy, antipathy, or simple animism.

To be sure, there is a way of defining magic that focuses on the intended force of an action, rather than the type of power invoked. This way of conceiving magic has its main roots in sixteenth-century religious debate and gained currency in anthropological writings of the late nineteenth and early twentieth centuries.[14] According to this approach, the central feature of religion is that it *supplicates* God or the gods, and the main characteristic of magic is that it *coerces* spiritual beings or forces. Religion treats the gods as free agents, whose good

[12] J. G. Frazer, *The Golden Bough*, 3rd edn (London: Macmillan, 1913), 54.
[13] Lucille B. Pinto, "Medical science and superstition: A report on a unique medical scroll of the eleventh–twelfth century," *Manuscripta*, 17 (1973), 12–21.
[14] William A. Lessa and Evon Z. Vogt, eds., *Reader in Comparative Religion: An Anthropological Approach*, 4th edn (New York: Harper & Row, 1979), 332–62. See now Edward Bever, "Magic and religion," in Richard M. Golden, ed., *Encyclopedia of Witchcraft: The Western Tradition*, vol. 3 (Santa Barbara: ABC-CLIO, 2006), 692–8.

Fig. 2. Extraction of mandrake, from the thirteenth-century bestiary by William the Clerk of Normandy

will must be won through submission and ongoing veneration. Magic tries to manipulate the spirits – or impersonal spiritual forces seen as flowing throughout nature – mechanically, in much the same way as one might use electricity by turning it on or off. From this perspective, the border between religion and magic becomes difficult to discern. A person who tries to coerce God by using rituals mechanically can be seen as practicing magic; indeed, sixteenth-century Protestants charged that this was precisely what Roman Catholics were doing. In recent years, even anthropologists have tended to put little stock by this pat distinction, but in the general reading public it remains so deeply entrenched that many people see it as the natural meaning of the terms.

Unfortunately, this way of distinguishing magic from religion is unhelpful in dealing with the medieval material. First of all, the sources tell us little about precisely how medieval people conceived the force of their actions. Did the user of the Wolfsthurn handbook intend to coerce God by incorporating liturgical formulas into curative rituals, or did these rituals reflect a deep (if unsophisticated) faith and piety? The handbook itself gives no clue; nor do other, similar sources. Secondly, ordinary people in medieval Europe probably did not distinguish sharply between coercion and supplication. When they used charms such as those in the Wolfsthurn book, they surely expected their efforts to have influence; sometimes this influence might be coercive, and sometimes supplicatory, but there was ample room for uncertainty about which form it would take. Prayer could be likewise ambiguous: Christ had promised to do anything that his followers requested in his name (John 14:14), and a Christian with faith would surely expect this promise to be unfailing, but the attitudes of those who invoked Christ's name could run the gamut from magical incantation at one extreme to mystical piety at the other, and simple Christians were unlikely to analyze precisely where along this spectrum their own intentions lay. Indeed, people in premodern Europe probably viewed their medicine in similarly ambivalent ways: even if a cure was tried and "proven," the force of its influence in a given case would be hard to calculate in advance. In the case of demonic magic, there is still a third reason why it is unhelpful to focus on the intended force: there were magicians who thought they could coerce demons, but only because they had previously supplicated God and obtained divine power over the demons. If we start by assuming a fundamental distinction between coercion and supplication, we will make little sense of these complexities.

Some of the cases we will examine do indeed suggest that people using magic were trying to compel demons, or the powers of nature, or God. The intent to coerce was thus one characteristic of these particular magical acts. But intentions are so ambiguous, complex, and variable that it is unhelpful to take the intended force as the crucial and defining characteristic of magic in general.

In antiquity, in medieval Europe, and today as well, "magic" is used as an umbrella term for a variety of practices, and what they have in common may be difficult to specify. They may be linked mainly by association with their users: "magic" is what the *magoi* or magicians of the ancient world used, whether or not there was any common defining feature among their practices. Or they may be thought of together because they are mutually supportive: demonic magic is linked together with natural magic because the demons themselves exploit hidden powers in nature and teach them to mortals. No matter how careful we are in our usage, a term like "magic" will inevitably have a strongly connotative character and call up associations that cannot be foreseen. It is a useful term of convenience. For rigorous analysis and comparison, more limited and precise terms (such as "spirit conjuration") are more useful.[15]

The definitions given above for natural and demonic magic will be our starting-points, then, for exploring the role of magic in medieval culture, but only starting-points. We must bear in mind the rough edges. We must also realize that these definitions came from a particular class within medieval society, those with theological and philosophical education. In using their definitions we must be careful not to let their viewpoint overshadow entirely that of their unlettered contemporaries. The problem is a familiar one. Our knowledge of medieval culture comes mainly from that small segment of the population that knew how to write, and there is no shortcut from their mental world to that of the illiterate populace. The best we can do is read the documents sensitively, with the right questions in mind. In what ways did the literate elite share or absorb the mentality of the common people? Do some writings reflect the views of ordinary people better than others? Can we accurately reconstruct popular notions from learned attacks on them? Do the definitions of magic used by the intellectuals reflect or distort popular ways of viewing things? The intellectuals have the advantage of having formulated explicit theories and definitions for us to read and adopt. The rest of society also had its ways of thinking about the world, but its views are harder to reconstruct. Popular and learned mentalities were sometimes alike and sometimes different, and to see the relationship between them we must read the evidence carefully, case by case.

Definitions are ways of helping to see and make sense of the world – but they can also become ways of misunderstanding. If you are committed to the notion that all magic is either demonic or natural, what do you do with magic that is neither natural nor demonic, but rather angelic? People conjured angels in much the same way that they conjured demons. Critical observers could always maintain that the angels who came in response to conjuration were actually demons, and so what purported to be angelic magic was actually demonic, despite the claims of the practitioners. Someone who held that by definition magic is either natural or demonic would be swayed by those definitions to misperceive angelic magic as demonic.

What we will discover, particularly in comparing popular with learned notions, is that the history of magic is, above all, a crossing-point where the exploitation of natural forces and the invocation of demonic powers intersect. One could summarize the history of medieval magic in capsule

---

[15] Richard Kieckhefer, "Rethinking how to define magic," in Page and Rider, *Routledge History*, 15–25.

form by saying that at the popular level the tendency was to conceive magic as natural, while among the intellectuals there were three competing lines of thought: an assumption, developed in the early centuries of Christianity, that all magic involved at least an implicit reliance on demons; a grudging recognition, fostered especially by the influx of Arabic learning in the twelfth century, that much magic was in fact natural; and a fear, stimulated in the later Middle Ages by the very real exercise of necromancy, that magic involved an all too explicit invocation of demons even when it pretended to be innocent. But at this point we are getting ahead of our story.

The classic anthropological definitions of magic may now seem outdated, and early anthropologists' ways of distinguishing between magic and religion may now seem questionable, but does that mean anthropology is no longer relevant to the study of magic and its history? By no means. Anthropology still raises crucial issues and suggests ways of seeing magic in its social and cultural context. Sometimes close parallels emerge between medieval Europe and other settings, but it can be perhaps even more instructive when the study of another culture shatters our expectations and forces us to raise new questions. Gananath Obeyesekere, for example, has shown how religious authorities in Buddhist, Hindu, and Muslim shrines of Sri Lanka work sorcery for their clients by invoking the powers of deities and saints. Obeyesekere challenges traditional distinctions between religion and magic. Perhaps more importantly, he has found that the clients are not criminal personalities, but rather law-abiding middle-class citizens who have been pushed against a wall by their enemies and see no recourse other than sorcery.[16] Obeyesekere's findings do not oblige us to assume the same was the case in medieval Europe, but they do call into question any simple link between magic, even in its maleficent forms, and criminality.

Many of the practices dealt with here as "magic" might be perceived as nonmagical, or spoken of in more neutral terms. Charms, divination, and alchemy, for example, might not be thought of as magical; even to refer to unofficial ritual formulas as "charms" might be seen as showing a bias in classification. A historian of these practices may prefer to emphasize that they *need not* have been seen as magical, and may want to avoid the connotations of "magic," which could be either negative or positive, magic being both suspect and alluring. A historian of magic, however, has reason to stress that they *could be and often were* seen as

---

[16] Gananath Obeyesekere, "Sorcery, premeditated murder, and the canalization of aggression in Sri Lanka," *Ethnography*, 14 (1975), 1–23.

having a magical aspect, and will want to underscore precisely those ambiguous connotations.

The Magical Power of Words and of Imagination

Even if we follow the medieval sources in recognizing magic as falling into two basic types, demonic and natural, we can see the problems created by this dichotomy when we look at the ways these sources deal with two key issues: the magical power of words and the magical efficacy of the imagination. If words had magical efficacy, was this because they communicated the magician's will to the demons and moved the demons to carry out that will? Or did words have some kind of inherent power analogous to the occult virtues in gems and plants? And if the magician's will could bring about changes in the world through the force of the imagination, did that imply a kind of psychological magic that could be classed as "natural?" Or was the magically efficacious imagination a power distinct from those of both demonic and natural magic?

Many people in medieval society assumed there was magical power in words, particularly in names. The fourteenth-century writer Berengar Ganell began his *Summa of Sacred Magic* with a definition: "Magic is the science of binding evil and good spirits by the use of God's name, by their own names, and by the names of things of the world." It follows that "magic is a science of words," for every name is a word, but unlike other sciences of words (grammar, rhetoric, and others), magic deals with words that can coerce a spirit. Ganell goes on to say that bread is changed into the body of Christ with words, God created the world with words, and Christ performed miracles with words.[17] Making no clear distinction between sacramental and creative words, or between the miraculous and the magical, Ganell held that words have inherent power, and names especially hold magical power.

Frequently, the words used in magic are addressed to someone or something, and in those cases the magic has what Nicolas Weill-Parot refers to as an "addressative" character.[18] When demons or angels were conjured, the words of the conjuration addressed to these spirits were the

---

[17] Damaris Aschera Gehr, "Beringarius Ganellus and the *Summa sacre magice*: Magic as the promotion of God's kingship," in Page and Rider, *Routledge History*, 237–53; and Kassel Universitätsbibliothek 4° MS astron. 003: *Magica est sciencia artandi spiritus malignos et benignos per nomen dei et per nomina sua ac per nomina seculi rerum.*

[18] Nicolas Weill-Parot, "Astral magic and intellectual changes (twelfth–fifteenth centuries): 'Astrological images' and the concept of 'addressative magic,'" in Jan N. Bremmer and Jan R. Veenstra, eds., *The Metamorphosis of Magic from Late Antiquity to the Early Modern Period* (Leuven: Peeters, 2002), 167–87.

chief means of summoning them and getting them to do as one wished. But this was by no means the only addressative form of magic. Charms could be addressed to the illnesses they were meant to cure, or to the plants whose power they were meant to enhance. Magic that attempted to bring down and exploit the power of the heavenly bodies could be addressed to the stars and planets themselves or to the spirits seen as linked with them.[19] Objects that one might have thought inanimate could be addressed. The shoulder blade of a gray amphibian could be conjured or solemnly commanded by the Trinity, the passion of Christ, God's names, and so forth, to drive a woman mad with love.[20]

It could always be said that the real power resided in the spirits, or in the heavenly bodies, or in the plants and other objects used for magic, and that the words were merely instruments of persuasion, supplication, or command. Theologians such as Thomas Aquinas and Jean Gerson regarded the addressative formulas of magic as communication with demons, who were the effective agents of magic. Other theorists, however, such as Roger Bacon, saw words themselves as having magical efficacy. One possibility was that words channeled the force of the soul and served as the connection between the person acting (the magician) and the one acted upon (whether a patient, a client, or a victim). The process might be seen as working especially well at moments when astrological factors were properly aligned. Alternatively, as Nicole Oresme argued, the magical power of words could be produced by the qualities of the sound, independent of any meaning the words might have.[21] Among theorists, then, the power of words could be explained in terms of either demonic or natural magic.

If we look at the writings of the magicians themselves, however, one important fact becomes clear: the words that have magical effect are not just any words, but names (of God, or the gods, or of various types of spirit) and references to sacred persons and events (perhaps from the life of Christ, perhaps from Norse mythology). Whatever we think of the relationship between magic and religion, magic attains much of its power

---

[19] For the role of names also in Jewish magic, see Gideon Bohak, "Jewish magic in the Middle Ages," in David J. Collins, ed., *The Cambridge History of Magic and Witchcraft in the West: From Antiquity to the Present* (Cambridge University Press, 2015), 286–91.

[20] Leif Søndergaard, "Polyphony and pragmatism in Scandinavian spells c. 1300–1600," in Louise Nyholm Kallestrup and Raisa Maria Toivo, eds., *Contesting Orthodoxy in Medieval and Early Modern Europe: Heresy, Magic and Witchcraft* (New York: Palgrave, 2017), 117.

[21] See especially Béatrice Delaurenti, *La puissance des mots: "Virtus verborum": Débats doctrinaux sur le pouvoir des incantations au Moyen Âge* (Paris: Cerf, 2007); also Peter Murray Jones and Lea T. Olsan, "Medicine and magic," in Page and Rider, *Routledge History*, 303.

by tapping into the sacred and making magical use of sacred names and sacred narrative. That is not necessarily to say that God or the gods are the agents who work the magic behind the scenes. It is, rather, to say that there is power in the sacred that is mediated by names and other words and can be exploited for magical effect. This source of power is usually not demonic; although names can be used to coerce the demons, the names themselves may be sacred. But neither does this source of power reside within the natural world, as magical plants and gems do, or magically efficacious rays emanating from the stars and planets. The theorists may view words as instruments of either demonic or natural magic, but the way words actually function in magic suggests that something else is going on that is not fully explained in terms of either demonic or natural powers.

It makes a difference whether the words used in magic are spoken or written.[22] When they are spoken they attest to the power of presence: the magician who speaks or perhaps intones the formulas stands in relationship to a client and often claims authority to command spiritual forces that also become present. The psychological effect of the magic, which would have been difficult to disentangle from its physical efficacy, could be greatly enhanced by the coordination of magical words, magical gestures, and magical objects in a skillful performance. Spoken magic might resemble liturgical language, and its power could be heightened by recollection of familiar authoritative liturgy. But it could also incorporate apparent nonsense words, *voces magicae* (magical voices or sounds), whose unfamiliarity and sheer weirdness could evoke a sense that unusual powers were being invoked, that contact was being made with a spiritual world that understood the magician's uncanny utterance.

When the words are written, should we say that they attest to the power not of presence, but of absence? Perhaps to some degree that formulation is fitting. Written words survive when the writer is no longer present. Particularly for the illiterate, writing may in itself seem to have a kind of magical character that is not obviously linked to personality or performance. The mystery of writing may be extended by use of cipher to remind even the literate that meaning can be cloaked as well as revealed by language. Words inscribed on a sheet of parchment or some other medium may be scraped off into a drink, suggesting that the ink itself

---

[22] See here David Frankfurter's two articles, "Spell and speech act: The magic of the spoken word," in David Frankfurter, ed., *Guide to the Study of Ancient Magic* (Leiden: Brill, 2019), 608–25, and "The magic of writing in Mediterranean antiquity," ibid., 626–58. While focused on antiquity, Frankfurter's discussion is relevant to the study of magic generally.

that has once been formed into characters and words retains magical efficacy, with no personal presence required. Still, the contrast between presence in the spoken word and absence in the written word cannot be pressed too far. Written magical words are often meant as scripts for performance. They can be seen as channels of vicarious presence: the author or scribe lives on in the written medium.[23] And when a book gives formulas for conjuring spirits, the spirits themselves may be seen as present within the book's pages.[24] Rather than speaking here of absence, we might speak of ambiguous presence: the written magical word evokes presences that may be less manifest than those uttering the spoken word, but are not absolutely absent.

If words had magical efficacy, so did the imagination. Most basically, some apparently marvelous effects could be explained by the power of suggestion. In his discussion of divination and superstitions, Ralph Higden suggested why these might at times seem valid:

> when good things are expected to happen, then minds are much strengthened and so, by their more strenuous action, labours are improved: when, on the contrary, evil is suspected, the mind weakens and acts sluggishly so that, through lack of spirit, evils are not restricted, but allowed free rein.[25]

A subtler approach to the magical efficacy of imagination came ultimately from Arabic notions. One concept of magic that the West took over from Arabic culture, called *nīraj* in the Arabic texts, involved direct influence of one spirit upon another: that of a man over a woman whose love he wished to constrain, that of a person seeking to bind another in obedience, that of a human over an animal.[26] But if there was any one faculty that could have magical efficacy it was the imagination, which could be seen as a means for bringing the magician's will to effect directly, without necessarily involving either demonic powers or hidden virtues in nature – unless "nature" was taken to include the powers of the mind and soul. It is relatively easy to recognize how imagination could have psychosomatic or emotional impact: a woman who thinks powerful magic has been worked on her behalf may find strength in childbirth, a

---

[23] For a fascinating example of a text that channels its author, see the case of Tom Riddle's diary in J. K. Rowling, *Harry Potter and the Chamber of Secrets* (London: Bloomsbury, 1998).

[24] Kieckhefer, *Forbidden Rites*, 5–6.

[25] G. R. Owst, "*Sortilegium* in English homiletic literature of the fourteenth century," in J. Conway Davies, ed., *Studies Presented to Sir Hilary Jenkinson* (London: Oxford University Press, 1957), 289. See also Jean-Marc Mandosio, "Peter of Zealand," in Page and Rider, *Routledge History*, 273–4.

[26] Charles Burnett, "Arabic magic: The impetus for translating texts and their reception," in Page and Rider, *Routledge History*, 73–4.

man who thinks his sexuality has been cursed may become impotent, a suiter who has worked love magic may be more bold in his advances, and friends who discover that separation magic has been cast over them may begin to draw apart. But the magical power of imagination was not limited to such psychological workings; it was thought to alter the material world.

The Arabic philosopher and scientist Avicenna (ca. 980–1037) had argued that the imagination conceives of something in the material world and then "the spirit itself emits rays that move external things, like the thing of which it is the image." While Avicenna did also write about psychosomatic effects, passages of this sort are talking about something different. The thing imagined and the thing in the external world have the same form, and imagination brings about effects that are not purely psychological. The imagination becomes an active force, entering into the outer world. Avicenna's theory was transmitted to the West along with the widely known work of al-Kindi (801–73).

The efficacy of words and that of the imagination were linked. Nicholas Oresme suggested that the imagination of the hearer is affected by certain physical properties in the words themselves, rather than the signification of the words. Disturbance of the imagination in turns affects the body.[27]

At the beginning of the sixteenth century, Andrea Cattani took this theory to extremes in the magical powers he ascribed to a "prophet," who has a higher nature to which lower natures must submit, so that he can heal or injure, transform the elements of the natural world, bring about storms or famines or epidemics, cause discord or harmony through the force of his will, or repel enemies in battle with the power of his gaze.[28]

Writers who viewed magic as largely a matter of illusion sometimes emphasized the role of the imagination in creating illusions. The theologian William of Auvergne held that the sense of sight is the sense most easily deceived, and this vulnerability applied also to the power of imagination that was the inner sense corresponding to outer vision. Vision and imagination could be led astray through gazing at a shiny, reflective surface, which had the effect of dazzling the outer vision so that objects in the imagination would be mistakenly recognized by the intellect as real. Specially prepared lamps and candles might have a similar

---

[27] Bert Hansen, *Nicole Oresme and the Marvels of Nature* (Toronto: Pontifical Institute, 1985).

[28] Paola Zambelli, "Imagination and its power: Desire and transitive or psychosomatic imagination," in Zambelli, *Astrology and Magic from the Medieval Latin and Islamic World to Renaissance Europe: Theories and Approaches* (Farnham: Ashgate, 2012), article II, esp. 10–25.

effect. The eye of an Indian turtle and the heart of a hoopoe could bring on a deep slumber or awaken terror that made a person vulnerable to illusions. Objects in the natural world thus played a role in creating illusions, and demons too could contribute toward this effect. When lone voyagers on the roads of Brittany found themselves in a marvelous castle where they could enjoy a rich feast and make love to a beautiful woman who appeared as a queen, all of which would suddenly vanish, the entire experience was crafted by a demon who excited the power of the imagination to mistake a cow for a beautiful queen and stinking mud for a castle. Similar theories about the power of imagination were developed by Thomas Aquinas, Nicole Oresme, and others under William's influence.[29] Did these experiences fall under the heading of either demonic or natural magic? They could involve either or both forms of power, but the power central to these illusions was neither type of outer influence, but the inner, psychological force of imagination.

In the writings of the magicians themselves we cannot expect to find this idea that imagination by itself can have magical effect. The magicians put their trust in rituals they performed, in spirits they conjured, and in powerful objects they exploited. But when the magician was held in awe by others, or when the witch was feared as someone capable of cursing, observers probably did suppose that individuals capable of magic did have the extraordinary ability to change things with the force of an imaginative will, even if normally they relied on salves and potions, talismans and rituals. Behind all the apparatus of either natural or demonic magic stood a commanding presence whose imaginative will could make powerful use of all these instruments and might even, at times, do without them.[30]

Once again, then, the history of magic includes in its purview a force that the theorists will incorporate into their notions of demonic and natural magic, although it may not fit obviously or comfortably into either of these categories.

Plan for this Book

One of the clearest distinctions between high and popular culture in medieval Europe is that intellectuals derived many of their conceptions of magic from their reading of classical literature. Before we can

[29] Robin Goulding, "Illusion," in Page and Rider, *Routledge History*, 312–30. See also *Magie et illusion au Moyen Âge* (Aix-en-Provence: CUERMA, 1999).

[30] See Mandosio, "Peter of Zealand," 273–4, on imagination as important for effecting or resisting magic.

understand how classical and medieval notions related to each other, and how writers around the thirteenth century began to cast off the classical mantle, or at least wear it differently, we must examine this inheritance from antiquity. That will be the task of Chapter 2, which will deal with the period up to about A.D. 500; the rest of the book will deal with magic in western and central Europe from about 500 to around 1500.

If the classical culture of the ancient Graeco-Roman world was one major source of medieval magic, the traditional culture of the Germanic and Celtic peoples was another, and we will turn to this in Chapter 3. In this chapter we will see how a critique of magic formulated in antiquity – by pagans as well as Christians – was transmitted to medieval churchmen and applied now to the indigenous cultures of northern Europe.

Chapter 4 will argue that certain forms of magic were so widespread that they formed a "common tradition," found among both clergy and laity, among both nobles and commoners, among both men and women, and (with certain qualifications) among townspeople and country people, in later medieval Europe. This is not to say that such magic was always and everywhere the same, but its basic forms were essentially similar wherever it occurred. Most importantly, it cannot be assigned to any particular subgroup.

In Chapter 5 we will look at the notions of magic prevalent in the courtly culture of later medieval Europe. The chronological focus here will be the twelfth through the fifteenth centuries, when courts had become established in many parts of Europe as major cultural centers. Geographically, this chapter will center mostly on France and on other countries influenced by French culture. The point, however, will not be simply to examine a particular region, but to analyze a distinctive attitude toward magic that seems to have become prevalent around the twelfth century: a more or less romantic and, at times, quite fanciful notion of magic.

Something else was happening around the twelfth century: the importation of Arabic learning into western Europe, which brought with it new conceptions of the occult sciences, including astrology, alchemy, and related areas of natural magic. By the thirteenth century, the material brought in from Arabic culture was so widespread and so influential that intellectuals had to undertake fundamental reconsideration of their views on magic. We will trace this development in Chapter 6.

One of the most widespread forms of magic in the later medieval West involved the invocation and conjuring of angels, which will be the subject of Chapter 7. This form of magic is particularly rife with ambiguities: it is difficult to distinguish from nonmagical devotion, it has strong links to astral magic, and because the angels who respond to the magicians' call might be taken for demons in disguise, angelic magic becomes entangled with demonic magic. This form of magic is worth examining precisely because its ambiguity helps us realize how complex a factor magic was in the medieval West.

Again, at about the same time, a more sinister magic began to take hold in certain corners: the explicitly demonic magic of necromancy (a word that was originally used for conjuring the spirits of the deceased). Conjuring of demons appears to have flourished mainly in a kind of clerical underworld. This will be the subject of Chapter 8. As we will see, this demonic magic, like angelic magic, has links to the rise of the new learning derived from Muslim culture, yet it is not simply an offshoot of that development.

At every stage we will try to relate the theory and practice of magic to its various cultural contexts. Doing so will inevitably involve some artificiality, since society cannot be divided neatly into different cultural settings. The same individual might be a courtier and also a member of that intellectual avant-garde that was importing Muslim forms of magic. Or he might be a courtier and also a figure in that clerical underworld that practiced necromancy. Historians can set up all the conceptual walls they want, but they should not be surprised when medieval people pass through them freely, like ghosts. Nonetheless, the categories can prove useful even if they are not mutually exclusive.

Finally, in Chapter 9, we will see how Church and state reacted to all these forms of magic. We will survey the moral condemnations by theologians and preachers, the prohibitions enacted by legislators, and the prosecution by both ecclesiastical and secular courts. It might be interesting to deal with these matters within each chapter: to show how the authorities reacted first to the "common tradition" of magic, then to each of the new developments in the twelfth and following centuries. Yet the authorities who condemned and prohibited magic tended in so doing to conflate its various forms, and the judges who prosecuted people for magic often charged them with different kinds of magical offense in the same trial. To see how different types of magic became confused with each other in condemnation, legislation, and prohibition, we must reserve all this for the final chapter, which will serve to sum up what we have examined elsewhere.

2 The Classical Inheritance

Magic was part of life in ancient Greece and Rome, Egypt and Palestine, indeed throughout the ancient world; and certain forms of magic – protective amulets, curse tablets, spells for love, and many other types – were so widely used that it is tempting to say that magic does not really have a history, but is everywhere and always the same. But magic does have a history. Changes in the forms of magic may often be hard to trace, but it is easier to see shifts in attitudes toward magic, ranging from broad tolerance to fierce condemnation and repression. It is possible also to detect some differences over time in the sorts of people most likely to use magic or be suspected of using it. And as commerce, conquest, missionary campaigns, and translation projects brought different cultures into contact, magic was one form of tradition often appropriated across cultural boundaries.

Speaking in very general terms, the rise of the Roman Empire (traditionally dated from 27 B.C. to 476 A.D.) brought a series of related changes: a strong sense that magic was distinct from and threatening to the pure and dignified religion of Rome, harsh legislation against magic, and a conviction (shared by certain pagan writers) that magic was worked by untrustworthy if not simply malevolent *daimones* or "demons." Divination was feared as potentially a tool of political opposition that could forecast the death of an emperor. In literary texts, witches were now portrayed more than before as supernaturally evil characters.

Roman armies had conquered Egypt shortly before Augustus was declared the first emperor, and the land once ruled by pharaohs was among the places thought of as swarming with magicians, including the temple priests. Such priests were among the professional magicians whose services were increasingly available for purchase. They were literate and expert in ritual. They produced and owned books that gave instruction in magic and could be seen as bristling with magical power. To be sure, the colonized lands were not the only places magic was practiced. It could be found in Rome, in the back alleys and in wealthy estates. But it was often represented as a vice of foreigners, of priests and charlatans who populated colonized lands and brought their perfidy to Rome, and distrust of magic was thus linked with the colonizer's suspicion of subject peoples. Egyptian priests had long been viewed as exotic wonder-workers, and now they bore that reputation in an Empire whose ruling classes viewed magic with horrified fascination.[1]

All these trends were found among pagans, but were shared by early Christians, and they would continue in medieval Christendom. Early Christian writers passed on to their medieval successors much that they shared with pagan contemporaries in the time of the Roman Empire: their severe condemnation of magic, their conviction that it relied on evil demons, their belief that it threatened the society of the righteous, and their distrust of indigenous religion in lands now annexed to a Christian cultural world. A study of medieval magic must thus begin by looking at magic in antiquity and both pagan and Christian attitudes toward magic.

Evidence for Magic in Antiquity

Archaeological evidence provides vivid details from the magic of antiquity. For example, in 1934 a lead plate dating from the era of the Roman Empire was unearthed in London. Someone had taken the trouble to rip it from a building, write an inscription on it, and pound seven nails through it. The inscription reads:

I curse Tretia Maria and her life and mind and memory and liver and lungs mixed up together, and her words, thoughts and memory; thus may she be unable to speak what things are concealed.[2]

One can only conjecture what sort of scandal lay behind this chilling curse. We do know, however, that it is not an isolated case. Through much of the Roman Empire, people with enemies to dispatch might try doing so by writing a curse on some object, usually a small lead tablet. To heighten the magical efficacy they would often transfix the object with a nail and bury it or drop it into a well, where it could take its place amid the powers of the netherworld.[3]

Archaeologists have also turned up amulets made from magical gems, especially in Egypt. These present magic in a less obviously sinister form, since they could serve for protection or healing, but they could be put to

---

[1] David Frankfurter, "The consequences of Hellenism in late antique Egypt: Religious worlds and actors," *Archiv für Religionsgeschichte*, 2 (2000), 162–94.

[2] R. G. Collingwood and R. P. Wright, *The Roman Inscriptions of Britain*, vol. 1 (Oxford: Clarendon, 1965), 3–4.

[3] John G. Gager, *Curse Tablets and Binding Spells from the Ancient World* (New York: Oxford University Press, 1992).

other ends as well. One such gem (Fig. 3a) has a picture of a mummy, with the inscription "Philippa's child Antipater sleeps." The person using the gem evidently wanted a certain Antipater to sleep like a mummy, which is a not very subtle way of saying he wanted Antipater dead. Another gem shows a female figure, possibly the goddess Isis, with a long spiral of meaningless letters around her. On the reverse is an inscription asking that one Achillas be brought back to a certain Dionysias. In other words, a woman named Dionysias was using the gem for love magic, in hopes that it might bring Achillas to her. Evidently it failed, since a further inscription in a cruder hand reads, "Bring him back or lay him low." If the gem would not work for love magic, perhaps it could work better for more sinister purposes.[4]

While these gems have short formulas inscribed on them, much fuller texts are to be found in the magical papyri: sheets of papyrus with magical writing on them in Greek or in the demotic language of Egypt. The abundance and explicit character of these texts make them some of our most important sources for the magic of antiquity. Fourth- and fifth-century Egypt was rife with these papyri, though the oldest known example comes from the first century B.C. The general flavor is suggested by this formula for love magic:

I adjure you, demon of the dead ... cause Sarapion to pine and melt away out of passion for Dioskorous, whom Tikoi bore. Inflame his heart, cause it to melt, and suck out his blood out of love, passion, and pain over me ... And let him do all the things in my mind, and let him continue loving me, until he arrives in Hades.[5]

The papyrus goes on to list magical names and characters. Other such papyri sometimes repeat long magical words, progressively abridged with each repetition, such as:

ablanathanablanamacharamaracharamarach
ablanathanablanamacharamaracharamara
ablanathanablanamacharamaracharamar
ablanathanablanamacharamaracharama

And so forth, until nothing but the initial "A" remains.

In the same era, magicians in the Mediterranean world were devising other magical words, like "abracadabra" and "abraxas," to use on

---

[4] Campbell Bonner, *Studies in Magical Amulets, Chiefly Graeco-Egyptian* (Ann Arbor: University of Michigan Press, 1950), nos. 151 and 156.
[5] *The Greek Magical Papyri in Translation*, PGM xvi, ed. Hans Dieter Betz (University of Chicago Press, 1986), 252.

Fig. 3 (a and b). Magical gems from late antiquity

amulets or papyri. Still other papyri tell how to transfer insomnia from one person to another by writing an inscription on a seashell, or how to make a woman disclose her secrets while sleeping. For the latter purpose one takes a strip of hieratic papyrus, inscribes it with powerful names and characters, wraps it around a hoopoe's heart that has been marinated in myrrh, and puts it in an appropriate place on the sleeping woman's body. It is remarkable that any of this material has survived, considering that the Roman government took a dim view of such things; in a single year, the emperor Augustus (63 B.C.±A.D. 14) is said to have had two thousand magical scrolls burned.

It would be difficult to distinguish here between magic and religion. The people who used these amulets and spells invoked all the powers they knew, and the strongest of these were the superhuman ones. Not only do the magical papyri and other sources contain endless appeal to the deities; they also ascribe their magical formulas to the kindness of those gods who have taught such things to mortals.

Fig. 3 (*cont.*)

Who was writing these magical papyri, and why? Two theories have
been proposed, both based on the plausible assumption that the texts
were written by priests officiating at Egyptian temples which no longer
enjoyed patronage from the pharaohs, now that Egypt had been incorporated in the Roman Empire. One theory holds that the imperial Romans
thought of Egyptian culture as ridden with superstition and magic, and
the priests went along with this stereotype in an effort to gain a new kind
of patronage for their magical skill. If people elsewhere in the Roman
Empire viewed them as exotic wonder-workers, this reputation could be
turned to profit, and so they offered love magic and rituals to summon
deities for all comers, including fascinated visitors to Egypt. The other
theory holds that the magical papyri were meant to be secret and were
written not for potential patrons, but for the priests themselves, as a way

of reinforcing their own sense of identity. Even under Roman authority, they upheld the traditions that made it possible for them to do all sorts of marvelous things once they had been initiated and become identified with their high god. The period of the Roman Empire was one in which magic was increasingly done not by amateurs, but by professionals, of whom these Egyptian priests were prime examples.[6]

Christian authorities warned incessantly against this occultism, but their warnings went unheeded in many quarters, even within the Christian fold. The magical papyri often use Jewish and Christian names for God or Christ among their other magical formulas. One magical gem had "ho ōn" (Greek for "the Existing") inscribed on it, surely as an allusion to the God of Exodus 3:14; and an otherwise meaningless series of letters on this amulet discloses an echo of the Hebrew Tetragrammaton "YHWH," again, a name for God (Fig. 3a). Far more explicit is a gem from around the third century that shows Christ cruci- fied, with kneeling figures on either side of him, the inscription "Jesus M[essiah]" written in Aramaic, and magical characters on the reverse side (Fig. 3b). While it may be that non-Christian magicians were draw- ing on the power of the Christian God, it seems likely that Christians themselves were dabbling at times in magic.

All this material is available to us because of archaeologists' and antiquarians' diligence, but little of it was known in medieval Europe. What did survive above ground, in fair abundance, were the writings of Greeks, Egyptians, and Romans *about* magic, and these had a profound influence on medieval culture. The scientific and philosophical literature of antiquity, even when it did not deal expressly with magic, helped to form medieval notions of what was possible and impossible in the phys- ical world, and thus contributed to the medieval understanding of magic. Fictional literature in classical Greek and Latin provided stories about magic that could be cited, often as fact, in medieval writings. The Bible itself, and extrabiblical (or "apocryphal") literature similar to the books of the Bible, contributed further stories about magic. And Christian writers from the early centuries of the Church's history carried on a continuous diatribe of condemnations, interpretations, and prohibitions directed against magical practice, all of which helped to refine the notions of magic that persisted among churchmen throughout the Middle Ages. Medieval Europeans thus inherited a wealth of writings about magic; the

---

[6] The first view is that of Frankfurter, "The consequences of Hellenism;" the second is that of Kyle A. Fraser, "Roman antiquity; the imperial period," in Collins, *Cambridge History of Magic and Witchcraft*, 115–47.

way they used this inheritance depended on how they interpreted this mass of varied and often problematic material.

Scientific and Philosophical Literature

The intellectuals of antiquity might look askance at magic, but their attitudes were usually ambivalent. One of the best examples is the *Natural History* of Pliny the Elder (ca. A.D. 23–79), a compendious survey of all the sciences. Drawing from personal experience and from numerous earlier authorities, Pliny gives a picture of the heavens, Earth and its peoples, animals, plants, drugs, minerals, and metals. In his discussion of plants and their medicinal uses (books 20–27), he rarely includes magical cures, though he does occasionally tell of popular customs such as using a herb for an amulet. When he turns to the curative powers of animals and their effluvia (books 28–30), however, the picture changes. He starts by acknowledging that much of what he is going to tell will arouse disgust; he does not mind, since he is only interested in providing information that will help people. He proceeds to catalogue the curative and other powers of animal bodies, and in the process he often cites exotic and apparently senseless ingredients. He mentions eating spotted lizards, imported from abroad and boiled, as a cure for dysentery. The remedies he gives often seem to rely for their effect on hidden and symbolic powers; he does not refer to these powers as magical, but they are the sort that later writers would cite in discussing natural magic. Elsewhere he mentions a belief that the tongue of a live frog, set over the heart of a woman while she sleeps, will compel her to answer all questions truthfully. Dirt from a wheel rut can heal the bite of a shrew-mouse, because the effects of the bite, presumably like the mouse itself, "will not cross a wheel rut owing to a sort of natural torpor." Pliny clearly does not place equal faith in all such prescriptions. Often he hedges by ascribing them to the magi or to common lore: "they say" this and "they do" that. He reports that "hyena stones," taken from the eyes of hyenas, bestow prophetic gifts on a person if they are placed under the tongue, "if we can believe such a thing." It is even possible to read his entire section on the medicinal use of animals as essentially a catalogue of follies. Yet he takes the trouble to accumulate all this lore, allegedly as an aid to human health, and he seems unwilling to dismiss altogether even those formulas that he distrusts. In any event, later readers did not take him to be skeptical, but attached the authority of his name to every manner of marvel.

It is in his discussion of gems and their powers (book 37) that he is perhaps most wide-eyed. The diamond is so hard that nature's "most powerful substances," iron and fire, cannot break it, yet it can be shattered if soaked in warm goat's blood. Here, more than anywhere else, he says, the principles of sympathy and antipathy can be seen at work, principles which lie at the heart of his science. He presumably means that the ignoble blood of the goat can undo the nobility of the diamond because of the antipathy of these two substances. But then he goes on to ask how this unexpected efficacy could have been discovered, and he replies that it must have been the deities who were responsible, for "reason is not to be sought in any part of nature, but rather will."

When Pliny speaks expressly of magic he is referring not to his own methods, but to those of the magi, and for these exotic charlatans he has nothing but contempt. If there were any value at all in their concoctions, the emperor Nero would have been a formidable figure indeed, since he studied the magical art with its best teachers, but in fact he was a man of little accomplishment. Magic has the shadow of truth only because it makes use of poisons. A magician may supplement his toxins with the mumbo-jumbo of rituals and spells, but it is the poisons themselves that have effect. No sooner has Pliny dismissed magic, however, than he again hedges: "There is no one who is not afraid of spells and incantations," evidently even scientists and philosophers.[7]

Much the same ambivalence shows in other scientific writers. Dioscorides (first century A.D.), whose work on the medicinal use of animals, plants, and minerals is a classic of early pharmacology, could not withhold his awe at the wondrous powers of certain stones. For this he was ridiculed by the famous physician Galen (ca. A.D. 130–ca. 200), who decried magic, yet recommended gathering a herb with the left hand, preferably before sunrise, for maximum effect. More important for future development was Galen's notion that certain drugs work in a wondrous manner not because of any particular ingredient or quality in them, but by virtue of their "whole substance." He did not yet speak explicitly of occult powers, but he laid the ground for this notion by suggesting that a plant or animal could have marvelous curative force not reducible to any specific property. Seneca (ca. 4 B.C.±A.D. 65), in his scientific writings, at times used Pliny's device of reporting marvels of nature as common belief rather than as truth. Yet he had profound confidence in the validity of divination: the movement of planets, the falling of meteors, the flight of birds, and especially the occurrence of

---

[7] Quotation from *Natural History*, vol. 10, xxxvii.15, trans. D. E. Eichholz (Cambridge, Mass.: Harvard University Press, 1962), 211. Further material from Georg Luck, trans., *Arcana Mundi* (Baltimore: Johns Hopkins University Press, 1985), 38.

thunder and lightning served for him as portents of future events. For these men, the occult powers and signs within nature were not inherently magical. Magic was a parody of such things, the practice of the infamous magi. Yet their scientific writings provided material for what later writers would indeed call magic. The same is true of the "herbals," or books about medicinal herbs, which provided a lush growth of lore about the wondrous powers of plants.

The most important classical writings in this area, vital for their impact on occult science both in antiquity and in later ages, were works on astrology. Forms of astrology arose in ancient China, India, and elsewhere, but the astrology passed down to the medieval West was developed in Mesopotamia and then in the Greek-speaking world. Astrology was built on the back of astronomy, as articulated by Aristotle (384–322 B.C.) and others. Two principles were of particular importance. First, the stars and planets were seen as made of a "fifth essence," superior to the four essences (earth, air, fire, and water) found on Earth. Second, the revolution of these heavenly bodies was responsible for developing life and promoting action on Earth. Aristotle's "prime mover," the ultimate divine being, was totally self-absorbed, remote from Earth, and exercised influence only through the mediation of these celestial bodies. This is not to say that Aristotle believed one could predict earthly affairs by observing the heavens. He did think that the motion of the heavens affected things below, however, and this premise was an important step toward justifying astrology on philosophical grounds.

The figure who took the further step of refining and defending astrological science was the Egyptian astronomer Ptolemy (second century A.D.). His impact on medieval science was far-reaching. Until Copernicus' heliocentric theory gained acceptance in the sixteenth century, it was Ptolemy's model of the cosmos that most intellectuals took for granted: a universe in which Earth was at the center, and the planets and stars revolved about it in complex patterns. In his *Tetrabiblos*, he explained in detail how the heavenly bodies affect human life. Fully aware of objections to astrology, he gave reasoned replies to its critics. He did not believe the stars absolutely determine human conduct; their power could be resisted. (In this respect, Ptolemy differed from certain Stoic philosophers, who believed human life was fully determined, and who saw astrology and other forms of divination as ways of knowing and thus bracing oneself for inevitable fate.) While Ptolemy's work was not available in Latin until the twelfth century, and before then was known in western Europe only indirectly, its eventual translation was a powerful stimulus to revived interest in astrology.

Medieval writers were indirectly influenced by early critics of astrology and divination, such as Carneades (219–126 B.C.) and Cicero (106–43 B. C.). In his treatise *On Divination*,[8] Cicero ridiculed the notion that the gods communicate messages in dreams, which are in fact merely confused and ambiguous recollections from waking life. Besides, if the gods wanted to communicate their truths to mortals they could find some better and more dignified way than to "flit about" people's beds and "when they find someone snoring, throw at him dark and twisted visions," which he has to take the next day to some interpreter. The diviners believe that Jupiter sends us warnings by means of thunderbolts. Why, then, does the god waste so many valuable thunderbolts by flinging them into the ocean, or onto deserts, or at people who pay them no heed? The defenders of divination claim that long and careful observation lies behind this science, but Cicero is doubtful. When and where have people systematically gathered data about the entrails from sacrificial animals, or the flight of birds, or the movements of the stars and planets? Other writers, such as Sextus Empiricus, tried to distinguish carefully those things which are determined in advance and those which are left to chance or free will. The former will occur in any event, whether foreseen or not, and in the nature of things the latter cannot be foreseen; thus there is little point in divination.

Skeptics like Cicero and Sextus might fulminate all they wanted; the crowds of people waiting for magicians' and diviners' services grew no thinner, and intellectuals would continue to find justification for their own practice of the occult arts. The Egyptian city of Alexandria, one of the largest and ethnically most diverse cities in the Roman Empire, was a focal point for the practice and development of magic and for its philosophical articulation. It was largely in Alexandria that cryptic and allegorical writings on certain crafts began to emerge – crafts such as metalworking and glassmaking, in which technical secrets were guarded jealously from outsiders – which laid the foundations for what would later be called alchemy. Also commonly associated with Alexandria, though in fact of uncertain provenance, is a body of second- and third-century Greek writings on philosophy, astrology, alchemy, and magic, which posterity ascribed to "Hermes Trismegistus," or "Hermes the Thrice-Great." Hermes himself was a Greek god of cunning and invention, generally identified with his Egyptian counterpart Thoth. When the treatises ascribed to this figure had gained renown, others were added to the collection, which over the centuries underwent revision and

---

[8] Cicero, *De senectute, De amicitia, De divinatione*, trans. William Armistead Falconer (London: Heinemann; New York: Putnam, 1927), 214–537.

translation many times over. Readers disinclined to suppose that a real god wrote these works ascribed them instead to three "philosophers": the biblical Enoch, Noah, and an Egyptian king.

More important for philosophical development was Plotinus (ca. A.D. 205–70), who articulated a school of Platonic thought known as Neoplatonism. His biographer tells how an envious rival tried to harm him by directing stellar rays against him, and Plotinus not only withstood these magical forces, but actually deflected them onto the magician. Whether true or not, the story accords with the philosopher's own ideas. In his *Enneads*, Plotinus explains both magic and prayer as working through natural sympathetic bonds within the universe. Beings on Earth are linked with each other and with the heavenly bodies in an intricate, living network of influences. Whether we know it or not, we are constantly subject to the tug of magical influences from everywhere in the cosmos: "every action has magic as its source, and the entire life of the practical man is a bewitchment." When people discover these forces they can employ them for their purposes. Thus, when a person prays to the gods, or to the divine heavenly bodies, the act takes automatic effect: "The prayer is answered by the mere fact that one part and the other part are wrought to one tone, like a musical string which, plucked at one end, vibrates at the other also."[9] Those who are truly wise, however, can cultivate the higher powers of the soul by turning inward in contemplation, and can thus become immune to magical forces directed at them. Such persons may still be affected by spells and incantations in their lower, unreasoning powers, and may in fact suffer death, disease, or other misfortune, but their true, essential selves will remain unaffected. This doctrine no doubt brought great consolation to a small philosophical elite.

Plotinus' followers Porphyry (ca. A.D. 233–ca. 304) and Iamblichus (d. ca. 330) further refined these theories. The Neoplatonists also worked out extravagant rituals for invoking the gods and heightening their own magical powers. Such philosophically grounded magic was known as "theurgy," and its practitioners fancied themselves far superior to the adepts of lower magic or "goetia." Many early Christian thinkers, such as Augustine, wrestled with Neoplatonic philosophy and derived much inspiration from it, but had little use for such notions and practices as these. Certain Neoplatonists of medieval Europe were fascinated by the notion of the cosmos as a great, harmonious, living organism, but not by Plotinus' theory of prayer and magic. In the fifteenth century, Humanist

---

[9] *The Enneads*, iv.4.41, trans. Stephen MacKenna, 3rd edn (London: Faber & Faber, 1966), 323 (adapted).

proponents of Neoplatonism rediscovered Plotinus and again argued for this conception of magic.

The influence of classical authors on medieval culture was often more indirect than direct. Sometimes a classical author was better known through a later, derivative work. Often a scientist or philosopher of antiquity held such authority among later generations that much later works would capitalize on that authority by claiming him as their author. Thus we have works written centuries after Aristotle's death, but claiming to be written by him, and other writings falsely ascribed to Pliny and other authorities. This tradition of false ascription continued for centuries, so that a medieval library might be well-stocked with the writings of pseudo-Aristotle and other impostors. Among the works imputed to Aristotle were books of magical experiments, alchemical and astrological treatises, works on the hidden powers of gems and herbs, and manuals of chiromancy and physiognomy that told how to read the future from people's hands and faces. Some of these writings were, in fact, ancient; others were medieval. Sometimes their authorial claims were based on some suggestive passage in the authentic writings of Aristotle, but often there was no such link.[10] One of the more frequently copied medical works of medieval Europe was a herbal falsely ascribed to "Apuleius the Platonist" of Madaura (second century). This work was often embellished with pictures of various plants, including the standard picture of a dog uprooting mandrake. Even when a work was correctly ascribed it might have undergone serious revision. Thus, Dioscorides was known to medieval readers specifically for the sections of his work dealing with plants, and even this material was handed down in a form that Dioscorides himself would not have recognized. One medieval charm even concludes with the preposterous claim, "This was used by Plato and me."[11]

Some of the works which had the strongest impact on medieval culture were writings of late antiquity which strike a modern reader as far more naive than the works of Ptolemy, Plotinus, or even Pliny. Among these later authors, one of the more influential was Marcellus Empiricus of Bordeaux (ca. 400), who mingled fragments of earlier medicine with the folk traditions of Gaul. If some of his treatments involved Latin incantations, Marcellus had others in gibberish (*crissi crasi cancrasi*, or *sky, cuma cucuma ucuma cuma uma maa*), or in Greek, or at least in Greek letters.

[10] Lynn Thorndike, "The Latin pseudo-Aristotle and medieval occult science," *Journal of English and Germanic Philology*, 21 (1922), 229–58.
[11] Jerry Stannard, "Greco-Roman materia medica in medieval Germany," *Bulletin of the History of Medicine*, 46 (1972), 467.

He told how to transfer a toothache to a frog, and how to use the blood of various birds as a remedy for illness.

It is tempting, perhaps, to conclude that the standards of science were low in antiquity and sank still lower in late antiquity. This would be unfair for many reasons, mostly because the works mentioned here are chosen not to represent classical science at its best, but for their impact on medieval magic. Medieval writers drew continually upon their ancient forebears for inspiration, but often they viewed the culture of antiquity through a glass darkly, and some of the classical writings they used seem mere parodies of better works. The task of medieval Europeans was not only to preserve classical culture, but also, at times, to recover it, and at times to improve on it.

Fictional Literature

The distinction between fictional and nonfictional literature may be misleading: apart from the borderline cases, or works in which fiction blends with or rests upon fact, there is the thorny problem of how a work was understood by its audience. Many a work of fiction has been taken as fact by later or even contemporary readers. Particularly the medieval readers of classical texts had a tendency to read them as "authorities," with a status not unlike that of the great philosophers or historians of antiquity. In medieval writings it is thus not uncommon to find the stories of Homer or of Apuleius cited as if they were events of history. This is not to say that medieval readers always read naively: while some conflated fiction with fact, others did not, and even those who did often had moral reasons for wanting to set aside the distinction and deal with fiction as if it were fact. In any case, the works of classical literature containing stories of magic are important for the influence they had on medieval understanding of magic. Indeed, they had greater impact on learned theories of magic than on medieval literature: medieval scholars, more than medieval storytellers, were steeped in the classical tradition.

When medieval writers wanted to cite a classical example of magic, one of the tales they were most likely to recall was from Homer's Odyssey (eighth century B.C.). During his travels Odysseus lands on the island of the seductive sorceress Circe. She disposes of his companions by turning them into swine (Fig. 4). Odysseus protects himself by using a magic herb given him by the god Hermes. While he lingers on the island, Circe instructs him in the method for conjuring forth the shades of the dead. What he performs is necromancy, in the original sense of that term: he summons the spirits of the deceased to a trough in which he offers them

Fig. 4. Circe with Odysseus and companions, from a fifteenth-century manuscript of Boccaccio, *On Famous Women*

sheep's blood to drink, and when they come to imbibe this life-giving fluid, he has them foretell the future. This story was well-known in medieval Europe, especially as retold by Ovid (43 B.C.–ca. A.D. 17). Rabanus Maurus (ca. 780–856) argued that the transformation into swine could only be fiction because God alone can change things from one nature into another. But he had to *argue* this point; it did not seem self-evident. Indeed, his influential predecessor Isidore of Seville seems to have taken the story of Circe as a factual account, and cited it alongside stories from history and the Bible. Reluctant to deny the factuality of the event, however, most theologians concluded that such incidents involved delusion of the senses. John of Frankfurt (d. 1440) advanced a different argument: if the poets speak of people being transformed into beasts, this is meant only metaphorically, the way one speaks of a glutton as a pig.

The literature of Greek and Roman antiquity often recounts the magic used by women against their unfaithful lovers, either to win them back or to destroy them. In some cases, the woman seeks the aid of a known expert in magic. Virgil (70–19 B.C.), for example, shows Dido in the *Aeneid* soliciting the services of a famed priestess to work magic against Aeneas when he deserts her to sail off and found Rome. In one of his plays, Seneca (ca. 4 B.C.±A.D. 65) depicts Heracles' wife using the services of a witch to form a love charm; thinking she has learned the art and can find magical plants on her own, the wife accidentally gives her husband poison. *The Witch* by Theocritus (third century B.C.) is a kind of incantatory lyric, depicting a young woman of Alexandria who tries by magical means to regain the lost affections of her lover. In the process, she tells the story of their affair, and one can imagine her feverishly rubbing her hands together as she lists the panoply of magical devices she is using. Alas, her libations, herbs, pulverized lizards, and magic wheel all fail her, as does her invocation of the Moon and its goddess Hecate. It is only in Virgil's retelling of the story in his eighth *Eclogue* that her magic succeeds in bringing back the lover.

While these abandoned women appear in a sympathetic light, other female magicians play the role of Evil Incarnate, particularly in literature of the Roman imperial period.[12] The poets recount in detail the terrifying appearance, foul character, and unspeakable deeds of these hags. Lucan (A.D. 3–65) describes the witch Erichtho as one whose awesome spells force the gods to heed her command:

Haggard and loathly with age is the face of the witch; her awful countenance, overcast with a hellish pallor and weighed down by uncombed locks, is never seen by the clear sky; but if storm and black clouds take away the stars, then she issues forth from rifled tombs and tries to catch the nocturnal lightnings.

---

[12] Fraser, "Roman antiquity," 128.

She creates zombies for her service, feasts on the bodies of children, and snatches corpses from sepulchers for her enjoyment:

the witch eagerly vents her rage on all the limbs, thrusting her fingers into the eyes, scooping out gleefully the stiffened eyeballs, and gnawing the yellow nails on the withered hand.[13]

She even murders unborn babes "to offer them on a burning altar." Perhaps only Medea can rival her for sheer horror. Even Horace's witch Canidia, who buries a child alive and uses its liver for a love potion, is less monumentally evil than Erichtho.

In quite a different vein, Roman literature sometimes presents magic from a satiric viewpoint. Horace (65–8 B.C.) recounts the disgusting nocturnal rituals of two hags in his *Satires*. They conjure the spirits of the dead, and they use image magic. The god Priapus, embodied nearby in a wooden statue, has to put up with their repulsive behavior until he eventually puts an end to it by releasing an explosive burst of air from his posterior, whereupon the terrified witches scurry away so fast that one loses her false teeth and the other drops her wig. Even more bitingly satirical is Lucian of Samosata (A.D. 117–ca. 180), whose writings constitute a passionate crusade against superstition. He tells of a magician who, for a handsome fee, charms the Moon down from the sky and brings a clay image of Cupid to life to win a woman's favors for his client. He succeeds, but we discover that the client might have accomplished the same end by giving the money directly to the lady. In another story, Lucian provides the prototype of the sorcerer's apprentice: the magician's assistant who brings a pestle to life, only to find that he cannot control it, and that when chopped in two it becomes two uncontrollable pestles.

Apuleius of Madaura (second century) – the "Apuleius the Platonist" to whom a herbal was pseudonymously ascribed in later centuries – was accused of magic and had to defend himself in court by ridiculing the very practices he was alleged to have engaged in. In his partly autobiographical story of *The Golden Ass*, however, magic plays a vital role. The main character is a young man who meets a seductive young witch and her more experienced mistress. They perform their magic with herbs and ointments, parts of human bodies taken from graves and gallows, metal plates with magical inscriptions – in short, the standard materials for witchcraft. Not knowing better than to fall in with such folk, the hero finds himself transformed into an ass. It is only when he discovers the

---

[13] *The Civil War*, vi. 515–20, 540–3, trans. J. D. Duff (Cambridge, Mass.: Harvard University Press, 1928), 343.

goddess Isis that she rescues him from this plight. The story lends itself to different readings: as an entertaining satire, or as a symbolic account of how a bumbling youth gets transformed into a real human being through the power of Isis. Medieval authors cited it as yet another classical authority, and had to deal with its evidence that magicians could transform people into animals. Was this metamorphosis real or only apparent? Augustine, who discussed this phenomenon at some length, refused to commit himself on the case of Apuleius, but shrugged his shoulders and remarked that the story might be fact or it might be fiction. Later theologians would agonize. They insisted that these metamorphoses could not be real, but they felt obliged to deal with the evidence they read in Apuleius. Johannes Vincentii (ca. 1475), for example, opined that Apuleius, like the companions of Odysseus, was a victim of diabolical machinations: the Devil lulled him into a deep sleep and he then had him dream about being transformed.

Doubtless this literature was originally intended to entertain, but also to instruct. When it parodied magic, it served as a kind of antimagical propaganda; deliberately or not, its authors were thus supporting the efforts of Roman authorities to curb the practice of magic, and it is not surprising to find that a writer such as Horace was closely linked with the emperor Augustus.

Conceived as contributions to Western culture, these writings are important perhaps most of all because they develop the stereotypes of the female magician or witch. In this early literature, as centuries later in trials for witchcraft, the witch tends to be either a young seductress using her magic to promote her amorous purposes, or else an ugly hag with awesome and sinister power. Neither of these persistent stereotypes is designed to flatter women, even if the seduction motif could be more sympathetic in tone. If medieval Europeans had known no other sources for misogyny, they could easily have learned it from these texts.

The Bible and Biblical Apocrypha

The Bible is replete with stories of wondrous events. For the most part, these are miracles worked by divine power: miraculous escape from bondage, healing, or resurrection. Certain passages, however, are about magical wonders worked by powers other than God's. And even the miracle stories are sometimes reminiscent of magic in the outer details of what occurs, even if the underlying cause for these wonders is not magical.

When the Old Testament deals explicitly with magic, it is to condemn it. The biblical authors do so at times through straightforward command, as in the often-quoted text of Exodus 22:18, "You shall not permit a sorceress to live." Elsewhere the point is made through stories about the punishment for dabbling in magic. King Saul, who had banished all practitioners of the occult from his kingdom, nonetheless consulted the "witch" of Endor before going into battle against the Philistines (1 Samuel 28). This woman summoned the prophet Samuel from the dead, and Samuel grudgingly came forth, only to proclaim that because of Saul's misdeeds he would be defeated in battle and killed. Christian interpreters as early as Hippolytus (ca. 170–ca. 236) were sure that the spirit who appeared to Saul was not really the ghost of Samuel, but merely a demon posing as the prophet.

The most important set piece for biblical and later religious literature is the story of the wonder-working contest between the magicians and God's own agents. In Exodus 7:8–13, Aaron impresses Pharaoh with his power by throwing down his rod and having it turn into a serpent. Pharaoh's magicians do the same thing "by their secret arts": each of them casts down his rod, and all the rods become serpents. But to demonstrate the superior power of the Hebrews and their God, Aaron's rod then devours all the other rods. Again when the prophet Elijah encounters the pagan priests of Baal, he wins a miracle-working contest with them on Mount Carmel (1 Kings 18). In medieval literature on magic, however, it is the story of Pharaoh's magicians that figures prominently; Isidore of Seville and other writers cite this as proof that God's miracles are superior to the Devil's magic.

The New Testament presents one classic example of an evil magician, Simon Magus of Samaria (Acts of the Apostles 8:9–24). Simon had impressed the people with his wonder-working. Confronted with the superior powers of the Christian Apostles, however, he offered money for a share in their power, but the Apostle Peter, outraged by this offer, insisted that such power could not be bought. By the second and third centuries, Christian authors were elaborating at length upon this simple story and converting Simon Magus into an arch-heretic and rival of Peter. (Because the Apostle Peter also bore the name Simon, the two figures were aptly paired as foes: Simon Magus versus Simon Peter.) The apocryphal Acts of Peter, a sort of novella purporting to tell the Apostle's deeds not related in the Bible, describes one miracle contest at length. Simon Magus feigns revival of a dead man by using trickery to rouse a few feeble movements in his body, but only Peter is genuinely able to bring the man back to life. Frustrated and robbed of his following, the magus announces that he is going to fly up to God. When he rises up, however, Peter's prayer brings him crashing back down, and soon afterwards he dies. A similar version of the story, which remained popular in medieval culture and became enshrined in the influential *Golden Legend* of the thirteenth century, makes it clear that when Simon Magus rises into the air he is borne aloft by demons, and what Peter does is merely dispel them.

Another passage from the New Testament presents magicians in quite a different light: the story of the magi who come to honor the newborn Christ (Matthew 2:1–12). The Gospel clearly represents them as honorable figures, and medieval legend even represented them as kings. Defenders of magic could thus argue that the magical arts hold a position of dignity, since magicians were among the first to revere Christ. One response to this argument, first made in the second century, was that while certain forms of magic were legitimate under the Old Testament, the New Testament had changed all that: the magi had submitted to Christ, symbolizing the abdication of magic before Christ's power.

It could always be argued, of course, that Christ himself and his followers performed magic. Indeed, this was a common theme in controversy between Christians and pagans as early as the second century. The pagan writer Celsus (second century) claimed that Jesus had learned the magical arts in Egypt: the techniques for "blowing away" illness, creating the illusion of food, and making inanimate things seem to move as if alive. This argument could find support in the Gospels. When Jesus' power suffices to cure a woman who merely touches the fringe of his garment, and when Christ then exclaims, "Someone touched me, for I perceive that power has gone forth from me," one might well wonder what sort of power this is (Luke 9:43–8). When he cures a deaf-mute by putting his fingers in the man's ears, spitting, and touching his tongue (Mark 7:32–4), or when he heals a blind man by anointing his eyes with clay made with his own saliva (John 9:1–12), these procedures could easily seem magical. Elsewhere, especially in Matthew's Gospel, Christ is seen healing people without such techniques, merely by his word, with a simple command such as "be clean," "arise," or "rise, take up your pallet, and walk." Yet this lack of magical ritual did not dispel all suspicion of magic: some Jewish opponents even argued that Christ was a magician specifically because his words themselves had such power.

For the early Christians, Christ's miracles were important not only in themselves, but for their broader religious significance. At times, Jesus healed people and declared that he did so because of their faith. On occasion, the physical healing was linked to spiritual cleansing: Christ cured both body and soul. Miracles are thus closely tied to the fundamental purposes of the Gospel, the kindling of faith and the preaching of repentance. They also have eschatological significance: they are part of a spiritual warfare between the kingdom of God and the rival kingdom of

Satan. The paradigmatic miracles, especially in the Synoptic Gospels, are exorcisms, but even the healing of physical disease can be seen as involving conflict with the forces of evil, or with demons. When Jesus drives out demons or deprives them of their force, he is striking a blow on behalf of God's power in the world. As he says at one point, "if it is by the Spirit of God that I cast out demons, then the kingdom of God has come upon you" (Matthew 12:28; Luke 11:30). Yet a pagan or a Jew might respond that whatever broader or symbolic force it may claim, magic is still magic. Apuleius' transformation into an ass might also count as having symbolic meaning, but that does not exclude it from the category of magic.

Realizing that the techniques and the broader relevance of miracles were not decisive in this argument, early Christian writers did not usually focus on these matters. Instead they either made or presupposed one central, crucial point: that magic is the work of demons, while miracles are the work of God. What this amounted to, of course, was the claim that the Christian God is true and the pagan gods are false, which is precisely what the Christians were saying. They lived in mixed communities, side by side with pagan neighbors, practicing the same trades and patronizing the same shops, and they claimed no ethnic distinction. The main factor that set them apart in their minds is that they worshiped the true deity and followed the true religion. That claim was for them, first of all, a truth, and secondly, the sole basis for their existence as a group. And one clear corollary to this belief was the firm distinction: pagans worked magic, but Christ worked miracles. The two might appear to be alike, but just as a dog is different from a wolf and a tame pigeon differs from a wild one, "so also what is accomplished by God's power is nothing like what is done by sorcery".[14]

If the Gospels were problematic, the Acts of the Apostles must have been more so. This book of the Bible has several stories in which the Apostles' power seems to resemble that of magic. Individuals who break the code of the early Christian community are suddenly struck dead (4:32–5:11). Peter's shadow has the power to cure (5:12–16), as do handkerchiefs and aprons that he has touched (19:11). The Apostles overcome the power of other magicians on more than one occasion, and when magicians at Ephesus are converted, they bring forth books of magic to be burned (19:13–19). Indeed, this book shows the Apostles carrying out a systematic campaign against what they saw as magic. From the pagan or Jewish viewpoint, however, the Apostles seemed merely to

---

[14] Origen, *Contra Celsum*, ii.51, trans. Henry Chadwick (Cambridge University Press, 1953), 105.

have a superior form of magic. Here, again, the sole Christian counter-argument was that the Christian God was the true deity, and whatever the Apostles accomplished, even if outwardly it resembled magic, was in fact a manifestation of God's power working through them.

Magic, Early Christianity, and the Graeco-Roman World

The same arguments that were made about Christ and his Apostles applied to later generations of Christians. They might readily be accused of magic because they ascribed power to an executed man, Christ, and to the cross on which he was executed. People in the Roman world often attributed special power to those who had died violent or untimely deaths; the spirits of these victims were especially sought in necromancy. Apuleius mentions the belief that fingers and noses from crucified individuals have great power, and both he and Lucian refer to the notion that nails from a cross possess magical potency. Christian actions, as well as Christian symbols, could arouse distrust. Tertullian (ca. 160–ca. 225) warns Christian women that if they marry pagan husbands they are inviting trouble: "Shall you escape notice when you sign your bed, or your body; when you blow away some impurity; when even by night you rise to pray? Will you not be thought to be engaged in some sort of magic?"[15] Christian exorcists could command the demons by using powerful and secret names. Indeed, the name of Jesus held such power against demons that in the words of one Christian writer, "there have been cases where it was effective even when pronounced by evil men."[16] Little wonder that when Christians were persecuted they were sometimes charged with magic. Yet Christians continued to insist that it was not they, but the pagans who were the real magicians.

The conflict between Christians and pagans rested, finally, on their differing notions about magic and its place in society. For pagans who opposed magic, it was reprehensible because it was secret and antisocial. It was a force that worked against society, from within society itself, and for that reason it had to be uprooted. The pagans did not care what gods you venerated, so long as you did so openly and did not call on them for help in performing evil. If you did invoke the gods' help for evil, what you were doing was both religious and magical; the realms were not distinct,

---

[15] *Ad uxorem*, ii.5, quoted in Stephen Benko, "Early Christian magical practices," *Society of Biblical Literature, Seminar Papers*, 21 (1982), 13.

[16] Pseudo-Clement, *De virginitate*, i.10, 12; quoted in Benko, "Early Christian magical practices."

since magic relied on aid and instruction from the gods. For the Christians, magic was reprehensible because it was the work of demons. These were evil spirits, ultimately subject to God, but they paraded as gods and received veneration. Christians could not complain about secrecy because they themselves were secretive. But invocation of false gods, whether secret or open, was wrong no matter what its purposes. Veneration of these gods was inseparably bound up with magic and therefore was not authentic religion. By distinguishing sharply between Christianity (which alone was true religion) and paganism (which had magical reliance on demons at its heart), early Christian writers in effect introduced a distinction between religion and magic which had not previously been made and which was not easily understood, except from a Christian viewpoint. It was a short step from saying that paganism was inauthentic religion to maintaining that it was no religion at all, but mere idolatry and magic. This new way of disjoining magic from religion remained part of the Christian heritage for centuries to come, and was joined only around the thirteenth century by a new emphasis on specifically natural magic as a kind of third term.

In short, the pagan definition of magic had a moral and a theological dimension, but was grounded in social concerns; the Christian definition had a moral and a social dimension, but was explicitly centered on theological concerns. Between these two different models there was little room for discussion. The two sides might agree on their moral principles, since both pagans and Christians found the evil purposes of magic repugnant, but morality was not at the heart of the issue from either perspective.

Early Christian writers tended to see all forms of magic, even ostensibly harmless kinds, as relying on demons. Tatian (second century) viewed herbs, amulets, and other accoutrements of magic as having no power in themselves; they are nothing but a kind of signal-system devised by demons so that human beings can communicate their desires. Reading these signals, the demons act accordingly. Divination, too, is carried out only with the aid of demons. By pretending to serve human beings, the demons in fact ensnare them into their service. Clement of Alexandria (ca. 150–ca. 215) saw the pagan poets as largely responsible for trapping people into this service through the bewitchment of their song. Thus, when Christians converted others to the faith, they conceived this as a victory over the forces of hell. St. Anthony of Egypt (ca. 251–356), a popular religious leader in one of the great centers of magic, is supposed to have declared, "Where the sign of the cross is made, magic loses its power and sorcery fails." Then according to his biographer, Anthony went on to taunt the pagans:

Tell me, therefore, where now are your oracles? Where are the incantations of the Egyptians? Where are the delusions of the magicians? When did all these lose their power and cease but at the coming of the cross of Christ?[17]

To grasp the force of this argument, we must realize how demons were perceived by pagans and by Christians. For most pagans, *daimones* (Latin *daemones*) were neutral spirits, intermediate between gods and human beings and capable of serving either good or evil purposes. But some philosophers held them in deep suspicion, and Christians shared that attitude. And Christianity, like Judaism, offered an explanation for the perfidy of demons: they were angels who had turned against their creator and given themselves wholly over to evil.

The variations on this theme that had the greatest impact on medieval culture were those by Augustine, particularly in his classic book *The City of God*, and in his work *On Christian Teaching*.[18] Augustine wrote *The City of God* in response to the argument that the Roman Empire had declined after becoming Christian. It is Roman religion, he says, that is grounded in necromancy and other magical arts. Following earlier writers, Augustine insists that all magic is worked by demons. These evil spirits first instruct people how to perform magic rituals, and how to make use of magical stones, plants, animals, and incantations; when the magicians make use of these things, the demons come and carry out the desired deeds. Augustine does acknowledge certain marvelous powers in nature itself. He recognizes the mysterious qualities of the magnet, the power of goat's blood to shatter the otherwise indestructible adamant, and the salamander's capacity to survive fire. Furthermore, he concedes that certain powerful substances, perhaps medicinal herbs, may cure sick people if they are bound to their bodies or suspended over them. While he thus recognizes the efficacy of what would later be called natural magic, however, he does so grudgingly and always remains suspicious that demons are somehow at work in these matters. If magical images, words, or incantations come into play, his suspicion is only confirmed.

---

[17] St. Athanasius, "Life of St. Anthony," ch. 78–9, trans. Sister Mary Emily Keenan, in Roy J. Deferrari, ed., *Early Christian Biographies* ([New York]: Fathers of The Church, 1952), 203.

[18] Augustine, *Concerning the City of God, against the Pagans*, viii–x, trans. Henry Bettenson, new edn (Harmondsworth: Penguin, 1984), 298–426. See Robert A. Markus, "Augustine on magic: A neglected semiotic theory," *Revue d'Études Augustiniennes et Patristiques*, 40 (1994), 375–88; repr. in Everett Ferguson, ed., *Christianity in Relation to Jews, Greeks, and Romans* (New York: Garland, 1999), 253–66; and Fritz Graf, "Augustine and magic," in Bremmer and Veenstra, *The Metamorphosis of Magic*, 87–103.

Opposition to magic came partly from a sense that it posed an alternative to Christian prayers. It was a competing system of practice, a rival to Christian ways of coping with adversity. Thus, John Chrysostom (ca. 347–407) preached against women who use magic when their children are sick, rather than using the one true Christian remedy, the sign of the cross. These women would never think of taking their children to the pagan temples in the hope of obtaining a cure through overt idolatry. Yet the Devil has deceived them into thinking that the magic they use at home is something other than idolatry. They use amulets and incantations; they bind to their children the names of rivers and other magical words, presumably written on slips of parchment. Rather than using properly Christian means, they call on folk healers with their bags of magic tricks. "Christ is cast out, and a drunken and silly old woman is brought in."[19]

While there is no reason to think that women alone practiced magic, both pagan and Christian writers ascribed it primarily to them. Tertullian charged women generally with a propensity toward such things: fallen angels taught women the special and secret powers of herbs, because women more than men are subject to the deception of these evil spirits.

For some writers, magic is more than merely an artificial system of signals worked out by demons. It is an objectively real system of powers which the demons know and teach. This is the thrust of Tertullian's notion that demons taught women about magical herbs; the magical powers were already there within the herbs, but it was through demons that women learned about them. For the Egyptian writer Origen (ca. 185–ca. 254), it is words that have magical power, and especially names. The names of demons, if pronounced in the right way, can be used to invoke them, command them, or exorcise them. These names must be used in their original forms; they cannot be translated into different languages or they will lose their power. Various names for God and for Christ, too, have prodigious force, as Origen's pagan compatriots knew when they invoked "the God of Abraham."

While most of these early Christian writers associated magic with paganism, there were others who saw it as a craft exercised by heretical Christians. Simon Magus was the prototype of the heretical magician; when Irenaeus (ca. 130–ca. 200) wrote his voluminous attack on the heresies of his day, he recounted how Simon had learned all the magical arts in his effort to rival the Apostles, and how he and his disciples used incantations and exorcisms in an effort to win a following. Occasionally,

---

[19] Homily 8 on Colossians, in Philip Schaff, ed., *A Select Library of Nicene and Post-Nicene Fathers*, 13 (New York: Scribner, 1905), 298.

these attacks on heretics indicate specific forms of trickery used to deceive people. To persuade the multitudes of their magical power, heretics use chemicals to change the colors of liquids, or they speak through hidden tubes to make people hear mysterious voices. Even if demons are involved, however, magic can still entail a kind of fraud: by duping people's senses, they make them think they see banquets spread before them when in fact there is no real food, or they make inert matter appear to live and move. So too, demons can persuade people that they have foreknowledge of future events when they only rely on their cunning to make plausible conjectures about the future.

While this is the general drift of early Christian thought regarding magic, there are exceptions. Julius Africanus (ca. 160–ca. 240) recommended magical techniques for healing, for growing crops, even for making love charms and destroying enemies in combat, without seeing any of this as demonic. He was a Christian layman, writing for the high society of imperial Rome rather than for the edification of fellow Christians. Even so, his views could hardly have won the approval of any churchmen who might have seen them. Other Christian writers took nuanced views regarding the occult. Firmicus Maternus (fourth century) encouraged the Roman authorities to extirpate paganism and the magic and divination linked with pagan temples, yet seems to have found astrology a valid and legitimate science. These may appear to be isolated and insignificant examples, but it is more likely that they spoke for untold numbers of compromisers whose thought never found its way into writing, or whose writings have not come down to us.

Furthermore, the Roman intellectual world was still by no means wholly Christian even in the fourth and fifth centuries. Neoplatonist writers like Martianus Capella (fourth century) were still interested in philosophical interpretations of mythology, in which various types of gods and other spirits function as the forces behind magic and divination. And Macrobius (fifth century), whose major work seems to have preceded his conversion to Christianity, believed firmly in the occult powers of numbers, in the prophetic significance of dreams, and in the virtues hidden within nature. Their works might at times be found on the shelves of a medieval monastic library, alongside those of Augustine and other foes of magic. Yet the tendency was clear: as Christianity became dominant, magic fell ever more under suspicion.

The Church not only preached against magic, but also passed ecclesiastical legislation against it. The decrees (or "canons") of regional assemblies (or "synods") eventually became the basis for the church's "canon law," which even in its early forms condemned magic. In 306, a synod in the Spanish town of Elvira proclaimed that people who had killed others by sorcery (*maleficium*) should not be allowed to receive communion on their own deathbeds, because such deeds could not be accomplished without "idolatry," which is to say the invocation of evil spirits. The Synod of Ancyra in 314 required five years of penance for those guilty of divination and magical cures, and ten years for those who procured abortions by magical means. In 375 the Council of Laodicaea forbade the clergy themselves to practice sorcery and related arts or to make magical amulets, while those who wore such amulets were to be excommunicated.

From the early fourth century, the Church had far greater influence because the emperors themselves were mostly Christian and subject to persuasion by the clergy. In earlier centuries, Roman law had punished magic only when it was used to inflict harm. The laws of the Roman Republic had threatened severe punishment, possibly even death, for those who used magic to arouse storms, to steal crops, or to summon the deceased. Under the emperor Tiberius (reg. A.D. 14–37) provisions that had earlier applied to poisoners now were extended to magicians as well: all who endangered the life of others by magic could be punished by death. The same punishment later applied to those who used love magic. It was after the conversion of the emperors to Christianity, however, that magic of all kinds became a capital offense. In 357 Constantius threatened beheading for all those who used any form of magic or divination, and these severe measures were repeated in the codes of Theodosius II in 438 and Justinian in 529. Even people who wore magical amulets to ward off disease might now be executed. The pagan writer Ammianus Marcellinus (ca. 330–ca. 398) complained that anyone who consulted a soothsayer or used "some old wife's charm" to ease his pains was liable to capital punishment. The emperor Valentinian I (reg. 364–75) prescribed death for those who went out at night and engaged in "evil imprecations, magic rituals, or necromantic sacrifices," terms which a judge might construe either strictly or broadly. In 371 some people who used divination to predict the death of Valentinian and the name of his successor were brought to court in a sensational trial and later executed. Soon afterward, the censors' bonfires consumed massive piles of magical literature, and people who owned books that might be seen as even remotely offensive burned them in advance to avoid the scandal of public exposure.[20]

---

[20] A. A. Barb, "The survival of the magic arts," in Arnaldo Momigliano, ed., *The Conflict Between Paganism and Christianity in the Fourth Century* (Oxford: Clarendon, 1963), 110–25, with quotations translated.

By the sixth century there was a new kind of society and a new culture in Europe which needed to take stock of the heritage bequeathed to it from antiquity. The Roman Empire had already become officially Christian, but then in the fifth century, Germanic peoples from northern Europe had moved southward and westward and taken control of England, Gaul, Italy, Spain, even northern Africa. The lands that they conquered became effectively severed from the old Roman Empire; only the eastern part of the Empire survived this disintegration. The breakdown of central authority in the West also meant a change in the context for culture. Knowledge of Greek language and literature became rare in the West. As different vernacular languages evolved, command of Latin became the privilege of a clerical elite. Just when the old Roman cultured classes were becoming Christian, these classes lost the status they had previously held within society. New rulers, unfamiliar or only vaguely familiar with Roman traditions, governed the West. The first task confronting the Church was to convert these rulers and their subjects to the Christian and Catholic faith. In the process, not only the converts, but the faith to which they were converted underwent a change, as elements of pre-Christian culture became grafted onto the new, medieval Christianity. However much churchmen repeated early prohibitions of magic, they now had to contend with new forms of magical belief and practice that took deep hold within Christian culture.

3   The Twilight of Paganism: Magic in Norse and Irish Culture

Norse tradition tells of a conflict between two earls of tenth-century Norway in which both the parties, named Hakon and Thorleif, resorted to magic. Thorleif disguised himself as a beggar, went to the court of Hakon, and under the pretense of singing a poem in his honor, recited a curse that caused Hakon to lose his beard and much of his hair, to itch uncontrollably between his legs, and to suffer a lingering illness. In revenge, Hakon invoked the goddesses Thorgerd and Irpa, who aided him with their "trollish and prophetic powers." They made a human figure out of driftwood, placed a heart inside it, and sent it to Thorleif, who promptly died.[1]

Our source for all this is a literary account, not a straightforward history. Indeed, the earliest recorded version of the tale is from the fourteenth century, and what it attests is not the actual practice of magic in pre-Christian Scandinavia, but rather the recollection of that magic at a time when it could arouse a mixed reaction, combining horror with amusement. Precisely in this respect, however, the story gets to the heart of the problem in working with the pre-Christian magic of northern Europe: most of our information comes from after the conversion, and our fullest sources are fictional accounts that combine actual magical practice with fanciful embellishments. We know in principle that magic in later medieval Europe represented a fusion of diverse influences, some from Graeco-Roman antiquity and some from the early Germanic and Celtic cultures. To get at the latter sources, however, we have to rely heavily on inference from late and problematic materials.

Ireland was among the first of North European lands in which Christianity gained a strong foothold, roughly in the fifth century. The Scandinavian countries were among the last: Denmark around the ninth century, Norway and Sweden in the tenth, Iceland officially in the year 1000. What it means to gain a "strong foothold" obviously varies from

[1] Jacqueline Simpson, "Olaf Trygvason versus the powers of darkness," in Venetia Newall, ed., *The Witch Figure* (London: Routledge, 1973), 178–9 (quotation trans. by Simpson).

55

case to case, but the conversion and support of a monarch with some measure of central authority is usually seen as a turning-point, and the establishment of Christian institutions such as monasteries and dioceses could aid in persuading the populace to embrace new beliefs and practices, which did not necessarily mean abandoning old ones.

For the history of magic, the difference in dating is crucial. At the time the Scandinavian lands were made officially Christian, there were already networks of dioceses and monasteries through most of western Europe to provide support for missionary efforts, and literate clergy were available to help secular rulers administer their lands and codify their laws. Being part of the Christian world meant, among other things, being integrated into a network of culture and authority. By this time, both secular and Church authorities were better than before at record-keeping. From the time shortly after the conversion of Scandinavian countries, we thus have a rich variety of sources that tell us something about magic in those lands: secular and ecclesiastical law codes, trial records, and other official documents.[2] For Ireland, our early sources are fewer and we have to rely somewhat more on materials with a folkloric quality, particularly saints' lives. In both cases, the missionaries and their successors, the bishops and monks, were like the cultured Romans who looked down their noses at the unwashed masses over whom they ruled. We can see traces of this mentality both in Ireland and in Scandinavia. But the sources that preserve those traces are different in these two contexts. This chapter will focus, then, on magic in regions with relatively early and relatively late appropriation of Christian culture.

Conversion and Pagan Survivals

The newly arrived peoples who now dominated western and central Europe eventually converted to Christianity, partly through assimilation to the Christian culture already present in the late Roman Empire, and partly through the efforts of foreign missionaries. The process took several generations, from about the fifth to around the tenth century. In bold outline: the Gauls and the English converted in the sixth and seventh centuries (partly through missionary efforts of the Irish, who had become Christian slightly earlier); in the seventh and eighth centuries, missionary monks from the British Isles preached to the Germanic peoples on the Continent; last to be included in the newly formed

---

[2] Stephen A. Mitchell, *Witchcraft and Magic in the Nordic Middle Ages* (Philadelphia: University of Pennsylvania Press, 2010), carefully traces the sources available in different Scandinavian countries.

European Christendom were the Slavic peoples of eastern Europe and the Scandinavians from the north, who joined this new cultural mainstream around the tenth century.

All of these dates, however, are approximations. Chroniclers usually took the year of a monarch's baptism as the official date for conversion of a kingdom. If we look more closely we will almost always find that there had been some Christians in the land beforehand, perhaps queens who had come from Christian countries and had brought their chaplains along, and perhaps also merchants from abroad. Nor did the rest of the country automatically follow the king's baptism. Indeed, effective conversion of the countryside might take several further generations. Yet if converting the monarch was neither the first nor the final step in Christianization, it was nonetheless a crucial step, which ensured the dominance of Christian institutions. Once the king was baptized, a network of monasteries, bishoprics, and local churches would soon displace pagan temples, and Christian clergy would displace the pagan priesthood. Once the traditional structures dissolved, people would naturally turn to Christianity for their religious needs. The process did not occur overnight, however, and even when it was accomplished some elements of the earlier culture would inevitably survive.

Accommodation to certain elements of pagan culture was common (though not universal) missionary practice in the early Middle Ages. Pope Gregory the Great (reg. 590–604) told his missionaries to England that they should not demolish pagan temples, but reconsecrate them and use them as Christian churches; they should endow pagan festivals with Christian meaning rather than prohibiting their observance. So too, the missionaries incorporated elements of what we are calling magic into their new cultural synthesis. Monks who traveled about as missionaries would often encounter magical charms, perhaps containing the names of Germanic gods; they would write them down so that other monks would know what to expect on the mission field, and perhaps they would devise Christianized versions of the same formulas. Thus, a famous early German charm tells how Woden was riding a horse through the woods when its leg was sprained and the god had to heal the afflicted limb. Later versions replace Woden with Christ, portrayed as riding his horse into Jerusalem, or with other Christian figures. While pagan priests were forbidden to continue their rites, the kings continued to be seen as descended from the gods and as sources of magical power and protection for their realms. There was little the Christian priest could do about these vestiges from the earlier culture.

Yet toleration had its limits. Monks and other churchmen usually drew the line at explicit veneration of the old gods, and they forbade practices that might be construed as involving such veneration. As an anonymous preacher in the early Middle Ages protested, "All those who believe they can prevent hail by means of inscribed lead tablets or charmed horns are no Christians, but rather pagans." Following early Christian writers, they identified the traditional gods as demons, and thus all magic that called on the services of these gods, explicitly or implicitly, was seen as demonic magic.

The traditional cultures of northern Europe, like those of the Roman Empire, linked religion and magic without distinction. In Germanic mythology, for example, the god Woden (or Odin) was himself a master of magic who had gained power over the magical runic alphabet and could use its characters to perform wondrous deeds. An Old English healing charm might invoke the power of this god; indeed, an English book of charms from long after the conversion to Christianity still contained a spell referring to Woden. In early medieval Europe, therefore, the churchmen had to continue the fight begun by their predecessors in the Roman Empire, and the logic of their argument was essentially the same. In both eras, orthodox opinion held that pagan religion was no true religion, but mere demon-worship, and that magic was inseparably linked to this demonic cult.

People who had performed magic might repent of their misconduct, and might go to a priest for confession. If so, the priest would probably have a "penitential," or manual telling him what penances to impose for these and other sins. The early medieval penitentials furnish ample evidence for the varieties of magic priests expected to hear from the newly converted peoples of Europe. One such handbook has a section on the worship of pagan idols, and under this heading prescribes varying lengths of penance for those who have performed "diabolical incantations or divinations." The author continues, drawing in part upon a canon from the Synod of Ancyra:

He who celebrates auguries, omens from birds, or dreams, or any divination according to the custom of the heathen, or introduces such people into his house, in seeking out any trick of the magicians – when these become penitents, if they belong to the clergy they shall be cast out; but if they are secular persons they shall do penance for five years.

The penitentials could be more specific: they condemned the use of magical potions to procure sterility, abortion, death, or love; they took seriously the belief that people can steal milk, honey, and other substances by magic, and kill animals with mere glances and words; according to these sources, women who boasted that they could arouse love or hatred, or that they could steal people's goods through magical means, were to be driven from their parishes. One penitential says that a person who "drives stakes into a man," meaning presumably an enemy's image, should fast for three years.[3]

Churchmen had occasion to condemn not only pagan practices, but also pagan beliefs. Around 820, Bishop Agobard of Lyon wrote against the superstitious belief that sorcerers could arouse hail and thunderstorms; only God, he insisted, controls the weather. On one occasion, the people of his region accused four unfortunate souls of having sailed about in the air on magical ships, from which they pilfered the fruits of the fields. Agobard concluded sadly that in his day folly had taken the upper hand, and Christians believed things which in better days even pagans would reject. An anonymous penitential, which got incorporated in Burchard of Worms' influential collection of canon law around 1020 and thus enjoyed wide circulation, rejected the belief that magic can disturb the weather, influence people's minds, or arouse love and hatred. The same source also dismisses the belief that people can be transformed into animals. All such notions seemed to infringe God's prerogative as creator. The canon *Episcopi*, probably from a ninth-century Frankish synod, condemned the belief of certain women that they rode through the air at nighttime on the backs of animals, in the company of the goddess Diana. For believing in such things, rather than for participating in them, these churchmen prescribe penance. Yet most of the synodal and penitential literature concerned itself with what people did, not what they thought, and most churchmen railed against magic rather than the belief in magic.

When we attempt to analyze the actual magical practice of the northern European peoples, however, we are on treacherous ground. Apart from occasional references to very early customs in Roman historians such as Tacitus, and condemnations by early medieval monks, we have little in the way of written record. The archaeological evidence usually tells us little: if excavation of a grave turns up a horse's tooth that has been pierced so it can be hung around a person's neck, is that an indication that this tooth once served as a magical amulet? If so, for what purpose? And why is it buried in the grave? Answers to these questions remain frustratingly speculative.

Two main areas for exploration nonetheless present themselves. The Norse peoples of Scandinavia remained pagan longer than most in northern Europe and left vestiges of their pre-Christian culture even after

---

[3] John T. McNeill and Helena M. Gamer, trans., *Medieval Handbooks of Penance* (New York: Columbia University Press, 1938), especially 38–43, 198, 228ff., 305ff., 329–41, 349ff. See now Jacqueline Borsje, "Love magic in medieval Irish penitentials, law and literature: A dynamic perspective," *Studia Neophilologica*, 84, suppl. 1 (2012), 6–23.

their conversion in roughly the tenth and eleventh centuries. There are narrative sources from the time after the conversion which reflect the customs and the mentality of the pre-Christian Norse regions, particularly the sagas from Iceland. Traditional Norse beliefs persisted in some quarters through the late Middle Ages and beyond. Runic charms from the fourteenth century still make allusion to material from Norse mythology, and appeal to Odin for financial success continued into the post-medieval era.[4] Pre-Christian motifs can be found also in the writings of the Irish, who had converted to Christianity much earlier. We cannot reconstruct an entire pagan culture from these remnants, but we can at least catch glimpses of what it must have been.

Runic Inscriptions

In a culture where writing is uncommon, it may sometimes appear magical. Even ordinary script may seem to bear extraordinary power, and it is not surprising when people in search of magical weapons or magical protection seize upon the written word. The English chronicler Bede (ca. 673–735) tells of a Northumbrian captive whose brother, thinking him dead, had masses said for his soul. Wondrously, the prayers loosened the captive's fetters and set him free. His captors, however, not knowing the cause of this strange development, immediately asked if he was carrying magical writing on his person. For them, magic must have seemed intimately bound up with writing.

One of the clearest examples of this mentality is the use of the runes, the alphabet of Norse culture of Scandinavia and Iceland. Runes were developed as early as the first century and were used by among Germanic peoples in several lands, but it was the Norsemen who retained and used them well into the medieval era. They were inscribed on weapons and jewelry, bones and wooden sticks, metal plates and rocks. They were used for ordinary writing, but clearly it did not take long for them to develop magical associations, and the very word "rune" can refer not only to an alphabetic character, but to a whispered secret or secret knowledge, and thus also an instrument of magic. We read in Norse stories about people who used runic inscriptions to work various types of magic: to gain victory in battle, to detect poison and split open a drinking-horn that contains a poisoned drink, to ensure fertility, to procure love, to affect the weather. A stick with runes carved on it invokes the Earth and Sun, along with "holy Mary and the Lord God himself,"

---

[4] Mitchell, *Witchcraft and Magic*, 50, 54; Søndergaard, "Polyphony and pragmatism in Scandinavian spells," 111–26.

for healing of malaria. One source speaks of the runes as having power even to revive the corpse of a hanged man. In *Egil's Saga* we hear of runes carved on whalebone to aid a sick woman. But they are, alas, the wrong runes, and when Egil finds them he comments sardonically that people who do not know their runes should leave this business alone. Then he carves the right ones, and the woman immediately revives.[5]

Various objects bearing runic inscriptions have been found from Scandinavia, Iceland, and the part of England that was occupied by the Danes. It is not always possible to ascribe precise magical intent to the inscriptions, but sometimes magical effect was clearly intended. A sixth-century amulet made from the bone of a fish and discovered at Lindholm in Sweden bears the name of the god Týr, and also has combinations of runes that cannot have ordinary significance and probably are meant to convey magic power. One portion of the inscription, for example, reads "aaaaaaaaRRRnnn;" repetition of magical runes in this manner seems to have been common. Such inscriptions also occur at burial sites as protective amulets on stones inside or near the graves, to stave off evil powers or to bind the deceased to the grave and keep them from wandering.

Runic stones, generally memorials to the deceased, often featured pre-Christian motifs such as a depiction of Thor's hammer, even if they were erected after the conversion to Christianity. An eleventh-century memorial stone from a parish church in Gotland featured a cross (clearly a Christian symbol) and a dragon represented in an interlace pattern (a motif from pre-Christian tradition, if not overtly pagan); the runic inscription declared that the stone was a memorial to a deceased man who had gone on an expedition and been betrayed by some Wallachian people, and so "may God betray those who betrayed him" (Fig. 5).

There was inevitably regional variation. In eastern Sweden, for example, conversion to Christianity was more often voluntary than in other Scandinavian lands, and less frequently coerced by rulers, and in that region the inscriptions on rune stones are less likely to invoke the god Thor or contain references that missionaries might see as magical.[6]

The Norse Sagas

Various genres of medieval literature make incidental reference to magic. *Beowulf*, for example, tells of a magical amulet set in a warrior's helmet as

[5] Mindy MacLeod and Bernard Mees, *Runic Amulets and Magic Objects* (Woodbridge: Boydell & Brewer, 2006).
[6] Birgit Sawyer, *The Viking-Age Rune-Stones: Custom and Commemoration in Early Medieval Scandinavia* (Oxford University Press, 2000), 124–45.

Fig. 5. Runic stone from Sjonhem parish church

protection. For sustained and realistic depiction of early Germanic magic, however, there are few sources as revealing as the Norse sagas. To speak of these documents as realistic is not to say that they are faithful in every particular to real life, or that they were read in that way. More than most types of medieval literature, however, they depict magic as occurring amid realistic accounts of everyday situations: in the thick of family feuds, in the exercise of judicial business, in the ordinary grind of life, not in a fantasy world or an idealized or enchanted realm.[7]

The verse sagas were written in Iceland around the thirteenth century, yet they are commonly set in a much earlier era, the period just after the conversion of Iceland to Christianity in A.D. 1000. The poets assume that the culture of their land has become at least nominally Christian, but they tell of people clinging to ancient beliefs and pagan practices. Thus they are a treasury of information, not so much for pre-Christian magic, but for Christian perception of that early magical practice.

The role of sorcery in this literature is manifest, for example, in *Grettir's Saga*, written in the fourteenth century but portraying events of the eleventh.[8] Like most sagas, this one is essentially a story of ruthless violence between families. The hero, Grettir, ends his days in exile on the lonely island of Drang, a rocky protrusion from the sea off the coast of Iceland. Before he goes to this refuge he bids his mother farewell. She warns him:

Be on your guard against treachery, but you will be slain by weapons. I have had some very strange dreams. Keep clear of sorcerers, for there are few things stronger than witchcraft.

The premonition turns out to be well grounded. Grettir's chief enemy, finding himself unable to attack Grettir on the island, solicits the aid of his old foster mother, who practiced sorcery before the conversion and still remembers its secrets. Reluctantly, the feeble old woman agrees to help. She goes along with others to Drang in a boat, but Grettir recognizes her and hurls a stone that breaks her thigh. Eventually she recovers from this injury and then proceeds against Grettir with savage cunning. Taking some men with her, she goes down to the coast and looks for driftwood. She finds a heavy tree-trunk, has the men scrape a smooth surface on it, then carves runes on it. She smears her own blood into the runes, chants a few spells, walks backwards and counterclockwise around the trunk, and has the men push it out into the sea. She puts a further spell on it, so that even though the wind is blowing toward land, it drifts quickly out to Drang. The next day Grettir goes to look for firewood and

---

[7] François-Xavier Dillmann, *Les magiciens dans l'Islande ancienne: Études sur la représentation de la magie islandaise et de ses agents dans les sources littéraires norroises* (Uppsala: Kung. Gustavs Adolfs Akademien för svensk folkkultur, 2006), presents in considerable detail the historical context for the magic and the magicians of early Iceland.

[8] *Grettir's Saga*, chs. 69 and 78–80, trans. Denton Fox and Hermann Pálsson (University of Toronto Press, 1974), 158–64.

finds this very tree, but rejects it as an "evil tree, sent to us by evil." The same thing happens the next day. The third day, however, a slave goes searching for wood, and unknowingly brings back the cursed trunk. Grettir begins chopping it before he recognizes it, but his axe glances off and strikes his leg, causing a deep wound. When the wound grows worse he knows he has been afflicted by sorcery. Weakened, he is unable to defend himself when his foes finally storm the island, and thus they are able to kill him with a blow to the head. When other people in Iceland learn what has happened, they hold Grettir's enemy guilty not for killing Grettir but for having recourse to witchcraft, and thus they banish him from Iceland. "Then it was adopted as law," the saga tells us, "that all sorcerers should be outlawed."

In various ways, the magic used against Grettir typifies the sorcery in the sagas. The magician is a specialist who performs services for others. She deploys ceremonies and magically charged objects, but her main source of power is the spoken and written word: the spells she chants over the tree-trunk and the runic inscription she carves on it. Others in her society find magic reprehensible, not because it is violent, but because it is unfair. One is supposed to kill enemies in honest combat, not through the furtive rituals of sorcery. Perhaps most importantly, the magic here and in other sagas takes place within the familiar context of Icelandic life. The witch is an old woman with special knowledge, but there is no suggestion that she is anything other than human, or that she is an outsider to Icelandic society. Nor is the situation that gives rise to magic anything out of the ordinary.

The effects of magic in the sagas are diverse. It may be offensive or defensive, but in either case it is almost always a means for confronting or evading one's enemies. It can kill them by ensuring they will be wounded in battle or by raising a storm while they are at sea. When accused of using magic, the magician can use further magic to kill the accuser. Short of bringing death, sorcery can make life miserable. It can keep a man from having intercourse with his wife. Magic can change people into animals so their enemies will not find them, or bring darkness and mist to confuse a pursuer. In a battle, a magician's glance can cause weapons to go blunt, a magical spell can prevent soldiers from protecting themselves, and a magically impenetrable shirt can make a warrior invincible. The evil eye is feared especially when the magician is apprehended; those who seize the sorcerer thus often put a sack over his head. Occasionally the sagas refer to healing magic, but even when someone claims to be using healing arts, she may in fact have evil intent. *The Saga of Droplaug's Sons* tells of a fighter named Grim whose leg becomes wounded in combat and festers. A woman comes to him claiming skill in medicine. She bandages his leg, but it only grows worse, and soon he dies. It turns out that the woman is in fact a witch, the friend of a man Grim has killed, and now she has taken her revenge.

The magicians of the sagas are almost always thoroughly sinister characters, surly and unpopular, and sometimes they are explicitly connected with paganism. When they commit their foul deeds, everyone agrees that they should suffer death or at least banishment. On occasion they are said to have learned their art from teachers, and small bands of assistants sometimes help by saying responses or chanting spells. One saga even refers to an entire family of sorcerers, "very skilled in magic," who have been driven from their home, presumably because of this reputation. For the most part, however, they operate by themselves, whether for their own ends or on behalf of clients. Often they have animal spirits that aid them. At times they also keep visible animals; one has twenty large black cats to protect him, and because of his spells they scare all and sundry with their demonic glares and yowling. The magicians do not usually need elaborate equipment. A staff, a cloth or animal skin, a "troll's cloak," or a platform will suffice.

The role of spoken or chanted spells in the magic of the sagas can scarcely be exaggerated. An episode in the *Laxdaela Saga* demonstrates how incantation might work. An entire family of sorcerers approaches their enemy's house at night and begins chanting. At first the victims are merely confused, though the incantation sounds pleasant. Soon the householder realizes that a spell is being worked against someone in the family, and he cautions everyone to keep awake but not look outdoors. Nonetheless, everyone dozes off except a twelve-year-old boy at whom the spell is directed. He becomes restless, goes outdoors, walks toward the sorcerers, and immediately drops dead.

The relationship between sorcery and Norse paganism is somewhat elusive. The sorcerers' opponents typically see magic as a practice supposedly given up when Iceland converted to Christianity. Sorcery is part of a culture that Icelanders are supposed to have forsworn at baptism as one of the Devil's works. In that sense it is a "pagan survival." Yet there is no hint that it is part of an organized pagan religion that has gone underground; neither here nor elsewhere is there evidence for persistence of a pagan cultural system. Nor does the magic of the sagas seem to be connected integrally with veneration of the Norse gods. While the sorcerers' magic may sometimes make reference to the gods, and may sometimes resemble the magic practiced by the gods, it seldom involves appeal to the gods. As elsewhere in Christianized Scandinavia, sorcery and heathen worship seem to have been seen as essentially different things, even if they might overlap at points. It was Christian writers who conflated these categories, telling stories about pagan deities who aid magicians with their "trollish powers," and it was later preachers who popularized that conflation.

While much of the magical lore in these tales can be traced to Germanic antiquity, and sometimes there are echoes of the magical power ascribed to the Norse god Odin, there is also evidence for absorption of non-Germanic beliefs. In some ways the magic of Iceland resembles that of the Sámi and other Arctic peoples. Like the shamans of the far North, Icelandic magicians are sometimes portrayed as having special psychic powers while asleep or in trance. Like Siberian magicians they can transform people into unexpected shapes to prevent their detection. Like Sámi wizards they can attack their enemies in the form of animals such as the walrus, and in Icelandic as in other northern stories the magicians in animal form are sometimes confused with the animal spirits that protect them. There are parallels even among Inuit shamans, who are known to enter ecstasy while lying on platforms and covered with skins: practices found or at least suggested in the sagas.[9] Yet another pathway, that of Arctic cultural systems, thus converges with those we have already located in our study of magic.

In other ways, however, the sagas represent a situation distinctive to Iceland. The society that they reflect, built on small-scale farming and fishing, is far more settled than it had been prior to conversion. Despite its geographical isolation, Iceland had cultural and ecclesiastical links within Scandinavia and with Europe generally. It had vernacular translations of essential Latin literature. Perhaps precisely because of its geographical isolation, however, its cultural elite had to remind people of the need to keep up the ties with civilization. The sagas, written down after several generations of oral transmission, reminded people of a distant age seen as one of heroic conflict.[10] Parts of the old Scandinavian tradition are darkly portrayed. Much as Horace and Lucian poked fun at sorceresses in an age when the Roman authorities were campaigning against real-life sorcery, so now the writers of the sagas depicted the unsavory powers of magic as a reminder of those bad old days to which Iceland should not return. In the process, these authors left a lively record of how sorcery was thought to work. They were writing stories about a particular kind of social turmoil, and the magic they depicted was part of the shading they used in painting this canvas.

---

[9] H. R. Ellis Davidson, "Hostile magic in the Icelandic sagas," in Newall, *The Witch Figure*, 37–8.

[10] Stephen A. Mitchell, "Scandinavia," in Page and Rider, *Routledge History*, 141.

Quite different are the magical motifs in the "eddas," which preserve much more of Norse mythology than do the sagas: while the distinction is by no means absolute, it is fair to say that the sagas deal more with human beings, and the eddas are our chief source for the gods. For the history of magic as it was actually practiced in human society, the eddas are thus the less important documents, yet it is important to bear in mind that the eddas also refer to magic and that the magical themes here are not altogether distinct from those in the sagas. Perhaps the most famous tale from the eddas, and for our purposes the most important, is that of how the god Odin hung on a tree, fasting and exposed to the elements, until he was rewarded by gaining mastery of the runes and their magical powers. For a divine as well as for a human magician, then, magic is a force closely linked with writing. What this myth conveys more vividly than the sagas is a sense of how magic assumes ascetic preparation: here, as in other early European cultures, magical force issues from one who has performed heroic disciplines, mastered the body and strengthened the soul, and with intense effort of will has gained access to otherwise hidden energies.[11]

Irish Literature

Celtic literature also contains magical themes, generally closer to those of the eddas than to those of the sagas. Like Norse literature, that of Ireland and other Celtic lands comes down to us primarily in later medieval redactions, from the twelfth and later centuries, and its pagan elements are reminiscences of an earlier culture, but the pre-Christian past was a much more distant memory for the Irish. Furthermore, the vestiges in Irish literature come more from mythology than from popular conceptions of how magic was actually performed; in that respect, the Irish materials resemble the eddas more than the sagas.

Christian missionaries saw traditional Celtic religion as a rival tradition and might see it as entailing magic, but matters were not always straight-forward and clear. The "Breastplate of Patrick" includes verses meant to protect against "the black laws of paganism" and "the spells of women and smiths and druids." The breastplate itself might seem like a form of countermagic, but the source of power is crucial: the text invoked God, the angels, and the saints for protection, and Christians would scarcely have viewed appeal to those powers as magic. Another old Irish formula, "A Chant for Long Life," invokes "the seven daughters of the sea who

[11] A. G. van Hamel, "Oðinn hanging on the tree," *Acta Philologica Scandinavica*, 7 (1932–33), 260–88.

form the threads of the long-lives youths," and "my silver warrior, who has not died, who will not die." It further calls upon "Senach of the seven ages, whom fairy women fostered on the breasts of inspiration." Here the allusion to pre-Christian belief is evident, yet the work has been ascribed to a learned Christian cleric, much of the formula is straightforwardly Christian, and it has been suggested that the "sevens" refer to the seven gifts of the Holy Spirit. Even if the author was deliberately absorbing traditional Irish lore, he would surely not have thought of his formula as pagan magic rather than Christian religion.[12]

The link between fairies and human beings is a prominent motif in the Irish tradition. One twelfth-century Irish work, for example, tells how hunters come upon a Fairy Hill, inhabited by twenty-eight warriors, each with a charming woman. Accepting their hospitality, the hunters spend the night in the hill. An earlier Irish source tells how Conle the Redhaired begins to hear the voice of a love-struck and alluring fairy. She invites him to join her in the Fairy Hill, where there are everlasting feasts, no cares, and no death. Fearing her enchantment, Conle obtains from a druid a musical charm with which he can ward off her allurement. She goes away for a time, but as she departs she throws him an apple which nourishes him for an entire month. Then she returns, warns Conle against the demonic power of the druids, prophesies the coming of St. Patrick to convert the Irish, and beckons for Conle to come away in a crystal boat. At last he succumbs to her entreaties and is never again seen among mortals. What we have here is clearly a Christianized version of earlier lore; fairies are more often interpreted in medieval Christendom as demons, but here the fairy allies herself with the forces of goodness and faith against the pagan druids.[13] As we shall see (in Chapter 5), the same ambivalence can be found in Continental romances as well: fairies have both good and evil sides, and while they can represent primal paganism, they can also be said to hold the Christian faith.

From a Christian perspective, the druids were generally seen not simply as pagan priests, but as magicians. Yet the sources do not all speak with one voice. Early medieval literature describes the druid Cathbad as an admirable sage or seer, while late medieval literature shows the druid Mog Ruith as a dubious figure, largely modeled on Simon Magus (or "Simon the Druid"), who sends magical beasts to attack his enemies, produces bloody rain, and sets things on fire by

---

[12] John Carey, *King of Mysteries: Early Irish Religious Writings* (Dublin: Four Courts Press, 1998), 127–38.

[13] Kenneth Hurlstone Jackson, ed., *A Celtic Miscellany: Translations from the Celtic Literature*, rev. edn (Harmondsworth: Penguin, 1971), 143–5, 164–5.

breathing on them.[14] Stereotyping of non-Christian tradition did not necessarily arise from direct encounter between pagans and Christian missionaries, but could be part of a romantic fascination with missionary heroes of the distant past.

Themes that appear in secular Celtic literature often show up in saints' lives as well. These texts, too, survive mostly in high medieval versions from well after the conversion. Both secular and saintly heroes, for example, were able to survive long periods beneath water. St. Colman mac Luachain once remained submerged for an entire day and night, while the aquatic fauna amused him by running races. Borrowing, perhaps, from early Celtic stories of gods and heroes, the biographers of Irish saints often told wondrous tales of their power over fire as well as water: they could produce fire from their fingertips, or carry it in their hands.

Irish saints were famous for their cursing. Frequently they used curses taken from the Psalms. Fishermen refused to give St. Brendan fish, and as punishment the saint cursed fifty streams and left them barren. When a local king got on the wrong side of St. Ruadan, the saint and his fellow monks used various forms of cursing – chants, bell-ringing, and fasting – which, according to the saint's biographer, killed twelve members of the king's household and ultimately destroyed his royal residence. St. Maedoc threatened to curse a king, but was induced to turn his curse against a stone, making it split. Monks on areas of the Continent that had come under Irish influence had a tradition of liturgical cursing against their enemies.[15]

To be sure, the sources represent these monks as exercising righteous anger and wishing to bring their adversaries to repentance. They could also inflict curses on their foes, and they often used this power against

---

[14] Mark Williams, "Magic in Celtic lands," in Page and Rider, *Routledge History*, 129–30; also Aideen M. O'Leary, "Constructing the magical biography of the Irish druid Mog Ruith," in Albrecht Classen, ed., *Magic and Magicians in the Middle Ages and the Early Modern Time: The Occult in Pre-Modern Sciences, Medicine, Literature, Religion, and Astrology* (Berlin: De Gruyter, 2017), 219–30.

[15] Ksenia Kudenko, "In defence of the Irish saints who 'loved malediction,'" in Ilona Tuomi, John Carey, Barbara Hilliers, and Ciarán Ó Gealbháin, eds., *Charms, Charmers and Charming in Ireland: From the Medieval to the Modern* (Cardiff: University of Wales Press, 2019), 65–77; Dorothy Ann Bray, "Malediction and benediction in the lives of the early Irish saints," *Studia Celtica*, 36 (2002), 47–58; Lester K. Little, *Benedictine Maledictions: Liturgical Cursing in Renaissance France* (Ithaca, New York: Cornell University Press, 1993). For other use of biblical material and even masses to bring harm and death, see Klaus Schreiner, "Volkstümliche Bibelmagie und volkssprachliche Bibellektüre: theologische und soziale Probleme mittelalterlicher Laienfrömmigkeit," in Peter Dinzelbacher and Dieter R. Bauer, eds., *Volksreligion im hohen und späten Mittelalter* (Paderborn: Schöningh, 1990), 329–74.

thieves, druids, and other enemies of all that was good and holy.[16] When a druid confronted St. Patrick (ca. 390–ca. 460?), for example, the saint raised him high in the air and then let him dash upon the rocks, like Simon Magus. Patrick also challenged the druids to wonder-working contests, as Simon Peter did with Simon Magus, and as the prophet Elijah did with the priest of Baal (I Kings 18). In one tale, a druid put into a hut made of green wood was burned alive, while Patrick remained unharmed when fire was set to his hut of dry wood. Doubtless it is possible to represent such stories as exercises in divine righteousness. If it is easier to see the saints as magicians casting spells on their adversaries, we must remember that for the writers and readers of this literature, the saints were not magicians precisely because they worked with divine aid. We are constantly reminded in certain texts that Patrick's miracles redounded to his glory and to God's. The druids, like the priests of Baal and like Simon Magus, are the true magicians because their power comes not from God but from demons. Righteous as all this cursing may be, cases of this sort make it harder to distinguish between magic and religion. Rituals worked for harm may seem more magical than religious, but magicians, like saints, may see their destructive magic as provoked and righteous.

Both Norse and Irish literature – and more broadly, Germanic and Celtic traditions – demonstrate that the beliefs of early Christian writers remained very much alive in medieval Europe. When medieval authors condemned magic as demonic, their perceptions were rooted in the experience of missionaries, propagandists, and other churchmen. In some cases, the magic of the Germanic and Celtic peoples made explicit appeal to the traditional deities. Even when it did not, Christian critics tended to assume an implicit link to pagan worship, and thus veneration of demons, simply because this magic was rooted in the same pre-Christian culture that had fostered veneration of the old gods. Those who contended that all magic is, by definition, demonic would have met little argument from the missionaries of early medieval Europe.

[16] Carolus Plummer, ed., *Vitae sanctorum Hiberniae*, vol. 1 (Oxford: Clarendon, 1910), introduction, cxxix–clxxxviii.

4   The Common Tradition of Medieval Magic

Part of the inheritance passed down from classical antiquity to medieval and modern Western culture is the notion of magic as something performed by special individuals. It is the magi, or magicians, who perform magic. Whatever similarities their operations may have to the work of others around them, "magic" remains a negative term associated with a suspicious class of practitioners.

When we look at the people who were in fact using varieties of magic in medieval Europe, however, it becomes hard to sustain the stereotype. Instead of finding a single, readily identifiable class of magicians, we find various types of people involved in diverse magical activities: monks, parish priests, physicians, surgeon-barbers, midwives, folk healers, and diviners with no formal training, and even ordinary women and men who, without claiming special knowledge or competence, used whatever magic they happened to know. The monks and priests who practiced magic were able to write much earlier and more widely than laypeople, and left more records of their magic, but this does not mean that they engaged in these activities more often.

Further complicating matters, people could move from one category to another. The library of the monastery of St. Augustine in Canterbury was richly stocked with works on various forms of magic, but these were largely brought into the monastery by three men who had cultivated this interest before they had entered and continued studying magic after becoming monks.[1]

Nor is there reason to think that these various practitioners engaged in wholly different kinds of magic. There is every indication that monks learned about medicinal and magic herbs from laypeople as well as from classical authors, that lay practitioners learned healing charms from monks and priests, and that before medicine became a university subject there was little to distinguish physicians from lay healers. One can thus

---

[1] Sophie Page, *Magic in the Cloister: Pious Motives, Illicit Interests, and Occult Approaches to the Medieval Universe* (University Park: Pennsylvania State University Press, 2013).

speak of a "common tradition" of medieval magic. Magic might be common in more than one way: it might be practiced by many people, it might be known even to people who did not practice it, and it might be generally accessible because it was practiced by relatively few specialists.[2] Fundamentally, however, the term as used here has negative force: it refers to magic that is not anyone's particular specialty. It does not mean that such magic was found universally in medieval society, or that it persisted wholly unchanged through the centuries. What it does suggest is that much of the magic in medieval Europe was distributed widely, and that it was not regularly limited to any specific group. It was not specific-ally the practice of monks, or women, or physicians. In later chapters we will examine other types of magic that were somewhat more specialized, but first we must survey this common magical tradition.

This chapter will deal mainly with materials from the twelfth through fifteenth centuries: a time when Christianity, pervaded with accretions from folk culture, was accepted throughout Europe. Numerous manu-scripts have survived from throughout this period, most especially from the fifteenth century, and from them we are richly informed about the magic of the age. We will also look at some earlier materials that show how magical beliefs and practices evolved and fit into the culture of medieval Europe.

Practitioners of Magic: Healers and Diviners

There is ample evidence that monks studied medicine within their mon-asteries and did what they could to absorb and transmit the medical knowledge of antiquity. When Cassiodorus (487–583) laid out a curricu-lum of studies for monks, he recommended the herbal ascribed to Dioscorides, the works of Hippocrates, Galen, and other Greek or Latin medical writers. During the early medieval centuries, it was the monks who copied out manuscripts of these and other classical authors. This is not to say that monks were training to become physicians. Rather, medical knowledge was a small part of the general education that they were expected to obtain; it was one portion of their inheritance from antiquity. Each monastery was expected to have an infirmary for its ailing and aged members, and in it the monks were most likely to apply whatever medical learning they had acquired. They might also provide medical aid for the poor, for travelers, and for pilgrims who came visiting at their monasteries. In many cases, the care of such outsiders gave rise to

[2] Catherine Rider, "Common magic," in Collins, *Cambridge History of Magic and Witchcraft*, 304.

early hospitals, distinct from the monks' own infirmaries. Around 940, for example, a hospital was founded at Flixton in Yorkshire for the care of these lay patients. Some monks gained such skill as healers that they were sought outside the monasteries by lay patients, even by royalty.[3]

To the extent that classical medicine entailed magical elements, or that the monks picked up new forms of medical magic from the culture around them, they would be practicing magical cures. Or rather, they would be using what later authors called magic. The early medieval monks would not have thought of themselves as dabbling in the magical arts. Without scruples, however, they would use mandrake for its mysterious curative powers, and they might also use charms to drive away the "elves" that were causing sickness.

Monks were not the only healers in early medieval Europe. There were also lay practitioners, known in England as "leeches," though we know little about them. Evidently some of them were itinerant. They had some kind of training, probably more practical than theoretical, and probably amounting to a kind of apprenticeship. They too might have some access to the medical writings of antiquity, though they did not have the systematic education of the monasteries available to them, and must have relied all the more on folk medicine and informal observation. While it is difficult to make comparisons, they, even more than the monks, probably used forms of medicine that later writers would call magical.

What applied to monks would apply as well to some of the diocesan clergy, at least those priests who had some kind of systematic education. Rabanus Maurus proposed that all such clerics should have medical knowledge, but realities fell short of this ideal, and indeed only a minority of the clergy would have any formal education at all. At least up to the thirteenth century, rural priests seem to have been essentially grassroots purveyors of ritual, happy to oblige their parishioners with uncritical use of such rites as they could perform. Typically they came from village families, and might have minimal education beyond a wobbly command of Latin. Their training, much like that of informal healers, was essentially a kind of apprenticeship. Bishops of the thirteenth and following centuries tried to amend the situation: they tried to enforce higher standards of education for local clergy and to eradicate magical and

---

[3] On healers and healing, see Robert Steven Gottfried, *Doctors and Medicine in Medieval England, 1340–1530* (Princeton University Press, 1986); Nancy G. Siraisi, *Medieval and Early Renaissance Medicine: An Introduction to Knowledge and Practice* (University of Chicago Press, 1990); Faith Wallis and Paul Edward Dutton, eds., *Medieval Medicine: A Reader* (University of Toronto Press, 2010); Danielle Jacquart, *Le milieu médical en France du XIIe au XVe siècle* (Geneva: Droz, 1981); and Rider, "Common magic," 320–6.

superstitious use of rituals, but they were struggling against deeply ingrained custom.[4]

While ordinary parish priests may have dabbled in medicine, they were more likely to practice other forms of magic. The sort of duty a village priest might be expected to perform is clear from an eleventh-century ritual for infertile fields. The ceremony extends through an entire day, starting before sunrise, with the digging of four clumps of earth from the four sides of the affected land. It is presumably the local priest who is supposed to sprinkle these clumps with a mixture of holy water, oil, milk and honey, and fragments of trees and herbs, while reciting in Latin the words that God said to Adam and Eve, "Be fruitful and multiply, and fill the earth" (Genesis 1:28), followed by further prayers. The clumps are then carried to church, where the priest sings four masses over them. Before sunset, the clumps are taken back out to the fields, where, fortified with a day's worth of ritual, they will spread the power for growth to all the land.[5] Homespun ceremonies of this kind might remain purely religious, with no admixture of magic, but the possibilities for combining the two were always present.

If the leeches and the parish priests had only meager education, there were other practitioners in medieval society with even less formal training. Most societies have informal healers and diviners recognized as such by their clients, but not by any sort of certifying authorities or official teachers. Different people can adopt this role. Folklore researchers in modern times have found that the rules regarding the practice of popular healing vary widely from place to place, even within Europe. In some areas the healers are mostly women; in others they are predominantly men. Sometimes the secrets of healing can be passed only from women to women or from men to men, but in other regions the gender must alternate with each transmission. In some places the healers are thought to possess inherited powers, and if charms are passed to people without these gifts they will have no force, but elsewhere there are recognized procedures for acquiring the powers without inheritance.[6]

---

[4] Patricia A. DeLeeuw, "The changing face of the village parish, I: The parish in the early Middle Ages," in J. A. Raftis, ed., *Pathways to Medieval Peasants* (Toronto: Pontifical Institute, 1981), 311–22, and Joseph W. Goering, "The changing face of the village parish, II: The thirteenth century," in Raftis, *Pathways to Medieval Peasants*, 323–34.

[5] G. Storms, *Anglo-Saxon Magic* (The Hague: Nijhoff, 1948), 172–87. Storms suggests that the priest was pagan, but this seems unlikely. See now Ciaran Arthur, *"Charms," Liturgies, and Secret Rites in Early Medieval England* (Woodbridge: Boydell, 2018), 87–91.

[6] Irmgard Hampp, *Beschwörung, Segen, Gebet: Untersuchungen zum Zauberspruch aus dem Bereich der Volksheilkunde* (Stuttgart: Silberburg, 1961), 15–17.

We have no reports from systematic field workers in medieval Europe, but the situation then is not likely to have been less varied.

If it is impossible to generalize about the sort of people who became unofficial healers, it is equally hopeless to generalize about the techniques they used. One Danish leechbook gives a variety of prescriptions – dropping a woman's milk into a man's urine to tell whether he will live, writing a Latin prayer on a doorpost to protect livestock from robbers and wolves, smearing leek juice on one's penis to keep one's wife from having sex with another man, and so forth – along with more ordinary medical recipes.[7]

Matteuccia di Francisco, a woman of Todi who was tried for sorcery in 1428, used a range of healing techniques alongside other forms of magic. She taught people to cure illness by taking a bone from an unbaptized baby out to a crossroad, burying it there, and saying various prayers and formulas on that spot over nine days. She knew how to counteract curses. When a man found a strange feather in his pillow and suspected it had been put there to cast a spell on him, he took it to Matteuccia, who destroyed the spell by means of an incantation, then told the man to take the feather home and burn it. Matteuccia could also transfer ailments, and did so on one occasion to cure a client's lameness: she took a potion with thirty different herbs, enhanced its power with an incantation, and cast it out onto the street so that the lameness might be transferred from the client to an unsuspecting passerby. Many of her clients were women. She gave a contraceptive formula to a priest's mistress: she was to take ashes from the burnt hoof of a female mule, mix them with wine, and drink them. But Matteuccia's real specialty was love magic. She recited incantations over herbs, then gave them to women as love potions. She gave women lotions for their hands and faces which would arouse men's affections. When the mistress of a priest complained that he had not had relations with her for a long time, but beat her, Matteuccia took a wax image and placed it on a fire, while the client recited words comparing the wax to the priest's heart; after this ceremony, the priest loved the woman passionately and did her bidding.[8]

Matteuccia was obviously a recognized specialist. Clients came to her, sometimes from out of town, to obtain various kinds of magic in exchange for money. Not all folk practitioners would have been as bold as she was: some might have been wary of using overtly magical techniques, and some might have been more scrupulous about the purposes

[7] Mitchell, *Witchcraft and Magic*, 47.
[8] Candida Peruzzi, "Un processo di stregoneria a Todi nel 400," *Lares: Organo della Società di Etnografia Italiana-Roma*, 21 (1955), issue 1–2, 1–17.

they served. Yet others may have been even more daring than she: unofficial exorcists, for example, who would go about driving demons out of people to cure their ailments. The theologian John of Frankfurt had little patience with such vigilante attacks on demons. Popular exorcists, he complained, take hold of people with natural illness and try to cure them with savage rituals, torturing them with cold water, strangling them, and beating them with switches. If the victims are not mad already, they can be driven mad with such treatment.[9] We know of one such exorcist who competed with the local clergy around Florence. By using strange rituals with a candle and incantations, he managed to cure a ten-year-old girl, though she was left weak after the rigors of his exorcism.[10]

If some people were known as healers, others were known as diviners or fortune-tellers. No doubt these categories overlapped, and no doubt there were monks and priests who engaged in divination as well. We have manuals for fortune-telling that may have been written by monks, either for fellow monks or for lay readers, though both the authorship and the audience are often obscure. When the duchess of Gloucester wanted assurance of her husband's future good fortune in 1441, one of the people she went to was Margery Jourdemayne, who was known as a "witch," but seems to have been known especially for her divination. Along with two distinguished scholars from Oxford, one a noted astrologer and the other an eminent physician, Margery aided the duchess in foretelling the duke's future and in working image magic to ensure an heir. This, at any rate, is what the defendants admitted when they were brought to trial; whether they performed further magic is unclear.

Some of the business of these folk practitioners – the healing, if not the divining – must have been siphoned off by the rise of university-trained physicians around the twelfth century.[11] There had been places where one could obtain scientific medical education in earlier years: medical study had been available at Salerno as early as the tenth century. The growth of universities in the thirteenth century brought more systematic medical training, integrated into the curriculum of scholastic education then emerging. After taking several years of formal coursework and passing examinations, the physician would be formally certified as such. One might expect that the rise of the medical profession brought about

[9] Joseph Hansen, ed., *Quellen und Untersuchungen zur Geschichte des Hexenwahns und der Hexenverfolgung im Mittelalter* (Bonn: Georgi, 1901), 79.

[10] Gene A. Brucker, "Sorcery in early Renaissance Florence," *Studies in the Renaissance*, 10 (1963), 13–16.

[11] Vern L. Bullough, *The Development of Medicine as a Profession: The Contribution of the Medieval University to Modern Medicine* (New York: Hafner, 1966).

the abolition of magical techniques, but since classical writings were still the foundation of medical education, the distinction between medicine and magic remained no clearer than it had been in antiquity.

The earlier types of practitioner remained in demand, especially among poor folk who could not afford the fees of university-trained doctors. It was not long before physicians with official credentials began challenging the right of other healers to practice their arts. Articulate medical writers steeped in formal medical theory would rail against those with merely empirical command of the healing arts. Popes in the second quarter of the fourteenth century supported the physicians' efforts to suppress medical care by uneducated practitioners. English physicians tried in the 1420s to secure an Act of Parliament prohibiting the practice of medicine without a university education, and specifically excluding women from all medical practice, though these efforts were in vain.

The distinction between physicians and surgeons emerged fitfully in medieval culture. Often the terms were interchangeable. When medicine became a subject for study at the universities, however, the dirty work of surgery remained at first outside the curriculum in many places, and thus a clearer distinction emerged: physicians were university-educated men who practiced internal medicine, while surgeons had less exalted credentials and cut into people. Physicians in the thirteenth and following centuries did their best to secure control over surgeons (and apothecaries as well); the surgeons responded by setting up their own schools and attempting to gain professional recognition in their own right.

Further down the social ladder were barber-surgeons, whose business was not simply cutting hair, but also bleeding people and performing other routine medical care. Much of medieval medicine was based on the notion that bodily humors must be kept in proper balance; to relieve people of excessive blood, it was common to bleed them regularly. Such operations might be routine and minor, but they still required knowledge of where to puncture the skin, how much blood to withdraw, and how to stop the flow. Preventing infection was not yet a subject for systematic study, but the trained barber-surgeon would have known that there are certain times of the month or of the year when a patient should not be bled, and would have observed these strictures.

Surgeons and barber-surgeons may have been less inclined toward magic than other practitioners. Their hands-on approach to health precluded some of the more exotic remedies that prevailed in internal medicine. Yet they were not wholly immune to the allure of magic. The biography of Antoninus Pierozzi (d. 1459), archbishop of

Florence, tells that he once went to a local barber-surgeon, and while the man was taking care of him the prelate asked how he had gained medical knowledge without command of Latin. The man replied in all innocence that a monk had given him a book from which he learned all he needed to know. The archbishop asked to see the book, and the barber-surgeon happily complied. To his astonishment, Antoninus found the manuscript filled with incantations "and things and signs pertaining to the evil and magical arts." It is difficult to know how to interpret this description. It might have applied quite literally to a compilation such as the Munich handbook, though the barber-surgeon would not have been likely to mistake that for anything else. More probably it contained prescriptions like those in the Wolfsthurn handbook, in which case the archbishop's reaction was overstated.[12]

Medical manuals from medieval Europe often have gynecological and obstetric information alongside other material, which suggests that general practitioners (to use modern parlance) might deal with these matters. For aid in childbirth, however, most people would go not to physicians, but to midwives. They, too, might engage in practices that others would call magical: there is ample evidence, for example, that amulets of various kinds were used to aid in childbirth, and a midwife might be expected to know and use such techniques.[13] In the later medieval centuries, when medicine had taken steps toward professional status and the notion of legal control had been established, midwives in some parts of Europe were officially licensed. Yet their training remained practical rather than theoretical or academic, and people with higher education no doubt saw them as unsophisticated. Not surprisingly, this unprestigious career was left to women, and this was virtually the only sort of health care that women were widely and officially allowed to provide in these later centuries.

The practice of midwifery could at times involve serious forms of magic. In the early fifteenth century, a woman of Paris named Perrette was practicing as a licensed midwife with clients even from the aristocracy. Against her better judgment, she became involved in a scheme to cure a certain nobleman of leprosy by irregular means: in exchange for a sum of money, she was to obtain the body of a stillborn infant, whose fat would be used for an unguent. After great hesitation she procured the needed corpse, only to find herself incarcerated under suspicion of

---

[12] *Acta sanctorum*, May, vol. 2 (Paris and Rome: Palmé, 1866), 339.

[13] William D. Paden and Frances Freeman Paden, "Swollen woman, shifting canon: A midwife's charm and the birth of secular Romance lyric," *Publications of the Modern Language Association*, 125 (2010), 306–21.

witchcraft. Eventually her friends appealed to the king for a pardon, which she obtained.[14]

There were also outright quacks, who claimed medical competence they did not have. One in London, in 1382, tried to cure a woman by giving her a piece of parchment with a prayer on it, which he alleged had special medicinal value. Another, earlier in the century, had been importing spoiled wolves' meat for its curative virtues. In both cases, the authorities made a point of showing that the culprits were in fact neither physicians nor surgeons. Apart from practicing unorthodox medicine, they were guilty of impersonation.[15]

Physicians soon found themselves competing not only with the earlier, traditional practitioners, but with a new sort as well: the occasional mendicant friar who developed skill in medicine. The mendicant (or "begging") orders, such as the Franciscans and Dominicans, arose in the thirteenth century. They distinguished themselves for their preaching and other religious service, especially in the towns, and became immensely popular and influential. Many of them went to the universities for their education, and before long they became prominent as scholars. Those who had studied the liberal arts might in the process obtain at least a smattering of medical knowledge, and some made it a special interest, even though they were forbidden to obtain medical degrees. There is evidence of Dominicans and Franciscans who provided medical care, especially for those who could not afford professional physicians. One medical treatise, ascribed to a Friar Randolf, is explicitly intended as a guide to those who would provide medical help for the poor, but do not have the requisite knowledge or the means to hire physicians. Drawing on the most authoritative sources, this author laid out systematically all the basic principles of medicine.[16]

There were, finally, the nonspecialists: people such as the compiler of the Wolfsthurn handbook, who probably had no special competence, but would gladly make use of magical techniques helpful in coping with the problems of daily life. In the fourteenth and fifteenth centuries, partly because literacy was increasingly common among the laity and partly because paper was beginning to become available (as an alternative to the more expensive parchment) as a material for books, European towns were flooded with popular writings on all topics. Medical writings taught

---

[14] Thomas Rogers Forbes, *The Midwife and the Witch* (New Haven: Yale University Press, 1966), 13–38.

[15] Bullough, *The Development of Medicine*, 104–5.

[16] Peter A. Cant, "*Thesaurus pauperum*: An edition of B.M., MS. Sloane 3489, a fifteenth-century medical miscellany with introduction, notes and glossary" (King's College London Ph.D. thesis, 1973).

people how to heal themselves: how to let their own blood, how to examine their own urine, what herbs to use in treating their ailments. Books of charms proliferated. Manuals for divination, long known in monastic and clerical circles, became common now among the laity. These and other materials, which had previously circulated for the most part in Latin, were increasingly available in the various vernacular languages. If the late Middle Ages saw a flowering of popular education generally, they were also a golden age for magic. Now one no longer needed to be a specialist. Anyone could learn the magical arts, and many people evidently did so.

These, then, are the *dramatis personae*, the characters we will see on the stage of medieval magic. They are a diverse company, and their interaction was unpredictable. Yet they did interact: scarcely any form of magic was the exclusive preserve of any of these groups. It was a monk who gave the Florentine barber-surgeon his book of magic. Margery Jourdemayne had a record of collaborating with clerics in the occult arts. Professionals might be jealous of nonprofessionals, but that was all the more reason for the latter to plunder the medical knowledge of the former via popular manuals that disseminated up-to-date medical techniques. The culture of the age was by no means uniform, but the distinctions that did exist – social, professional, and geographical – were remarkably fluid.

Medical Magic: Herbs and Animals

The varieties of medical practice in medieval Europe can already be gleaned from two Old English manuals, both of which show how the pre-Christian culture of northern Europe became grafted onto Graeco-Roman tradition.[17] The first is generally known as the leechbook (or "doctor-book") of Bald, because a poem incorporated in it refers to a man named Bald as having it written out for him. Living well before the rise of universities, Bald must have been an informally trained leech. The use of the vernacular language suggests that he was a layman, though the occasional use of Latin indicates that he was a man of some culture. On the other hand, some of his formulas require either saying masses or having masses said over the healing herbs; these materials probably came

---

[17] For both, see Storms, *Anglo-Saxon Magic*. See now Christine B. Voth and Debby Banham, eds., *Bald's Leechbook and Leechbook III: Old English Medicine in British Library, Royal 12. D. xvii*, Dumbarton Oaks Medieval Library (Cambridge, Mass.: Harvard University Press, 2021). On healing magic more generally, see Rider, "Common magic," 310–15.

from a clerical or monastic setting. His book dates from the tenth century, though it includes much earlier material, some of it classical. It cites the authority of "Pliny the great physician" for some of its prescriptions, it takes over bodily a treatise by Alexander of Tralles (ca. 525–ca. 605), and it also draws from Marcellus Empiricus. It starts in orderly fashion, dealing first with ailments on the outside of the body from head to foot, then covering internal illnesses. Then it adds a jumble of prescriptions that borrow heavily from Christian ritual: such things as incense, holy water, and prayers figure prominently in this third section.

The character of this leechbook is difficult to indicate, since it is a collection from various sources. On the whole it is a reasonably sober distillation of classical medicine, yet it did not lack elements of what later authors would call natural magic. Consider, for example, its prescription for skin disease:

Take goose-fat, and the lower part of elecampane and viper's bugloss, bishop's wort, and cleavers. Pound the four herbs together well, squeeze them out, and add a spoonful of old soap. If you have a little oil, mix it in thoroughly and lather it on at night. Scratch the neck after sunset, and silently pour the blood into running water, spit three times after it, then say, "Take this disease and depart with it." Go back to the house by an open road, and go each way in silence.[18]

The first part of the prescription is ordinary herbal medicine, but the procedure for transferring illness to running water, with its attendant rituals and taboos, can more readily be perceived as magical.

The second of these compilations, the *Lacnunga*, is from the eleventh century and has a much stronger leaning toward magic.[19] Many of its prescriptions are from European folk culture: that of the early English themselves, or of the Celts or the Norsemen, all of which traditions would have been familiar in Britain. Intermingled are remedies taken from the ancient culture of the Greeks, Romans, and Jews. While the *Lacnunga* is anything but a coherent treatise on medicine, there are recurrent themes that afford insight into the compiler's view of diseases, their causes, and their cures. One of the most important sources of illness is the mischief-making of elves, whom Christian theologians and moralists would identify with demons. The book tells how to cure "elf-shot," meaning disease caused by the invisible but all too perceptible assault of these elves. More than many leechbooks, the *Lacnunga* prescribes Christian prayers to be recited in Latin over the ingredients used for medicine. One healing salve, for example, is made of butter from a

---

[18] Storms, *Anglo-Saxon Magic*, 165 (adapted).
[19] Edward Pettit, ed. and trans., *Anglo-Saxon Remedies, Charms, and Prayers from British Library MS Harley 585: The Lacnunga* (Lewiston: Edwin Mellen Press, 2001).

completely red or completely white cow, to which fifty-seven specified herbs are added. The mixture must be stirred with a stick on which the names "Matthew, Mark, Luke, and John" are inscribed in Latin. Several charms or incantations are then sung over the salve. This book may also be the work of a lay leech, though the heavy influence of Christian liturgy points, perhaps, to monastic influence.

The same kind of material found in these two books can be read in later works as well, and most of it can be found on the Continent as well as in England. The materials prescribed in this literature tend to be quite simple, at least until they are compounded by the healer: herbs and other plants, portions of animal bodies, and the effluvia of animals are the stock ingredients for drugs. While some of these medicines are specifics, any given plant is likely to have multiple uses. Thus, mandrake is recommended for afflictions of the eyes, wounds, snakebite, earache, gout, baldness, and numerous other complaints.[20] The oak and vervain had diverse magical uses, and merited separate treatises outlining their wondrous properties.[21] If healing virtue was sought from animal bodies, each organ was likely to have its special function. Thus, a short treatise on the uses of the vulture, which has survived in a manuscript from Gaul around the year 800 and in many other versions, gives minute instructions on how to use each portion of the bird. The skull, wrapped in the skin of a deer, cures headaches. Its brains, mixed with unguent and stuffed into the nose, are effective against head ailments. The kidneys and testicles cure impotence if they are dried out, pulverized, and administered in wine.[22]

The authors of these materials do not reflect explicitly on the relationship between medicine and magic, nor do they indicate which of their cures have "occult" as opposed to ordinary power. Doubtless they would have argued that the curative value of all their remedies was borne out by experience. Even modern pharmacology often relies more on trial and error than on theoretical notions of how chemicals will work, and medieval healers seem to have worked essentially the same way. If they claimed that cat faeces could cure baldness or a quartan fever,[23] they would support this claim not so much with theoretical explanation as

---

[20] E.g. British Library, MS Harley 5294, fol. 43[r-v].

[21] Jerry Stannard, "Magiferous plants and magic in medieval medical botany," *Maryland Historian*, 8 (1977), no. 2, 33–46.

[22] Loren C. MacKinnery, "An unpublished treatise on medicine and magic from the age of Charlemagne" (with translation), *Speculum*, 18 (1943), 494–6; A. A. Barb, "Birds and medical magic," *Journal of the Warburg and Courtauld Institutes*, 13 (1950), 316–22.

[23] British Library, MS Harley 1585, fol. 74[r].

with appeal to their own experience. "An experienced woman told me," says the compiler of one work, "that after she had been weighed down by frequent childbearing she ate a bee, and after that she no longer conceived."[24] Precisely why this or that remedy worked was not the healer's concern. Given this apparent indifference to causes, the distinction between occult and manifest power perhaps seems beside the point: what mattered was whether a remedy worked, not how it did so.

Without doing violence to the mentality of the healers, however, we can identify certain features of their work that do point in the direction of magic – or, more precisely, what a critical observer could see as magical.

First, the preparation of the drug often involves observance of taboos; though these may strike us as having no obvious role in the healing process, they are important for maintaining the purity of the healing substance or for enhancing the power of the healer. The ashes from burnt ravens are effective against gout and epilepsy, for example, but only if the birds are taken live from their nest, carried without touching the ground or entering into a house, and burned in a new pot.[25] One should go out barefoot, or in silence, to pick a herb; or one should abstain from sexual contact before gathering herbs. One should dig a herb from the ground without using an iron implement: a common requirement, perhaps showing that the magic in question predates the use of iron in prehistoric Europe. The killing of magical animals, too, can involve such taboos: the vulture should be killed with a sharp reed, not a sword, and before its decapitation the killer should say, "Angel Adonai Abraham, on your account the work is completed."

Secondly, the choice of healing ingredients was sometimes dictated by the symbolic considerations of sympathetic magic. Thus, animals known for their strength, their speed, or their ferocity are preferred over gentler beasts, and often a male animal such as a bull, a hart, or a ram is indicated because it is physically stronger than the female and thus, by extension, has greater healing potency. Patients with jaundice are to be given earth-worms to drink in stale ale, but the worms must be the sort with "yellow knots" to counteract the yellowness of jaundice. In this case, the author insists on grinding the worms so small that the patient will not recognize them, "for loathing," but this is merely an element of common sense in an otherwise magical prescription.[26]

[24] British Library, MS Sloane 3132, fol. 57^v.
[25] Henry Ellis, "Extracts in prose and verse from an old English medical manuscript, preserved in the Royal Library at Stockholm," *Archaeologia*, 30 (1844), 397.
[26] Warren R. Dawson, ed. and trans., *A Leechbook or Collection of Medical Recipes of the Fifteenth Century* (London: Macmillan, 1934), 154–5.

Thirdly, even apart from the rise of systematic astrology, medical procedures often involve explicit or implicit attention to the effects of the heavenly bodies. Certain plants can cure lunacy if they are wrapped in red cloth and tied around the lunatic's head under a specified astrological sign while the Moon is waxing. One should go out before sunrise to pluck a herb. Fragments of bark are more potent if they come from the eastern side of the tree, where they can absorb the rays of the rising Sun.

Fourthly, use of arcane language, whatever other significance it has, at least suggests that the cure involves mysterious ingredients or processes. Old English charms often include language that seems like gibberish, sometimes mingled together with recognizable language. A charm for dysentery, said to have been delivered from heaven by an angel, includes this mixture of words, which has fragments of Latin, Greek, and Hebrew:

Ranmigan. adonai. eltheos. mur. O ineffabile. Omiginan. midanmian. misane. dimas. mode. mida. memagartern. Orta min. sigmone. beronice. irritas. venas. quasi dulaþ. fervor. fruxantis. sanguinis. siccatur. fla. fracta. frigula. mirgui. etsihdon. segulta. frautantur. in arno. midoninis. abar vetho. sydone multo. saccula. pp pppp sother sother.

One interpretation of such passages is that they come from the garbling of scribes who do not understand what they are copying. A second is that deliberate use of strange language allowed a performer-healer to make a deeper impression on the patient and others. A third suggests that this language was a kind of "spirit code" used in coercing demons or other spirits. And a fourth interpretation is that early English scholars and those on the Continent associated with them knew of early Christian theories of language and deliberately used elaborate ciphers, combinations of languages, and manipulations of language to render their language more obscure and challenging, to give their texts a veil of secrecy, to reproduce the primordial language spoken before the Tower of Babel, and sometimes to add an element of playfulness. They knew the legend of an angel that gave the early monk Pachomius knowledge of a "mystical language" so that he and others might communicate with each other using a "spiritual alphabet."[27] These theories are not mutually exclusive. Modes of language devised by writers with a sophisticated grasp of language theory could have been imitated by others with less learning and used by healers for stronger performative impact.

---

[27] Arthur, *"Charms," Liturgies, and Secret Rites*, 169–214, develops the fourth interpretation and discusses the others. The idea of a "spirit code" is from Leslie K. Arnovick, *Written Reliquaries: The Resonance of Orality in Medieval English Texts* (Amsterdam and Philadelphia: Benjamins, 2006), 27–59. See also Jones and Olsan, "Medicine and magic," 301.

These ways of approaching the healing process seem to have been common to healers of all sorts, not just the monks and priests, or the lay practitioners, or members of any other group. Even if such factors were of less importance in the medicine of the universities, they were not uprooted altogether: as we will see in a later chapter, astrological considerations became, if anything, more important in formal medical study. The people who used these magical cures may not have reflected deeply on the causes they were invoking or the philosophical implications of these causes, but when later writers decreed that certain cures appealed to "occult powers" in nature, they were not seriously distorting the realities of medical practice.

A further complicating factor is that the use of herbal magic, if it cannot be rigorously distinguished on the one hand from science, has links on the other hand to religion. Herbs and ointment were often compounded with holy water, and it becomes artificial to distinguish between its function as "holy" and its role as "water." Popular and monastic manuals for healing, at least, not infrequently encouraged their readers to say prayers over the herbs. One prayer written specifically for this purpose is quite straightforwardly religious rather than magical:

O God, who at the beginning of the world commanded the verdant plants ... to grow and multiply, we offer humble and suppliant prayers that you may bless and consecrate in your name these herbs, gathered for medicinal use, so that all who take potions or unguents made from them, or apply them to their wounds, may deserve to obtain health of mind and body.[28]

The same essential notion is conveyed graphically by a herbal that depicts Christ and Mary standing beside a large cluster of foliage; Christ has his hand extended in a gesture of blessing (Fig. 6). The meaning would have been clear to any medieval reader: Christ's blessing is what bestows or enhances the healing power of the herbs.[29]

Charms: Prayers, Blessings, and Adjurations

If the boundary between natural magic and religion is elusive in the case of medicinal herbs, it is all the harder to distinguish the magical from the religious in verbal formulas. These are of three basic types. First there are *prayers*, which have the form of requests and are directed to God, Christ, Mary, or a saint. Second there are *blessings*, which have the form of wishes

[28] British Library, MS Sloane 783B, fol. 214ᵛ.
[29] See the apocryphal legend about Jesus collecting herbs for Mary, in A. Vögtlin, ed., *Vita beate virginis Marie et salvatoris rhythmica* (Tübingen: Litterarischer Verein in Stuttgart, 1887), 94–5.

Fig. 6. Christ blessing the herbs, with Mary, from a fourteenth-century herbal

and are addressed to the patients. Third there are *adjurations or exorcisms*, which have the form of commands and are directed to the sickness itself or to the worm, demon, elf, or other agent responsible for it. The term "exorcism" is usually reserved for an extended ritual expressly directed against demons, but the border between these and adjurations is fluid.[30] To categorize all such formulas as "charms," a term that could be seen as

---

[30] Hampp, *Beschwörung, Segen, Gebet*, 136–40. For a far more intricate typology and analysis, see now especially Marcello Barbato, ed., *Incantamenta latina et romanica: Scongiuri e formule magiche dei secoli V–XV* (Rome: Salerno Editrice, 2019), xxvii–xcv.

prejudicing the question how far they are magical, is mainly to make a point about their manner of use: they were scripts for performance, often sung, and indeed the word "charm" derives from a Latin word for "song."

It is clear even from the Wolfsthurn manual how prayers can play a role in otherwise magical practices. Often these are snippets from the Christian liturgy, removed from their context and used without any sense of their meaning. The standard prayers known throughout Christian society are also used: the Lord's Prayer, the Hail Mary, sometimes the Creed. To keep cattle from harm, one is advised to sing the liturgical "Agios, Agios, Agios" around them every evening. If such prayers were used by themselves, there would be no reason to refer to them as magical. When a charm for toothache begins with an appeal to "Lady Moon," what we have is evidently a vestige of pagan religion, but in most cases the prayers used are clearly Christian. Often the manuals advise saying these prayers three times, and it is tempting to read magical significance into that fact, but of course the number three stood for the Trinity, and in healing, as in the liturgy, threefold repetition of a prayer could be in honor of the Trinity. At times, the prayers are linked with magical rites or taboos, as in a twelfth-century manuscript, evidently from Germany, which gives a prayer to be written out on five wafers. The patient, who must be barefoot, removes the wafers and eats them, then says a further prayer.[31] When linked with explicitly magical embellishments of this sort, the prayers themselves seem to take on a magical character – not because of their intended force (which we cannot judge), but because emphasis appears to lie on the observance of religiously irrelevant conditions surrounding the formula.

Much the same can be said about blessings, which take the general form, "May God bless you ..." or "May God heal you ..." If these were used by themselves they would be clearly religious and not magical. The explicitly religious character of these formulas becomes especially clear when the manuals suggest saying further prayers *after* one has been cured. There is no suggestion in that case that the prayers are intended for direct practical effect; rather, they express gratitude to God or to his saints. In short, prayers and blessings can be used alongside magic and can be integrated with magic, but they are not inherently magical.[32]

---

[31] Lynn Thorndike, *A History of Magic and Experimental Science*, vol. 1 (New York: Macmillan, 1923), 729–30. Another prayer is meant to be written on a piece of bread, which should then be crumbled and fed to hogs for their protection.

[32] Joseph Klapper, "Das Gebet im Zauberglauben des Mittelalters, aus schlesischen Quellen," *Mitteilungen der schlesischen Gesellschaft für Volkskunde*, 9 (1907), pt. 18, 5–41.

Adjurations are more problematic and require closer scrutiny. Sometimes they involve simple commands, repeated perhaps three times. One brief Old English charm goes, "Fly, devil; Christ pursues you. When Christ is born the pain will go." A German adjuration addressed to a worm enjoins it to "go out" from the patient's marrow into his veins, then from his veins into his flesh, and so forth until it is outside the body altogether. The same progressive weakening of the illness is found in a charm for a cyst:

May you be consumed as coal upon the hearth. May you shrink as dung upon a wall. And may you dry up as water in a pail. May you become as small as a linseed grain, and much smaller than the hipbone of an itch-mite, and may you become so small that you become nothing.[33]

Often the power of an adjuration is enhanced by appeal to persons, things, or events that are sacred and therefore powerful. The disease or the demon is adjured by the cross or the blood of Christ, or by his burial, or by the Last Judgment. The adjuration is still addressed to the sickness or its cause rather than to God or a saint, but the sickness is commanded "in the name" or "by the power" of someone or something holy. This does not necessarily mean that either the disease or the holy person is being coerced, or that the ritual is seen as having mechanical or binding effect. A command leaves open the possibility of refusal; the sickness or demon may not depart. The healer is locked in a kind of combat with the evil power of the disease, and relies on sacred powers as aids in this battle.

In both blessings and adjurations, the sacred events of the Bible or of Christian legend might be more than simple sources of power: they could serve as archetypal events, directly analogous to the healing process itself. Just as the spear of Longinus pierced Christ's side and then came out, so too may some iron implement come out of a wounded patient. Just as Mary suffered anguish when she saw Christ hanging on the cross, so too "must you suffer, O worm!" One of the most popular instances of this formula was the Jordan charm, found as early as the ninth or tenth century. The original version tells how Christ and St. John were approaching the river Jordan, and Christ told the waters to stop flowing. Later variants refer to the baptism of Christ in the Jordan, or to an apocryphal tale of how Christ and John (or Mary) stopped the torrent so they could pass over to the other bank. In any case, the stopping of the water becomes an archetype for the clotting of blood. The formula may be a blessing, in which case the key notion is: "Just as the Jordan stopped, so may your blood stop

---

[33] Storms, *Anglo-Saxon Magic*, 155 (with translation).

flowing." Or it may be an adjuration addressed directly to the blood. In some later versions, this charm is made into an adjuration against disease, weapons, fire, animals, even thieves, all of which are commanded, like the Jordan, to stand still in one or another sense.

The authority of the charms is sometimes enhanced by ascription to a saint. The "charm of St. William," for example, was allegedly given to the holy man by Christ himself as a remedy for worms, cankers, festers, and various forms of gout. Another charm was said to have been devised by St. Eustace for the benefit of a woman in great pain. A common variation on this theme is the blessing or adjuration woven into an apocryphal story, with a character in the legend actually speaking the healing words. In these cases, the legend itself becomes the charm, and the words ascribed to the holy person are the operative portion. The charm for toothache from the Wolfsthurn book is a case in point. When Christ finds Peter sitting on a rock and holding his jaw because a worm is rotting his tooth, Christ himself in most versions adjures the worm or the toothache to depart. A charm that derives from early Jewish and Byzantine sources is that of three angels who, while walking on Mount Sinai, encounter a demon. They ask where he is going, and he says he is off to inflict pain on a certain person. The angels then adjure him by the Father, Son, and Holy Spirit, and by Abraham, Isaac, Jacob, all the patriarchs, prophets, Apostles, martyrs, confessors, virgins, and all saints of God, not to harm that person. The earliest Western version of this charm is a Latin text from the tenth century. Some later examples have multiple demons, who recite a long list of bodily organs they intend to afflict when they attack their victim.

As we have seen, early charms were found among the pagans of northern Europe and were written down and adapted when these areas were converted. At a later stage, perhaps beginning around the eleventh century, Christian monks and priests began writing new charms that were not derived from pagan models. Many of these appear in similar form through much of Europe, apparently sent or taken from one monastery to another. Originally in Latin, they were translated sooner or later into the vernacular languages. A still later phase in the evolution of charms came around the fourteenth and fifteenth centuries, when lay influence asserted itself once more. Certain formulas were now composed originally in the vernacular, or at least expressed in poetic forms long popular in the vernacular languages. Thus the three-flower charm, first found in a French Swiss manuscript from 1429, tells of three roses planted in a garden, or perhaps by Christ's tomb. In some versions, this charm begins in the first person singular: "I went to a garden ..." In any case, the names of the three roses are given, the third usually being "Blood-Stand-Still" or some variation. The folk poem itself ends up as a healing charm.

While rooted in popular culture and developed by monks, charms could be used by physicians as well. John of Gaddesden (ca. 1280–1361), who was court physician under Edward II and was mentioned by Chaucer as an eminent medical authority, recommended the use of such methods, and while John of Mirfeld of St. Bartholomew's Hospital expressed some skepticism on these matters, he nonetheless copied out several charms for whatever benefit they might provide.[34]

Exorcisms, which tend to be much longer than charms, often involve a complex mixture of liturgical and folkloric elements. There was no firm distinction between official exorcisms used by the higher clergy and popular exorcisms devised by lower clergy or even laypeople. The Church did not yet have fixed rituals for universal use in expelling demons, and in the nature of things exorcisms were put together ad hoc or else borrowed from someone else's invention. In some cases they might be reminiscent of standard Christian rites, even if elements of folklore intrude:

In the name of the Father, and of the Son, and of the Holy Spirit, amen. I conjure you, O elves and all sorts of demons, whether of the day or of the night, by the Father, and the Son, and the Holy Spirit, and the undivided Trinity, and by the intercession of the most blessed and glorious Mary ever Virgin, by the prayers of the prophets, by the merits of the patriarchs, by the supplication of the angels and archangels, by the intercession of the Apostles, by the passion of the martyrs, by the faith of the confessors, by the chastity of the virgins, by the intercession of all the saints, and by the Seven Sleepers, whose names are Malchus, Maximianus, Dionysius, John, Constantine, Seraphion, and Martimanus, and by the name of the Lord + A + G + L + A +, which is blessed unto all ages, that you should not harm nor do or inflict anything evil against this servant of God N., whether sleeping or waking. + Christ conquers + Christ reigns + Christ commands + May Christ bless us + [and] defend us from all evil + Amen.

Each time the exorcist finds the cross marked on the page, he is to make the sign of the cross over the afflicted person.

Elsewhere the formula of exorcism draws more heavily from folklore, as in one which begins by "conjuring" and "adjuring" the elves and all diabolical enemies that they may have no more power over the patient. (The words *coniuro* and *adiuro* are used interchangeably for "command.") The exorcist calls on all God's saints to cast these "accursed elves" into the eternal hellfire that is prepared for them. He implores Jesus to send his blessing so that these wretched elves will no longer harm

---

[34] H. P. Cholmeley, *John of Gaddesden and the Rosa medicinae* (Oxford: Clarendon, 1912), 48–52; Percival Horton-Smith Hartley and Harold Richard Aldridge, *Johannes de Mirfeld of St. Bartholomew's Smithfield: His Life and Works* (Cambridge University Press, 1936), 44.

the patient in head or brain, nose, neck, mouth, eyes, hands, and so forth through the various members and organs of the body. He commands Heradiana, the "deaf-mute mother of malignant elves," to depart. As the exorcism progresses, it shifts at random, addressing now the patient, now the elves, and now the heavenly powers.[35]

If both those exorcisms seem only marginally magical, a third one steps unquestionably across the border. If you see a man or woman seized by a demon, the manuscript in question instructs, you should take a piece of parchment and write on it the sign of the cross and the opening of the Gospel according to John. Then you should scrape the words off the parchment into a bowl, and give these scrapings to the afflicted person to drink, along with holy water. If the first potion does not work, a second or even third application may be necessary. This "charm" is given on the best authority: a demon taught it to a possessed person, and it is tried and proven.[36]

While adjurations and exorcisms were usually intended for individuals suffering bodily or mental affliction, they could be put to other purposes as well. Thieves and soldiers might be adjured. Demons responsible for hail, likewise, could be addressed, as in an eleventh-century charm: "I adjure you, O Devil, and your angels ... I adjure you, O Mermeut, with your companions, you who have power over tempests." While such formulas normally sought to drive evil beings away, the same language could also be used to keep helpful beings from leaving. Thus, one fourteenth-century manuscript has a charm addressed to bees: "I conjure you in the name of the Father, and of the Son, and of the Holy Spirit, O you handmaids of God who produce wax for God's service, not to withdraw or flee from me ..."[37]

While most charms fall into the three categories we have been discussing, there is a fourth type that is less common, but more explicitly magical: incantations articulating the meaning of sympathetic magic. A pregnant woman who fears miscarriage or misshapen offspring is instructed to step three times over a grave. If there were no charm for her to use, we might be able to conjecture that she is performing sympathetic magic, expressing victory over death. The point is made explicit, however, by a charm she is supposed to say in the process: "This as my

---

[35] British Library, MS Sloane 962, fols. 9^v–10^r, and MS Sloane 963, fols. 15^r–16^v.

[36] Bodleian Library, Oxford, MS e Mus. 219, fol. 187$^{r–v}$.

[37] Max Siller, "Zauberspruch und Hexenprozess: Die Rolle des Zauberspruchs in den Zauber- und Hexenprozessen Tirols," in Werner M. Bauer, Achim Masser, Guntram A. Plangg, and Eugen Thurnher, eds., *Tradition und Entwicklung: Festschrift Eugen Thurnher* (Innsbruck: Institut für Germanistik der Universität Innsbruck, 1982), 129; Hampp, *Beschworung, Segen, Gebet*, 125.

help against the evil late birth, this as my help against the grievous dismal birth, this as my help against the evil lame birth."[38]

If we ask what it is that qualifies the first three categories of charm as magic from a medieval perspective, we find that they are, for the most part, borderline cases. When speculative minds in the later medieval centuries began reflecting on natural magic, one of the questions that they considered was whether words by themselves, just like certain herbs and other objects of nature, held special powers. Many people believed that verbal formulas could have such inherent power, and these charms would be prime examples. Thus, for *some* medieval people, charms would count as magic. Other people would have been hard-pressed to distinguish between them and purely religious prayers. And perhaps the majority of users would simply not have reflected on the question: if the charms worked, that was more important than *how* they worked.

Protective Amulets and Talismans

Herbs, animal remedies, and charms were used mostly to cure diseases that had already set in. Amulets, on the other hand, were typically meant as protective devices. Unlike the other forms of magic we have discussed, amulets served psychological purposes somewhat more than physical ones: they ensured health of the mind more than that of the body. They could ward off disease, to be sure, but more often they protected their bearers against the attacks of visible and invisible enemies. Whereas herbal and animal cures were usually ingested or applied directly to the body, amulets worked through mere proximity. A potion would be swallowed and an unguent was for anointing, but an amulet was merely to be carried about on one's person. Herbal and animal cures were depleted with use, but amulets could be retained for long or repeated deployment.

Nonetheless, the use of amulets represents essentially a variation on these other forms of magic. This is clear from the nature of the objects used as amulets, which for the most part fall into two categories: plants and parts of animals' bodies. The materials used are essentially the same as those we have already examined, but the way they are applied differs. And the mode of employment usually indicates that occult virtues are assumed to lie within these objects. A hare's foot, bound to the left arm, will enable a person to go anywhere without danger. The right foot of a hare, or the heart of a dog, will keep dogs from barking. Sprigs of rosemary, put at a person's door, will keep venomous snakes away.

---

[38] Storms, *Anglo-Saxon Magic*, 197.

Carried on one's person, rosemary keeps evil spirits at bay, and a spoon made of its wood has power against poisons. If five leaves of a nettle plant are held in the hand, they will ensure safety from all fear and fantasy. Heliotrope, gathered under the sign of Virgo and wrapped in laurel leaves along with the tooth of a wolf, will keep people from saying anything bad about its bearer. If mistletoe is carried on one's person, one will not be condemned in court. If a person goes out in the sign of Virgo before sunrise, collects various herbs, says three Pater Nosters and three Ave Marias, then carries the herbs on his person, no one will be able to speak evil against him, or if they do he will overcome them. If heliotrope is placed at the entrance to a church where adulteresses are present, they will be unable to leave the building until it is removed. The list could be extended indefinitely.[39]

Even in their mode of employment and in their purpose, amulets do not differ absolutely from other magical substances. For example, unguents as well as amulets can serve for prevention: by anointing yourself with the blood of a lion you can keep yourself safe from all other beasts, and if you smear lion fat over your body you will be secure from snakebite.[40] When herbs are used for ligatures or suspensions, bound to or hung from the body, they became similar to amulets. Indeed, the distinction breaks down altogether in a prescription given for demonic possession. In discussion of one plant that goes by various names, including "the herb of Solomon," the author of a herbal tells how St. Augustine learned of its power to expel evil spirits. The saint had learned this lore from an anonymous philosopher. He had occasion to use this knowledge when a noble and pious woman complained to him that her daughter and son were both troubled by demons. He recommended that she take this herb and suspend it around their necks, and when she tried the remedy, it worked. The cure is even more dramatic in the accompanying drawing (Fig. 7), which shows the herb – magnified to enormous dimensions, presumably for identification – being held up to the possessed youths, who are so far beside themselves that attendants must hold them up from behind. The herb is, however, doing its job, and demons are flying from the victims' mouths.

While talismans are generally similar to amulets in purpose and in mode of employment, historians sometimes treat them separately. The distinguishing feature is that talismans, unlike amulets, have written

---

[39] Bodleian Library, Oxford, MS Wood empt. 18, fols. 32^r, 34^r; MS e Mus. 219, fol. 187^v. British Library, MS Sloane 3132, fol. 56^r; MS Sloane 3564, fols. 34^v–35^r, 37^{r-v}. Ellis, "Extracts in prose and verse," 396.

[40] British Library, MS Harley 1585, fol. 66^v.

Fig. 7. St. Augustine recommending a herb for exorcism, and the herb taking effect, from a fourteenth-century herbal

words, or at least letters, inscribed on them. The power of such inscriptions is at least as great as that of plants and animals. Many in medieval society, including the noted medical authority Bernard Gordon (d. ca. 1320), believed one could ward off epileptic attacks by carrying the names of the biblical magi on one's person, written on a slip of parchment. One manuscript gives series of letters from the alphabet which, if written out and carried, will have wondrous effect: one series, to be hidden under the right foot, will silence the bearer's enemies; another, to be held in the left hand, will win favors from potential benefactors. Another manuscript gives a series of names for God which, if borne on one's person, will protect against fire, water, arms, and poison. If a pregnant woman has this formula on her, she will not die in childbirth. Then the author hedges, adding a condition: whoever carries such a sequence of divine names *and looks at them each day* will not die by sword, fire, or water, and will remain unvanquished in battle.[41]

Perhaps the most famous device used on talismans was the magic square with the SATOR-AREPO formula:

---

[41] Bodleian Library, Oxford, MS e Mus. 219, fol. 186^v; MS Wood empt. 18, fol. 9^{r-v}.

S	A	T	O	R
A	R	E	P	O
T	E	N	E	T
O	P	E	R	A
R	O	T	A	S

These words make no obvious sense. Their interest lies largely in the fact that the square reads the same four ways: from top to bottom, from left to right, from bottom to top backward, and from right to left backward. The origin of the square has been disputed, but one popular theory takes it as an anagram for the opening words of the Lord's Prayer in Latin, "Pater Noster," laid out as a cross, with a double "A" and "O" for Christ the Alpha and Omega (Book of Revelation 1:8). It was used as early as the first century; it is found in a house at Pompeii. In medieval Europe it served various magical purposes. It could be inscribed on cloth and placed over the womb to aid a woman in childbirth, and if carried on one's person it could win the favor of all those one met.[42]

Small metal plates called "laminas" were often carried on the body for healing wounds and overcoming infertility, although they could be put to other uses as well. These could be inscribed with crosses, astrological figures, magic squares made of numbers that yield the same total when added in any direction, and other devices. Those meant for fertility often had brief prayers to the "holy mothers" Elizabeth, Ann, and Mary. Similarly eclectic combinations of text and diagram could be inscribed within circles laid out together on parchment that could be folded and borne on one's person to protect against sudden death, demons, attacks by animals or insects, and other dangers.[43] People who wore laminas may have done so because of some specific concern; those who wore talismans with multiple protective circles may have been plagued with multiple anxieties, but it is perhaps more likely that they (or the scribes from whom they purchased these talismans) were simply repeating the range of issues typically averted with such magical protection. They were magical equivalents of modern multivitamins, and they guarded against all sorts of contingencies that people may not have been keenly alert to.

What connection did these amulets and talismans have with the Church's sacramentals? The question is not easy to answer. Certainly, some of the holy objects provided or sanctioned by churchmen seem reminiscent of amulets. Wax blessed on the feast of the Purification was

---

[42] Storms, *Anglo-Saxon Magic*, 281; Bodleian MS Wood empt. 18, fol. 32[r].

[43] Sophie Page, "Medieval magical figures: Between image and text," in Page and Rider, *Routledge History*, 435–42; V. Karpenko, "Between magic and science: Numerical magic squares," *Ambix*, 40 (1993), 121–8.

thought effective against thunderbolts. Ringing of church bells could safeguard the parish from storms. The *Salernitan Regimen*, a popular medical compilation, recommended the "Agnus Dei" (a wax lamb blessed, in principle, by the pope) as protection against various evils, including death by lightning. Long sheets of parchment or paper, inscribed with prayers and then rolled up, could protect their bearers against sudden death, wounding by weapons, the slander of false witnesses, evil spirits, tribulation, illness, danger in childbirth, and other afflictions.[44]

The relics of saints also seem at times to have served as amulets. When Count Rudolf of Pfullendorf brought relics of the biblical patriarchs back from the Holy Land, they imparted peace, fertility, and good weather everywhere he took them. Wax taken from the tomb of St. Martin of Tours and placed atop a tree could protect the surrounding vineyard from hail. Carried into battle, relics could secure victory over the foe. Yet it is dangerous to focus on such reports in isolation from other factors in the veneration of saints. These holy persons might work on Earth through their physical remains, but their devotees knew that their souls were in heaven, interceding before God. They had annual feast days that would be celebrated; in the meantime they could be addressed in prayer. Their deeds on Earth were recorded in legend and recalled in preaching. They had personalities, specific desires, and the ability to punish those who offended them. It is thus misleading to assume that their relics were seen as having *inherent* power, only loosely connected to their spiritual presence. Even the unsophisticated in medieval Europe seem to have had a lively sense that the saints were real persons, subjects for both imitation and awe. They may still, on occasion, have treated their relics as magical amulets, but concrete evidence for this is rare. The danger for the historian lies in the temptation to strip away the religious context by a process of abstraction and then take the magical remainder as the essence of popular piety.

Similar difficulty surrounds popular veneration of the Eucharist. The twelfth and thirteenth centuries saw escalating devotion to the Eucharist, or to the host that the priest consecrated during the mass. This was the age when the theological doctrine of transubstantiation was being refined: no longer content with the vague assurance that Christ was somehow present in the consecrated host, theologians now proposed that the "substance" of bread was miraculously replaced with that of

---

[44] Keith Thomas, *Religion and the Decline of Magic* (London: Weidenfeld & Nicolson, 1971), ch. 1; Curt F. Bühler, "Prayers and charms in certain Middle English scrolls," *Speculum*, 39 (1964), 270–8.

Christ each time the priest pronounced the words of consecration, despite the remaining "accidents" or appearances of bread. Fortified by this doctrine, popular piety now demanded to *see* this miraculously transubstantiated host, and the custom spread of having the priest elevate it over his head after the consecratie so that people at mass could behold it. Popular belief soon held that a person who saw the consecrated host during mass would be safe from harm for the rest of the day. On the feast of Corpus Christi, the host would be carried in procession through town and then out to the fields to ensure fertility of the crops. Laypeople allegedly carried the process further, stealing or otherwise obtaining consecrated hosts to protect themselves against wounding or drowning, to cure their diseases or procure fertility, to prevent storms or to gain riches. At times, they might heighten the power of the host by writing Bible verses or magical charms on it. From one source we learn that peasants were using the Eucharist to protect their livestock: a twelfth-century nun told how Christ came to her in a dream and complained, "They have made me into a swineherd and concealed my body in the stall so their cattle will not succumb to the plague."[45]

In short, the Eucharist lent itself at least as much as saints' relics to use as a magical amulet. This form of abuse may in fact have been easier, since the connection between the consecrated host and Christ's historical life was less apparent, and for that reason it may have been easier to conceive the host as having inherent power. Reformers in the fifteenth century complained that people who were venerating the consecrated host seemed little interested in receiving the same host in communion; this is not quite the same as saying that they viewed it as a magical amulet, but it is a related complaint, based on the observation that people were missing the authentic significance of the Eucharist.

People in medieval Europe who noted and protested against these abuses were not likely to call them magic, but rather superstition, which in this context meant the improper use of a holy object. One corollary to the intellectuals' ways of defining magic is that they had little reason to reflect on the similarities between what they called magic and what they termed superstition. They would scarcely have said that improper use of relics or the Eucharist was an example of *demonic* magic. Demons might tempt people to such abuse, but the abuse itself did not involve the conjuring of demons, even implicitly. Nor was it a case of natural magic when the power being used came from God and the saints. From the theologians' and preachers' viewpoint, relics and hosts were not *natural*

---

[45] Peter Browe, "Die Eucharistie als Zaubermittel im Mittelalter," *Archiv für Kulturgeschichte*, 20 (1930), 134–54.

repositories for occult power; they were not analogous to sprigs of rosemary or organs from vultures.

These distinctions surely corresponded in some measure to the sensibilities of ordinary people. It was not just the theologians who recognized the saints as personal beings, or who knew that the Christ who came in the form of a wafer was the same as the Christ who would come one day as judge. Yet for many people the practical implications of this theology seem to have been less straightforward. Whatever religious meaning these holy objects had, they were immediate sources of potential power. If one could ask the peasant whether the host that he concealed in his stable was similar to some herb that might have served to protect his horses, he might well have said that of course it was not: it had far greater power, and that is why he used it. Practically, however, he was using the host as if it were an amulet, and the theoretical implications would perhaps not have come to his mind. At least one late medieval critic did draw a parallel between certain devotions and magic. Peter of Zealand said the clergy were happy to have laypeople bring images of body parts into the churches as votive offerings, although they worked in the same way as the astral magic that they condemned. A theologian would have reminded Peter that astral magic and votive offerings appeal to fundamentally different sources of power, and that they do *not* work in the same ways. As far as the concrete forms of ritual action were concerned, however, Peter's argument might seem compelling.[46]

Sorcery: The Misuse of Medical and Protective Magic

If it is difficult at times to distinguish magic from science or from religion, it is all the more difficult to separate "white" (helpful) magic from "black" (harmful) magic, or medical and protective magic from sorcery. Much depends on one's point of view, and while it is not customary to speak of "gray magic," there are indeed gray areas between these categories.

What if a healer attempts a cure and the patient only grows worse? Some may assume that the healer was in fact trying to harm the patient. Someone with special knowledge of healing herbs may, after all, know other herbs that can bring sickness and death – or so people in

---

[46] Mandosio, "Peter of Zealand," 273. On the complex relationship between magic and religion, see now Catherine Rider, *Magic and Religion in Medieval England* (London: Reaktion, 2012); and Edina Bozóky, "From matter of devotion to amulets," *Medieval Folklore*, 3 (1994), 91–107.

premodern Europe seem often to have reasoned. Apart from the healer's intentions, the remedy may have been the wrong one, and if a magical cure backfires it may count as sorcery by virtue of its effect. Different but equally great problems arise with love magic. If a magician uses magic to inspire adultery, a God-fearing Christian may easily brand this as sorcery. But what if the same magician uses love magic to help a woman regain her husband's affections? Is this, too, a form of sorcery? Many in medieval society would have assumed so.

A fifteenth-century manuscript tells a story about a woman who has been given a charm written out for her to use against headache. When the woman shows the formula to her confessor, however, he realizes it is actually not a healing charm, but a curse meant to inflict headaches on her and others as well, ending with the notion that thirty devils should carry her off.[47] The moral of the tale is clear: using charms is risky business, because they may not be what they seem to be, and demons may play an unexpected role.

Much of our information about sorcery comes from the records of prosecution: we hear from some disgruntled peasant, for example, that an old woman who lives near him has bewitched his cows or his children. The most common allegation when people are brought to court for magic is that they have caused bodily harm or even death. In some places, love magic is also a frequent basis for prosecution. In theologians' and lawyers' eyes, love magic seems to have counted as sorcery even if used by a wife to regain her husband's affections; it was a means for constraining the will, and that in itself was evil.[48] Elsewhere, especially in and around Switzerland, we find people taken to court for magically inducing storms to destroy their neighbors' crops. A German charm of the tenth century enjoined the Devil in Christ's name not to cause any harm "through destructive rain, through frost, through storms, or through the murmured incantations of sorcerers." Sorcery itself must have appeared as a force of nature, focused on individual agents yet linking them with cosmic powers. On a smaller scale, theft was also punished at

---

[47] Alfons Hilka, "Altfranzösische Zaubersprüche," *Zeitschrift ür romanische Philologie*, 37 (1913), 463–4. William Paden (personal communication 2020) translates the Old French text as "Your head hurts and [but] it doesn't usually hurt you. / May pain come to anyone who wishes you well. / Go to your mother, and she will make you some [pain?]. May thirty devils carry you off." A Provençal version of the same text concludes (again in Paden's translation), "And thirty devils will carry you off."

[48] Richard Kieckhefer, "Erotic magic in medieval Europe," in Joyce Salisbury, ed., *Sex in the Middle Ages: A Book of Essays* (New York: Garland, 1991), 30–55; Rider, "Common magic," 316–17.

times as an act of sorcery, on the assumption that the thief had broken in or removed an object by magical means.

The techniques for sorcery were essentially the same as those for medical or protective magic: potions, charms, and amulets, often with accompanying rituals. The difference between positive and negative magic lay not in their basic conception, but in the purposes they served. Sorcerers who gave people food and drink to do them harm might be accused of "poisoning" them, the distinction between normal and occult powers being as difficult to define here as elsewhere. A Swiss woman in the early fifteenth century allegedly killed a man by giving him a "poisoned" apple, but she was being tried as a sorceress, not simply as a murderer. Love potions might include herbs, ashes, and other materials. Like Heracles' wife in the play by Seneca, women who used love magic at times confused lethal poisons with aphrodisiacs. A woman at Lucerne in the mid-fifteenth century, for example, was accused of making this mistake and was punished by banishment from the town. Another woman confessed that she had given a man her menstrual blood as a love potion, but when he died soon afterward she refused to believe her magic was the cause.

Charms used with evil intent are usually known as "curses." Such a formula was often simply an inverted blessing or adjuration, and had the same structure as these. Like a blessing or adjuration, a curse might make appeal to the events of sacred history or religious legend. At Innsbruck in 1485, a baptized Jewish woman was accused of reciting a blasphemous spell to arouse as much pain in her enemy's head as Mary had in her body when she bore Jesus. Better attested is the use of a charm for love magic: "May N. love me as much as Mary loved her Son when she gave him birth."

Because these curses would be uttered in secrecy, the victim would have little reason to know what they were or even that they had been uttered, and for that reason they probably show up in the court records much less often than they were actually used. For different but equally obvious reasons, the victims of sorcery could not present as evidence potions that had been consumed. What the accusers did have to show the judges were magical amulets that had been left under their thresholds or beds to do them harm. Often these amulets were bundles of noxious powders, human faeces, wood from a gallows, or other such materials. One sick woman checked under the threshold of her home and discovered the bodies of three small black animals, like mice, wrapped in cloth.

The rituals used for sorcery typically involved sympathetic magic. A witness at Lucerne in 1486 told that she had seen two neighbors performing a strange ritual at a well: one of them reached behind herself into the well and drew water over her head three times, and soon it began to hail. If sorceresses stole milk from cows, it might be by "milking" a knife stuck into a wall. Or physical harm could be worked by image magic, the most notorious of sympathetic techniques: when a person's image is pierced with pins or otherwise afflicted, the symbolic harm to the image causes real harm to the victim. Thus, a sorcerer in fourteenth-century Coventry experimented with a wax image of a neighbor. When he drove a lead spike into the image's forehead, the neighbor went mad and began shrieking with pain. After several weeks of this agony, the sorcerer drove the spike into the image's heart and the neighbor died.

Not surprisingly, sorcerers were often thought to use the Church's holy objects and rituals for their transgressions. Seeking supernatural power wherever it was to be found, they would not scruple to bend holy things to their purposes. Fear of such sacrilege might be expressed in anti-Jewish propaganda. An epidemic that spread through Aquitaine in 1321 led to the rumor that lepers and Jews had poisoned the wells with a magical mixture of blood, urine, plants, and the consecrated host. As early as 1130, when the archbishop of Trier gave the Jews of his archdiocese the choice of converting to Christianity or being banished, he died soon afterward, and Jews were charged with having had a wax statue of him baptized, then slowly melting it over a fire to cause his death. Heightened veneration for the Eucharist in the thirteenth and following centuries brought intense fear that the consecrated host would be stolen from churches and used for sorcery. Stories were told of how a woman might kiss a man while holding the host in her mouth to increase his love for her. In one famous case, a woman who did this was punished with inability to see the consecrated host even when it was elevated during the mass. Only when she touched a relic of St. Bridget of Sweden was she released from this affliction. Such stories tend to have a breathless, legendary air about them, but there is nothing inherently implausible about the fear that holy things might get used for unholy ends.

Manuscripts with formulas for medical magic sometimes include material that a theologian or judge would consider as sorcery. The procedures recommended in these manuscripts do not seem different, in principle, from those hinted at in court records, but because we have further detail it becomes easier to see how this magic resembles the herbal concoctions used for healing.[49]

---

[49] British Library, MSS Sloane 3132 and 3564; Bodleian Library, MSS e Mus. 219 and Wood empt. 18.

These manuscripts often prescribe aphrodisiacs, which would have been seen by outsiders as means for love magic. To·arouse a woman's lust, one manuscript advises soaking wool in the blood of a bat and putting it under her head while she is sleeping. The testicles of a stag or bull, or the tail of a fox, will arouse a woman to sexual desire. Putting ants' eggs in her bath will arouse her so violently that willy-nilly she will seek intercourse.[50] More questionable still is the advice of one compiler that if you write "pax + pix + abyra + syth + samasic" on a hazel stick and hit a woman on the head with it three times, then immediately kiss her, you will be assured of her love. A woman, on the other hand, can arouse her husband to love by mixing a herb with earthworms and giving it to him in his food.

Herbs can serve for other kinds of sorcery as well. If teasel is given in food or drink along with a tooth, presumably ground up, it will cause all who ingest it to fight with each other until they consume the juice of another herb. There are many kinds of potion that can make a man impotent, or at least diminish his sexual desire. Eating the flowers of the willow or poplar can do so, "as is proved from long experience." Indeed, a man could be rendered impotent for the rest of his life by being so careless as to imbibe forty ants boiled in daffodil juice. Perhaps the most extravagant claim is that sage, allowed to decay while surrounded by dung, will give rise to a bird with a serpent-like tail; if people are touched with the blood of this bird they will lose their senses for at least fifteen days, while if the serpent is burned and then the ashes are cast into a fire there will at once be terrible thunder.

We need not assume that all such instructions were penned with an equally straight face. Medieval people did seriously believe, however, that bewitchment could cause impotence, and when King Lothar II was unable to consummate his marriage because he was magically impeded, Archbishop Hincmar of Rheims (806–82) was called on to decide whether the affliction was sufficient grounds for the king to dismiss his bride and marry a different woman. The question arose again later, absorbing the attention of leading canon lawyers and other churchmen in the eleventh and twelfth centuries. The solution to the problem was that separation from the bride was allowed if remedies had failed, and

---

[50] W. L. Wardale, "A Low German-Latin miscellany of the early fourteenth century," *Niederdeutsche Mitteilungen*, 8 (1952), 5–22. The prescription concludes with the instruction to write "amet lamet te misael," of which only *amet* ("may she love") and *te* ("you") are intelligible. The same manuscript has other counsel for heightening sexual pleasure and for quelling passion.

remarriage was permitted if the cause of the first failure was clearly magical. In short, sorcery was serious business indeed.

Magically induced impotence is particularly interesting because it was a matter of concern to theologians, canon lawyers, and physicians, who read and were influenced by each other's work. They were influenced also by popular belief and practice – by the problems that people raised when they claimed to suffer from magically induced impotence. Once scholars in various disciplines began reading and commenting on each others' work, they might get caught up in this academic discourse and lose sight of popular concerns. But those concerns came back in focus in the thirteenth century, when theologians and canonists, eventually joined by physicians, came under the sway of a movement of pastoral reform that tried to respond to lay needs and to instruct and regulate the religious and moral life of the laity.[51]

For sorcery, as for healing magic, the power of herbs might be enhanced by use of charms. One fourteenth-century formula, superficially Christian, is addressed to a plant:

In the name of Christ, amen. I conjure you, O herb, that I may conquer by Lord Peter ... by the moon and stars ... and may you conquer all my enemies, pontiffs and priests and all laymen and all women and all lawyers who are working against me ...[52]

If the same basic techniques were used for both positive and negative magic, it is not surprising that these techniques could also be used as protection against sorcery, or as countermagic for use against a curse that someone was inflicting. One formula from 1475 is explicitly identified as a charm for use against "a wicked witch." While worded as a charm, it is intended as a talisman: it is to be written out and carried on one's person, for protection "in sleeping, in waking, in drinking, and especially in dreaming." It reads:

In nomine Patris, etc. By the power of the Lord, may the cross + and passion of Christ + be a medicine for me. May the five wounds of the Lord be my medicine +. May the Virgin Mary aid and defend me from every malign demon and from every malign spirit, amen. + A + G + L + A + Tetragrammaton + Alpha + O ...[53]

The physician Arnold of Villanova wrote a treatise *On Bewitchments* around 1300, in which he gave numerous remedies for impotence caused

[51] Catherine Rider, *Magic and Impotence in the Middle Ages* (New York: Oxford University Press, 2006).

[52] Thorndike, *History of Magic*, vol. 1, 598 n. 1 (with translation of quotation).

[53] John Brand, *Popular Antiquities of Great Britain*, ed. W. Carew Hazlitt, vol. 3 (London: Smith, 1870), 73.

by magic. In some cases, he says, men who are unable to have sexual relations with their wives can be cured by human means; in other cases, divine aid is necessary. Sometimes the bewitchment is caused by use of some object which can simply be removed: the testicles of a rooster placed under the bed of the married couple, or an inscription with characters written in bat's blood. There are further natural expedients to use: fumigation of the bedchamber with the bile of a fish will counteract the bewitchment (Tobit 6:16–17 and 8:4, in the Old Testament apocrypha), as will smearing or sprinkling the walls with the blood of a black dog. For more difficult cases, Arnold prescribes an elaborate exorcism in which the opening verses from the Gospel of John are written and immersed in a liquid, which the couple drinks. Leaves, flowers, and fruit are placed over burning coals to drive away the meddling demon. The assumption here seems to be that the magic in question can be either natural or demonic: in the former case, natural countermagic will suffice, but in the latter, one must resort to an exorcism.[54]

Divination and Popular Astrology

The forms of magic so far examined were ways of manipulating nature to affect one's destiny. Divination was a means for knowing a destiny that was foreordained. As we have seen, early medieval writers thought of magic primarily as a series of divinatory techniques, all of which, like the rest of magic, relied on demonic inspiration. Roughly half of Isidore of Seville's section on magicians deals with diviners, and his schema had lasting influence. While other forms of magic attracted increasing attention in later medieval Europe, divination lost nothing of its appeal for the populace or its horror for moralists.[55]

The varieties of divination were legion. "Oneiromancy" or interpretation of dreams remained popular, as did treatises suggesting how to interpret them. Popular oneiromancy might involve simple equation of dream content with future events: dreams about water, for example, might signal death by drowning. On a more sophisticated level, the "dream books" of writers such as Hans Lobenzweig (mid-fifteenth century) made careful allowance for the social status and physical condition of the dreamer and contained complex rules for interpreting dreams. Observation of signs in nature seems also to have retained its importance. The elaborate norms that the Romans had developed for augury may have been lost, but a primitive sort of popular augury could discern the

---

[54] Hansen, *Quellen und Untersuchungen*, 44–7. Cf. British Library, MS Sloane 3132, fol. 56ʳ.
[55] Rider, "Common magic," 315–16.

future from the calls of birds. The number of croaks uttered by a raven could be a sign of changes in the weather, because that bird was so sensitive to conditions of the air. One woman, we are told, asked a cuckoo how long she would live, and when the bird cried five times she concluded she had five more years, but of course this story was told to debunk the superstition, and we cannot assume it is a fair report of something that actually happened. Chiromancers made more show of subtlety, with their claim that they could read on people's hands how many spouses they would have, what promotions lay in store for them, or whether they were fated to die on the gallows.

Scholarly astrology, based on detailed observation of the heavens, seems to have been rare in Europe until the twelfth century, but popular astrology was perennial. Usually the popular form referred more to phases of the Moon than to motions of the other heavenly bodies, for the fairly simple reason that the Moon could more easily be seen and its movements more readily understood. Detailed charts told which days of the lunar cycle were good or bad for various activities. Such written material may have originated among people with some education, but the mentality was not specifically learned.

Other signs of the future could be detected in the skies as well, and they were often treated in the same kind of mock-systematic fashion. One of the more common means of prognostication was interpretation of thunder. The direction it came from might be significant: if it sounded in the east, for example, it portended great bloodshed in the coming year. Even more important, perhaps especially in regions where thunderstorms are relatively rare and might not occur in most months of the year, was the month in which the thunder was heard. A chart from the fourteenth century shows "what thunder signifies in each month," complete with simple drawings that make the future clear. If it thunders in January there will be strong winds, abundance of fruit, and war. Thunder in February means death for many people, especially the rich. The most cheering prospect on this generally bleak chart is reserved for the end of the year: if thunder occurs in December, it portends a rich harvest in the land and peace and concord among the people.

Certain days of the month are more propitious than others, and certain days of the year are exceptionally unlucky. Murders, battles, and other misfortunes are especially likely to occur on the "Egyptian days," though by knowing these in advance one can take precautions. One leechbook says there are thirty-two evil days in the year, apart from local variations:

Whoever weds a wife on any of these days, he shall not long have joy of her. And whoever undertakes any great journey shall never come back again, or some misfortune shall befall him. And he that begins any great work shall never make an end thereof. And he that has his blood let shall soon die, or never be well.[56]

Casual superstitions of all sorts were used to foretell one's fate. Those who found halfpennies or needles could congratulate themselves on their good luck, unless they were so foolish as to dispose of these discovered objects, in which case the luck would turn against them. It was lucky to find a horseshoe or an iron nail, or to meet a hare as it was escaping from hounds. To encounter a raven or an ass was unlucky. Some people believed it could be bad luck to meet a monk or priest unless one made the sign of the cross; a favorite anecdote for preachers told how a woman took this precaution to avert misfortune on meeting a priest, but the cleric cast her into a muddy ditch and thus proved her superstition ineffective. Whether such beliefs fall within the realm of magic, however, even on medieval terms, is doubtful. Early medieval authors who spoke of "the magical arts" would have reserved the term for divinatory or other practices that involved some measure of systematic correlation between signs and future events. The term "art" in this context referred to a systematic body of knowledge, and few would have accorded the dignity of this title to a casual superstition.

Not all forms of divination were passive, or required mere observation of signs present in the world. Certain forms, which seem to have become especially popular in the fifteenth century, but could be found much earlier, required active operation of the person foretelling the future. These varieties of divination might be referred to as "experimental."[57] Opening a book at random and reading the passage that first meets one's eyes is a time-honored method. Another means of prognostication, found in antiquity and developed in medieval sources, involves rolling of dice. One late medieval manual instructs its user on how to roll dice as a key to whether they will obtain some desire.[58] For the lucky person who rolls three sixes, the book gives this verse:

> You that have cast three sixes here
> Shall have your desire this same year.
> Hold you stable and worry you not,
> For you shall have the desire that is in your thought.

---

[56] Dawson, *A Leechbook*, 328–9.
[57] See now Matthias Heiduk, Klaus Herbers, and Hans-Christian Lehner, eds., *Prognostication in the Medieval World: A Handbook* (Berlin: De Gruyter, 2020).
[58] W. L. Braekman, "Fortune-telling by the casting of dice: A Middle English poem and its background," *Studia Neophilologica*, 52 (1980), 3–29.

The good fortune is not reflected in the quality of the verse, which is no literary masterpiece, but still it is no doubt welcome. The player who casts two sixes and a two will also have the desired object, but much adversity along with it. Those who roll a six and two fours are told to give up their notions. Fortune-telling devices of this sort can be traced back to the ancient Greek Oracles of Astrampsychus and the fourth-century *Lots of Saint Gall*. Arabic versions were influential in the later medieval West. Such techniques could always be used for serious divination, but perhaps lent themselves better to use as party games. Sometimes the techniques involved are extremely elaborate, with several charts to consult and movable pointers to turn before one receives counsel. A work called *The Lots of the Twelve Patriarchs* involves rolling dice, consulting a table, and being led to rhymed answers to standard questions. That work includes some answers critical of fortune-telling (such as "If you go where blind Chance goes / Chance is apt to break your nose!"), but reaching these answers would require the impossible roll of only "one" from a pair of dice.[59]

A book of fortune from fifteenth-century Germany has a complicated system of prognostication that works something like a complex board game or a sequential treasure hunt, in which one clue leads to another (Figs. 8a and 8b).[60] No doubt those consulting the book could find it entertaining, especially if they did so in groups, although there was also a serious side to the quest for counsel. The book has a knob on the front cover that the user can twist, causing a metal image of an angel on the other side of the cover to point to the name of one of twelve Apostles. The user then goes to a list of questions: whether a sick person will recover from illness, whether a pilgrim will return home, and many other matters for inquiry. Having selected an Apostle and a question, the user then consults a table that leads to one of a series of circles, and inscriptions in those circles will then lead to one of twenty-four "books," or lists of versified responses. For example, if the twisting of the knob leads to the choice of the Apostle James, and if the question is whether a pilgrim will return home, the user is led from one device to another before reading a verse warning that the pilgrim "will come back sick and quite unwell / that is the fate I have to tell."

Certain techniques of experimental divination make use of the same kinds of objects that are used in manipulative magic; these techniques typically occur in the same manuscripts as other forms of magic. Herbs,

---

[59] T. C. Skeat, "An early mediaeval 'book of fate': The *Sortes XII patriarcharum*, with a note on 'books of fate' in general," *Mediaeval and Renaissance Studies*, 3 (1954), 41–54.

[60] Marco Heiles, *Das Losbuch: Manuskriptologie einer Textsorte des 14. bis 16. Jahrhunderts* (Wien-Köln-Weimar: Böhlau, 2018), 58–67, 467.

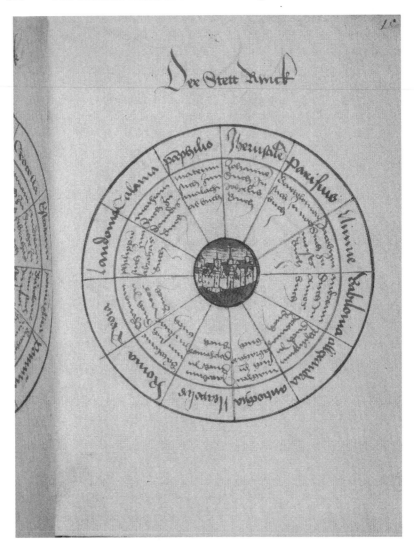

Figs. 8a and 8b. Fortune-telling circles with inscriptions keyed to various cities and to clerical orders and positions, from a book of fortunes by Heinrich Meise of Würzburg

for example, can aid in the detection of a thief: if heliotrope is placed under the head of a sleeping person from whom something has been stolen, that person will be able to see the thief and his whereabouts in his dreams.

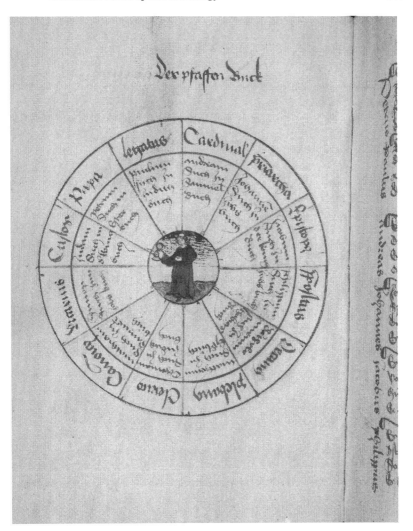

Figs. 8a and 8b. (*cont.*)

Such techniques can also serve the purposes of medical prognosis. If a healer holds vervain against a sick person's hand and asks how he fares, the vervain will enable the person to give a correct answer; the patient will live or die, according to the answer he or she gives. The physician John of Mirfeld gives a series of techniques combining prognosis with prognostication, including one specimen of "onomancy," or divination through calculations based on names:

take the name of the patient, the name of the messenger sent to summon the physician, and the name of the day upon which the messenger first came to you; join [the numerical values of] all their letters together, and if an even number result, the patient will not escape; if the number be odd, then he will recover.[61]

We may be surprised to read such techniques in the work of a leading and generally hardheaded practitioner, but the surprise comes from our modern expectation of a strict distinction between science and magic.

The manuscripts containing divinatory procedures sometimes include elaborate techniques to detect a thief. Write the formula "+ Agios Crux + Agios Crux + Agios Crux Domini" on virgin wax and hold it over your head with your left hand, and in your sleep you will see the thief. If you suspect someone, write certain letters on a piece of bread and give it to the suspect to eat, and if he is guilty he will be unable to swallow it. If there are several suspects, one manuscript recommends inscribing elaborate formulas on a piece of bread, reciting various prayers, and then administering the bread to the suspects. Alternatively, in a procedure known as Abraham's Eye, one can draw a picture of an eye on the wall, gather all the suspects, and watch to see which one weeps from his right eye. If he denies having stolen the missing object, drive a copper nail into the eye on the wall, and when you strike the nail, the guilty person will cry out as if he himself had been struck: a clear case of sympathetic magic.[62]

Detection of a thief or location of stolen goods might be linked to magic that would restore the lost property. A fourteenth-century Flemish manuscript, for example, uses a kind of sympathetic magic as a way to discover and regain a stolen object. It is based on the legend that after Christ's crucifixion, his cross was buried until St. Helen sought and discovered it. Just as the earth yielded this holy relic, so too the earth itself should now disclose the stolen goods. To invoke the power of the cross itself, the diviner lies four times on the ground, once in each of the compass directions, with arms stretched out in the form of a cross, and each time recites a formula commanding the cross of Christ to fetch back the thief and the stolen goods.

Magical procedures can also be used to obtain secret information directly from another person, and since the goal here is to gain knowledge, one might class these operations as forms of experimental divination. If you put the heart and left foot of a toad over the mouth of a

---

[61] Hartley and Aldridge, *Johannes de Mirfeld*, 71 (with translation).

[62] Page, "Medieval magical figures," 434–5; see also Chiara Benati, "Painted eyes, magical sieves and carved runes: Charms for catching and punishing thieves in the medieval and early modern Germanic tradition," in Classen, *Magic and Magicians*, 149–218.

sleeping man, for example, he will immediately reveal to you whatever you ask him.

It is reasonably clear how divination might be taken for a species of demonic magic. Augustine had explained in his treatise *On the Divination of Demons* that, while evil spirits do not have truly prophetic knowledge of the future, they can make conjectures that are informed by their keen perception, their ability to move about quickly, and their rich store of experience, and it is these conjectures that are communicated to human beings in divination. What was less obvious was how divination could count as natural magic. The people who spoke of occult virtues in nature were usually thinking of powers that could be put to use, rather than natural signs of future events. Yet they were not wholly inattentive to prognostication. William of Auvergne, for example, speaks of a "sense of nature," a kind of extrasensory perception that enables a person, for example, to detect the presence of a burglar. Animals can also have this sense, according to William. Sheep use it to guard against wolves, and by means of it vultures know when there is going to be a battle (and thus, for them, a feast). Still other authors ascribed prognosticatory signs to God, who has bestowed them on humankind to help people brace themselves for future misfortune. The Flemish writer Venancius of Moerbeke catalogues numerous forms of divination ("the varieties of prognostication are practically infinite," he says), and laments that God's efforts to warn people meet all too often with unconcern or incomprehension.[63] But to view divination in these terms is to take it clearly outside the realm of magic and place it within the sphere of religion.

The Archaeology of Magic

Written sources tell us how magic was done, how its effects were supposed to work, how people feared and condemned it. Sometimes they tell us in some detail about particular circumstances in which people used magic. Apart from written sources, however, we also have archaeological evidence for magic. It can be difficult to interpret, but it is sufficiently abundant that it cannot simply be ignored.[64]

Objects buried along with a corpse could be meant for magical effect. At times, people were buried with jewelry bearing inscriptions that were elsewhere used to ward off illness. Wooden staffs are often found in or beside coffins, perhaps a tradition surviving from pre-Christian Norse

[63] Roger A. Pack, "A treatise on prognostications by Venancius of Moerbeke," *Archives d'Histoire Doctrinale et Littéraire du Moyen Âge*, 43 (1976), 311–22.

[64] Rider, "Common magic," 309–10.

culture, in which a staff might be used in a magical ritual, but now possibly reinterpreted as a staff aiding in the journey of death and purgation. When women were buried with spindle whorls in their graves, the point may have been simply to affirm their role as home-makers, but elsewhere spinning of thread and weaving of cloth were linked with charms or incantations thought to have magical potency, and the whorls left in graves often had letters inscribed on them, probably to enhance their magical efficacy. When pebbles of quartz were placed in the mouth or hand of a corpse, or antique coins and jewelry were buried with people, these objects could have been meant to protect the deceased. When a coffin was lined with ash taken from a domestic hearth, this may have been a way of restraining the dead from leaving the grave.[65]

In other cases, the magical intention can be inferred from evidence of some ritual enacted with its placement, or from similarity to objects and inscriptions known as magical from other sources. Objects deposited in cultivated fields could also serve magical purposes, particularly if there was some sort of ritual act accompanying their placement. Small vials or ampullae usually used by pilgrims to carry water or other substances from shrines were first deliberately damaged and then placed in fields. Coins were first bent and then deposited.[66] Graffiti inscribed on medieval church walls include curses, pseudo-Hebrew characters meant as symbols of angels, and apotropaic or protective figures of various kinds. Pentangles on church walls may have been meant as protection against demons, and geometrical designs were perhaps scratched by simple scissors as protective devices.[67]

Archaeological evidence of magic is often inarticulate. Without the interpretive aid of inscriptions on the objects discovered, and without contemporary explanation of what was intended, the magical associations of grave goods or other objects can only be conjectured. Still, the cumulative evidence of objects placed in particular unexpected places suggests that many objects placed in graves, or in buildings, and many devices scratched on church walls, were meant for symbolic purposes that can best be conceived as magical. Even if we cannot know more

---

[65] Roberta Gilchrist, "Magic for the dead? The archaeology of magic in later medieval burials," *Medieval Archaeology*, 52 (2008), 119–59.

[66] Roberta Gilchrist, "Magic and archaeology: Ritual residues and 'odd' deposits," in Page and Rider, *Routledge History*, 383–401.

[67] Matthew Champion, "Magic on the walls: Ritual protection marks in the medieval church," in Ronald Hutton, ed., *Physical Evidence for Ritual Acts, Sorcery and Witchcraft in Christian Britain: A Feeling for Magic* (New York: Palgrave Macmillan, 2016), 15–38.

precisely what the purposes were, it is worth noting this evidence for what may have been among the most widespread forms of medieval magic.

The archaeology of magic could of course be seen as a subfield within the broader field of magic and material culture. Talismans, crystal balls, mirrors, rings and other jewelry, even narwhal tusks taken for unicorn horns can all be studied as evidence for the history of magic, and sometimes their function is clarified by inscriptions on them, by textual reference to them, or even by surviving instructions for their manufacture and use (for example, a manuscript that explains how to make a magical Mirror of Floron).[68] What archaeology adds is the local contextualization provided by the depositing of material, and the evidence for ritual use associated with that depositing.

The Art of Trickery

Not all magic in medieval culture was serious. Just as there were forms of divination intended for entertainment, so too there was other magic that aimed to amuse: performative magic that would arouse wonder at the magician's virtuosity, and practical jokes that would give amusement at least to the one who played them.

The notebook of Thomas Betson (late fifteenth century) is instructive in this regard.[69] Betson was a monk at Syon Abbey in Middlesex. He seems to have been a pious man, but also a prankster and a dabbler in magic, and his notebook includes instructions on how to perform various tricks. Take a fine hair from the head of a woman, for example, and attach it to a hollowed-out egg. You will be able to move the egg about, holding the other end of the hair in your hand, and no one will see the hair because of its thinness. You can even hang the egg in a house, and "many people will think it is being held up by nothing at all." Or use a bit of wax to attach one end of a hair to a coin; pull on the other end of the hair, and the coin will move, and "many people will think it is done by magical art." Put a beetle inside an apple with a hole in its center, and when the beetle rocks the apple people will think the fruit is moving by itself. Was Betson counting on an exceptionally gullible audience? Not

---

[68] Sophie Page, "Love in a time of demons: Magic and the medieval cosmos," in Sophie Page, Marina Wallace, Owen Davies, Malcolm Gaskill, and Ceri Houlbrook, *Spellbound: Magic, Ritual and Witchcraft* (Oxford: Ashmolean Museum, 2018), 19–63. Published to accompany a museum exhibition, this volume devotes considerable attention to the material culture of magic.

[69] St. John's College, Cambridge, MS E.6. For other materials here cited, see Bodleian Library, MS e Mus. 219, MS Wood empt. 18, and MS Ashm. 1393; British Library, MSS Sloane 121 (a particularly rich source) and Sloane 3564.

necessarily. Presumably he performed for people who wanted to be entertained, were willing to suspend their disbelief, and could be amused by even a simple "magic" trick if it was executed with panache. Betson also copied down instructions for much more sophisticated operations, for making images appear by elaborate arrangement of mirrors, or for producing interesting optical effects with a coin and a dish of water, and thus it seems he was not merely a buffoon.

Betson's moving apple finds its analogue in several other objects made to appear self-moved: loaves of bread that dance about on a table or leap through the house, dead fish that jump out of a pan, hollow rings and eggs that seem to roll about of their own accord. Numerous manuscripts tell how to perform tricks with fire: how to make a candle that cannot be extinguished; how to cause a great flame to rise up from a pan full of water. Likewise there are formulas for creating special light effects that will produce illusions, such as making men appear headless, or making people look so large that their heads seem to be in the heavens while their feet remain on Earth. Often these "experiments" require basic knowledge of chemistry, though the last of them calls for simpler ingredients: oil, centaury, and blood from a female hoopoe. Any well-stocked kitchen would have had the onion juice required for secret writing or the strong red wine whose vapor could turn a white rose red.

Other forms of entertainment required equipment and manual dexterity. For example, the magicians' instructions tell how to release tied hands by cutting the rope with a concealed knife. From artistic evidence we know that certain tricksters used the classic ball-and-cups game to deceive onlookers by sleight of hand. The subject is common in fifteenth-century German art; late in the century, Hieronymus Bosch (ca. 1450–1516) did a drawing of this motif, and early in the following century he executed a painting of it. Like earlier artists, Bosch pokes fun at the folly of the spectators who are duped by the clever illusionist.[70]

In other cases, the tricks that later medieval magicians had up their sleeves were examples of pure mischief, inflicted on unsuspecting victims. The manuscripts tell how to frighten a companion by making a torch explode in his face, how to make people itch in their beds, how to turn them black as they bathe, how to make their dinner meat appear raw or wormy, and so forth *ad infinitum* and, no doubt, *ad nauseam*.

---

[70] Kurt Volkmann, *The Oldest Deception: Cups and Balls in the 15th and 16th Centuries*, trans. Barrows Mussey (Minneapolis: Jones, 1956); Mark Crane, Richard Raiswell, and Margaret Reeves, eds., *Shell Games: Studies in Scams, Frauds, and Deceits (1300–1650)* (Toronto: Centre for Reformation and Renaissance Studies, 2004).

Magic of this kind might find its way into various sorts of manuscript. Sometimes it appears in collections of medical material or in general potpourris of magical lore. One medical miscellany from Germany contains a great deal of straightforward medical lore, but mixes in with it prescriptions for invisibility ("take two eyes from a black frog ..."), for making people appear headless, for finding stolen goods in one's dreams, and so forth.[71] There were special compilations devoted specifically to magical tricks, of which *The Supplement to Solomon* is one of the better-known. It would be difficult to say who would have used this material. A monk might, but so might a physician. Professional qualifications were clearly less important than a stage personality and a desire to entertain.

Almost all of the surviving sources for such magic date from the fourteenth and fifteenth centuries. It may be that the vogue did not set in until that late. What is perhaps more likely is that similar tricks were known much earlier, but that they did not get widely recorded until the fourteenth and fifteenth centuries, with the proliferation of popular written material. Some evidence of earlier practice does survive: William of Auvergne tells how a magician can make a house appear full of snakes by burning a snakeskin in a place filled with sticks or rushes, so that the flickering of the flame makes these things appear to be writhing serpents. Indeed, many of the tricks with fire seem inspired by Byzantine experiments with "Greek fire," intended primarily for military use.

What historical significance, if any, attaches to this trickery? For various reasons, we must at least take passing cognizance of all this, even if we do not dwell upon it. It is, first of all, one element in the medieval complex of notions associated with magic, and if we do not take it into account, our notions of what medieval people meant by magic will be incomplete. This side of magic may not be primary in medieval culture, as it is in modern culture; when fifteenth-century townspeople thought of magicians, they probably did not think first of all about stage performers pulling rabbits out of hats. Yet the performative element is one component of medieval magic. Furthermore, it became linked in complex ways with other, more sophisticated or more sinister forms of magic, as we will see. Joachim Ringelberg in the sixteenth century referred to such tricks as entertaining diversion from otherwise taxing studies, and perhaps they served this function in earlier centuries as well. There is no reason to think this trickery was exclusively a learned craft, but when taken over by scholars it might well provide light distraction from their study of astrology, alchemy, and other heady pursuits.

---

[71] Wardale, "A Low German-Latin miscellany."

Magical tricks were also the stuff of literature, particularly the fabliaux: short, often bawdy tales of the high and late Middle Ages, usually telling the exploits of those lower classes that were presumed incapable of noble conduct. In one fabliau, a swindling enchanter is said to be able to transform a cow into a bear, and another can create coins out of little fragments of debris. A peasant taken in by such tricks sets out to make a fortune by such means, but ends by giving his soul to the Devil. Elsewhere the authors play upon the double sense of the word "enchant": the magician is one who can enchant the audience itself with his deceiving tongue. Yet another fabliau tells of a peasant from whom two thieves steal a ham, whereupon the peasant regains the meat by trickery. Both the original theft and the subsequent recovery are said to be cases of "enchantment." An English poem of the fifteenth century, "Jack and His Stepdame," follows in the tradition of the fabliaux. A stranger gives Jack various magical favors, including a pipe that causes its hearers to dance about madly. Taken to court as a "great necromancer" and a "witch" for this and other pranks, Jack begins playing his pipe and causes everyone present to dance and tumble until they promise to let him go free.[72]

The power of Jack's magical pipe might be mysterious, but most magical trickery, even in the fabliaux, worked in natural ways – like the other forms of magic we have surveyed in this chapter. The powers in question were occult in only a crude sense: the magician knew them full well, but tried to keep them hidden from the audience or the victims. What we have here is thus, in a sense, a parody of natural magic. Thomas Betson does not say that the effects of his simple tricks will *be* magic, but that many people will *think* they are magic. Or perhaps we should say that for lack of an immediate explanation, people who wished to be entertained would suspend their disbelief and pretend for the moment that the magician had awesome powers over nature. For the bulk of the populace, however, this distinction would have been a fine point.

[72] Raleigh Morgan, Jr., "Old French *jogleor* and kindred terms: studies in mediaeval Romance Lexicology," *Romance Philology*, 7 (1954), 301–14; Melissa M. Furrow, ed., *Ten Fifteenth-Century Comic Poems* (New York: Garland, 1985), 67–153.

5   The Romance of Magic in Courtly Culture

The word "magic," like many related words, began as a term of abuse, but has taken on more positive connotations. Particularly the adjectival forms of these words, "magical," "enchanting," "charming," "fascinating," and even "bewitching," now stand for objects and experiences that are out of the ordinary, but alluring and attractive.[1] This shift in usage came after the Middle Ages, but for background to it we must turn to the portrayal of magic in medieval courtly culture, and especially in the literary romances written for that culture. People at court clearly recognized that certain magical practices could be sinister and destructive; there is ample evidence that kings and courtiers feared sorcery at least as much as commoners did. In their imaginative literature, however, they were willing to accord it a different status and to consider, without horror, the symbolic uses of magical motifs. Sorcerers in courtly literature were figures in an enchanted realm. On one level this literature offered escape from the humdrum realities of life, but on a deeper level it reflected the social and psychological complexities of courtly society, and made possible for medieval and for modern readers a richer understanding of that life.

The court as an institution and a cultural center had existed well before the twelfth century – the court of Charlemagne (reg. 768–814) at Aachen is a classic instance – but it was during that century in particular that rulers of all sorts began rivaling each other to establish glamorous and impressive courts as tokens of their own splendor. Not only kings had magnificent courts, but also dukes and counts, popes and bishops, and lesser rulers. Women might exercise political and cultural dominance at certain courts, as did Eleanor of Aquitaine (ca. 1122–1204) and her daughter Marie of Champagne (1145–98). Clerics left a profound mark on some courts, but rulers elsewhere prided themselves on their freedom from clerical influence. In any case, rulers

---

[1] For parallel cases, see the nouns "glamor" and "prestige." I owe this list and the observation about it to Barbara Newman.

surrounded themselves with officials, advisers, servants, physicians, relatives, and friends. Among their advisers and aides might be astrologers and magicians. And among the entertainers who came to court there might be minstrels to celebrate the exploits of fictional courtiers in a world charged with enchantment.

Magicians at Court

It has been argued that the medieval court, particularly from the thirteenth century on, was an especially good breeding ground for magic. The main reason for this, it is suggested, is the disparity between two levels of power at court. On the one hand, there are the officials formally invested with power by the lord: chancellors and chamberlains, treasurers, ambassadors, and others. On the other hand, there are the throngs of courtiers who have no formal claim to power, but who for various reasons nonetheless wield informal power: relatives and friends of the lord, clerics and mistresses, poets and physicians, and a coterie of servants. Individuals in both groups could rise meteorically to high favor and then plummet. Apart from the inevitable rivalries *within* each of these groups, there was more basic tension *between* them. To the extent that those with unofficial power sought to displace those with official power, the two classes would hold each other in constant suspicion. Those seeking royal favor might use sorcery in doing so. As we will see more fully in a later chapter, there were methods prescribed specifically for gaining favor at court. Love magic could be used by a prospective wife or mistress. And various forms of magic could dispose of rivals and other enemies. Foreigners at court, such as monarchs' mothers-in-law, might have dynastic and other interests different from those of other courtiers, and they might be unscrupulous and surreptitious in their pursuit of those interests. Even when magic was not actually used, the tensions at court could easily lead to suspicion of its employment. In brief, courtly society was ridden with magic and fear of magic.[2]

There is much substance to this picture. In the late fourteenth and early fifteenth century, allegations of sorcery proliferated in the context of rivalry between the French royal family and the dukes of Burgundy. Key figures included King Charles VI ("the Mad") (reg. 1380–1422), his brother Louis of Orléans (1372–1407), and Duke John the Fearless of Burgundy (reg. 1404–19). Magicians were brought in to cure the king of

---

[2] Edward Peters, *The Magician, the Witch, and the Law* (Philadelphia: University of Pennsylvania Press, 1978), 110–37. See also now Jean-Patrice Boudet, "Magic at court," in Page and Rider, *Routledge History*, 331–42.

his madness, and magicians were thought responsible for causing his affliction. Louis was accused of engaging a team of magicians and having them consecrate to demons his sword, his dagger, and his ring. He was accused of using love magic to constrain women, and of trying to murder his royal brother. One of the king's physicians confessed to making a magic image and consecrating it to demons to exercise power over the duke of Burgundy. This physician was condemned and burned, along with his books of magic. A treatise against divination that was dedicated to Duke John gives testimony to the occult practices for which courtiers were notorious. As Jan Veenstra comments, "Like hot air and other volatile substances, beliefs and practices concerning magic and divination have a tendency to rise rather than move down."[3]

Magical assassination and love magic were common allegations in the French court during the early fourteenth century, and they were not uncommon in the English court throughout the late Middle Ages. In 1316, a sorceress who was being interrogated accused Mahaut of Artois, mother-in-law of Philip V of France (reg. 1316–22), of using magic to reconcile the king with her daughter. More seriously, she had supposedly used poison (whether magical or ordinary) to kill Louis X (reg. 1314–16) and secure Philip's succession as monarch. In 1441 the duchess of Gloucester was charged with using image magic against Henry VI of England so that her husband the duke might rise in power and perhaps gain the throne. Nor was the papal court immune from such intrigue. Perhaps the best-known cases in which magic was suspected in the papal curia come from the pontificate of John XXII (1316–34). The most celebrated instance of all was that of 1317, in which the bishop of Cahors was executed for involvement with an alleged Jewish magician and other shadowy figures in an attempt on John's life. Not content with poisons, the conspirators allegedly tried to smuggle into the papal palace magical images, with inscriptions attached to them, concealed in loaves of bread.[4]

Yet it is misleading to portray the situation at court as different in principle from that elsewhere. There were rivalries and animosities in all walks of life that led to the use and suspicion of magic; the historical record gives little warrant for taking the courts as distinctive in this regard. We know more about magic at court than in many settings because the records are much more ample. Magic in a rural village might

---

[3] J. R. Veenstra, *Magic and Divination at the Courts of Burgundy and France: Text and Context of Laurens Pignon's* Contre les devineurs *(1411)* (Leiden: Brill, 1998).

[4] Frans van Liere, "Witchcraft as political tool? John XXII, Hughes Géraud, and Matteo Visconti," *Medieval Perspectives*, 16 (2001), 165–73.

pass unnoticed, but magic at court was likely to arouse the interests of chroniclers and other writers. In many cases – indeed, in all the cases cited above – even when courtiers were charged with magic, it was not they but outsiders, common people brought in *ad hoc* from the towns or villages, who are actually supposed to have done the deed.

Within courtly society itself, diviners seem to have been very much in demand. This is the burden of the complaint by John of Salisbury (ca. 1115–80): in a long section of his *Policraticus*, he deplores the various magical arts to which courtiers are tempted, but when he turns to specific forms and examples, what he delivers is, in effect, a treatise on divination. His references are almost entirely to the literature of antiquity, and readers who hope to find in his work details about the practice of magic or divination at court will be disappointed. Yet he clearly feels it important, in giving moral guidance for courtiers, to expose the ways and errors of augurs, astrologers, chiromancers, interpreters of dreams, crystal-gazers, and diviners of every stripe. From other sources as well, we know there were often astrologers at court and (as we shall see in a later chapter) they gained special popularity there in the twelfth century.

Apart from diviners and astrologers, rulers might find employment for other specialists in occult practices. Johannes Trithemius (1462–1516), though not the most reliable of witnesses, tells of an archbishop of Trier who depleted his treasury in buying books of alchemy and hiring alchemists. One of his successors retained his own alchemist for twelve years, until the alchemist went off to serve the duke of Württemberg.

The case of Conrad Kyeser is instructive.[5] Evidently a physician by training, Kyeser did service on the battlefield and as a diplomat, for Duke Stephan III of Bavaria-Ingolstadt, among others. He fell from favor, first because of his role in the crusade that terminated in disaster at Nicopolis in 1396, and secondly because he took the wrong side in imperial politics at the turn of the century. To satisfy his ambition and regain favor, he decided to write a great work on warfare, his *Bellifortis*, which he dedicated to the emperor Rupert. The work is replete with descriptions and pictures of marvelous, fanciful engines of war, torches that cannot be extinguished (thanks to technology borrowed from Byzantine sources), and various kinds of herbal and animal magic. The hide from the breast of a deer, he says, will give special protection against wounds in battle, and feathers or hairs from animals killed in the hunt will guide arrows to their goal. Perhaps the most remarkable feature of the collection is that

---

[5] Conrad Kyeser, *Bellifortis*, ed. Götz Quarg (Düsseldorf: VDI, 1967).

the text is all put into elaborate and often dense Latin verse. One of the most perplexing sections is one where Kyeser recommends making a candle out of used wax, tow, and the brine from the umbilicus of a newborn baby. "You can carry it where you will, on a moon-lit night, and you will see its effect." Then he adds that a lantern can be made if fat from a hanged man is added to the concoction. The text is accompanied by a picture showing a castle (probably Karlstein, outside of Prague) with a trumpeter on a tower, a new Moon in the sky, a naked impish figure riding toward the castle on a long stick, and another such figure carrying a candle (Fig. 9). Was this simply another recipe for a magical light, or did Kyeser intend some other effect? The author was a man of considerable education and some practical skill as a physician and an engineer, but he was also fond of covering his practical counsel with a dark cloak of mystery. Did he hope to impress the emperor more effectively in that way? If so, we have no indication whether he succeeded.

Royal and aristocratic courts were also graced with various kinds of entertainers whose repertoire might include performative magic. Chrétien de Troyes (ca. 1140–ca. 1190), describing the fictional marriage of Erec and Enide, tells how minstrels from all over the countryside came to provide entertainment for the occasion: "one leaps, another does acrobatics and another performs magic tricks; one tells tales, one sings, others play on the harp," and so forth.[6] Another fictional work recounts how a magician, renowned for his feats of "necromancy," "enchantment," and "conjuration," is brought to court to entertain the hero. He can turn stones into cheese, cause oxen to fly, or have asses play on harps – or so it seems to his astonished audience. He appears to cut off someone's head, but the severed head turns out to be a lizard or a snake.[7] Other magicians in literature can turn animals into knights, make water run uphill, increase the size of rooms, or conjure forth hundreds of knights to joust with each other. Their accomplishments may have exceeded those of real-life magicians, but they provided a high standard for emulation. Nonfictional accounts sometimes wrote disparagingly of such magic: Roger Bacon and Marsilio Ficino both expressed disdain for the sleight of hand, ventriloquism, and illusions of performative magicians. Neither Bacon nor Ficino was writing specifically about magicians at court, and we can perhaps assume that the performers who did go to

---

[6] Chrétien de Troyes, *Arthurian Romances*, trans. D. D. R. Owen (London: Dent, 1987), 27.

[7] For this and numerous other examples, see De La Warr Benjamin Easter, *A Study of the Magic Elements in the Romans d'Aventure and the Romans Bretons* (Baltimore: Furst, 1906). I have also used extensively Easter's dissertation, from Johns Hopkins University, of which his published book is a portion.

Fig. 9. Magical activities at a castle, from Conrad Kyeser's *Bellifortis*

court had more sophisticated versions of the tricks performed in the marketplace. The less accomplished magicians, like most popular performers, could expect only revilement from respectable society. At times, indeed, the "illusions" enacted at court seem to have involved elaborate and expensive staging of entertainments, done very much by craft rather than through necromancy.[8]

One might suppose that there were two distinct categories: astrologers and other diviners to serve as advisers at court and provide serious counsel for practical use, and minstrels and mimes who could lighten the life at court with their stories about magic and displays of magic. The case of Conrad Kyeser, however, should caution us against such a simple distinction. He sought to win favor at court with a book that mixed hardheaded technology with an air of fantasy. In this respect, he was probably not exceptional. Magicians who could do extraordinary things and astrologers who claimed to read the future in the stars were individuals who could arouse wonder. Their skills might also have practical relevance, but in any event the state of wonder would in itself be gratifying. They could be both counselors and entertainers. Their counsel was probably taken with selective seriousness, heeded when their courtly patron found it plausible and prudent, but otherwise taken – in both senses of the word – lightly.

Magical Objects: Automatons and Gems

When literary texts spoke of magical spectacles provided for the entertainment of courtly audiences, the wonders they recounted had their counterpart in the real life of the courts. The technology for creating mechanical men and beasts had been known since antiquity: Philo of Byzantium and Hero of Alexandria had written treatises on such things. In the early medieval centuries, this technology was better preserved in the Byzantine and Muslim worlds than in western Europe. When traveling Westerners encountered mechanical angels that blew trumpets, or clocks on which mechanical horsemen signaled the passing hours, they were understandably awestruck. In the tenth century, Liutprand of Cremona visited the imperial court at Constantinople and reported on the marvelous Throne of Solomon displayed there:

Before the emperor's seat stood a tree, made of bronze gilded over, whose branches were filled with birds, also made of gilded bronze, which uttered different cries, each according to its varying species. The throne itself was so marvelously fashioned that at one moment it seemed a low structure, and at another it rose high into the air. It was of immense size and was guarded by lions,

---

[8] Laura H. Loomis, "Secular dramatics in the royal palace, Paris, 1378, 1389, and Chaucer's 'tregetoures,'" *Speculum*, 33 (1958), 242–55.

made either of bronze or of wood covered over with gold, who beat the ground with their tails and give a dreadful roar with open mouth and quivering tongue.[9]

By the thirteenth century, the technology for such devices had become widely known in the West. All that was required to build them was money, which meant that they were typically playthings for the nobility. In the late thirteenth century, the count of Artois fitted out a palace at Hesdin with automatons, a room equipped to create the illusion of thunderstorms, and, among many other such curiosities, "eight pipes for wetting ladies from below and three pipes by which, when people stop in front of them, they are whitened and covered with flour."[10]

To appreciate the fascination with these devices, we must bear in mind that major advances were occurring in mechanics and engineering in and around the thirteenth century. This was the age that saw the birth of vertical windmills, the rebirth of stone bridges, and numerous other developments. It comes as no surprise to find Roger Bacon stimulated to speculation that must have struck most contemporaries as wild-eyed: seagoing ships can be made which a single man can steer, and which move more rapidly than if propelled by oarsmen; a fast-moving vehicle can be constructed that goes without being pulled by any living being; a flying machine can perhaps be made, with artificial wings moved by a crank; optical devices might strike terror into an army by creating the illusion of a great opposing force. Bacon's readers might be impatient for such developments, but in the meantime they at least had mechanical birds and illusions of thunderstorms to keep them enchanted.

No matter how well-known these mechanisms became, writers of fiction persisted in teasing their readers with the suggestion that such things were done by "necromancy." But it was not only in the realm of fiction that mechanical wonders might seem magical: when the fifteenth-century physician Giovanni da Fontana laid out schemes for making clocks, mechanical carriages, combination locks, alchemical furnaces, and many more such devices, he evidently took pride in the reputation he gained as a demon-conjuring magician. Similarly, when Conrad Kyeser devised military machines in the early fifteenth century, he took no pains to distinguish his skill in engineering from his fascination with magic: one of his battle wagons took the form of a giant cat with its claws outstretched in a threatening gesture. One scarcely knows

---

[9] William Eamon, "Technology as magic in the late Middle Ages and Renaissance," *Janus*, 70 (1983), 175 (with translations of quotations).
[10] Eamon, "Technology as magic," 176.

whether medieval people beholding such wonders did so in a spirit of awestruck terror, in a mood of playful fascination, or with a mixture of both.

It was probably a different combination of attitudes that inspired the collection of magical gems. There is little about these that one could call playful; rather, they were marks of that sumptuous magnificence in which courtiers would rival each other. Royalty and nobility had no exclusive hold on precious gems, not even on those with magical power. A grocer named Richard de Preston, for example, is known to have donated to St. Paul's at London a sapphire with virtue to cure ailments of the eyes, and doubtless there were other commoners who obtained and kept such items. In the nature of things, however, those with political power had more wealth than most people to spend on these jewels, and their life at court called for a habit of extravagance which made the display of gems normal. All the better if a precious stone not only looked beautiful and advertised its bearer's magnificence, but also cured diseases and performed other wonders.

It is not surprising, then, that most of the magical gems for which we have evidence were found at court. Inventories of royal or aristocratic treasuries afford numerous examples. A ring from the late fourteenth century, discovered at the Palace of Eltham, is set with five diamonds and a ruby, and has an inscription promising luck to its wearer. Charles V of France (reg. 1364–80) had a stone which could aid women in childbirth, and an inventory of the ducal treasury of Burgundy in 1455 lists a similar item. Hubert de Burgh was accused in 1232 of having taken a gem from the king's treasury which bestowed invincibility in combat; allegedly he had given it to one of the king's enemies. Various kinds of stone were prized for their ability to detect poison, a function that would always prove helpful at court. One chronicle suggests that when gems were in proximity to poison, they would break out in a kind of sweat. Such notions may seem fanciful, but clearly they were meant seriously. Thus, in 1408, the duke of Burgundy had a stone set in a ring as a means for detecting poison.

Quite often, the magical power of the stone itself was enhanced by that of inscriptions. One example which in many ways typifies the tendency is a fourteenth-century ring from Italy (Fig. 10). The ring itself is gold. It is set with a "toadstone." This stone, which counted as precious, allegedly came from the head of a toad, though actually it was a fossil derived from a certain kind of fish. The ring is inscribed with two lines from the Gospels, *Iesus autem transiens per medium illorum ibat* (Latin for Luke 4:30, "But Jesus passed through their midst") and *Et verbum caro factum est* (John 1:14, "And the Word became flesh"). There is precedent for use

Fig. 10. Italian ring, fourteenth century

of both of these texts on talismans.[11] Similar examples can be found from many parts of Europe from the thirteenth century onward.

In more than one way, the power of gems could be linked with that of the saints. Reliquaries with saints' bones in them were sometimes set with gems, presumably to render honor to the saints thus enshrined, but perhaps also to heighten the wonder-working power of the relics. A different kind of link is to be found in legend: St. Edward the Confessor (reg. 1042–66) was said to have given a ring to a beggar, who took it with him to Rome and brought it back just before the monarch died. The ring, thus sanctified, was enclosed in Edward's coffin until 1163, when it was removed and used to cure epilepsy. In a case like this, religion fuses altogether with natural magic.

Books called "lapidaries" set out in detail the wondrous properties of gems. The genre was known even in antiquity, but for medieval Europe the classic was the *Book of Stones* by Bishop Marbode of Rennes, from the late eleventh century. Marbode claims no originality for the contents of his work, but says that he is putting a previous collection into verse form for the reading of a small circle of friends, presumably people close to the episcopal court. God himself, Marbode affirms, has endowed precious stones with singular power. While herbs contain great strength, that of jewels is far greater. The sapphire, for instance, has a wide range of physical effects. Being inherently "cold," it can counterbalance excessive bodily heat and reduce perspiration. If pulverized and administered in

[11] O. M. Dalton, *Franks Bequest: Catalogue of the Finger Rings, Early Christian, Byzantine, Teutonic, Mediaeval and Later … in the Museum* (London: British Museum, 1912), 142.

milk, it is good for ulcers, headaches, and other ailments. Furthermore, it has spiritual and moral powers. It dispels envy and terror, induces peacefulness, and even renders God favorable to supplication.

Other lapidaries, mostly following Marbode, further disseminated such lore, telling the magical uses of each precious stone: one could cure gout and eye diseases, another could defend against madness and wild beasts, yet another could render a garment fireproof. Several stones were prized for their luminosity. Stones can even aid in theft: a burglar need only sprinkle a crushed magnet over hot coals, and the occupants of the house will mysteriously depart, leaving the place easy prey for burglary. Certain gems aid in "prophecy": placed presumably in the speaker's mouth, they educe truths that would otherwise remain hidden. Or they can be used to compel others to divulge the truth. A man who doubts the chastity of his wife, for example, can place a magnet against her head while she is lying in bed, and if she has been unfaithful she will fall onto the floor. There were some who doubted these wondrous powers, but others vigorously defended such notions. Gervase of Tilbury (ca. 1152– ca. 1220) ridiculed the scoffers, and told how Solomon himself was the first to perceive the magical virtues of gems.

While the lapidary was never exclusively a courtly genre, medieval lapidaries seem to have been especially popular at court. One such work was even ascribed to a monarch, Alfonso the Wise of Castile and León (reg. 1252–54), and the printed editions of one French lapidary say that it was translated from Latin for the sake of René of Anjou (1408–80). In the later Middle Ages it is likely that the genre had a far wider audience, and even works written originally for courtly consumption might reach non-courtly readers, as did other, more specifically courtly forms of literature. It is tempting to see the lapidary as a kind of user's manual for the wonder-working gems found in the royal or aristocratic treasury, but there is only rough correspondence between the gems listed in the lapidaries and those known to have been worn or otherwise used at court. One can imagine a courtier delighting in the knowledge that the sapphire induces prophecy. One can even imagine the courtier experimenting, with results we can only conjecture, to test the truth of this knowledge. It is difficult not to suppose, however, that we have once again come upon the border between instruction and entertainment. Much as a faithful Christian would listen with awestruck belief or suspended disbelief to reports of miracle-working relics, so too a medieval European might read with awe this information about magical gems. In both cases, the sensation of wonder would be reason enough for listening or reading, and wonder is a state that seldom notes carefully the bounds between fiction and fact.

Further ambiguity surrounds these magical gems: we can assume that their powers were usually seen as natural, but some authors toyed with the notion that they might be repositories of demonic power. One lapidary advises that by pulverizing a gem called diadochos and sprinkling it with water, one can evoke the forms of demons and of the dead.

Magic in the Romances and Related Literature

Even explicitly fictional writings would of course reflect certain realities of courtly culture: they are unhelpful as sources for events, but invaluable as guides to attitudes and values.[12]

French poets of the twelfth century composed extended verse narrations, which were most often based on the chivalrous adventures of King Arthur and his circle. Their stories provided common stock for later romances as well, in France, Germany, and England. While they were set in the immemorial past, in the fantasy world of Arthur's court, they often projected onto that setting the customs of the author's own day: knights in these romances met at tournaments, fought in battles, and went to court more or less the way the author and his audience might do. Yet the Arthurian world of the romances was less predictable than the familiar world of ordinary experience. It was inhabited by monsters of popular mythology, occasionally by angels and demons of Christian lore, and quite regularly by fairies borrowed from Celtic literature.

We know little about most of the authors of these romances. One of the most important, Chrétien de Troyes, wrote in the second half of the twelfth century and was patronized by Countess Marie of Champagne (1145–98) and by the count of Flanders, in whose courts he evidently composed his romances for oral reading. Other writers of romances also seem to have been patronized by rulers, though there is ample evidence that the genre soon moved outward to noncourtly settings: that people in the towns, for example, were reading romances originally written for courtiers, or else adaptations or translations of these romances.[13] The border between "courtly" and "popular" romances is difficult to define with any clarity. What is clear is that even when the romances were not written for a courtly audience, they remained courtly in their content,

---

[12] See now Corinne Saunders, "Magic in literature: Romance transformations," in Page and Rider, *Routledge History*, 355–70; and Corinne Saunders, *Magic and the Supernatural in Medieval English Romance* (Cambridge: Boydell & Brewer, 2010).

[13] John Lough, *Writer and Public in France, from the Middle Ages to the Present Day* (Oxford: Clarendon, 1978), 7–30.

portraying and glamorizing the lives and adventures of kings, knights, and others at court.

The romances differ strikingly from the sagas in their conception of the foci for magical power. In the sagas, power inheres mainly in words; in the romances, it resides more in objects. First, when characters have been wounded, they are healed by wondrous herbs and unguents, usually administered by women: not necessarily major figures in the stories, but nurturing and kindly souls who happen to be on hand when a character needs magical refreshment. Secondly, there are love potions, such as Tristan and Iseult accidentally drink. Thirdly, the romances abound in luminous and otherwise magical gems, often set in rings, generally used to preserve the characters from danger. One such gem proves its ability to protect the hero from water, fire, and weapons when he has himself thrown into a river with a millstone tied to himself, then walks into a raging fire, and finally enters a duel.[14] Fourthly, there are artifacts with marvelous properties: serving dishes that present themselves for use; mechanical birds, lions, chessmen, and angels that appear alive; mechanical heads that talk with their makers; swords that bring sure victory; boats that sail of their own accord to wondrous harbors unknown to their hapless riders. The world of the romances seems at times a vast toy shop stocked with magical delights. Magical objects of this fourth variety often resemble the automatons and other mechanical wonders actually manufactured for courtly entertainment, and doubtless the fictional and real examples appealed to courtiers for the same mixture of motives: the allure of machines combined with the mystery of the unexplained. Chaucer (ca. 1340–1400) set forth an array of such marvels in *The Squire's Tale*, which is clearly indebted to the romance tradition.

The romances sometimes describe marvelous objects with an element of humor, irony, even self-parody. Luminous gems, for example, may not be an unmixed blessing. If they are set in a bed and blaze brightly through the night, it may be necessary to cover them up if anyone wishes to sleep. And magical unguents may have power that is wondrous to the point of comic effect. Thomas Malory (ca. 1400–71) tells how Sir Gareth beheads another knight and Dame Lynet anoints his severed head and trunk, puts them back together, and thus, in effect, glues his head back onto his body. Gareth then cuts the knight's head off again, chops it into a hundred pieces, and throws the fragments out the window into the

---

[14] Gautier d'Arras, *Eracle*, lines 981–1132, ed. Guy Raynaud de Lage (Paris: Champion, 1976), 31–6.

castle moat. Even so, Lynet glues the pieces back together with her extraordinary ointment and revives the victim.[15]

The romances often lay down conditions for use of these objects. A magic bridge may be crossable only by those who possess all knightly and godly graces. A boat may give passage only to riders innocent of treachery, treason, and boasting; a passenger who utters a boast may be plunged immediately into the water. A gate may close on a knight who is proud, until he humbles himself in prayer. A magic castle may be invisible to cowards. The Siege Perilous, or "dangerous chair," may only be sat upon by a paragon of all knightly virtues. A magical sword may bring unfailing victory, but only for one who uses it in a righteous cause. An extension of this notion is that of the magical object that only a true ruler can use: Arthur shows himself as heir to the throne of Britain by drawing the sword Excalibur from a stone, and Havelok the Dane proves himself ruler of Denmark by blowing a magic horn.

The purveyors of magical objects are often fairies, immortal beings who live in the "Land of Fairy," but occasionally enter the world of mortals and favor certain individuals with magical gifts. The romance *Escanor* bristles with magical objects made by fairies: an entire castle full of them, including a wondrous bed with shining jewels. Elsewhere the fairies provide magical boats, a marvelous tent made of silk, gold, and cypress, or a soft coverlet that protects people from harm, even from harmful thoughts. They may fall in love with human males and attempt to seduce them away to their own world. When they wish to enter the human realm, they typically do so at night. They wander in forests and linger by fountains. The ambivalence regarding fairies sometimes found in Irish literature can be seen in the romances as well: they have both good and evil sides, and while they can represent primal paganism, they can also be spoken of as "good Christians." They can bestow favors or destruction, according to their individual character, whim, or purpose. They serve other purposes as well, but one of their main functions is to keep the romances well-stocked with magical paraphernalia.[16]

Secular magic blends at times into religious observance. Things that are holy in Christian cult can substitute for magical objects, and things that are inherently powerful can have their power enhanced through sacred names or rituals. A sword may have the name of Jesus inscribed on it or relics placed on its pommel. Certain romances tell of people

---

[15] Sir Thomas Malory, *Le Morte d'Arthur*, vii. 22–3, ed. Janet Cowan, vol. 1 (Harmondsworth: Penguin, 1969), 272–5.

[16] See now Michael Ostling, ed., *Fairies, Demons, and Nature Spirits: "Small Gods" at the Margins of Christendom* (London: Palgrave Macmillan, 2018).

anointed with the very unguent used on Christ's body; one tells how Perceval uses such an unguent to heal his own wounds, to resuscitate his horse, to revive a dead enemy (whom he kills again as soon as the experiment has worked), and then to cure other warriors.[17] When the romances are reworked by clerical or monastic authors, these religious elements come much more clearly to the fore. The classic case is *The Quest of the Holy Grail* (early thirteenth century), which takes the theme of the wonder-working chalice of the Last Supper as its central motif, rich with theological and liturgical associations.

Some writers feared that these magical motifs were too superstitious to be redeemed. In the fifteenth century, John Gerson complained that the French passion for romances had accustomed people to all sorts of fabulous and superstitious beliefs. Doubtless he was right in seeing the fascination for romances as one part of a broader interest in fabulous lore, though it seems less obvious that these poems were in themselves the cause of this preoccupation.

In many romances, magic is central to the plot. The entire story may revolve about relations between lovers whose fate has been sealed by a magic love potion, or a hero may find himself besotted with love for a fairy who has enchanted him. Magical healing, resuscitation, and shape-shifting may be integral to the plot, or the narration may hinge on magical distortions of time, as when a hero spends a few moments in an enchanted castle and emerges to find that winter has turned to spring.

Often, however, magic is less important in itself than as a symbol or indicator of some psychological state. Indeed, the same instance of magic may function differently in different versions of the same story. For one author, the love potion that Tristan and Iseult drink magically and irreversibly seals their fate; for another, the magical character of the potion is unclear, and the potion serves as a symbol or pointer, calling attention to the psychological interaction between the lovers. Similar variation can be seen in the romances of King Horn. When Horn goes into battle, all he needs to conquer his enemy is a glance at a ring given him by his beloved. In popular versions of the romance, it is clear that the ring is exerting magical force, but the courtly Anglo-Norman *King Horn* is more subtle, and leaves open the possibility that the moving force is in fact the hero's love. Again, when a magician makes the dangerous coastal rocks of Brittany seem to disappear in Chaucer's *Franklin's Tale*, the event itself is not as important as reactions to it: no one even goes to the coast to verify that the magic has occurred, but the reported success

---

[17] Chrétien de Troyes, *Perceval: The Story of the Grail*, trans. Nigel Bryant (Cambridge: Brewer, 1982), 222–5.

of the magician's power sets in motion a series of crises in the characters' lives. Pliny and other sources relate the notion that leprosy can be cured with the blood of an innocent person; what is distinctive about the story of *Poor Henry*, by Hartman von Aue (ca. 1200), is that the patient is cured of his moral flaws – and thus also of the leprosy that symbolizes those flaws – not by the actual use of a young girl's blood, but by the realization that she is willing to be sacrificed for his sake.[18] In all of these cases it would be misleading to say that because magic occurs in the story, the tale is one about magic. In the more subtle and skillfully crafted romances, the focus is usually on inward states of mind and soul, which may be just as mysterious as any magic, and the magical motifs function as ploys for developing the inner lives of the characters.

The subordination of magic to psychology is especially clear when the plot hinges precisely on the non-use of a magical object. In *The Two Lovers*, a story by Marie de France (late twelfth century), the suitor is required to carry his beloved up a high mountain before he can marry her. He is too proud to drink the magic potion that will enable him to do so, and though his love is thus shown to be as strong as magic, his exertions kill him. Chrétien de Troyes also plays upon the non-use of magic in *Yvain*. The hero goes in search of adventures, equipped with a ring from his bride that will protect him from all adversity. In a year he is to return to her, but a year passes and he fails to return. In the meantime, he has not used his ring, but his possession of it tells us something important: it is not adversity that has held him back, but his inability to balance his quest for adventure with commitment to his bride.[19]

The plot of a romance often presents magic as part of a preestablished situation: a castle has been enchanted, or a sword has had a spell cast on it, at some time prior to the action in the romance, whether by a human adversary or by a fairy. The adventure now narrated involves the *disenchantment* of the place or object, the undoing of the original enchantment. In *The Book of Lancelot of the Lake*, the hero enters a wood and discovers a band of knights and damsels, singing and dancing around a chair that bears a golden crown. As soon as he joins them he loses all memory and is trapped in the dance. When he sits on the chair and has the crown placed on his head, however, the enchantment is broken. He then learns how the dancers were enchanted many years beforehand, and how they could not be released until the "best and handsomest knight in

---

[18] Saul Nathaniel Brody, *The Disease of the Soul: Leprosy in Medieval Literature* (Ithaca, New York: Cornell University Press, 1974).

[19] Helen Cooper, "Magic that does not work," *Medievalia et Humanistica*, n.s., 7 (1976), 131–46, used here extensively.

Fig. 11. Lancelot releasing captives from a magic dance, from a fourteenth-century manuscript

the world" sat on the chair and wore the crown (Fig. 11). The hero works the disenchantment without intending or even knowing how to do so. He simply pursues adventure into an unknown realm, where the magical power of his very person suffices to break the enchantment. (There are other romances in which disenchantment requires some heroic effort.) Only afterward do hero and reader learn the background to the original spell; the romances delight in presenting their heroes with mysterious situations and pitting them against disguised adversaries, and their willingness to undertake adventures without key knowledge is one test of their prowess.[20]

The magicians depicted in the romances are almost always secondary figures, foils for the heroes. Whether allies or antagonists, they serve mainly to aid or challenge the heroes in their quest for adventure and in their attainment of knightly virtue. Merlin, tutor of King Arthur, is the offspring of a demon father who raped his human mother, and from his father he inherits magical and prophetic powers. He aids Arthur by casting a spell on enemy troops, causing them to fall asleep, and he prophesies the

---

[20] *The Vulgate Version of the Arthurian Romances*, ed. H. Oskar Sommer, vol. 5 (Washington: Carnegie Institute, 1912), 120–4, 148–52, with English glosses.

outcome of future combat.[21] In the major Arthurian sources – from Geoffrey of Monmouth's fanciful but seminal *History of the Kings of Britain* (twelfth century) to Thomas Malory's grand summation of Arthurian lore in the *Morte Darthur* (fifteenth century) – Merlin demonstrates his wondrous powers early on and then is quickly dispatched, allowing Arthur to mature on his own, without preternatural help. Arthur's sister Morgan le Fay (i.e. "the Fairy"), at times nurturing and helpful, is nonetheless mainly a thorn in Arthur's side. According to Malory, she learned "necromancy" in a nunnery where she was sent as a girl. She has learned her lessons well: she provides healing unguents; to evade capture, she transforms herself, her horse, and her companions into marble blocks; she devises a splendid jewel-studded mantle, which bursts into flame when worn; and out of love for Lancelot she kidnaps him with an enchantment that puts him to sleep. At one juncture a foreign king solicits the aid of Morgan and a friend of hers, asking them to "set all the country in fire with ladies that [are] enchantresses." In case after case, her mischief serves not merely for incidental interest but as provocation to the heroes, who must exercise their own cunning to evade her traps. In other romances as well, the heroes' knightly prowess is tested, proved, and reinforced by conflict with magicians. Gawan, in Wolfram von Eschenbach's *Parzival* (early thirteenth century), heroically withstands a series of ordeals, culminating in hand-to-paw struggle with a hungry lion, and his success breaks the spell by which the wizard Clinschor holds a castle full of hapless captives. Clinschor himself, however, does not even appear in the romance: his story is told by other characters, but he remains mysteriously in the wings, leaving the stage to Gawan.

Is the magic of the romances natural or demonic? Generally the question is not addressed explicitly, even if there are clues pointing in one direction or another. When the visiting knight in Chaucer's *Squire's Tale* appears with a complement of magical artifacts, bystanders immediately begin speculating on possible natural causes for their wondrous powers. If a sword can slice through thickest armor and inflict incurable wounds, perhaps that is because it has been tempered in some special way with the proper chemicals. Elsewhere the reader or audience is teased with deliberate uncertainty about a magical device, which may be fashioned by "craft" (natural means) or "necromancy" (diabolical agency). Clinschor may be intended as a demonic magician, but Wolfram gives only indirect suggestions to that effect.

In the romance of *Wigalois* (thirteenth century), the pagan magician Roaz of Glois appears as an explicitly demonic magician. Early in the work we are

---

[21] See now Stephen Knight, *Merlin: Knowledge and Power through the Ages* (Ithaca, New York: Cornell University Press, 2009).

told that he has given himself to the Devil, who in return performs wonders and secures land for him. In the end, however, the hero Wigalois defeats him in single combat. Wigalois himself is protected by a slip of parchment with a prayer written on it, and by the sign of the cross which he has made on approaching the castle. As the hero fights with his heathen foe, Roaz' richly adorned wife looks on from her high seat, flanked by maidens who illuminate the scene with tall candles. The presence of these women, and the recollection of Wigalois' own beloved, has a powerful effect on the fighters, giving them strength for their combat. A manuscript of this romance, copied and illustrated in 1372 by a Cistercian monk under the patronage of the duke of Brunswick-Grubenhagen, depicts this scene with a vivid splendor, designed to evoke a sense of enchantment (Fig. 12).

Even when magic was most explicitly demonic, then, it held a kind of romantic fascination. The demons themselves may not be glamorized, but their magical effects do take on a wondrous aura. The rulers and courtiers for whom such material was originally written would surely not have been dazzled and entertained by genuine demonic magic in their midst, but within the realm of imaginative literature they were willing to take a more nuanced view. Magic might be evil, but it had its allurements. The magic dance in *The Book of Lancelot* was originally devised by a clever cleric as an entertainment for a lady whose favors he sought. The cleric's ruse may have been worked by necromancy, and it may eventually have palled, but the reader can understand why the lady would succumb to this temptation. It would be too much to suggest that the romances portray demonic magic sympathetically, but not too much to say that they make its dangerous attractions clear.

It was not only the Arthurian tradition that provided magical lore for writers of romances. During the twelfth and thirteenth centuries the ancient poet Virgil, long revered for his great learning, came to be seen as a maker of magical artifacts. Legend had it that he was a powerful magician who had benefited the city of Naples with various wondrous devices: by his astrological arts he set up a bronze fly that kept other flies from infesting the city; setting a piece of meat in the wall of the meat market, he ensured that other meat would not spoil; he used apotropaic magic to keep venomous snakes from the city; he placed carved figures in a city gate that caused people entering in through that gate to have good or evil fortune, depending on which side they inclined toward; he planted a garden with a plant that could give sight to blind sheep; he erected a bronze trumpeter that could avert the noxious fumes from a volcano (Fig. 13a).[22] At a later stage in the formation of this legend, however, Virgil was no longer just a natural

---

[22] Gervase of Tilbury, *Otia imperialia: Recreation for an Emperor*, ed. and trans. S. E. Banks and J. W. Binns (Oxford: Clarendon, 2002), 576–85.

Fig. 12. Combat of Wigalois with Roaz the Enchanter, from a
fourteenth-century manuscript

magician devising wondrous benefactions by astrological means, but a
conjurer of demons who released them from a bottle by smashing it. One
legend, reminiscent of the story of Aladdin, told how he gained his knowledge of the occult arts from twelve demons whom he had released from a

Fig. 13a. Virgil's magical devices for the city of Naples, from *Book of the Marvels of the World*, manuscript of ca. 1460

Fig. 13b. Virgil breaking a bottle containing demons, from a fourteenth-century manuscript

bottle in which they were trapped (Fig. 13b).[23] To some extent, the legend of Virgil intersected with the romance tradition. Wolfram represented Clinschor as the poet's nephew, and some of Virgil's magical inventions (especially a mirror that reflects events from all over the Roman Empire) are adapted and included in the story of Clinschor. In the compilation *Dolopathos*, Virgil teaches the hero's son astrology, and in *Escanor* he even tutors a fairy in the magic arts.

An entirely distinct body of material, which also became subject matter for romances, pertained to Alexander the Great and those in his service, such as Aristotle. Stories of Alexander are replete with gems that counteract the enchantments used in combat, wondrously fashioned animals with mechanical birds on their antlers, and other magic. When certain of Alexander's "barons" are transporting gems, demons assault them physically, and invisible hands hurl sticks and stones about their camp; the precious stones turn out to be owned by the demons, who jealously guard them for their occult powers. When Alexander establishes possession of them, they prove their magical power by protecting him from wild beasts and demons.

With the stories of Alexander, however, we enter a new area of inquiry. These legends had been preserved in various traditions: Greek, Latin, Arabic, Armenian, and so forth. While much of the Alexander tradition was known in earlier medieval Europe, it was supplemented in the later Middle Ages by new lore, which entered into the West as part of a large body of material ascribed to Alexander's tutor Aristotle. If these tales are relevant to the study of courtly romance, they are also part of a different topic: the infusion of Arabic learning that significantly altered Western notions of philosophy, science, and magic.[24]

---

[23] Allegra Iafrate, *The Long Life of Magical Objects: A Study in the Solomonic Tradition* (University Park: Pennsylvania State University Press, 2019), 67–69.

[24] George Cary, *The Medieval Alexander*, ed. D. J. A. Ross (Cambridge University Press, 1956).

The common tradition of magic was by no means uniform, but varied its themes from time to time and from place to place. One turning-point in the history of magic came in the twelfth century, with the rise of a new kind of learning that included scientific astrology, astral magic, and alchemy. The common tradition itself had incorporated elements of classical lore: remedies from Pliny or from Marcellus Empiricus, for example, were included in medieval leechbooks. But the new learning claimed to be more deeply rooted in ancient philosophy and science, and presented itself in a more rigorous and sophisticated guise. Like most forms of scholarship it lent itself to popularization, and thus the boundaries between the common tradition and the new magical learning did not remain rigid. Yet the fact remains that in the twelfth century something new was introduced, however complex its relationship with the older tradition became.

One qualification must be made at once. The people who studied astrology and alchemy in the twelfth and following centuries would not usually have thought of themselves as magicians. Their *enemies* might so brand them: those conservatives who harked back to Isidore of Seville included astrology, if not alchemy, under the heading of magic. It was only in later centuries, especially at the end of the Middle Ages, that practitioners began to see themselves as engaged in natural magic. In the meantime, however, both conceptual and practical links were forged between the new learning and the common tradition which make it impossible to study the one in isolation from the other.

The Transformations of European Intellectual Life

In very broad terms, there were two major factors that deeply affected the intellectual life of Europe in the later Middle Ages: first, the rise of universities out of earlier cathedral schools; and second, the importation of Arabic learning, including the transmission of Aristotelian philosophy and science from Arabic culture.

The major centers for learning in the early Middle Ages had been for the most part monastic. There were places one could go for medical study, and people with learning were sometimes attached to courts, but the only places that provided systematic education in a variety of subjects were monasteries. From the eleventh century, however, it was schools attached to the cathedrals that fostered most advancement in learning. Located in the towns, these cathedral schools provided education for some of the diocesan clergy, and also for people who, without intending to become priests, wanted preparation in the liberal arts so they could proceed to legal careers or service to rulers. If a cathedral school had a particularly eminent teacher, it might draw students from all across Europe; Latin was the language of instruction in any event, so linguistic boundaries posed no difficulty. In the second half of the twelfth century, a major further development occurred, the rise of universities. By the late fourteenth century there were universities throughout Europe, which continued to teach the liberal arts, but also had faculties for theology, medicine, and law.

If magic had any place in the university curriculum, it was only indirectly. Astronomy was one of the liberal arts, and could be taught in such a way as to include astrology, which traditionally was included among the branches of magic. Indeed, the borders between "astrology" and "astronomy" were fluid in medieval parlance, and the distinction between the two fields was drawn in various ways. Raymond of Marseilles equated the two terms, for example, while the *Mirror of Astronomy*, often and arguably ascribed to Albert the Great, distinguished the disciplines and dealt with both of them. What is most important for the history of magic is that the universities produced educated individuals who could go on to study learned forms of magic or "occult sciences," even if these were not subjects for formal study.

The cathedral schools and universities fostered a commitment to intellectual inquiry which led many scholars beyond an interest in the traditional texts. What this meant in most cases is that they wanted more knowledge about classical learning, which they could obtain from scholars in the Islamic world. Doing so was difficult: relations between Christendom and Islam had never been cordial, and·the Crusades had heightened the mutual antipathy. Yet there were border territories, particularly Spain and southern Italy, where historical circumstance had brought Christians and Muslims together, and in these places there was cultural contact and scholarly exchange.

Among the subjects which Islam had inherited from late Greek antiquity were astrology and alchemy. These sciences, to be sure, had undergone much change. Having been imported into Persia and India, Greek astrology had been developed and modified there, and Arabic astrologers learned and incorporated many of these adaptations. They had also had to respond to challenges within their own culture: Muslims had raised many of the same objections to astrology that Christian writers had posed and would soon revive, and writers such as al-Kindi (d. ca. 873) and Abu Ma'shar (787–886) had to confront this opposition in establishing astrology on a scientific basis and giving it an established place among the branches of learning. Alchemy, too, was developed among the Muslims, particularly by Jabir ibn Hayyan (ca. 721–ca. 815), known in the West as Geber (and not to be confused with an influential European alchemist of the later Middle Ages who adopted the same name).

During the eleventh century, when Christians of western Europe were fighting for the reconquest of Spain from the Muslims, they had only slight access to this Arabic learning, but in the twelfth century the floodgates opened. In the twelfth century, well over a hundred works were translated from Arabic into Latin, or else written in Latin specifically as paraphrases of Arabic learning. Magic was not simply one part of the body of material taken over into the Latin West – it was viewed as the culmination of Arabic learning.[1]

The earliest known translator of the period was Adelard of Bath (ca. 1080–ca. 1155), who translated works on astrology and astral magic, as well as an important set of astronomical tables. The most prolific was Gerard of Cremona, with sixty-eight known titles to his credit, including a handful of astrological writings. Abu Ma'shar's *Greater Introduction* to astrology became available in 1133, and Ptolemy's *Tetrabiblos* was translated in 1138. One of the most popular astrological works, a series of a hundred aphorisms falsely ascribed to Ptolemy under the title *Centiloquium*, was translated into Latin at least four times by the middle of the century. Often the translators worked in collaboration with Arabic-speaking aides, perhaps either Christians or Jews, who sometimes did the initial translation into Spanish or another vernacular tongue, leaving it to be put into Latin. Christians engaged in such labor might do so with uneasy conscience: one translator concluded his effort with the tag, "finished, with praise to God for his help and a curse on Mahomet and his followers."[2]

---

[1] Burnett, "Arabic magic," 71–84.

[2] Quotation translated by S. J. Tester, *A History of Western Astrology* (Woodbridge: Boydell, 1987), 53. For general information on the transmission of Arabic culture, see Charles S. F. Burnett, "Some comments on the translating of works from Arabic into Latin in the mid-twelfth century," *Miscellanea Mediaevalia*, 17 (1985), 161–71; Marie-Thérèse d'Alverny, "Translations and translators," in Robert L. Benson and Giles Constable, eds., *Renaissance and Renewal in the Twelfth Century* (Cambridge, Mass.: Harvard University Press, 1982), 421–62; Dorothee Metlitzki, *The Matter of Araby in Medieval England* (New Haven: Yale University Press, 1977); and Tester, *History of Western Astrology*, 147–53.

Fig. 14. Sign of Leo from the *Book of Nativities* by Abu Ma'shar, fifteenth-century Egyptian manuscript

It would be misleading to suggest a sudden revolution in medieval thought. While there were many in the twelfth century who absorbed the fruits of Arabic science, there were many more who rejected or ignored these developments. John of Salisbury, for example, rejected astrology, but for his knowledge of it drew mainly on Augustine, Macrobius, and Martianus Capella rather than the recently translated Arabic writers. Like most historical changes, the transformation of medieval learning took time for its full impact. By the thirteenth century no one could ignore the flood of Arabic texts that had poured into western Europe, but even then there were many who opposed it or rejected certain of its implications.

Although European scholars showed particular fervor in absorbing Muslim scholarship, in the process of doing so they absorbed Jewish influences as well. Jewish scholarship had long flourished within the Muslim world; as we have seen, Jews seem to have helped in the transmission of Arabic texts to the West. In addition, some Western scholars working in the occult sciences obtained access to specifically Jewish texts. One astrological work, for example, gives Hebrew names for the planets and for the signs of the Zodiac, and other data, and its prescriptions for divination require transliterating the letters of a person's name into the Hebrew alphabet for their numerical values.[3] Nor did Western scholars, preoccupied with these new discoveries, neglect earlier Latin materials: writings such as those of Julius Firmicus Maternus on astrology were now rediscovered.

The main beneficiaries of this new learning were men who had been trained in the cathedral schools and in the newly emerging universities. To be sure, the occult sciences did not remain their monopoly. Even in the twelfth and thirteenth centuries, clerical advisers to princes could convey to them the essence of this learning. To some extent in the thirteenth century, and far more in following centuries, Arabic writings and derivative compilations were translated into the vernacular languages for the benefit of laypeople. Throughout the later Middle Ages, however, these new forms of learning would have been primarily the preserve of those with formal education, the clergy and physicians in particular.

The Practice of Astrology

The most basic use of astrology was in making horoscopes, which would indicate the influence that the stars and planets had on a person at birth

---

[3] Charles Burnett, "Adelard, Ergaphalau and the science of the stars," in Charles Burnett, ed., *Adelard of Bath: An English Scientist and Arabist of the Early Twelfth Century* (London: Warburg Institute, 1987), 133–46.

or at any other juncture in life. Whether Arabic or Latin, a medieval horoscope was a complex diagram. It would have a central rectangle, surrounded by twelve rectangular or triangular segments (for the twelve astrological "houses"). Information given in these segments could pertain to the positions of the planets on the anniversary of the birth of the person for whom the horoscope was drawn up: Jupiter, for example, could be at a specific location in the constellation Aries. In the margins, the astrologer might give the positions of the planets eight years earlier, at the time of the person's birth. Some of the information, however, might pertain not to the subject himself, but to his father; as Ptolemy had recognized, a horoscope for a child can be used as a guide to the future of the child's parent.[4] One twelfth-century manuscript gives a series of four horoscopes, one of them labeled, "figure for the arrival of a certain person in England." The second has the caption inside a central square: "The question concerning the army of Normandy; and the conclusion is that it will not come." The third pertains to a deceased count of Anjou, and the fourth is a "figure for the commerce between two persons."[5] The astrological information given for these horoscopes points to 1151 as the year to which they refer. They all have political bearing, though their precise intent is obscure. The first one, for example, could be intended as a guide to what will happen if the unnamed person arrives in England, but more likely the question is *whether* he will do so. The question might have been whether Henry of Anjou (1133–89) would invade England with his Norman troops, in which case the horoscope might have been made by a friend of Henry (such as Adelard of Bath) or an enemy.

These horoscopes indicate some of the purposes that astrology served. First, knowing where the stars and planets were located at birth (or on the anniversary of a birth) could show how the heavenly bodies affected a person's character and general destiny. Marriages, career decisions, and other plans might be made accordingly. Secondly, astrology might be used for "interrogations": given a particular time for a trip, a marriage, a battle, or some other vital action, what outcome would this undertaking have? Thirdly, it might be used for "inceptions": given a specific undertaking, what would be the most auspicious moment to undertake it? In the second and third cases, the crucial factor would not be the configuration of stars and planets at birth, but rather their location at the present time or the near future.

---

[4] Bernard R. Goldstein and David Pingree, "Horoscopes from the Cairo Geniza," *Journal of Near Eastern Studies*, 36 (1977), 123–9.

[5] J. D. North, *Horoscopes and History* (London: Warburg Institute, 1986), 96–107; see also J. D. North, "Some Norman horoscopes," in Burnett, *Adelard of Bath*, 147–62.

Astrology had implications for medicine. A surgeon or barber-surgeon was supposed to know which signs of the Zodiac governed which parts of the body, because it was dangerous to operate or bleed a patient when the wrong constellation was dominant. Physicians, too, would need to know such things, and for that reason astrology was studied perhaps more systematically in medical schools than in other branches of medieval universities. The University of Bologna, eminent for its medical studies, had a professor to teach fledgling physicians how to gauge the influence of the stars on human bodies.

Astrological science was also deemed useful for rulers. Various forms of fortune-telling seem to have been popular at court, but none more than astrology. Even in ninth-century Gaul, we are told, all the great lords had their own astrologers, and a chaplain to William the Conqueror (reg. 1066–87) was so dedicated to astrology that it was said he would spend his nights gazing at stars rather than sleeping. After the infusion of Arabic science, astrology gained further prominence. Readers of the pseudo-Aristotelian *Secret of Secrets* would have learned from it how Aristotle was supposed to have advised Alexander the Great never to embark on war, indeed not even to eat or drink, sit down or rise up without consulting an astrologer. (The same book also mentions a stone which will secure victory in battle, and a Dominican who translated the work into French pondered why Alexander had to fight so hard when he had such power at his disposal.)

It is not always easy to tell whether astrologers' alleged influence was real or merely legendary. One wonders, for example, whether Guido of Montefeltro (d. 1298) really waited for his astrologer (standing atop a belltower) to signal the proper configuration of the stars before he galloped off into battle. Yet there is compelling evidence that many rulers did take astrology seriously. According to the chronicler Matthew Paris, the emperor Frederick II (reg. 1215–50) used astrologers to cast his children's horoscopes and to determine whether his plans were destined for success; he did not even consummate his marriage to the empress Isabella until the astrologers had announced the most propitious time for doing so. We might doubt the word of a chronicler, but there is other evidence of the emperor's interest. Michael Scot (ca. 1175–ca. 1235), whose early career had been devoted mainly to natural science, turned more to astrology when he came into Frederick's service. He advised the emperor regarding which phases of the Moon were best for seeking counsel, and told Frederick not to have his blood let when the Moon was in Gemini, for fear that he would be punctured twice rather than once. Scot himself tells us that the emperor deliberately went to a barber-surgeon at the proscribed time, to test this warning. The barber dismissed the advice and proceeded to let the emperor's blood, but then accidentally dropped his lancet on Frederick's foot and caused a serious wound.[6]

As S. J. Tester observed, the astrologers' function at court seems to have been ascertaining "when" rather than "what" or "whether."[7] They were charged with finding the most appropriate moment for any crucial act. One historian has surveyed more than two hundred key events in the reigns of the Habsburg dynasty, such as coronations, treaties, marriages, and battles, and has taken the positions of the stars (by medieval reckoning) for each of these events. Marriages turn out to have taken place at astrologically propitious times more often than other occurrences. This is scarcely surprising; it would be difficult to control the timing of battles and other affairs of state, but marriages could easily be postponed to await appropriate conjunctions of the stars.

The emperor Rudolph I seems to have been especially attentive to astrological concerns. Even his birth, while presumably not arranged by deliberate choice, portended an auspicious reign: he was born on 1 May 1218, when Mars and the Sun were in close and powerful conjunction, Mars being the planet of war and the Sun being a dominant influence for monarchs. He was crowned as emperor on 24 October 1273, when the same heavenly bodies were in conjunction. When he fought the most decisive battle of his career, again these bodies were in the most favorable conjunction possible, and he was married under a conjunction of Venus and Mercury. (A conjunction of Venus and the Sun might have been still more propitious, but such events occur only about every forty-three weeks, while Venus and Mercury are conjoined roughly twice as often.) Whether Rudolph had an official court astrologer is unknown, but these decisions may have been influenced by Henry of Isny, one of his closest confidants, who could have learned astronomy and astrology during his student years at Paris, and who was present when Rudolph was married. Several chronicles allege that Henry practiced sorcery and had dealings with demons, which may hint at an interest in astrology. In any case, it seems likely that someone with astrological knowledge guided Rudolph in timing key events. Among the Habsburg successors who seem to have continued this practice was the emperor Frederick III (reg. 1440–93), whose complex wedding

---

[6] Charles Homer Haskins, *Studies in the History of Mediaeval Science* (Cambridge, Mass.: Harvard University Press, 1924), 272–98.

[7] Tester, *History of Western Astrology*, 196.

arrangements may have become so by the need to accommodate both diplomacy and astrology.[8]

What we know for sure is that rulers did not appreciate having astrologers forecast the time and manner of their demise. As in the Roman Empire, so too in medieval Europe, predicting the death of a ruler was a hazardous business, at least bordering on treason. One of the men implicated along with Margery Jourdemayne in 1441 was an astrologer who, in his written work, had explained how to predict a person's death. When he helped show that Henry VI was teetering on the edge of the grave, the king needed an alternative horoscope to recover his composure.[9]

Not all monarchs were interested in astrology, and those who were attracted to it were not all drawn in the same ways. In England, Edward III (reg. 1327–77) seems to have been uninterested in astrology, and Richard II (reg. 1377–99) had a taste for fashion that is reflected in his sumptuous book on divination, but it was under Henry VI (reg. 1422–61, 1470–71) that king and courtiers began to take the reading of horoscopes seriously as a way of foretelling health and longevity.[10] In France, Charles V (reg. 1364–80) was famous for his library, which included 135 books of astrology and other occult arts, although also writings by critics of these arts. Charles founded a college for astrology and astrological medicine at Paris, had astrological writings translated into the vernacular, and obtained an astrological reading on his bride before marrying her.

Kings who took an interest in astrology might be judged variously by their subjects, depending in part on how they acquitted themselves generally as rulers. Peter IV of Aragon (reg. 1336–87) ruled with authority and was successful in combat, so his subjects tended to tolerate his interest in astrology, but his son John I (reg. 1387–96), weaker and more of a spendthrift, drew criticism for the same interest.[11]

When unaccustomed sights appeared in the sky, galvanizing public attention, the astrologers were the obvious experts to consult for guidance. Thus, in 1368 a comet appeared over much of Europe and

---

[8] Helmuth Grössing and Franz Stulhofer, "Versuch einer Deutung der Rolle der Astrologie in den persönlichen und politischen Entscheidungen einiger Habsburger des Spätmittelalters," *Österreichische Akademie der Wissenschaften, Philosophisch-historische Klasse: Anzeiger*, 117 (1980), 267–83.

[9] Hilary M. Carey, *Courting Disaster: Astrology at the English Court and University in the Later Middle Ages* (New York: St. Martin's, 1992).

[10] These distinctions are developed in Carey, *Courting Disaster*.

[11] Michael A. Ryan, *A Kingdom of Stargazers: Astrology and Authority in the Late Medieval Crown of Aragon* (Ithaca, New York: Cornell University Press, 2011).

provoked much speculation. A German or Polish astrologer, evidently writing in the service of some monarch or prince, saw the comet as a portent of misfortune for Scandinavia and other lands to the North. The fact that it appeared in the house of Taurus was a generally bad sign, portending widespread disease, warfare, death of cattle, conflagrations, frost that would ruin the harvest, and other calamities. Other characteristics of the comet gave warning of violent thunderstorms and of hot winds that would destroy crops. A French astrologer, perhaps also working in the service of a court, interpreted the comet as foretelling misfortune for England, since Parisians first saw it in the part of the sky more or less corresponding to the direction of England, and because it was first seen in the house of Taurus. This interpreter also pointed out that the planet dominant at the time the comet appeared was not England's planet Saturn, but France's planet Jupiter. In short, ill fortune for the enemy meant good fortune for one's own land, which was news that a monarch would be pleased to hear.[12]

Principles of Astrology

Astrology presupposed a certain view of astronomy, or the way the cosmos was structured. Certain facts would have seemed obvious to any medieval European. During the course of the day, the Sun travels in an arch across the southern sky, from east to west. Less obviously, over a year its position also changes vis-à-vis the twelve constellations that mark out the Zodiac: Aries, Taurus, Gemini, and the rest. For part of the year it will be in front of one of these constellations, and then it will move to be in front of another. The path that the Sun moves in, in relationship to these constellations, is roughly the same as that of the Moon, Mercury, Venus, Mars, Jupiter, and Saturn, which along with the Sun make up what were recognized in premodern astronomy as planets. At any given time, one could speak of the Sun as traveling in front of a particular constellation, and thus as in the "house" of one sign in the Zodiac, and so too each of the other planets would be in this or that house of the Zodiac.

This much would have been accepted as noncontroversial in medieval educated company. Because everyone recognized that the planets and stars circled the Earth in regular progression, the Zodiac itself became a symbol for the passage of time, and was represented as such in various artistic contexts. Signs of the Zodiac might occur, for example, in books of hours or prayerbooks for the laity. Their use did not commit an artist

---

[12] Hubert Pruckner, *Studien zu den astrologischen Schriften des Heinrichs von Langenstein* (Leipzig and Berlin: Teubner, 1933), 73–85.

or author to any theory about the *influence* that the stars and planets exerted.[13] The Zodiac by itself was, in modern terms, astronomical rather than specifically astrological.

Yet most Europeans would also have recognized that these planets and stars, and to a lesser extent other stars outside the Zodiac, did influence human affairs in various ways. Precisely what influence they held was intensely controversial. The Sun had obvious effects: it illuminated things, heated them, and dried them out. But astrologers held that the Sun, which is far more noble than earthly fire, could do many other things as well, and could work in subtle and occult ways. So, too, could the other heavenly bodies. All the planets and stars (and astrologers sometimes referred merely to "the stars" as shorthand for all the heavenly bodies) had some measure of power over earthly affairs, although it might be difficult to determine the nature and degree of a heavenly body's influence. The degree of power exerted by one of these bodies depended partly on its position in the sky. If it was just rising at the eastern horizon it was "in the ascendant," which was an especially powerful position. Directly overhead, it would also exert strong influence.

If one knew the identity and position of each planet and star, one could in large measure gauge the *degree* of its impact. The *nature* of that influence, on the other hand, was inherent in each star and planet, not something relative to its position in the sky. Each planet had its own nature, effects, and areas of influence. The Moon was feminine, watery (and thus cold and moist), powerful (especially during a person's infancy), and associated with madness (hence "lunacy") and chastity. Venus was feminine, airy (thus hot and moist), powerful in adolescence, and linked with sensuality. So, too, each of the other planets had its own special characteristics.

The path along which these heavenly bodies traveled was divided into twelve houses of unequal size, six of which were in the visible sky and the other six below the horizon. Thus, as a planet moved through the sky, it would pass through all twelve houses in succession. The area of life that the planets influenced would depend in part on what house they were in at a given time. A planet in the first house would have general influence on personality, while in the second house it would affect material fortunes, and in the third it would help determine the character of one's family. In other houses, a planet would influence relations with parents or spouse, sexuality and children, health, and so forth. Thus, if Mars happened to be in the tenth house at a crucial time, it could mean that

---

[13] Tester, *History of Western Astrology,* esp. 129.

one was destined to become a soldier, since Mars was warlike in nature and the planets in the tenth house influenced a person's career. The same planet in the eighth house would have very different meaning: that being the house governing death, it could portend death in battle.

The planets and stars exerted special influence at certain times, particularly birth. An infant just coming from the womb was still soft and malleable, and thus especially susceptible to the influence of the heavenly bodies. Having Jupiter in the ascendant at birth would be a generally good sign. If Mars were in the seventh house, one might expect a stormy marriage. Because the Wife of Bath in Chaucer's *Canterbury Tales* was born with Venus in the ascendant, however, she was fated to a lifetime of sexual passion. Apart from these influences at birth, any critical juncture in life would be an appropriate time to consult the positions of the planets. One would not want to enter battle when Mars was in a weak position, but one might wish to arrange a marriage for a time when Venus was dominant, or perhaps when Venus was close to (or "in conjunction with") the Sun, which would strengthen her influence.

To speak of certain people as "Sagittarians," for example, is to say that they were born at a time of year when the Sun was traveling in conjunction with Sagittarius. Modern popular lore has made this factor the very essence of astrology, but in astrological science it was merely one of numerous factors to be weighed in making any prediction. Among the many further complications is the association of planets with constellations: the Sun is most powerful when in the same house as Leo, for example, and Saturn is strengthened by Capricorn during the day and by Aquarius at night.

These were the basic principles on which astrology rested.[14] But whether its principles were correct or not was a controversial question, and many would have challenged them. One of the most influential discussions of the matter was in Augustine's *On the City of God*, which admitted that stars might *predict* future events, but denied that their motions could *produce* future events. Augustine and later writers rejected the notion that the stars exert a determinist force that would constrain human will. Even the predictive force of astrology was, at best, tentative and imperfect: otherwise how could one explain the cases of twins who, born under essentially the same astrological influences, nonetheless led very different lives? In following centuries, arguments against astrology came to be routine and derivative. Isidore of Seville acknowledged its

[14] For a more detailed presentation, see Wayne Shumaker, *The Occult Sciences in the Renaissance: A Study in Intellectual Patterns* (Berkeley: University of California Press, 1972).

role in predicting the weather, and allowed that the heavenly bodies influenced the growth of crops and even human health, but could not believe that the stars regulate human souls or that a person's fate could be read at birth in the stars. Other writers, such as Gregory the Great, borrowed his distinctions or expressed themselves in similar terms. The sheer weight of Augustine's and Isidore's authority was enough to render astrology suspect.

In later medieval Europe, certain basic applications of astrology were noncontroversial: its influence on the human body and on climate was generally accepted, and thus there was little objection to its use in healing or in predicting the weather. Far more problematic was its use in predicting human behavior. Helinand of Froidmont, a late twelfth-century Cistercian monk, argued that for the planets to have the kind of influence ascribed to them, they must have intelligent souls, and thus be either angels or demons; and if they are angels, how can they sometimes do evil? The most serious objection to astrology in the later Middle Ages was the danger of determinism: if the stars governed human affairs, did they not infringe human free will and divine omnipotence? Gerard of Feltre in the thirteenth century posed the problem sharply in his *Summa on the Stars*: "If the stars make a man a murderer or a thief, then all the more it is the first cause, God, who does this, which it is shameful to suggest."[15]

Even as a means for predicting human behavior, however, astrology had its defenders. The argument was essentially threefold: first, the astrologers and their advocates delimited carefully the claims that astrology could make; secondly, they provided examples suggesting that it actually worked; and thirdly, they provided philosophical and scientific support for its assumptions.

Those who defended astrology typically insisted on certain major qualifications. First, they insisted that while astrologers of antiquity actually worshiped the stars, those of their own age subjected the stars to scientific examination. This was, in large part, a tactic for undercutting the opposition of Augustine and other early Christian writers; they may have been right in opposing the idolatrous astrologers of their own era, but their arguments do not apply to later astrologers. Yet there were more difficult challenges, such as the problem of determinism, which seemed inherent in all astrology. Drawing on a distinction made even in antiquity, the defenders of astrology argued that the stars were not causes, but merely signs of future events. This did not altogether solve the problem of determinism, since even if the stars did not cause events,

---

[15] Paola Zambelli, "Albert le Grand et l'astrologie," *Recherches de Théologie Ancienne et Médiévale*, 49 (1982), 155.

their efficacy as signs might presuppose some determining cause. Thus, three further qualifications were vital: astrology could predict general trends, but not particular chance events; it could not predict with certainty; and the free human will could override the influence of the stars. Freedom of the will was the most important concern. Perhaps few people availed themselves of their freedom, yet in principle everyone had the power to overcome astral influences. Both Albert the Great (ca. 1200–80) and Thomas Aquinas agreed that the stars can influence the body, and that the body, in turn, can influence the soul. Thomas, in particular, argued that most people are ruled by their bodily passions or appetites; very few have the strength of intellect and will needed to overcome their bodily impulses. For the bulk of humankind, therefore, the influence of the stars upon the body will go unopposed. Yet the will remains free in principle, and those who exert themselves may counter the effects of the stars. The argument was usually supported with a maxim ascribed to Ptolemy: "The wise man rules the stars."[16]

Certain others in the thirteenth and following centuries were more enthusiastic and less critical about astrology. Guido Bonatti denied precisely such qualifications as Thomas maintained. For him, astrology held the key to all knowledge:

All things are known to the astrologer. All that has taken place in the past, all that will happen in the future – everything is revealed to him, since he knows the effects of the heavenly motions which have been, those which are, and those which will be, and since he knows at what time they will act, and what effects they ought to produce.[17]

Yet this extreme view was very much a minority opinion. Among philosophers and theologians from the late thirteenth century onward, the more common conclusion was that the stars and planets exert a strong, yet resistible influence on human affairs. Even this much was sometimes denied: Nicholas Oresme (ca. 1325–82), for example, maintained that the stars influence earthly objects only by shedding heat and light.

Further support for astrology came from appeal to what we would call case histories. One writer from the late twelfth century, for example, told how he had been at Jaffa when a new ship was about to sail. Being known as an astrologer, he was asked to determine what fate the stars held for this vessel. He calculated the position of the heavenly bodies, and began

---

[16] The usual forms were *Homo sapiens dominatur astris* or *Sapiens dominabitur astris*; *homo* would usually be read here, as often in medieval Latin, to exclude *femina*.

[17] Theodore Otto Wedel, *The Mediaeval Attitude Toward Astrology, Particularly in England* (New Haven: Yale University Press, 1920), 79 (with quotations translated).

trembling as he realized the ship was destined to founder. He himself escaped disaster by not boarding it, but the crew decided to set sail despite his warning, and soon after they left harbor the vessel was, in fact, shipwrecked. Another story, set in India, involved two boys, one a prince, whose horoscope suggested he should be a craftsman, and the other a weaver's son, whose horoscope indicated he should be a great dignitary. The outcome, of course, was that the two boys grew up as the stars decreed, not as their families expected. On the other hand, what about people born under the same stars but in fact destined to very different lives? In response to this challenge, the astrologers could cite a tale from Julius Firmicus Maternus about a king and a peasant who were born at the same time. The king ruled over his kingdom; the peasant, while deprived of the same kind of power, nonetheless was a dominant figure who ended up ruling in his own figurative realm. The logical extension of these stories was the claim that astrology actually rested on empirical study of numerous case histories. One writing of pseudo-Aristotle thus claims to report the results of a survey, in which horoscopes cast for twelve thousand men provided a proper database for astrology.

More than anything else, however, it was the philosophical and scientific grounding of astrology that gave it a respected position in the European intellectual world. Arabic astrologers such as Abu Ma'shar had refined the philosophical underpinnings for astrology, using eclectic but loosely Aristotelian arguments to show in systematic detail how the more perfect quintessence of the heavenly bodies could exert power over the lesser bodies on Earth. It was the backing of this philosophical cosmology that did most to ensure that astrology would gain credence in the universities of western Europe.

Astrologers might also gain a hearing in Neoplatonist circles. To be sure, there were Neoplatonists whose focus on the "intelligible" world of the spirit drew their attention away from the physical world, but there were also Neoplatonists influenced more by the cosmology of Plato's *Timaeus* and by the work of Macrobius. Those of the latter sort inclined to see the cosmos as an integrated totality, within which even divine influence is mediated through the stars rather than intervening directly upon Earth.[18] Even so, the Neoplatonist tradition disposed its adherents to see the cosmos as a *living* system, with complex and unpredictable influences, not as a system of mechanical and regular influences on

---

[18] Tullio Gregory, "La nouvelle idée de nature et de savoir scientifique au XIIe siècle," in John Emery Murdoch and Edith Dudley Sylla, eds., *The Cultural Context of Medieval Learning* (Dordrecht: Reidel, 1975), 193–218.

which a science of prediction might be based. It is one thing to say in the abstract that the macrocosm of the universe will exert constant impact on the microcosm of the individual human being. It is something quite different to isolate and analyze specific influences, and that was a tendency more to be expected from the Arabic synthesis of learning, with its grounding in Aristotelian cosmology.

While astrology could be useful in ascertaining the influence of the stars and predicting things that would happen, its underlying principles could also be helpful in explaining certain occult or mysterious phenomena within nature. This is a topic that arises in various philosophical writings of the thirteenth and following centuries, and one of the fullest treatments is to be found in Thomas Aquinas' treatise *On the Occult Works of Nature*.[19] The examples Thomas gives are phenomena we would not usually recognize as magical, and indeed he does not apply that term to them: he is trying to explain such things as the power of a magnet to attract iron and the power of rhubarb to act as a medicinal purgative. While his examples are thus quite ordinary, he nonetheless speaks of "occult" powers – those which cannot be ascribed to the physical makeup (or "elements") of the objects in question – and his reasoning would apply to other occult processes that would more often be called magical.

Thomas says at the outset that a higher agent can work through a lower one in either of two ways. The higher agent may impress some kind of "form" upon the lower agent, as when the Sun illuminates the Moon and causes it to become luminous. Or else it may simply use the lower agent as a tool, the way a carpenter uses a saw. When the lower agent consistently has the same effect every time it is applied, we must assume that the higher agent has impressed a form upon it; such powers are part of the essence of these lower agents. This is the case with the powers inherent in magnets and rhubarb. Where do these forms come from? Thomas, like Aristotle, sees the stars and planets as responsible for the generation and decay of all corruptible bodies: when a mineral is formed in the ground, or a plant grows in the soil, these processes can be traced to the influence of the heavenly bodies, which affect all things on Earth by their passing through the sky. It is the stars and planets, then, which by their motion impress those forms on magnets, rhubarbs, and all other things, endowing them with both ordinary and occult powers.

---

[19] Joseph Bernard McAllister, *The Letter of Saint Thomas Aquinas de Occultis Operibus Naturae ad Quemdam Militem Ultramontanum* (Washington, DC: Catholic University of America Press, 1939).

In writing this treatise, Thomas was not doing astrology, nor was he even addressing the question whether the stars can foretell human conduct. What he had in common with the astrologers was simply the belief, which both he and they found already worked out in Aristotelian cosmology, that the stars have influence on earthly persons and objects in ways that are not manifest (and are thus "occult"). It is sometimes argued that magic is not in fact a branch of science, but rather of technology; it would be more in keeping with medieval usage to say that it is a practical rather than a theoretical science. Yet it lent itself to theoretical explanation, and what Thomas was articulating was a theory of the cosmos that could suffice to account for a wide range of occult phenomena.

Astral Magic

In the same treatise, Thomas explicitly distinguished natural channels of astral influence (such as magnets and rhubarb) from those artificial astrological images sometimes used in magic: images bearing signs of the constellations or planets, through which the power of these heavenly bodies is drawn down and concentrated so that it can be used in magic. The latter, he says, can work only as tools of some extrinsic agent, by which he means a demon. Others would have disagreed, and argued that such images can have effect naturally, without demonic intervention, though this position is not easy to find in formal philosophical literature. Because this magic sought to change rather than merely learn one's destiny, its effect was entirely distinct from that of astrology proper, and for that reason it has been proposed that it be called "astral" rather than "astrological" magic.[20] Treatises on such magic made their way from the Arabic world to the West – works ascribed sometimes to known historical writers and sometimes to the mythical Hermes Trismegistus.[21]

How this magic worked can be seen, for example, in the instructions that Thabit ibn Qurra (ca. 836–901) gives for ridding a place of scorpions. The first step is to make an image of a scorpion out of copper, tin, lead, silver, or gold, while the constellation Scorpio is in the ascendant. One must write the name of this constellation and various other

---

[20] Frances A. Yates, *Giordano Bruno and the Hermetic Tradition* (London: Routledge, 1964), 60.

[21] See now Antonella Sannino, "From Hermetic magic to the magic of marvels," in Page and Rider, *Routledge History*, 153–68; Brian P. Copenhaver, *Hermetica: The Greek Corpus Hermeticum and the Latin* Asclepius (Cambridge University Press, 1992); Florian Ebeling, *The Secret History of Hermes Trismegistus: Hermeticism from Ancient to Modern Times*, trans. David Lorton (Ithaca, New York: Cornell University Press, 2007).

astrological information on the image, then bury it in the place that is to become free of scorpions. While burying it, one should say, "This is the burial of it and of its species, that it may not come to that one and to that place." It is still better to make four such images and bury them in the four corners of the place in question.[22]

This procedure may seem innocent enough, but Thabit and others recommended similar techniques for many purposes, not all so blameless. Astral images could help in recovering a husband's affections, gaining the favor of a king, recovering stolen property, destroying a town or any other place, inflicting illness, preventing a person from performing some action, bringing concord to enemies or enmity to friends. A physician might try to heal kidney disease by using a medal with an image of a lion and certain characters inscribed on it, a practice which the theologian Jean Gerson (1363–1429) wrote against. Sometimes the instructions called for writing the name of the victim on the image. Often they listed spices or herbs to be used in fumigating it. Incantations might also be recited over it: some treatises give names of spirits to be invoked as an aid in this magic. Once duly prepared, the image might be worn over one's heart or otherwise carried on one's person, though most often it was to be buried. The Latin preface to the translation of one such treatise recognized that this magic might give offense, but argued that God had given it to his servants as a tool for the good and for vengeance against malefactors. Granted, it might at times be misused; but should the axe be blamed if it is used sometimes for killing people rather than cutting down trees?

Thabit's procedures could be adapted for new purposes. Allegedly a physician working for Charles V of France expelled the English troops from French soil by adapting Thabit's instructions for driving away scorpions. Under the requisite astrological conditions, images that bore the names of the English king and his military officers were buried upside down, with their hands or arms behind their backs, and with the names of spirits that would torment them and drive them out of France. The magic worked "in no time, that is to say in a few months."[23]

Not all astrological images were alike. From an orthodox Christian perspective, an image that drew only on the powers of the heavenly bodies might be acceptable, but if the images were meant to be accompanied by prayers or images addressed to those heavenly bodies, or to the

---

[22] Lynn Thorndike, "Traditional medieval tracts concerning engraved astrological images," in *Mélanges Auguste Pelzer* (Louvain: Bibliothèque de l'Université, 1947), 217–73.

[23] Boudet, "Magic at court," 337.

spirits associated with them, or if they bore characters and words in unknown languages, they came closer to idolatry or to demonic magic. (Thomas Aquinas rejected this distinction and saw all astrological images as invoking demons, implicitly if not expressly.) One writer on astral magic distinguished various figures that could be used in this art: a figure could have a form corresponding to that seen in the heavens, as when the image of a lion was used and reflected the figure of Leo seen in the stars; or the figures could be letters or characters that bear no such resemblance; or there could be likenesses of heavenly images but not made in the ways prescribed by astrologers; or the figures of heavenly images could have characters or letters added to them; or there could be talismans that derive their power from conjurations, sacrifices, and suffumigations.[24] The first of these types served most obviously to channel effectively the powers as well as the forms of the heavenly bodies; the last was the most problematic.

The most famous work of astral magic was an Arabic text known in the West as *Picatrix*.[25] This was translated from Arabic into Spanish at the behest of Alfonso the Wise (reg. 1252–84) and then found its way into Latin. The author (or rather compiler, since the work is an unwieldy collection of related materials) professes a dualistic view of the world, in which spirit stands exalted above matter, yet the basic point of the work is to show how spirit itself, dwelling at its purest in the stars, can be brought down to Earth and can work upon matter. Occasional statements of grand principle are interspersed in a great mass of specific instructions. Inscribe a set of markings or talismanic signs on a piece of linen under the proper astrological conditions, add the name of a person, and set fire to the cloth, and the person named will be compelled to go wherever you want. Write other signs on a lead tablet and hide it in any habitation, and you will draw down the power of Saturn in such a way that the place will become depopulated. Elsewhere the reader is told to bury such images for the desired effects. Alternately, the power of the heavenly bodies can be channeled through "prayers." One chapter tells in detail how to pray to the planets, first listing the situations appropriate for petitioning each of them, then giving the properties of each and proposing formulas for prayer (which might well have served as models for the astral prayer in Chaucer's *Franklin's Tale*). As smoke rises from one's censer, one is to

[24] Jérôme Torrella (Hieronymus Torrella), *Opus præclarum de imaginibus astrologicis*, ed. Nicolas Weill-Parot (Florence: SISMEL, 2008), 120–1; Nicolas Weill-Parot, "Jerome Torrella and 'astrological images,'" in Page and Rider, *Routledge History*, 254–67.

[25] *Picatrix: A Medieval Treatise on Astral Magic*, trans. Dan Attrell and David Porreca (University Park: Pennsylvania State University Press, 2019).

invoke the planets by their names in various languages, praising them for their powers, and "conjuring" them to aid one's designs. The book also lists magical substances with wondrous properties: mandrake, laurel, the brain of a hoopoe, the blood of a bat, and so forth. Sometimes these suffice by themselves as potions, but elsewhere they are to be burned as "fumigations," and their smoke acts as a kind of incense to enhance the power of an image or a prayer. On occasion, the work speaks of constraining demons to perform one's will, but this theme is seldom explicit.

We find ourselves here in a particularly controversial area of the occult sciences, which shed disreputability upon the movement as a whole and enhanced critics' suspicions of astrologers generally.

Alchemy

Like astrology, alchemy was a form of occult knowledge that required extensive learning. Also like astrology, it arose in antiquity, lived on in the Byzantine and Muslim worlds, but survived in the West only in fragmentary form until Arabic materials were translated in the twelfth century. In 1144, Robert of Chester translated into Latin the first alchemical treatise ever accessible to Europeans. Soon he and other translators of the era made Westerners familiar with Arabic terms basic to chemistry and alchemy alike: "alkali," "naphtha," "alcohol," "elixir," and the word "alchemy" itself.

The essential point of alchemy is to discover the elixir or "philosopher's stone," which can transmute lead or other base metals into gold and silver. In their search for this elixir, alchemists would spend years working over increasingly complex furnaces and laboratories, attempting to refine, sublimate, fuse, and otherwise transform their various chemicals. In the process, they produced much improvement in the tools of experimentation; their furnaces and stills, for example, contributed to the techniques of later chemical experimentation.

Alchemists assumed an intricate system of affinities between chemicals and other forms of being. Like the astrologers, they assumed a consonance between microcosm and macrocosm. For their purposes, this link was suggested most fundamentally by the association between metals and planets: between gold and the Sun, silver and the Moon, iron and Mars, quicksilver and Mercury, and so forth. They thought that observation of the heavens could show the most favorable times for working with these metals and other chemicals. When alchemists work under a waxing Moon, for example, they obtain purer metals.

Like astrology, alchemy rested upon philosophical principles most clearly and authoritatively stated by Aristotle and developed by

Scholastic philosophers. Of particular importance was the notion that all matter is reducible to four elements (earth, air, fire, and water), which are further reducible to "prime matter." If all metals are composed of these same basic elements in various proportions, then should it not be possible to recombine the elements to obtain other, higher forms of matter? This was the alchemists' dream.

One fundamental theory behind Arabic alchemy and later Latin alchemy was the "Mercury-Sulphur theory," which viewed all metals as compounded of mercury (viewed as wet and steamy) and sulphur (thought of as dry and smoky). If these two metals are pure and are combined in optimal proportions, they produce gold. If they are impure or combined in the wrong proportions, they yield other metals, such as lead – but by purifying these baser metals and adjusting the proportions of mercury and sulphur the alchemist can transmute base metals into gold. Another key notion was the analogy between alchemy and medicine: just as the physician seeks to restore health by balancing the bodily humors, so too the alchemist transmutes metals by adjusting their qualities, using a medicinal "elixir" as an agent of change, so that lead, with its cold and dry properties, is turned into gold, with predominant hot and wet qualities. The "philosopher's stone" was similarly an agent that could make metals into incorruptible gold, while also curing corruption or disease in human and animal bodies.[26]

Another alchemical theory focused on the make-up of metals. A thirteenth-century Latin author, who wrote under the pseudo-Arabic name Geber, thought of metals as being composed of the infinitesimal particles that are put together in different ways: gold is made up of tiny particles packed closely together, while base metals have larger particles packed more loosely. Alchemists had powerful "medicines" that could alter this composition; one such medicine can produce gold, and another silver.[27]

The writings of the alchemists are often obscure and veiled in symbolism. Their opacity can be seen in one classic text that the alchemists claimed as their own: the *Emerald Table*, a series of cryptic sayings allegedly written on an emerald slab and discovered in the tomb of Hermes Trismegistus:

As all things were by the contemplation of one, so all things arose from this one thing by a single act of adaptation. The father thereof is the Sun, the mother the

[26] Lawrence M. Principe, *The Secrets of Alchemy* (University of Chicago Press, 2013), 35–44, 72.
[27] Principe, *The Secrets of Alchemy*, 54–8.

Moon. The Wind carried it in its womb, the Earth is the nurse thereof. It is the father of all works of wonder throughout the whole world. The power thereof is perfect.[28]

And so on. Alchemists explained that the "one thing" is the elixir, whose father is gold and whose mother is silver. Other sayings in the text were interpreted as referring to various procedures carried out in the alchemical laboratory.

Far more straightforward was a popular manual of alchemy from later medieval Europe, the treatise *On Alchemy* ascribed to Albert the Great. The greater part of this work was a practical, point-by-point introduction to the various tools and procedures of the trade: the kinds of furnaces used, the vessels, the chemicals, and the stages in preparation of chemicals. The author explains that "calcination" is a process of reducing a substance to powder by exposing it to fire, to remove the moisture that unites its component parts. "Distillation" is purification of a liquid by allowing its vapors to rise and be separated from the dregs. Among the most important chemicals are sulphur and mercury; before the philosopher's stone can be prepared, sulphur must be dissolved, whitened, and fixated as follows:

First, boil sulphur in strong acid for a whole day. Let it first be well ground, and remove the superabundant scum. Afterwards allow it to dry, grind it, and add as much of the prepared alum as I have taught, and put it into the vessel for sublimation for mercury, knowing that less fire is to be applied than for mercury. Turn down the fire and slowly sublime it for a whole day. Take it out in the morning and you will find it sublimed and black. Sublime it a second time and it will be white. Sublime it a third time, with salt added, and it will be very white. Again sublime it a third time, with salt added, and it will be very white. Again sublime it a third time and a fourth time up to the fixation point, and set it aside.[29]

This treatise also contains advice for the aspiring alchemist. It is important, the author insists, to have a house in a secluded place for alchemical work. He warns against starting to work without sufficient funds. And he admonishes the pupil to avoid all dealings with princes, who will harass the alchemist whether he is successful or unsuccessful, though for different reasons in the two cases. Many would-be alchemists, he says, fail through misunderstanding, debauchery and folly, carelessness, lack of funds, or irresolution.

---

[28] Translated in E. J. Holmyard, *Alchemy* (Harmondsworth: Penguin, 1957), 97–8.
[29] *Libellus de alchimia, Ascribed to Albertus Magnus*, trans. Sr. Virginia Heines (Berkeley: University of California Press, 1958), ch. 38 (translation adapted).

A particularly engaging introduction to medieval alchemy is the writing of Thomas Norton, an alchemist in fifteenth-century Bristol, who claimed that he had learned by age twenty-eight how to confect the elixir of gold. In his *Ordinal of Alchemy* he tells how he traveled over a hundred miles to find his master in this art, and in forty days he learned from him all of its secrets, but when he set about preparing the elixir back at home, his product was stolen from him twice.[30]

Even more than Albert the Great, Norton devotes himself to rendering wise counsel. He warns against trusting in superstitions, in false astrologers, and in necromancy, "for it is a property of the Devil to lie." For the work to proceed correctly, everything must be in proper concord. The alchemist's mind must be in accord with the work itself, properly stable and comprehending. The workmen must be in accord with the craft, working in orderly shifts. The instruments must be in accord with the work, all the vessels having the proper shapes and materials. The place too must be in accord with the work, without drafts or other disturbances. Places "where lechery is used" are inappropriate. And the work must be in accord with the heavenly spheres: it must be done under proper astrological conditions. Norton's insistent refrain is that people without the proper training in metaphysics and physics should leave alchemy alone, since they are doomed to failure. He laments that "every estate" has its hand in this art: everyone from popes and cardinals down to glaziers and tinkers. We need not take this claim entirely at face value; most other sources suggest that the practitioners were mainly clerics and physicians (in the late thirteenth and early fourteenth century, for example, the Franciscan and Dominican orders felt obliged several times to forbid their members to practice alchemy), yet Norton had perhaps met or heard of people of varied status who at least dabbled in the art.

He tells numerous stories of people who have met with hardship, even disaster, in their quest for alchemical gold. A priest near London, reputed to be "half a leech" because of his medical skill, determined that with the proceeds from his alchemy he would perform an act of service: he would build a bridge across the Thames. After long deliberation he decided that he would light his bridge with luminous carbuncles. But after still more deliberation he went nearly mad worrying about where he would find enough carbuncles for his purpose. After a year he had made little progress in his search for gold; he did not even have brass for his efforts. In another case, the king of England heard of a monk who had made 1,000 pounds of gold in less than half a day. When the monk was

---

[30] *The Ordinall of Alchimy by Thomas Norton of Bristoll, Being a facsimile reproduction from Theatrum chemicum britannicum* (London: Arnold, 1928).

dragged from his monastery and asked about his gold, he told a sad tale. He had accumulated enough gold to send 20,000 men to the Holy Land, and kept it for a long time, hoping to find a king who might go on crusade, but because of the trouble it had cost him he eventually cast it all into a lake. The king soon dismissed the monk, but others from the court, perhaps more credulous than their monarch, apprehended and detained him for several years, hoping to benefit from his art.

After several such cautionary tales, Norton proceeds to discuss the elements of alchemy. First there is the "gross work," the heavy labor of mining and working with minerals. The alchemist should not expend his efforts on such work but should leave it to servants. The "subtle work," on the other hand, falls to the alchemist himself, who must be trained in metaphysics and physics so that he will understand this work. The gross work must not be done by clerics (meaning here educated men); the subtle work can only be done by a cleric. An early manuscript of Norton's work suggests the respective roles of the educated master and uneducated servants: the servants are shown getting their hands dirty, while the master sits and gives directions. The alchemist himself must understand the effects of hot and cold, dry and wet. He must know, for example, that heat causes dry things to become white, as in the case of burnt bones or lime, while cold engenders whiteness in wet things, such as ice and frost. He must learn to recognize the states of things by color, odor, taste, and fluidity. Physicians distinguish nineteen different colors of urine, but alchemists have a hundred more colors they must recognize in their chemicals. Taste would be an excellent way to analyze substances, except that it can be dangerous. Norton tells of two foolish men who imbibed a bit of the "white stone" in hopes of relief from their sickness, but because they had taken it before it was fully prepared they became paralyzed until the alchemical master came with an antidote. Alchemists must also learn to distinguish various degrees of heat. One who has become a true master of the art will ultimately be able to produce not only the white stone (needed for production of silver), but the red as well (required for alchemists' gold). What he will discover is that the red stone is hidden within the white one and may be released by fire. "Then is the fair White Woman married to the Ruddy Man."

With curious frequency, medieval sources speak of alchemy as useful for health as well as wealth. The elixir has medicinal properties ascribed to it, as do other alchemical concoctions. Thus, in 1456, twelve men petitioned Henry VI of England for permission to practice alchemy: among them were two of the king's own physicians and another physician who was a friend of the duke of Gloucester. In granting permission for three of these petitioners to engage in alchemical work, the king recalled that the elixir was a medicine that would easily cure all illnesses, prolong

Fig. 15. Alchemical apparatus, from a fifteenth-century manuscript

human life in undiminished strength, cure wounds, and serve as antidote to all poisons. Only as an afterthought did the king add that transmutation of metals into "true gold and very fine silver" could help enrich his kingdom.[31] One key to this conception of alchemy is provided by the treatise *On Consideration of the Fifth Essence* by John of Rupescissa

---

[31] D. Geoghegan, "A licence of Henry VI to practise alchemy," *Ambix*, 6 (1957), 10–17 (with translation of quotation).

(d. ca. 1365). What seems odd about this work at first is that it applies the notion of the fifth essence to alcohol. It gives various means for distilling the alcohol found in wine, and it tells how to "fix the sun in our sky" by treating the alcohol with heated gold to enhance its already marvelous medical powers. Rupescissa may have been the first to use alchemical technology and vocabulary in this way.[32] One might suppose that his work is not really on alchemy at all, but what is more to the point is that many people seem to have been using alchemical techniques, equipment, and language for purposes other than simply trying to confect gold and silver. Clearly, Rupescissa was not unique in proposing that alchemy could produce new kinds of drugs from chemical rather than biological sources. In that respect, alchemy provided a breakthrough in inorganic pharmacology, however great or small the immediate payoff from this breakthrough may have been.

Alchemists were notorious for making fake gold and silver, which turned to dross when tested. Echoing a Psalm verse, Albert the Great lamented that this fraudulent gold "does not gladden the heart" like true gold. Chaucer conveyed a widespread view of alchemists in *The Canon's Yeoman's Tale*, which presents the alchemists as rogues who spend so much time around noxious chemicals that they smell like goats, and who rob people of their money by persuading them they can produce gold or silver. They can take silver pieces and insert them into a piece of charcoal, from which, not surprisingly, they then produce silver. Or they pretend to obtain it by stirring a crucible, but the stick they use is hollow and has silver filling inside it. They feign conversion of copper into silver, but they accomplish this feat only by having silver up their sleeves. Evidently, there were in fact alchemists who tried to pass off false gold or silver as the real item. To curb this practice, Pope John XXII stipulated that anyone who made or circulated such counterfeit gold or silver should pay a fine in real gold or silver equal in weight to the false metal. The pontiff provided special penalties for clerics caught in these practices.

Even Chaucer's storyteller, however, does not see all alchemists as scoundrels; some of them are merely fools. This attitude too was widely shared. Johannes Trithemius speaks with verisimilitude when he tells of several people who were ruined by alchemy. He speaks of a man who squandered a fortune in his alchemical pursuits, then disappeared and left wife and children behind. He knows of an abbot who left his abbey in

---

[32] Robert P. Multhauf, "John of Rupescissa and the origin of medical chemistry," *Isis*, 45 (1954), 359–67.

debt because of his alchemical research, and a Carthusian prior who wasted five or six years on these pursuits. Trithemius concludes:

Alchemy is a chaste whore who has many lovers but deludes them all and never falls into the embrace of any. She turns the foolish into madmen, the wealthy into paupers, philosophers into simpletons, and those she has deceived into talkative deceivers, for while they know nothing they profess to know all.[33]

Why, then, did many intelligent people take alchemy seriously? Partly, no doubt, because hope sprang eternal. Partly because other research was being done in the name of alchemy. But also because the allure of secret knowledge was in itself strong, and even stories of wretched failure could not deter those romantic intellects who craved the fascination of deep and mysterious learning.

The Cult of Secrecy and Books of Secrets

The European writings on astrology and alchemy may have reached a fairly broad audience by the fifteenth century, but they were seldom intended for the masses. Quite the contrary: the authors of these works often exerted themselves to restrict their own audience. This was especially true of alchemists, but astrologers, too, sometimes donned the cloak of secrecy. *The Mirror of Astronomy*, often ascribed to Alfred the Great, contains a solemn warning that its teaching should be kept secret; and for obvious reasons *Picatrix* is obsessed with this concern. The theme is common in works on magic generally. In his treatise on gems, Marbode of Rennes argued that if the common people learned of their mysterious powers, the value of the mysteries would be diminished. Roger Bacon quoted this text and others against the breaking of secrets, then suggested a series of ways to preserve the occult character of nature's own knowledge. A person writing about such things should use enigmatic phrases, invent secret words and alphabets, mix together different languages, abbreviate heavily, and so forth. The secrecy of magic was also the stuff of legends: Alexander Neckham (1157–1217), for example, told how Aristotle had certain of his subtler works buried along with him in a sepulcher so well-concealed that no one has found it, though when Antichrist comes he may be able to read these books.

When medieval writers used the term "occult," they used it in reference to the hidden powers of nature, but they did not typically use the term with reference to special branches of knowledge, or the "occult

---

[33] J. R. Partington, "Trithemius and alchemy," *Ambix*, 2 (1938), 53–9.

sciences." The latter term is nonetheless useful, first of all as a kind of shorthand for "sciences dealing with occult powers," but secondly as a characterization of the learning itself, which was something reserved for the few and concealed from the many. Those who studied these things studied hidden powers, and sometimes (not always) kept their knowledge about those powers hidden.

Alchemical writers warn constantly that their works must not fall into the wrong hands. The treatise *On Alchemy* ascribed to Albert warns against revealing the secrets of the art to anyone, but particularly "the foolish," who will fail in their efforts and in their frustration will envy those who succeed. Thomas Norton is even more insistent on this point. The art of alchemy is so holy that it must be taught orally, with the seal of "a most sacred, dreadful oath," and its deepest secrets must never be committed to writing. At one point Norton fears that he may be telling too much, and he adds, "But my heart quaketh, my hand is trembling, when I write of this most secret thing." When the alchemist grows old he may entrust his knowledge to a single suitable pupil, but no more than one. Otherwise evil people will gain the knowledge and use it to disrupt the peace and overthrow rightful princes.

The writers of magical manuscripts, alchemical and otherwise, did at times use cipher. Usually this involves nothing more than replacing each vowel with the consonant that follows it in the alphabet.[34] Thomas Betson, in what appears to be a relatively earnest mood, after discussing the interchangeability of astrological and alchemical terms, recommends using such techniques to keep the occult sciences from falling into the wrong hands, though he does not make it entirely clear which hands are the right ones. Another writer uses such cipher in a prescription for seeing hidden things:

So that you may see what others cannot see, mix the bile of a male cat [*de cbttp mbscxlp = de catto masculo*] with the fat of an entirely white hen [*gblllnf= galline*] and anoint your eyes with it, and you will see what others cannot see.[35]

Still another manuscript goes to the trouble of transliterating key words into runes, although the manuscript itself comes from southern

---

[34] Thf rfsvlt js spmfthjng ljkf thjs.

[35] St. John's College, Cambridge, MS E.6., fol. 7^r–8^v (the writer's alphabet does not include j, k, v, or w); Bodleian Library, MS Ashm. 1398, fol. 144^v. Cf. Bodleian MS e Mus. 219, fol. 186^{r-v}. For general information on medieval cryptography, see Bernhard Bischoff, "Übersicht über die nichtdiplomatischen Geheimschriften des Mittelalters," *Mitteilungen des Instituts für österreichische Geschichtsforschung*, 62 (1957), 1–27, esp. 4. For use of cipher in recipes for contraceptives, see Hartley and Aldridge, *Johannes de Mirfeld*, 44.

Germany, and how the author or scribe acquired his rather sophisticated command of the runic script is unclear.[36]

Why this emphasis on secrecy? Two reasons occur repeatedly in the literature: the subjective need to maintain an aura of mystery, and the alleged objective need to keep the secrets out of the hands of bunglers who will give magic a bad name by their very failure. In the case of alchemy, there is also a social motive, the fear that an indefinite supply of gold will only lead to misuse and laziness.[37] The factor one might expect to be cited is conspicuously absent: the magicians do not typically concede in private that their magic is a sham and that their tricks must be kept hidden so people will accord them greater power than they actually have. This argument might indeed have applied to performative magic, which plays a relatively minor role in medieval magic generally. For the most part, however, the magicians at least claim to be convinced that their magic actually does work. What needs to be guarded is not their means for deception, but the sources of their actual power. Even when they give instructions for harmful magic, the writers do not say that they are afraid of being caught and brought to justice. Rather, they say that their "experiments" must be kept secret because of their "great power."

This cult of secrecy can be explained in large part as an outgrowth of the cultural setting for magic. What we have called the common tradition was widely available in medieval society, but the new occult sciences were originally the possession of certain clerics. Doubtless there was much pressure to lower this barrier and share this extraordinary learning, particularly if it could be put into simpler form for popular consumption. The emphasis on secrecy came partly, no doubt, as a reaction to this demand for popularization. The scholars who held jealously to their occult learning were in effect declaring that they would not allow it to become debased through assimilation to the broader, common tradition; rather, they would preserve it in its purity and retain its power for themselves.

The insistence on secrecy highlights a dimension of the occult arts that might otherwise be less clear: their value simply as a form of knowledge. From the viewpoint of these writers, knowledge might *bring* power, but it also *was* power. Knowing mysterious things was in itself valuable, even if

---

[36] Hartmut Beckers, "Eine spätmittelalterliche deutsche Anleitung zur Teufelsbeschwörung mit Runenschriftverwendung," *Zeitschrift für deutsches Altertum und deutsche Literatur*, 113 (1984), 136–45. It is not only the material for explicitly demonic magic that is here disguised. For very different use of runes, see Charles S. F. Burnett, "Scandinavian runes in a Latin magical treatise," *Speculum*, 58 (1983), 419–29.

[37] Gerhard Eis, "Von der Rede und dem Schweigen der Alchemisten," *Deutsche Vierteljahrsschrift für Literaturwissenschaft und Geistesgeschichte*, 25 (1951), 415–35.

readers never acted on that knowledge. In extreme cases magic was intended for the sole aim of gaining knowledge: to learn all that happens on Earth, the secrets of everyone's mind, and even heavenly things, one manuscript recommends beheading a hoopoe at sunrise, under a new Moon, and swallowing its heart while it is still palpitating.[38] The point is not so much to gain control over the world, though magic might also accomplish that. More basically, it is cherished simply because it brings hidden things to light, or at least to the dim visibility of the shadows.

In keeping with this cult of the occult, works on magic were sometimes referred to as "books of secrets," even if they had only tenuous connection with this new learning, and indeed even if there was no real secret about their contents. In the later Middle Ages, a *Book of Secrets* ascribed to Albert the Great circulated quite widely. It contained various kinds of magic, none of it as sophisticated as technical astrology or alchemy; it was essentially a work of popularization, but with added glamor derived from the pretense of secrecy. By far the most influential work in this genre was the pseudo-Aristotelian *Secret of Secrets*, which one author with pardonable exaggeration has called the most popular book in medieval Europe.[39] Widely accepted as an authentic work by Aristotle, this book was well-known in its Latin version, was translated into nearly every vernacular language of Europe, and was even put into poetic paraphrase. It purports to contain Aristotle's instructions to his pupil Alexander the Great. In fact, it is a motley compilation of material, put together in several different Arabic versions during the early Middle Ages, long before its translation into Latin. Much of it is devoted to principles of statecraft and personal health, but natural magic also appears in its pages. Medicine, the powers of gems, astrology, and related topics are all included. The show of secrecy is carried beyond the title: much of the work, claiming to represent Aristotle's esoteric learning, is concealed in riddles and other cryptic formulas, and Aristotle exhorts Alexander not to violate the divine mysteries by letting the book fall into the wrong hands. One could hardly find a better example, however, of a further reason for this display of secrecy: the semblance of mystery is itself a splendid advertisement, and a way to ensure wide distribution of a work.

A further result of all this show of secrecy was the rise of legends about people who engaged in magic or were thought to do so. They claimed to

---

[38] British Library, MS Sloane 3132, fol. 56ᵛ. Bodleian Library, MS e Mus. 219, fol. 186ᵛ, gives instructions for more limited knowledge: to learn the language of the birds, take the heart of a hoopoe or the tongue of a kite and put it in honey for three days and nights, then place it under your tongue.

[39] M. Gaster, cited in Thorndike, "The Latin pseudo-Aristotle," 248–9.

have wondrous powers; very well, said the legend-mongers in effect, let us see their wondrous deeds! Men who had unexpectedly won favor at court, perhaps as advisers to monarchs, were subjects for legend formation. Equally vulnerable were scholars whose dazzling intellects aroused more envy than popularity, particularly if they had studied in Muslim lands or dabbled in scientific experiments. In chronicles especially, but also in treatises, correspondence, and other writings, the legends evolved.

Gerbert of Aurillac (ca. 940–1003) provides an early example of this process. As a student of philosophy and other disciplines, he had traveled to Spain (though not in fact Toledo, as legend always had it), where he studied logic. After returning to central Europe he was close to the court of the German emperors, and with their patronage he rose in dignity and power within the Church, eventually becoming Pope Sylvester II. By the late eleventh century, a cardinal named Benno was explaining Gerbert's rise to power in conspiratorial terms: not only he, but other popes had risen to their office by magic, and indeed throughout the century they had perpetuated a school of magic in Rome. Cardinal Benno told how Satan had promised Pope Sylvester he would not die until he celebrated mass in Jerusalem. The pope thought this meant he was safe, but one day he said mass in the Jerusalem church at Rome and was called to death during the liturgy, and in desperation he cut off his tongue and one hand to atone for his sins of necromancy.

Similar legends grew up around Michael Scot, Albert the Great, Roger Bacon, and many others.[40] Legends told about any of these figures might be transferred to others. The process was long familiar in hagiography, or legends of the saints, and stories of the necromancers constituted a sort of inverse hagiography. Thus, twelfth-century legend told how a public statue at Rome had an outstretched finger and bore the inscription "Strike here." Many people tried striking the finger itself, but Gerbert noted where the *shadow* of the finger fell at noon, returned to that spot at night, and dug an opening to a marvelous golden palace lighted with a magic carbuncle. Essentially the same tale was told of Virgil. More than one of these legendary wizards is supposed to have manufactured a head that would talk to him. Albert the Great was thought to have made a bronze head which was so talkative that Thomas Aquinas had to smash it with a hammer to keep it from distracting him in his studies; the same

---

[40] William Godwin, *Lives of the Necromancers: or, an Account of the Most Eminent Persons in Successive Ages, Who Have Claimed for Themselves, or to Whom has been Imputed by Others, the Exercise of Magical Power* (London: Mason, 1834).

invention is ascribed to Roger Bacon. Certain themes in these legends, such as distortion of time so that a few minutes seem like twenty years, are borrowed from (or by) the romances.

Of special importance in many of these legends is the magician's book of magic. Gerbert was said to have abducted two things from his teacher: his daughter and his book. In the legend of Virgil – which furnished material both for the romances and for these tales about scholarly magicians – we read that the poet's book of magic was buried along with him, and its discovery and exhumation is a story unto itself. The power of the book, and specifically the aura of mystery surrounding a book of magic, here finds eloquent expression.

The Renaissance Magus

Occult learning feeds perennially on antiquity, and when occultists cannot find ancient sources to suit their purposes, they will invent them. Arabic writers served the cause of occult knowledge in the West by making available the sciences of ancient Greece, much reworked over the centuries, and this infusion of ancient learning kept Western occultists busy for several generations. By the late fifteenth century, however, the Humanist movement led some occultists to dig deeper into the ground of classical antiquity, where they found further and (they thought) more authentic materials for their study.

The mythic figure taken as a kind of patron saint for this movement was Hermes Trismegistus, whose image appears on a mosaic pavement laid at the cathedral of Siena in the 1480s. Standing beside the Sibyls, Hermes is depicted here not as a magician, but as a supposed prophet of Christianity, though his connections with magic, astrology, and alchemy could hardly be put out of mind or distinguished altogether from his prophetic powers.

The Humanists of the fourteenth through sixteenth centuries were heirs to earlier students of antiquity, and while they conceived themselves as witnessing a renaissance (or "rebirth") of classical knowledge, they were in fact continuing a much earlier fascination with ancient Greece and Rome. Some of them had studied Greek; by the later fifteenth century, Byzantine scholars were readily available in Italy. To that extent, these Humanists had better access to the Greek texts of antiquity than had their twelfth-century forebears. They also had a great many more manuscripts of classical materials, and were able to read Greek or Roman works that earlier readers did not know. One finds among them, more than among their predecessors, an interest in classical learning inspired by secular as well as religious concerns. This last factor, however, had little relevance to their interest in magic: for them, magic was a religious phenomenon, related in complex and often problematic ways to traditional Christianity.

The late medieval and early Renaissance period saw the emergence of what has been called the "author-magician."[41] In broader areas of literature and scholarship as well, the period saw clearer claims to authorship being made and recognized: claims that the writer of a text was more than a compiler or commentator, that the writer was setting forth original ideas, narratives, and structures.[42] For magical writings, the fame of authorship could of course become notoriety. Still, theories of magic represented an important area of intellectual exchange, and increasingly the key works were no longer anonymously circulated or pseudonymously ascribed to the legendary magicians of antiquity, or to more recent scholars such as Albert the Great. Even if it was risky, or perhaps in part because of the risk, those who published theories of magic wanted readers to recognize them as magician-authors, figures whose authorship was grounded in the mastery of occult learning to which few had access.

Humanist scholars of the late fifteenth and early sixteenth centuries include some of the most vigorous devotees of magic. Marsilio Ficino combined his Platonic philosophy with a serious interest in medicine, and produced a treatise on astrological medicine grounded in Neoplatonic philosophy. Jacques Lefèvre d'Étaples (ca. 1450–1536) combined magic and astrology with a Pythagorean interest in the power of numbers. Johannes Reuchlin (1455–1522), a noted scholar of Hebrew culture, exalted the occult powers of names and other words. Johannes Trithemius, while disclaiming the title of magician, proposed a system of secret writing, argued the possibility of a sort of telepathic communication, and claimed to have revealed knowledge of many wondrous things.

It is Ficino who most fully represents the tradition of the Renaissance magus in the second half of the fifteenth century. When he was still a young man, Cosimo de' Medici commissioned him to translate from Greek the *Hermetic Corpus* ascribed to Hermes Trismegistus. Cosimo had already asked him to translate the works of Plato, but when a monk appeared in Florence with a Hermetic manuscript in hand, Plato had to wait: Hermes was considered (falsely) the more ancient authority and

---

[41] Nicolas Weill-Parot, *Les "images astrologiques" au moyen âge et à la renaissance: Speculations intellectuelles et pratiques magiques (XIIe–XVe siècle)* (Paris: Champion, 2002), 602–36.

[42] See especially Alastair Minnis, *Medieval Theory of Authorship: Scholastic Literary Attitudes in the Later Middle Ages*, 2nd edn (Philadelphia: University of Pennsylvania Press, 2010), and ongoing work by Daniel Hobbins.

thus the more important.[43] Years later, Ficino wrote his work *On Life* as a medical treatise based on astrological principles; the third and final section of this work, in particular, tells how to benefit as fully as possible from the positive influences of the stars (Fig. 16). He recommends "solar" objects above all for their beneficial influence: gold, chrysolite, amber, honey, saffron, the lion, and other repositories of that influence. Even people with golden hair are worth associating with because they transmit solar effects. Jupiter, too, radiated fine, life-supporting virtues; and the other planets' power could also be put to salutary use.

While Ficino also saw astral images as means for channeling the power of the stars and planets, he looked askance at such artificial techniques. He explained how inscribing figures on material things – thus making talismans of them – could help by disposing them to receive astral influences. He described how learned men of antiquity had put astral images on rings, and how one philosopher had lived 120 years by using such devices. In principle, however, he insisted that he was only describing such practices, not recommending them. Astral medicines, he said, were more potent than astral images for three reasons: the powders, liquids, unguents, and other such stuff used by astral medicine absorb the influences of the stars more easily than the hard matter used for images; being taken internally, medicines penetrate the body more effectively; and being concocted of many different ingredients, they capture more of the stars' or planets' essence than an image made from a single material.

Ficino was drawing on various sources for his astral magic.[44] He was one of the first Westerners since late antiquity to know the work of Plotinus at first hand, and he claimed explicitly to be providing a commentary on the work of this founder of Neoplatonic philosophy. Plotinus had seen all of nature as pervaded with magical influences, and Ficino captured the spirit of this notion with his maxim that "Nature is everywhere a magician." Yet he, unlike his predecessors in the West, also knew the later Neoplatonists such as Porphyry and Iamblichus, and drew heavily from their thought. The most important notion for him was that of a world soul or cosmic spirit, a concept found among Neoplatonists but traceable further back to the Stoics. This spirit is like the human spirit, but is found throughout the cosmos. Powers from this cosmic spirit are beamed toward Earth from the stars and planets, and the task of the magician is to discern and channel these powers. Of the various means for so doing, some are more material (especially stones and metals), while others are more

[43] Yates, *Giordano Bruno*, 1–19.

[44] D. P. Walker, *Spiritual and Demonic Magic, from Ficino to Campanella* (London: Warburg Institute, 1958), used here extensively.

Fig. 16. Preface to Ficino's *Three Books on Life*, from an early Renaissance manuscript

spiritual (words, songs, and so forth), and as a good Neoplatonist, Ficino ranks these means in a hierarchy with the more obviously material ones at the bottom and the spiritual ones at the top.

The kind of music Ficino had in mind as a means for channeling these cosmic influences is largely a matter for conjecture. We know from other writings of his that he used "Orphic" hymns, named after the magical song of Orpheus, the musician of Greek myth. Ficino speaks also of accompanying his own song on an Orphic lyre, though the words seem to have been more important to him than the melody or accompaniment, since it was words that bore meaning.

Other Renaissance mages, perhaps inspired by the same Neoplatonist preference for spiritual over material means for magic, shared Ficino's interest in exploiting the powers of music. Giovanni Pico della Mirandola (1463–94) spoke of Orphic hymns as a uniquely efficacious form of magic, and his contemporary Lodovico Lazarelli wrote a Hermetic dialogue in which Lazarelli himself is represented as leading the king of Aragon into ecstasy with his hymns. One of these compositions, a paean celebrating the power of human creativity as analogous to God's own creative power, begins: "Ah, my mind, ponder now these great mysteries. Who made all things from nothing? The word of the Father, alone. May he be blessed, this Word of the Begetter!" Having heard this hymn, the king exclaims that he is inflamed with love and stunned with awe, much as a person is stunned when touching a torpedo-fish! The same reverence for the magical power of music can be seen also in Reuchlin's work. While emphasizing the difficulties and hazards of magical hymnody, Reuchlin depicts an initiation into mystical knowledge through liturgical ceremony that involves preparatory hymns. We have few words for such magical song, and no melodies; indeed, the magicians may simply have improvised their music. What we know is not the precise nature of their singing, but the theoretical place it held in their thought.

Ficino and his fellows needed to defend these fascinations of theirs. Christ himself, Ficino argued, healed the sick and taught "his priests" to do so with words, herbs, and stones. Should it be scandalous, then, if Ficino (himself a priest) did likewise? Indeed, the magi of the Gospels were wise men and priests, and were held in high esteem. As for the underlying conception of magic, Ficino links his theories to a Neoplatonic conception of a living cosmos, and he professes only disdain for those who see the lowliest plants and animals as having life but deny that the cosmos itself is alive.

While most of these writers needed to defend themselves from attackers, Pico actually courted controversy. In 1486 he went to Rome and there set forth nine hundred theses for public debate. In these propositions, Pico upheld the value of natural magic, by which the forces inherent in nature are brought together and made efficacious, but he claimed also to have found a source of magical power far higher than those in nature. A young man of astonishingly broad erudition, Pico had become intensely interested in the Hebrew tradition of magic and mysticism known as the Kabbalah. In keeping with this fascination, he asserted that words can have magical power – but only words in Hebrew, which were taught to Adam and Eve by God himself, and which derive their power from having been spoken by God's own voice. Mastery of the Kabbalah can give a person unimagined magical skill, though a dabbler who uses the Kabbalah carelessly can be destroyed by demons. (When Pico spoke of "demons," he used the word in two senses: following the Neoplatonist philosopher Porphyry, he proposed that in addition to the demons normally so-called, there are powers within matter that can also be called "demons.") At his most enthusiastic, Pico insisted that magic grounded in the Kabbalah is the only effective magic.

Later in his brief life, Pico modified his tone and published a strong condemnation of the astrologers' errors. But even then he did not deny that there was such a thing as legitimate astrology or valid magic, and this later work can be read primarily as a defense of astral magic such as Ficino's, which Pico seeks to distinguish from the fatalistic astrology he is attacking.

Among those who hastened into the controversy with Pico was Pedro Garcia (d. 1505), who took up the opposite extreme by repudiating all magic as illegitimate. He doubted that there were such things as occult powers hidden in nature and manipulable by magicians. Or if there were such powers, the only way to learn about them was from the instruction of demons. And if these powers did exist they were highly unstable, unpredictable, and thus unserviceable for practical purposes. As for the Kabbalah, Garcia denied that it was an ancient tradition traceable to Moses; it was, he asserted, an offshoot of heretical Judaism springing from the Talmud.[45]

Pico's interest in the Kabbalah was shared by others, such as Lefevre d'Étaples and Reuchlin.[46] In his dialogue of 1494, *On the Wonder-Working Word*, Reuchlin reminds the reader of the magic that sorceresses in classical literature worked by the power of their words, but then argues that the most potent magic is not to be found in Greek or Egyptian

---

[45] Lynn Thorndike, *A History of Magic and Experimental Science*, vol. 4 (New York and London: Columbia University Press, 1934), 529–43.

[46] Charles Zika, "Reuchlin's *De verbo mirifico* and the magic debate of the late fifteenth century," *Journal of the Warburg and Courtauld Institutes*, 39 (1976), 104–38.

words, but rather in Hebrew. So too, real power was not to be found in those charlatans of Reuchlin's own day who ascribed their writings to Solomon and other worthies, but in fact practiced demonic magic. There is indeed power in natural magic: God has implanted occult properties in coral, for example, which give it value as an amulet. The focus of the dialogue, however, is the wonder-working power of names for God. In Exodus 3:14, God gave Moses the classic Tetragrammaton or four-letter divine name ("YHWH") which, like other Hebrew words, is spelled without vowels. Reuchlin uses the form "IHUH" for this divine name, to which he assigns a wealth of numerological symbolism and miracle-working power. The ultimate wonder-working word, however, is an expansion of this, "IHSUH," a variation on "Jesus." Like certain writers from early Christian centuries, Reuchlin exalts this name of Christ as having power to work multiple wonders. It can change rivers into wine, it protected Paul against serpents on the island of Malta, it gave other disciples power against dragons, and so forth. It must be used together with the cross; word and gesture combine to accomplish the highest of all forms of magic. Like Pico and other Humanist mages, Reuchlin shows himself here thoroughly orthodox, but more than Pico he stresses his eagerness to wed his occult learning to the Christian tradition.

The magic of these Renaissance mages might invoke supernatural as well as natural powers, and to that extent it transcends the categories we have been using. Once again, magic becomes linked to religion, but out of sophistication rather than naivety. On the other hand, however, the mages had to defend themselves against the charge of demonic magic. We have already seen that this argument arose in the debate over Pico, and the question appeared in subtler form in the writings of Ficino.

Repeatedly, Ficino insisted that he was advocating only natural magic.[47] His songs were not incantations addressed to demons. If images of any kind held magical power, it was not because demons inhabited them; in any case, he did not advocate worshiping demons, even if they were present in images. From various writings of his, we know that he did have a theory about demons and their place in the universe. Both the New Testament (e.g. Ephesians 6:12) and the Neoplatonist tradition conceived of spirits as present in the heavens, and Thomas Aquinas had thought of the heavenly bodies as guided by angels. In Ficino's view, the planets had good and bad spirits associated with them. He recognized other kinds of demons as well, some dwelling above the heavens, and others present on Earth. The planetary demons have bodies made of air

---

[47] Walker, *Spiritual and Demonic Magic*, 45–53.

or ether, and are involved in transmitting astral influences to Earth. Thus, while in his work *On Life* Ficino saw magic as a channeling of cosmic powers, he suggested elsewhere that astral influences are subject to demonic intervention, though he nowhere put the two theories together and concluded that magic can and should involve relations with these planetary demons. On at least two occasions he used astral magic to *expel* demons associated with Saturn, and thus he dabbled in a kind of astrological exorcism. He did not advocate *using* the powers of such demons. But the wary reader might well suspect that he was doing so in secret, and the suspicion would be all the more plausible since others in his day were in fact engaged in explicitly demonic magic. If Ficino, Reuchlin, and other Renaissance magicians took pains to distinguish their magic from the demonic sort, it was because both kinds of magic were very real – and the similarities between them, if not real, nonetheless appeared so to many onlookers.

7   Invocation and Conjuration of Angels

A healing charm found as early as the ninth century begins with a story about three angels who encounter a band of personified diseases. They ask where the diseases are going. One disease says he is going to dry out the bones, empty the marrow, and otherwise torment some servant of God. The others all have their evil designs. The angels adjure the diseases by the Trinity, the orders of angels, and various categories of saints not to harm their victim, but rather to depart and not return.[1] In this formula, the angels themselves are not adjured or conjured; they are the one who do the adjuring. Still, this is an example of how angels might function in healings, as they did in liturgy and other contexts. Prominent already in parts of the Bible and in early Christianity, they richly populated European folklore.

While magicians often sought to use hidden powers within nature, many of them claimed to work magic with the aid of angels. They might conjure angels to appear in a reflective surface and answer questions. They might perform elaborate rituals, with incense and magic circles and other devices, as well as conjurations, to summon angels and request or compel their assistance. Sometimes angels alone were invoked; often their aid was sought along with that of the saints and Christ. The prayer book of King Władysław III of Poland (reg. 1434–44) contains prayers to Christ, the Virgin, the Holy Spirit, and angels. For the most part, these prayers are standard liturgical and devotional formulas, but they have insertions asking for aid so the king can use a crystal ball to learn about the past and future and discover his subjects' secret plans.[2] Treatises of angel magic generally gave lists of angels' names, and sometimes also lists of divine names, because sacred names held sacred power, and reciting them was among the techniques used for the working of magic.[3]

---

[1] Barbato, *Incantamenta latina et romanica*, 28–32.
[2] Benedek Láng, "Central and Eastern Europe," in Page and Rider, *Routledge History*, 115.
[3] On this point, see especially Gehr, "Beringarius Ganellus," 237–53.

There were ambiguities inherent in other forms of magic, but the ambiguity in angel magic was all the greater. Angel magic could easily be confused with demonic magic, and might shade into nonmagical devotion, and it often had connections with astral magic. The magicians might claim they were summoning good angels, but what sorts of spirits actually came to their aid? St. Paul had warned that Satan can disguise himself as an angel of light (II Corinthians 11:14). Magicians claiming to work with good angels could thus be either deceived or deceiving, and the spirits who answered their summons could turn out to be in fact evil angels, or demons. Another form of ambiguity arose if the spirits invoked were taken to be good and unfallen, as the prayer book of King Władysław demonstrates: how sharply could magical appeal to angels be distinguished from the simple devotion that any Christian might pay to angels? When medieval sources defined two kinds of magic, natural and demonic, their schema tended to leave angel magic unaccounted for, and this is not surprising because angel magic could be perceived in fundamentally different ways.

There could also be ambiguity in the way angels were addressed. They could be invoked in prayer, or they could be conjured (or formally commanded, with formulas and rituals seen as constraining their will) in magic, but the distinction was not always clear. In this, as in other ways, religion and magic could be difficult to disentangle.

Not all medieval people thought about angels in the same ways. A simple view of things distinguished straightforwardly between unfallen and fallen angels: all angels were created good, but some rebelled against God, fell from grace, and became demons. The unfallen angels, those who remained good, resided primarily in heaven. They were organized in a hierarchy of choirs: the highest choirs of angels, called the Seraphim and Cherubim, remained around God's throne and never departed from heaven, but those in the lower orders were sent to Earth as God's messengers to humans. The term "angel" meant "messenger," although it was only those in the lower orders who actually served that function. The fallen angels, or demons, were expelled from heaven and cast into hell, which became their primary abode, although they too could come to Earth, mainly to tempt people and lead them astray. The chief of the demons was Satan, or the Devil, and the spirits who joined in his rebellion against God and became his followers were called demons. (To complicate matters, the distinction between the singular "the Devil" and plural "demons" was not always observed: demons were also sometimes called devils.)

From the time of St. Augustine onward, and under his influence, theologians and preachers usually honored this sharp distinction between the good, unfallen angels and those who rebelled against God and became demons. This distinction corresponded to St. Augustine's notion that all humans belonged either to the saved or the damned, to the city of God or to the earthly city: those who belonged to the city of God did so because they were moved by love of God even to the contempt of self, while citizens of the earthly city were those motivated by love of self even to the contempt of God. There could be degrees of goodness and of evil, but fundamentally there were two types of people, distinguished by their basic moral disposition. So too with angels, who were either good or evil. The deciding factor for angels, as for humans, was the orientation of their will: those whose will was directed toward God, or who willed to remain faithful to God, were distinguished from those whose wills had turned away from God.

Yet there were complicating factors, and some of these were rooted in the Bible. The Gospel of John refers to "the ruler of this world" (12:31, 14:30, 16:11), who could easily be identified as Satan, reigning not in hell but on Earth. Demons, too, could be seen as inhabiting the Earth: Graeco-Roman, Celtic, and Germanic cultures all referred to spirits such as fairies or elves, satyrs or other such beings, living perhaps inside hills or in woodlands, and Christians often identified these spirits, in fact, as demons. Both fallen and unfallen angels might also be seen as residing not in "heaven," where God and the saints reside, but in "the heavens," whether in the lower atmosphere or among the planets. The epistle to the Ephesians speaks of "the ruler of the power of the air" as a spirit working among the disobedient (2:2), which suggests a demonic abode not in hell or on Earth, but somewhere above the Earth. Alternatively, there could be good angels attached to the planets and moving them in their orbits. Scholastic theologians accepted the notion that the heavenly spheres to which the planets were attached were governed and moved by angelic beings.

Further complicating the picture, there might be neutral or intermediary spirits, neither fully good nor entirely evil. Elves and fairies could be thought of as implicitly belonging in this category, but some texts raise the possibility explicitly. This notion was often found in literature, even in Dante's *Divine Comedy*. It appeared in *The Navigation of Saint Brendan*, a widely read Irish text. Precisely how did it come about that there were neutral spirits? On one accounting, when Satan and other angels rebelled against God, some angels remained faithful and fought against these rebels, but there were some who did not take sides; these may have been cast out of heaven, but were not relegated to hell. Rigorous theologians might insist on a clear-cut distinction between the unfallen and fallen angels, but many orthodox writers held to a more complicated picture.[4]

There was conflict, then, between two rival conceptions of angels: what we might call a two-type view and a multiple-type conception. Not all Christians, and not even all educated orthodox Christians, held strictly to the standard two-type view of angels. There was room for neutral or intermediate angels. Spirits of the field and woodland might be intermediate rather than demonic. And if there were angels assigned to the planets, they might be purely good or purely evil, but there might also be multiple types of angels, in a system more complicated than the two-type model allowed.[5]

When angels of any sort were called upon by magicians, the summons usually took the form of an elaborate ritual. The category of angel magic thus overlaps with that of "ritual magic." Most magic has or at least can have a ritual aspect to it: charms and incantations were sung or chanted, magical herbs were harvested in particular ways and might have powerful words sung over them or inscribed on them, magical books and other paraphernalia of magic might be consecrated, and magical objects were sometimes placed on an altar while mass is being celebrated. Certain forms of magic, however, consist primarily of elaborate rituals, with lengthy conjurations interwoven with gestures, inscription of magical diagrams, and manipulation of magical objects. Most forms of angel magic and necromancy answer to this description, as does much astral magic. The term "ritual magic" can be used to cut across these other categories and call attention to the techniques magicians used, whatever the powers they were invoking. The same or similar rituals could be used to summon good or evil spirits, and to help the magician communicate with both, but also to protect against the threats and terrors of fallen spirits. In this discussion, however, the primary focus will be the powers that magicians called upon: the previous chapters of this book discussed what it meant to exploit hidden powers within nature, and the following chapter will deal with the overt conjuring of demons, but this chapter will focus on magicians who claimed to be summoning good angels and making use of their powers.

Magic Involving Angels of the Heavens

When Arabic texts were translated and circulated in the Christian West, from the twelfth century onward, one notion found in these sources had

---

[4] Richard Kieckhefer, "Angel magic and the cult of angels in the later Middle Ages," in Kallestrup and Toivo, *Contesting Orthodoxy*, 71–110.

[5] Coree Newman, "The good, the bad and the unholy: Ambivalent angels in the Middle Ages," in Ostling, *Fairies, Demons, and Nature Spirits*, 103–22.

profound influence on magic: the idea that each of the planetary spheres is moved by what Aristotle called an intelligence, which Muslims and Christians took to be angels. The seven planets, affixed to a series of clear concentric spheres surrounding Earth, were moved in their orbits by these angels assigned to them. But each of the angels might be seen as governing a collectivity of spirits, and the character of these angels who resided in "the heavens" was often ambiguous, and those who adhered to a two-type view of angels might categorize some or all of them as demons rather than unfallen angels, while those allowing a multiple-type approach could see them as distinct both from the angels in heaven and from the demons in hell.

The problems are amply illustrated by a treatise of angel magic contained in a fifteenth-century manuscript, called *The Book of Angels, Rings, Characters and Images of the Planets*.[6] The angels in question are associated with the seven planets recognized in medieval astronomy, including the Sun and the Moon. To call upon these planetary angels, the magician makes rings, inscribes the names and magical characters of the angels on parchment or some other medium, and offers birds or animals as sacrifices. With the aid of these angels, the magician could obtain transport on a black horse, win the love of a woman, create the illusion of armed soldiers or castles, turn a drink into a poison, arouse enmity between two people, or destroy whatever one wishes.

The treatise (at least much of it) is a work of angel magic, but what sorts of angels does it have in mind? For the most part, it explains how to call upon the planetary angels by inscribing their names and conjuring them, but it also tells how to conjure devils or devil "kings," who, again, are associated with the planets. A reader might be familiar with the notion that the celestial spheres to which the planets are attached are governed by angels, but nothing about this text – the ritual forms, the purposes served, the association of planetary angels with other spirits explicitly called devils – suggests that these angels are unfallen or even neutral. The title indicates that this is a book of angels, but the contents show why readers might be suspicious of magic claiming to work through angelic agency.

More nearly devotional was a text called the *Holy Almandal*, which gave instructions for the use of a wax tablet for which the treatise

---

[6] Juris G. Lidaka, "*The Book of Angels, Rings, Characters and Images of the Planets* attributed to Osbern Bokenham," in Claire Fanger, ed., *Conjuring Spirits: Texts and Traditions of Medieval Ritual Magic* (Stroud: Sutton; University Park: Pennsylvania State Press, 1998), 32–75. The text brings together materials that circulated independently, and approximately the first half involves angel magic.

was named.[7] This tablet was to have sacred seals inscribed on it – in particular, the star of Solomon and names of God – and was to be propped up on four lighted candlesticks. The text gives conjurations to be used to summon the angels. Incense placed below the almandal would rise up through holes in it, and its fragrance would further induce angels to come and respond to questions. The angels invoked in this magic are seen as residing in different regions of the heavens, designated by compass directions and by various "heights." In one manuscript, the text associates the angels expressly with signs of the Zodiac. The almandal is made of a different color wax for each category of angel. Representatives of angels from various altitudes will come and hover over the almandal, perhaps in the form of a beautiful youth, or an armed soldier clad in gold, or a seraph, or a white dove or lamb, or a woman bearing an olive branch. On appearing, an angel will ask what the magician wants, and the magician will say that his petition should be fulfilled, whatever it may be. The different categories of angel have power over different aspects of life, such as fertility, or acquisition of treasures, or changing of monarchies and empires, or enmities and battles. They bestow mastery of various arts: one category of angel endows the magician with knowledge of physics, medicine, and alchemy, while another bestows theology, metaphysics, and geomancy, and so forth.

A critical reader might wonder if the angels summoned by this ritual were in fact demons, but in several ways the text makes clear that the spirits who appear are good, unfallen angels. It says they are holy and chosen by God. One of the requests made of them is reconciliation with God. Contact with certain of these spirits bestows a degree of perfection that can convey assurance of salvation. Others can restore the intellectual powers that God gave Adam before his fall. Angels in one or another group can protect against demons and their illusions, or forcefully compel all spirits to uphold God's commands, although others can compel demons to observe agreements made with humans. The practitioner does not simply use the angels as instruments for magic, but develops a close and affectionate relationship with them. One historian speaks of this magic as "essentially a ritual of redemption and the perfection of human nature,"[8] which is indeed how it is represented in the text.

Like many forms of magic, that of the *Almandal* requires moral purity, at least for its instrumental value. An addition to the text in one

---

[7] Julien Véronèse, *L'Almandal et l'Almadel latins au Moyen Âge: Introduction et édition critique* (Florence: SISMEL, 2012).

[8] Jan R. Veenstra, "The Holy Almandal: Angels and the intellectual aims of magic," in Bremmer and Veenstra, *The Metamorphosis of Magic*, 196.

manuscript says it is good if someone engaged in this magic can be virginal, but since virgins are so rare, the operator should at least be "continent," which the writer takes to mean penitent. The same manuscript goes on to tell of someone who began using this magic, but he had a dream in which he was speaking with a beautiful girl and tried to reach out and kiss her. The next time he tried to summon an angel, it would not come until he did penance for this grievous sin.

It is worth noting that the *Almandal* is found in different forms in various manuscripts, and that the scribes who produced these manuscripts sometimes included new material that could affect the character of the work. Magical texts often vary, to greater or lesser degrees, from one manuscript to another, and for various reasons this is a feature frequently seen in works of angel magic. Sometimes the users adapted the texts in ways that attempted to make them seem more orthodox, less problematic. Sometimes they personalized them, fitting them into a program of magic and devotion that had special meaning and utility to the individual user. Given the inherent ambiguity of angel magic, this flexibility is not surprising: magical invocation of angels could resemble pious devotion, or demonic necromancy, or astral magic, and a user or scribe might wish to emphasize one of these links and downplay others.

Christians using the treatise might not be aware of its having Muslim precedent, although the syllable "al" (found also in "alchemy" and "algebra") might have suggested this origin to them. One plausible hypothesis is that the treatise underwent successive revisions, and survives in various forms, because of an ongoing effort to transform a type of Muslim magic meant to communicate with the Muslim spirits called jinn into a Christian ritual to commune with angels – but angels still strongly associated with the heavens.[9]

A twelfth-century work called *The Book of the Essence of Spirits* further shows how angels could be seen as useful in magic.[10] It would be less useful to a practitioner than either *The Book of Angels* or *The Holy Almandal*, but it sheds light on the philosophical theories that could underlie angel magic. This work rests on a kind of Neoplatonic framework in which all things come out of a divine source and return to that source, and it gives a theory of spirits that also shares much with Neoplatonic notions of angelic hierarchies. The anonymous author claims that he himself lived for thirty years in a desert region where he communicated with spirits. He speaks of three types of spirits: the highest ones dwell in the highest heaven and are incorruptible; below them are

---

[9] Véronèse offers this hypothesis.   [10] Page, *Magic in the Cloister*, 93–111, 147–59.

planetary rulers who reside further down amid the planets that they govern; and each of these planetary rulers commands spirits of a third type that come down to Earth, interact with humans, share human passions, come to the aid of magicians, and can be imprisoned within matter. The author does not expressly distinguish between "angels" and "demons" within this schema, but the hierarchy implies that all three groups occupy positions intended by their creator. Still, when the spirits under the command of the ruler of Mars are said to share the passion of violence, or when those under the ruler of Venus are said to share and promote lust, a theologian would find it difficult to see them as analogous to the angels in the orthodox Christian hierarchy of angels, who are sent into the world to guide and guard devout souls.

All three of these texts could be problematic for a critical reader, but in different ways. *The Book of Angels* prescribes sacrifice and other magical rituals to conjure planetary spirits for purposes that are in many cases clearly transgressive. The *Holy Almandal* is the text that most insists on the holiness of the angels, the purity of the practitioner, and the spiritual effects of the ritual, and while it sees the angels as coming from planetary realms, it makes the least reference to this connection, but the idea of a close friendship between the angels and the magicians could easily be confused with the bond between a magician and a demon sealed with a pact. *The Book of the Essence of Spirits* draws on a Neoplatonic framework that might at first sight appear traditional, but it depicts spirits who share in human passions to a degree that a critical reader would find troubling.

Jewish Angel Magic

The category of angel magic overlaps not only with that of ritual magic, but also with what is often called "Solomonic magic." From the twelfth century onward, many magical writings were ascribed pseudonymously to King Solomon. Magic might seem plausibly ascribed to Solomon, because in the Bible he has a double reputation: he is praised for his wisdom, yet he took foreign wives and turned to their gods (I Kings 3 and 11), so one could easily imagine that he was cunning as a magician and willing to exploit dubious spirits. The Jewish historian Josephus (37–ca. 100) represented Solomon as a powerful exorcist. And the late ancient *Testament of Solomon* gave a fictional account of how Solomon used a magic ring to compel demons to construct his Temple. In the later Middle Ages, works of various sorts were attributed to Solomon, and texts such as *The Bond of Solomon* and *The Key of Solomon* bear this attribution in their titles. Use of the hexagram (and later also a pentagram) as a magical device is also connected with Solomon, and specifically the notion that the magical ring he used to constrain demons was a signet ring inscribed with this device.[11] The image of Solomon as a magician king was so widely known that it served as at least one model for medieval monarchs who took an interest in the occult sciences, such as Alfonso X "the Wise" of Castile.[12]

The claim that a magical text or practice can be traced back to Solomon is connected to a broader tendency to link Christian magic with Jewish precedent. Christians had ambivalent attitudes toward Jewish magic and magicians.[13] Sometimes the accusation of working magic was part of a campaign of vilification directed at Jews, and sometimes Jewish magic was seen as simply ineffective. The *Sworn Book* ascribed to Honorius of Thebes says only Christians can work magic effectively; pagan magic is vain, and Jews cannot work effective magic because spirits are compelled to come by the power of God's holy names, but the Jews are not sealed with the Lord's seal, meaning the cross and the faith, and so the spirits are unwilling to respond truly to them. Yet Christian writers sometimes saw Jewish magic as grounded in an ancient and venerable tradition, and Christians sometimes recruited Jews as accomplices in magic. Christian magical diagrams often contained Hebrew or pseudo-Hebrew inscriptions, which again shows respect for a magical tradition seen as exotic, but also ancient and authoritative.

If there is any form of Christian magic that actually does resemble Jewish magic and may have been partly inspired by it, directly or indirectly, it is angel magic.[14] While the invocation of angels and other spirits associated with the heavens and the planets was inspired largely by Arabic sources, there were other types of angelic magic developed in Jewish circles and available for appropriation by Christians. Jewish magicians were fascinated with mysterious characters that might elsewhere be thought astrological, but by Jews were taken as letters in "angelic alphabets" that had to be deciphered.[15] Jewish texts of late antiquity refer to an angel called the Prince of the Torah (Sar-Torah), who could be conjured with divine names and would give the conjurer exceptional ability to learn and remember. Practitioners who had summoned this angel and benefited from his powers had gone on to become great rabbis. The ritual

[11] Julien Véronèse, "Solomonic magic," in Page and Rider, *Routledge History*, 187–200.
[12] Sebastià Giralt, "Magic in Romance languages," in Page and Rider, *Routledge History*, 99; Boudet, "Magic at court," 333.
[13] Katelyn Mesler, "The Latin encounter with Hebrew magic: Problems and approaches," in Page and Rider, *Routledge History*, 85–98.
[14] Michael D. Swartz, *Scholastic Magic: Ritual and Revelation in Early Jewish Mysticism* (Princeton University Press, 1996).
[15] Bohak, "Jewish magic in the Middle Ages," 279.

conjuration involved reciting divine names. One rabbi who had difficulty in learning used the magic ritual and testified that his heart was immediately enlightened, his eyes beheld the depths and pathways of Torah, and he never forgot what he had learned. A ritual called "opening the heart" could also improve one's capacity for learning. One text instructs, "If you want to perform the opening of the heart, purify yourself and take a cup of wine and say the psalm over the cup seven times and drink it. Thus one shall do three times in the morning and drink, and one's heart shall be opened to Torah."

Another set of texts told how angels could help in rising through the heavenly palaces or "Hekhalot" to behold God's chariot-throne or "Merkavah." This Hekhalot literature represents a form of mysticism, but it has in common with Jewish magic the reliance on the aid of angels for gaining revelations, and some Hekhalot texts give procedures for divination that involve summoning an angel to appear in a dream. In these traditions it seems clear that ritual purity is required because the angels demand it: they had protested when even Moses came into their midst, and someone practicing a magic ritual that involved the aid of angels had to be utterly free of any defilement.

One of the most important Jewish works of angel magic, the *Sefer ha-Razim*, was translated into Latin as the *Liber Razielis*, or *Book of Raziel*.[16] The opening sections of the book tell how Adam, on being expelled from Paradise, lamented his loss of knowledge, understanding, and wisdom. Seeing Adam's grief, God sent the angel Raziel to him with a book written on sapphire that would teach him all the wondrous powers available to him from the angels of the seven heavens. He would learn the causes of life and death, of good and evil. He would learn how to interpret dreams and visions. Demons would be in his power. He could send angels wherever he wished. He would be able to predict future events. Adam received this book and passed it down to his son Seth. Eventually it reached Noah, who pored over it constantly after disembarking from the ark. Abraham gave it to Isaac, Moses entrusted it to Joshua, and it came into the hands of Solomon, who used it to build the Temple and gain dominion over the winds, the demons, all the spirits of the air, and human souls.

The portions of the book dealing with the two lowest heavens are by far the longest. The first and lowest heaven is populated by seven "armies" of angels, while the second heaven contains angels organized into twelve

---

[16] Bill Rebiger, Peter Schäfer, Evelyn Burkhardt, Gottfried Reeg, Henrik Wels, and Dorothea M. Salzer, eds., *Sefer ha-Razim I und II: Das Buch der Geheimnisse I und II*, vol. 1 (Tübingen: Mohr Siebeck, 2009), 31–52.

"heights." The *Book of Raziel* lists by name the angels of both these heavens and of the heavens above them. Angels of the first two heavens have many positive and protective functions: they cure diseases, they establish love and goodwill between people, they promote friendship and peace, they run errands on command, they fetch men and women from a distance, they drive away wild beasts, they turn back flooding rivers and seas, they prevent harm to women in childbirth, they avert arrows and other weapons in battle, and they bestow high honors. But they also stir up wrath and combat, sink ships, destroy towns, afflict and destroy the practitioner's enemies, bring back the dead so one can speak with them, make it possible to speak with demons, and drive people mad by keeping them from sleeping. At times they are coercive: they bend the wills and impede the plans of potentates and others, and they can bind the tongues of rulers.

The text gives brief conjurations directed to the angels. It tells how to construct metal plates with the names of angels inscribed on them, to be worn or buried or otherwise positioned for magical effect. It gives rituals to be performed for magical goals. To counteract the will of a ruler or anyone else, for example, one should go out at midnight under a full Moon, barefoot and clean, wrapped in a new cloth, position oneself beneath the Moon, call out the names of the relevant angels, ask them to turn the will of enemies and make them friends, and write names and characters on a silver plate to wear around one's neck. The angels conjured for this purpose are able to strike terror into those who encounter them. When they walk about they bring storms and cause the earth to tremble. They speak harshly, with great wrath. In their hands they hold fiery staffs. Their faces are like rays of fire, and when they speak twelve thousand fiery rays shoot from their lips.

The angels of the third through sixth heavens are less vividly characterized, and their powers are not spelled out in such detail. The seventh and highest heaven is a realm of pure light, in which the angels dwell in the divine presence. While the *Book of Raziel* does refer at times to demons, the angels encountered in the seven heavens are not characterized as demonic, and at times the text refers to them explicitly as holy angels. Their holiness becomes more manifest in the higher heavens. But Judaism was not bound to the strict distinction between fallen and unfallen angels found in orthodox Christian theology; the idea of fierce and potentially destructive yet holy angels was more easily accommodated in Jewish writings.[17] If Christian magicians were seeking support

[17] Annette Yoshiko Reed, *Fallen Angels and the History of Judaism and Christianity: The Reception of Enochic Literature* (Cambridge University Press, 2005).

for their own multiple-type understanding of angels, they could easily find it in Jewish tradition.

In any case, Jewish and Christian traditions influenced each other in both directions, and both show inspiration from Arabic sources as well. The Jewish writer Yohanan Alemanno (1435–1505?) provides a striking example.[18] He wove Jewish, Muslim, and Christian traditions of magic into a synthesis grounded in his own cosmology. He drew on the *Book of Raziel*, the *Sworn Book* of Honorius, Arabic astral magic, and many other sources. In his synthesis, modeled on Dante's *Divine Comedy*, he journeys to his version of an Inferno, Purgatorio, and Paradiso, accompanied by a personification of the Torah. In the Inferno he learns how to use rituals to control the demons – for example, by tracing a circle on parchment and writing sacred names in the blood of a bat – and he is told to strike the demons with a wand if they disobey him. In the Purgatorio he learns about the angels who govern the planets and the Zodiac; while in the Paradiso he learns about the highest divine names. Alemanno associated with Humanists in Florence and is generally recognized as having taught Kabbalah to Giovanni Pico della Mirandola. Magicians might be devout Jews, Christians, or Muslims, but in their magical learning they recognized a wider fellowship.

Angel Magic as an Aid in Learning

For students who wanted to make better and more rapid progress in their studies – to improve their memory and understanding, and to master with ease the branches of learning they might be expected to know in the universities of the thirteenth and following centuries – the *Ars notoria* provided magical aid.[19] This was a set of prayers and meditative diagrams said to have been imparted to Solomon by an angel. Especially in one extended version of the *Ars notoria*, the role of angels and their names are repeatedly emphasized. The text is said to have been delivered to Solomon inscribed on gold tablets that the angel Pamphilus placed one night on an altar in his temple. The practitioner who uses the *Ars notoria*

---

[18] Gal Sofer, "The magical cosmos of Yohanan Alemanno: Christian and Jewish magic in the service of a Kabbalist," *Jewish Thought*, 2 (2020), 65–92.

[19] Julien Véronèse, *L'Ars notoria au Moyen Âge: Introduction et édition critique* (Florence: Sismel, 2007); Julien Véronèse, "Les anges dans l'*Ars notoria*: Révélation, processus visionnaire et angélologie," *Mélanges de l'école française de Rome. Moyen Âge*, 114(1) (2002), 813–49; Claire Fanger, "Plundering the Egyptian treasure: John the Monk's *Book of Visions* and its relation to the *Ars notoria* of Solomon," in Fanger, *Conjuring Spirits*, 216–49. Stephen Skinner and Daniel Clark, eds., *Ars Notoria: The Grimoire of Rapid Learning by Magic, with the Golden Flowers of Apollonius of Tyana*, Vol. I, Version A (Singapore: Golden Hoard Press, 2019), is amply illustrated.

after confessing his sins, fasting, and maintaining chastity will receive angelic visions in his sleep and will be given powerful memory, eloquence, understanding, and steadfastness. As he continues to use the magic, the operator will master the liberal arts and other branches of knowledge. It is angels who originally revealed this magic, angels who appear to the practitioner and inform him whether or not he is worthy to proceed in this art, and angels who produce the magical effects, which are achieved through invocation of their names. The role of angels is shown clearly in some manuscripts, in which angels are depicted accompanying the diagrams (Fig. 17). The user thus has visual reinforcement of the message conveyed in the prayers, which ask God to grant intellectual abilities by the power of angels' names, or beseech God to send angels as aids, or even call upon the angels themselves to be present and strengthen the practitioner's capacities. The angels are immensely powerful and may be fearsome: one of the diagrams used is called the mark of dread (*nota terroris*), because it depicts an angel's face. Still, they are said to be angels and not demons.

One of many glosses added to the extended version of the text tells a cautionary tale. King Solomon left his book out one day, and a friend of his happened to discover it and began reciting one of the prayers. But this man was guilty of drunkenness, unchastity, and other sins, so the four angels who would otherwise come to his aid began afflicting him and causing him to lose his sight, hearing, speech, memory, and understanding. He remained a madman to his dying day. The story echoes the tale of the sorcerer's apprentice: a person who comes upon a book of magic, uses it without authorization, and suffers dire consequences. In this case, however, the problem arises for specifically moral reasons, and the effects are the opposite of what the magic is designed to accomplish. It was not only uninitiated friends who had to be cautious: Solomon himself once made light of the magic entrusted to him, but then he repented and submitted to punishment.

The extended version of the *Ars notoria* takes a complex attitude toward necromancy. It claims that according to Solomon, the art of necromancy is contained in seven books, and it is only a minor sin to read and use five of them, but the remaining two are utterly forbidden because they involve offering sacrifice to malign spirits, sometimes even the offering of human blood. Elsewhere the *Ars notoria* suggests that certain exceptional individuals were allowed to use demonic magic. God permitted Solomon – and after him magicians such as Appolonius, Ptolemy, and Virgil – to constrain the evil spirits, invoking them by name, that they might obey him and carry out his will. They were allowed to bind and imprison the demons, offering them sacrifice,

Fig. 17. First *nota* of dialectic from a manuscript of the *Ars notoria*. Manuscript of 1360–75

even though to do so is (at least for others) seriously evil. How much more, then, is it permitted by God to beseech him, invoking his name, and to call upon his good angels by name, with fasting and chastity, for the sake of good deeds, gaining the favor of God and the holy angels, and then acquiring knowledge and wisdom.

The text contains lists of the names of holy angels, understood as invocations of these angels, intermingled with prayers in what the text claims are Greek, Chaldean, and Hebrew. While angels are invoked, ultimately the power they mediate is that of God. The prayers given are said to be composed of "mystical words." One of them begins with a series of names, including Hehyatham, Gessamagar, Hepymegabos, Hasazamay, and many others. It continues:

O God, my strength, the splendor of wisdom, king of the angels whose names I have recited, enliven me in your ways, sanctify your name in me, give me the power that you bestowed on your holy angels, confirm in me the wisdom and knowledge that you bestowed on Adam, and convert my heart toward obedience to you. Give me, then, O Lord my God, your holy angels, that they may observe and guard me and my sense and understanding for the fulfillment of your precepts, O wisdom and font of all wisdom. Give me today full knowledge of that art for which I labor and invoke your holy name...

The diagrams for learning theology are again accompanied by prayers, one of which asks God to receive the prayers of all the holy angels and all the celestial powers, that the practitioner may gain power to learn all of Scripture.

The *Ars notoria* was called that not because it was notorious, but because it makes use of "notes," meaning prayer formulas, along with meditative or magical figures that are also sometimes called notes. Yet this text was in fact also notorious. Roger Bacon mentioned it among the books of magic he thought should be banned. Thomas Aquinas singled it out for condemnation, assuming that the unknown names given in its formulas were those of demons. He repudiated it as unlawful because it involved alliance with demons, and also ineffective because illumination of the human intellect is not a function of demons.[20] The text of the *Ars notoria*, particularly in its most extended form, insists clearly that the angels invoked are holy, speaks of them as "heavenly spirits," and says they come to the practitioner's aid with God's permission. Thomas either did not know or did not believe these assurances. Perhaps he was familiar with the text only indirectly, or only with a shorter version that was less explicit and less emphatic about the unfallen nature of the angels

---

[20] Thomas Aquinas, *Summa theologiae*, II-II, qu. 96, art. 1.

invoked. Even if he knew the more extended versions with explanatory glosses, however, they might have struck him as protesting too much and arousing all the more suspicion that the angels were less holy than the text claimed.

A monk in the early fourteenth century, John of Morigny, was more clearly familiar with the *Ars notoria*.[21] He used it personally and left a harrowing account of its effects. His experience with both necromancy and the *Ars notoria*, as well as the circumstances of his writing an alternative form of magical devotions, can be found in his *Book of Flowers of Heavenly Teaching*. The prologue to this book gives something like an autobiography of a medieval magician. About four years after he entered the monastery of Morigny, a cleric gave John a book of necromancy, but someone recommended that he use instead the *Ars notoria*. At the outset he realized that the *Ars notoria* appears holy, but that it involves necromancy, meaning it is worked with the aid of demons. Indeed, soon after he said prayers from the *Ars notoria* he had a night vision, beginning with a sinister shadow appearing on a wall, then the Devil hovering in the air, then a figure in black descending into a field. After further disturbing visions, including one in which a man climbed through his window and demanded his homage, he came more and more to realize that the *Ars notoria* was hazardous. In one vision he fled from a demon, took refuge in a crowd, found a bishop in the crowd and confessed his sins to him, and on waking up realized his troubles were caused by using the *Ars notoria*, so he gave it up, but not fully. Even when he did set the *Ars notoria* aside, he lapsed into the practice of necromancy and began writing his own book of necromancy, although a voice came to him warning that he was a fool. Finally, he had an ecstatic dream of Jesus seated on a throne and dressed in a red toga; he begged for mercy, but he was punished with a beating, and he felt the pain from this punishment on waking and set aside his involvement in necromancy.

Magic is often learned in a master–disciple relationship, and in John's case his younger sister Bridget became his disciple. He shared the *Ars notoria* with her, thinking it could help her learn to read, and indeed it enabled her to learn quickly, but it also brought her demonic visions, until she had a vision in which she beat and crushed the demon, gave up

[21] John of Morigny, *Liber florum celestis doctrine / The Book of Flowers of Heavenly Teaching*, ed. Claire Fanger and Nicholas Watson (Toronto: Pontifical Institute of Mediaeval Studies, 2015); Claire Fanger, *Rewriting Magic: An Exegesis of the Visionary Autobiography of a Fourteenth-Century Monk* (University Park: Pennsylvania State University Press, 2015); Claire Fanger and Nicholas Watson, "John of Morigny," in Page and Rider, *Routledge History*, 212–24.

the *Ars notoria*, and began seeing visions of God and of the Virgin, after which she became a nun.

While many of his visions were sinister and threatening, John experienced a different set of dream visions of the Virgin Mary, who protected him and brought him to his conversion. She appeared to him in her cathedral at Chartres, where her silver image became alive and spoke to him. He also beheld a procession of angels in this cathedral, one of whom took him by his hand and brought him into their company. He received the Virgin's permission to write a book with a series of prayers that could serve the same purpose as the *Ars notoria*, but without the dangers it entailed. The Virgin could be a sharp critic, and evidently shared some of John's own doubts about the relationship between his new techniques and the *Ars notoria* he was supposed to have abandoned. At one point she charged that he was inserting "some nonsense about the angels which is not much use."[22]

The *Book of Flowers* is divided into three main sections. The shortest, the Book of Visions, recounts John's visions of the Virgin Mary and other sacred persons. The Book of Figures gives a series of diagrams on which the operator is expected to meditate; in an earlier version of the text these resembled somewhat the figures given in the *Ars notoria*, but in a later reworking they were replaced by images of the Virgin Mary more devotional and less overtly magical in character. The Book of Prayers, by far the longest of the sections, consists of prayers and hymns addressed mainly to the Virgin, to Christ, and to the angels. One subsection gives a set of thirty prayers directed first to Christ and then to the different choirs of angels: the Archangels for dialectic, the Thrones for rhetoric, the Principalities for "astronomy or astrology," and so forth, culminating in an appeal to the Cherubim for moral philosophy and the Seraphim for theology. The prayers do not have the structure or the character of conjurations, which would command the spirits by bringing spiritual forces to bear upon them. Rather, they call upon the angels – ranks of angels, not individual spirits – in the highly formulaic language of ritual, expressed as formal entreaty. For example:

Angels of understanding, Angels of memory, Angels of fluency, Angels of eloquence, Angels of skill, Angels of groundwork, Angels of steadfastness, Angel teachers of grammar ... I invoke, supplicate, and ask you, with power received from God, to come to me and be with me always, and guard my soul from every hindrance, and to uphold me, my understanding, my memory, my eloquence, my fluency, my skill, and my steadfastness, and may you teach me the

---

[22] Page, "Medieval magical figures," 443.

entire art of grammar, with the permission of our Lord Jesus Christ, whom I ask to release you that you may come.

There is ambiguity in more than one aspect of John's writing, first of all in his attitude toward magic, as the narrative of his experience makes clear. Even when he claimed to turn away from it, he found it alluring. At various points in the *Book of Flowers* he seems to remain committed to the mastery of magic. One of his thirty prayers asks the Seraphim for aid in mastery of the occult sciences, and another calls upon the Cherubim who preside over necromancy, aeromancy, pyromancy, and other occult arts. He even asks for knowledge and understanding of "all the arts of necromancy." Immediately, however, he clarifies: he wants to know and understand these arts, but not to carry them out. He realizes that readers may at first think the exercises in his book closely resemble the *Ars notoria*, but he insists that they are contrary in all respects. The *Ars notoria* is carried out in secret, and the operator is instructed not to reveal his visions, but John's exercises are meant to be done openly, and anything resulting from them that redounds to the praise of the Virgin should be made public.

There is ambiguity in his conception of visions. He typically says they began when he was in ecstasy and ended with his waking, which might seem to leave it unclear whether they occur in rapture or in dreams. Even when he speaks of himself as receiving visions in his sleep, he sometimes suggests that it is a sleep of ecstasy rather than literal sleep. Ultimately, however, he seems not to have thought of different modes of revelation as fundamentally different: divine inspiration can come through deeds, words, visions, dreams, or direct inspiration of the Holy Spirit, but the effect is the same regardless of the means.

All the tensions we can see in late medieval perception of magic – its alluring and yet threatening character, the claim that it can be orthodox and the counterclaim that it always remains suspect, the tug of war between angels and demons – are found here within the life and work of a single individual. John was harshly criticized during his lifetime, and his book was condemned, but he himself was his first critic, and the autobiographical sections of his work have a confessional quality to them that is exceptional in the history of magic.

Angel Magic as a Means for Gaining a Vision of God

In some ways the most daring work of angel magic is the *Sworn Book*, probably written in the early fourteenth century, and pseudonymously ascribed to one Honorius of Thebes.[23] This book begins by giving an obviously contrived account of how it came to be written. The pope and cardinals, moved by the influence of malign demonic spirits, set out to repress the art of magic. (This calls to mind the condemnation and prosecution of magicians under Pope John XXII around the 1320s, which may be a clue to the time when the book was written.) They alleged that magicians and necromancers, in opposition to the Church, were working toward the damnation of humankind by invoking and offering sacrifice to demons. The magicians were said to be leading people into error, attracting ignorant followers with their illusionist wonder-working. Aware of this campaign against them, the magicians held a council of eighty-nine masters from Naples, Athens, and Toledo, which chose Honorius, son of Euclid, a master of Thebes, to defend them. With the counsel of the angel Hocrohel, Honorius compiled a book that was called sworn or sacred because sacred matters were its source or its outcome, or because it was consecrated by angels and by the Lord. They determined that no more than three copies of the book should be made, and that it should be passed along to no one until one of the masters was near death, at which point he should find a worthy recipient. If no fitting recipient could be found, the master should have his copy of the book buried.

The prayer formulas in the first part of the book, which makes up over half of the book's length, can be used to gain a vision of God. The practitioner must confess his sins with true penitence, must avoid even seeing women, and must be set apart from evil and infirm men. The prayers are addressed sometimes to God and sometimes to the Virgin Mary. The book gives series of divine names, including a hundred names of God that the practitioner is told to write in ash around his bed. This part of the work does not straightforwardly and obviously have the character of angel magic, yet it does call upon the angels for aid. Many of the prayers are series of mystical names, such as Assaylemaht, Rasay, Semaht, Azahat, and so forth, and in some of the prayers these are identified as names of angels. An angel will appear to the practitioner in sleep and reveal whether his request to proceed with the ritual is granted or refused. One of the prayers is said to be useful in persuading

---

[23] *Liber iuratus Honorii: A Critical Edition of the Latin Version of the Sworn Book of Honorius,* ed. Gösta Hedegård (Stockholm: Almqvist & Wiksell, 2002); Honorius of Thebes, *The Sworn Book of Honorius:* Liber iuratus Honorii, ed. with English trans. Joseph Peterson (Lake Worth, Fla.: Ibis Press, 2016); Katelyn Mesler, "The *Liber iuratus Honorii* and the Christian reception of angel magic," in Claire Fanger, ed., *Invoking Angels: Theurgic Ideas and Practices, Thirteenth to Sixteenth Centuries* (University Park: Pennsylvania State University Press, 2012), 113–50.

the celestial spirits, against their natural inclination, to come down and speak with humans or compel aerial or earthly spirits to come and obey them.

The attainment of a divine vision is thus highlighted as the primary goal of the *Sworn Book*, but it is by no means the only goal. While the highest angels are those who reside in heaven and serve God alone, below them are planetary angels, and the second part of the *Sworn Book* suggests that they can be invoked to learn the powers of the planets and stars, to gain learning in general and knowledge of all the plants and animals, all the spirits of water or earth or hell, to know the hour of one's death, to have a vision of purgatory or hell, and so forth. The spirits of each of the planets are named, as well as the demons who are subject to them (Fig. 18). Then conjurations are given, addressed to the planetary angels and to the spirits under their command, of which this is a small excerpt:

I invoke you, O powers of the heavens, and [again] I invoke you, conjuring you by Ab, by Gap, by Abx, by Abra, by Abraca, by Gebra, by Abracala, by Abracasap, by Abracaleus, by Zargon, by Abrion, by Eleyon, by Sargion. I invoke you, therefore, you mighty angels, and in invoking I conjure you.

One of the conjurations directs the spirits to descend, to appear in benevolent form within circles that have been traced to receive them, and to respond truthfully to all questions.

Below the planetary angels are the spirits of the air, or the atmosphere closer to Earth. The *Sworn Book* says that the Church views these spirits as damned, but the spirits themselves say otherwise, and the text calls them neither good nor bad. But then it says some of these aerial spirits are good and work only for good purposes, and they cause harm only when compelled by divine power, while others are bad and cause harm, turning to good only when compelled by a higher power. The third sort of aerial spirit, neither good nor bad, but doing good or evil as required by one who invokes them, is the kind discussed in this part of the book. The spirits are listed by name according to the compass directions of the regions where they reside, and their bodies are described. Those of the west, for example, have large and full bodies, soft and phlegmatic, dark and shadowy in color, like clouds, with much swelling, eyes red and watery, hairless, with teeth like a boar's. To conjure these spirits, the practitioner draws a circle on the ground, inscribes the names of the relevant spirits, stands inside the circle, recites a conjuration, and, when they come, ceremonially calls their attention to what he has inscribed and to the "seal of Solomon," with its letters, characters, and figures, which he has brought before them.

Fig. 18. Angels of Mars and of the Sun, from Honorius of Thebes, *Sworn Book*. Manuscript probably early sixteenth century

The book has little to say about the final type of spirits, which it calls angels of the Earth, but in principle they can be invoked to find out about precious metals and stones, and in general how to find all things that are hidden. These spirits can also create the illusion of resuscitated and talking bodies of the dead. But the text warns that Christians rarely or never have dealings with these spirits, and their counsel is not trustworthy. They are still called angels, and those holding a multiple-type theory of spirits could recognize them as being angels of a particular type, although to those who hold to a strict two-type understanding of angels they sound a great deal like demons.

Angel Magic and Magical Figures

The *Ars notoria*, John of Morigny's *Book of Flowers*, the *Sworn Book*, and the *Almandal* all share one feature characteristic of angel magic, that being the use of magical figures. Diagrams of various kinds are used in other forms of magic as well: symbols of the planets are used in astral magic, and more or less elaborate circles occur in the demonic magic that will be discussed in the next chapter.[24] The diagrams used in angel magic are sometimes more devotional than those found elsewhere, but sometimes they resemble closely the figures used in astral or demonic magic.

The *Sworn Book* gives elaborate instructions for composing the "seal of God" that has a five-pointed star in the center, surrounded by seven-sided bands and a seven-pointed star, along with sacred signs, names of angels, and other inscriptions in and around this configuration. The practitioner can wear this seal on his person while compelling the spirits to come in pleasing form and do his bidding. He consecrates it, asking that with God's help it may be used to subdue heavenly powers and to subjugate, invoke, transmute, conjure, constrain, rouse up, gather, disperse, and bind aerial, earthly, and infernal ones, and to render them harmless, as well as to curry favor with humans, to pacify enemies or divide those who are at peace, to preserve or undermine health, to cure the infirm, to guard good people from bad, to avoid all bodily peril, to render judges favorable, to attain victory in all things, to mortify sins of the flesh and avoid those of the spirit, to augment one's wealth, and to stand among the elect at the last judgment and behold God's majesty. The interwoven sides of the pentagram, which flow in an unbroken continuum, have some resemblance to a knot, which Michael Camille

---

[24] Page, "Medieval magical figures," 442–5.

suggested was perhaps "the magical visual form par excellence."[25] Elsewhere such knotlike patterns serve as protective devices, binding the spirits that might otherwise threaten.[26] Something of that sort may be intended here as well, but the seal of God is mainly a device for compelling the spirits to do something, not a means for keeping them from action. A later magician, Berengar Ganell, took over the device of the seal and claimed it could serve not only to attain a vision of God, but to rescue a soul from purgatory. Others also took over the seal and produced metal versions that survive, including a metal matrix that could be used to form wax impressions.[27]

In most cases, as with this seal of God, the diagrams serve mainly to draw down the magical power of the heavenly bodies, to summon the spirits, or sometimes to protect the magician against potentially threatening forces. They are meant in those cases to have effect on the sources of magical power that are invoked, not mainly on the magician. The figures used in angel magic can also be used to conjure or to allure the spirits who are invoked. The diagram inscribed on the wax tablet called the Almandal is part of an apparatus meant to entice the angels and induce them to appear and communicate with the practitioner. Such figures often serve also to elevate the practitioner's mind and soul. They can work as meditative devices, tools for concentration and for empowerment.

The diagrams in the *Ars notoria* are meant to bring systems of knowledge before the practitioner's eyes and mind in a way that can easily be grasped.[28] They recall the use of images in works on the art of memory, except that here the graphic devices are meant also to elicit contact with the angels who impart the mastery one seeks. One manuscript of the *Ars notoria* gives a figure for the art of grammar in which a lion rests its hind paws and tail on five circles labeled for the parts of speech, while nine further grammatical terms are given in circles below, each with a configuration of lines and smaller circles beneath it. Another manuscript shows angels positioned alongside complex renderings of bands, circles, and intricate designs. These figures do not represent the learning of arts – they do not show students being taught by masters or by allegorical figures – but rather they serve as meditative devices that the practitioner

---

[25] Michael Camille, "Visual art in two manuscripts of the *Ars notoria*," in Fanger, *Conjuring Spirits*, 123.
[26] Champion, "Magic on the walls," 18, 20.
[27] Page, "Medieval magical figures," 444–5.
[28] Michael Camille, "Visual art in two manuscripts," 115–19; Sophie Page, *Magic in Medieval Manuscripts* (London: British Library, 2004), 39–44.

looks at intently, so that the process of inspection itself brings about contact with spirits who instill knowledge.

The figures in John of Morigny's *Book of Flowers* are of two sorts. There was an original set, of which only two stray examples survive out of ninety-one that were intended. One of these is a circle with smaller circles inside it; the smaller circles are accompanied by initials standing for the sacred name of God and for the intellectual powers of under-standing, memory, eloquence, and steadfastness. Text accompanying this figure suggests that it represents the "gate of paradise"; the practi-tioner using John's method is meant to meditate on this device and imagine himself standing at the gate of heaven. The other diagram features a five-pointed star with a cross and the words "of Jesus Christ" in the center, then letters in alternating red and black at the points of the star that spell out "Mary" (in black) and "beloved" (in red), and further words that make up a prayer for the owner of the book, named Geoffrey.[29] But figures of this kind clearly seemed too similar to those found in the *Ars notoria*, and the second one, despite the prayer inscribed in it, appeared too similar to diagrams used in necromancy. John thus abandoned this type of diagram and substituted a set of more clearly devotional figures, focusing on the Virgin Mary shown with her child. It is the latter set of figures that became standard in manuscripts of John's work. They are supposed to be closely linked to the prayers that accom-pany them. The purpose, however, remains the same: the practitioner is meant to meditate on the figures as an aid to gaining access to the knowledge imparted by sacred personages, Christ and the Virgin, through the mediation of angels.

Angel Magic and Devotion to Angels

If angel magic was difficult to distinguish on the one hand from demonic magic, it could be similar on the other hand to purely orthodox and even standard devotion to angels.[30] The archangels Michael, Gabriel, and Raphael were biblical figures and referred to as saints. Their names were taken as personal names, fully parallel in this respect to names taken from the saints. Michael was commemorated on the liturgical calendar, along with the saints; October 29th came to be the feast of Saint Michael and All Angels. Each individual was thought to have a guardian angel. Prayer to the angels was not only allowed, but encouraged. Some saints had one or more guardian angels whose names they knew. Angels were thought of

---

[29] Fanger, *Rewriting Magic*, 91–8.   [30] Kieckhefer, "Angel magic."

as sources of revelation, and some saints' lives told of the revelations they had received from angels. Ascent to the higher stages of mystical spirituality could also be seen as promoted by angels.

Critics of angelic magic might view it as heretical, or superstitious, or idolatrous, but how could angelic magic be distinguished from this ordinary devotion to angels? Works such as the *Ars notoria* and John of Morigny's alternative set of rituals were found at times in monasteries, and their users might think of them as more devotional than magical. What was it that marked the boundary between devotion to angels and angel magic? Was it when angels' aid was sought in the acquisition or revelation of knowledge? The saints, too, received revelations from angels. These revelations typically came to the saints spontaneously, without their seeking them, but if they remained devoted to their angel companions, over time the distinction between spontaneous and cultivated revelation would not be absolute; and in any case, people at the time did not take this as a defining distinction between devotion and magic. Did devotion to angels become magical when the angels were named? No, again there were saints who had named angel companions. Did devotion pass over into magic when it took on the trappings of ritual? Clearly not; rituals of various sorts, official and unofficial, could be recognized as pious and not in any sense magical. Was the aid of angels thought of as magic when it circumvented the institutional channels of the Church's sacraments and the university's instruction? Private devotion as a complement to the liturgy and sacraments was never in itself problematic, and if people were allowed to study in their rooms, relying on whatever memory aids they found useful, there could be no objection to having angels as study aids to enhance performance within the universities.

One key factor to bear in mind is that even though devotion to angels was an important part of medieval religion, it could never be regulated in the same way as devotion to the saints. Saints could be canonized, which meant they were carefully vetted by the institutional Church, but nobody ever canonized an angel. The veneration of saints often centered on their physical remains, their relics, which were usually located in churches and subject to ecclesiastical control, but there were no bodily relics of the angels to be guarded in shrines. Even the two-type conception of angels was rivaled by the multiple-type view, which could claim the support of influential hagiography and the work of so exalted a poet as Dante. In short, devotion to angels and even the conception of angels had gray areas, and angel magic exploited and magnified these.

In the end, what distinguished angel magic from more purely acceptable devotion to angels was largely context. If angels were venerated alongside the approved saints, and in basically the same ways (with patronage, and liturgical observance and private prayer, but without relics), and if the people who venerated and even received revelation from angels were in all other respects faithful to the Church's traditions and authority, then there would be no problem. But forms of angel worship that departed from the norm and from the usual contexts of liturgy and devotion could easily become suspect. And if suspicions arose about the practitioners themselves, their practices could easily be called into question, because any angel could have its status challenged by those who saw demons lurking everywhere.

8   Conjuration of Demons

John of Salisbury, in his *Policraticus*, tells of an experience from his own youth. He was studying Latin from a priest, using the Psalms as the texts for study. As it happened, however, his teacher was an adept in the divinatory art of crystal-gazing, and abused his position of trust by making John and a somewhat older pupil participate in these activities. The idea was to anoint the boys' fingernails with some sacred chrism so that images would appear reflected in the nails and would impart information. Alternatively, a polished basin might be used as the reflecting surface. After certain "preliminary magical rites" and the requisite anointing, the priest uttered names "which by the horror they inspired, seemed to me, child though I was, to belong to demons." The other pupil declared that he saw "certain misty figures," but John himself saw nothing of the sort and was thus ruled unqualified for this art. John goes on to say that almost all the people he knew who engaged in such practices were punished later in life with blindness and other afflictions. He knew only two exceptions, including the priest who had taught him Latin; both of these men repented and entered into religious life as monks or canons, and even they were punished somewhat for their offenses.[1]

What should we make of John's recollection that the priest had recited the names of demons? Was this the fruit of childish imagination or faulty memory? One might think so, except that the Munich handbook (discussed in Chapter 1) contains detailed instructions for conjuring demons in precisely the way that John recounts, and for the same purpose. The magic of the Munich manual is explicitly demonic, and there is no reason to doubt that the rites of John's Latin teacher were equally so.[2] Evidently what we have here is an example of the demonic magic that seems to have been practiced rather widely in the later Middle Ages.

---

[1] *Frivolities of Courtiers and Footprints of Philosophers*, ii.28, trans. Joseph B. Pike (London: Oxford University Press, 1938), 146–7.
[2] For the Munich manuscript, see above, Chapter 1, n. 3.

This story is not the first indication in the West that such practices were known. A century earlier, Anselm of Besate had put together a series of accusations against his cousin Rotiland. The charges were intended as a rhetorical exercise, and we need not take them seriously as charges against Rotiland in particular, but on the other hand we cannot rule out the possibility that Anselm intended his portrayal to have verisimilitude, and in later centuries similar accusations were being made very much in earnest. Rotiland is supposed to have gone out of town one night with a boy, buried the lad up to his waist, and tortured him with some kind of acrid fumes. As the boy underwent this abuse, Rotiland supposedly recited a formula that began, "As this youth is held captive in this place, so may girls be captive to my love." Part of his incantation was in "Hebrew, or rather diabolical, words," though the characters given in the account are actually garbled Greek letters. To avenge his mistreatment, the boy later stole Rotiland's "notebook of necromancy," and Rotiland conjured up a dead man "by diabolical art" to recover the book. This conjurer is supposed to have committed a second offense in the company of a Saracen or Muslim physician; this time he is charged with using the hand of a dead person to break into a house, and with murder as well.[3] This account proves little, but raises the question whether demonic magic was being used even in the eleventh century, and whether we have here a fanciful elaboration of actual experience.

Both John of Salisbury and Anselm of Besate were speaking of "necromancy." Originally the term had meant divination (*mantia*) by conjuring the spirits of the dead (*nekroi*). Circe was the classic necromancer of Graeco-Roman tradition, and the witch of Endor was the archetypal necromancer of the Bible. When medieval writers interpreted such stories, however, they assumed that the dead could not in fact be brought to life, but that demons took on the appearance of deceased persons and pretended to be those persons. By extension, then, the conjuring of demons came to be known as necromancy; this was the ordinary meaning of the term in later medieval Europe.[4] It took on a wide range of

---

[3] Karl Manitius, "Magie und Rhetorik bei Anselm von Besate," *Deutsches Archiv für Erforschung des Mittelalters*, 12 (1956), 52–72.

[4] High and late medieval sources more often use the form "nigromancy," which was taken as equivalent to "necromancy." While "necro-" comes from a Greek word for the dead or a corpse, "nigro-" comes from the Latin for the color black and calls to mind the negative associations of blackness. A strong case can be made that historians should use the more common medieval form "nigromancy," with all its complexity of both denotation and connotation. See Jean-Patrice Boudet, *Entre science et nigromance: Astrologie, divination et magie dans l'Orient médiéval (XIIe–XVe siècle)* (Paris: Sorbonne, 2006), 92–4; and especially Boudet, "'Nigromantia': Brève histoire d'un mot," in Alessandro Palazzo and Irene Zavattero, eds., *Geomancy and Other Forms of Divination* (Florence: SISMEL,

meanings: it could still refer to conjuring the dead; it could apply to explicit conjuring of demons; it could be a general term for magic, used to translate the Arabic *siḥr*. Sources could even refer to "necromancy according to physics," and by this, what they have in mind is natural magic. In any case, necromancy often referred to explicitly demonic magic. Other forms of magic might be taken as implicitly demonic, and even a person who wore an amulet or recited a charm might be suspected of implicitly demonic magic. The necromancer, however, actually invoked demons or the Devil, and often did so by invoking their names, whether familiar or unfamiliar.[5]

For someone holding to the mainstream two-type understanding of angels, distinguishing rigorously between the fallen and the unfallen types, there was no room for ambiguity, and seldom much room for uncertainty: someone conjuring demons for unsavory purposes, and taking precautions lest they appear in threatening form or manner, was involved with fallen and radically evil spirits. As we have seen, however, not everyone accepted this two-type understanding. There could be various forms of spirit, some of them neither quite good nor altogether evil, and residing primarily neither in heaven nor in hell. When people referred to demons, too, they might have the fallen and utterly corrupt angels of hell in mind. They sometimes spoke of "demons," but meant something like the classical Greek *daimones*, lesser gods or guardian spirits. One interlocutor in Plato's *Symposium* spoke of *daimones* as mediators between the gods and mortals. As the gods were increasingly thought of as unattainably distant from human beings, far beyond the reach of the smoke that rose from sacrificial offerings, mediators were needed, and the *daimones* played that role. But not all of them were reliable, and pagan writers such as Plutarch and Porphyry railed against the evil *daimones* who could not be trusted, and against the magicians who wittingly or unwittingly invoked these evil spirits.[6] Early Christian writers were heirs to this suspicion. Yet not all writers, pagan or Christian, were willing to brand all demons as evil. In medieval sources, the spirits of the heavens might sometimes be called angels, but might also be called demons and were not necessarily untrustworthy. Cecco d'Ascoli spoke of demons who live in the North and have a noble nature, knowing the secrets of the world's elements

---

2017), 445–62. In English, however, "nigromancy" readily brings to mind modern connotations of blackness that do not quite coincide with medieval connotations and can cause confusion.

[5] See now Frank Klaassen, "Necromancy," in Page and Rider, *Routledge History*, 201–11.

[6] Fraser, "Roman antiquity," 130–5.

and responding readily to the invocation of persons who share their noble nature, staying and conversing familiarly in the households of the noble, but hurling stones and dung in the homes of the ignoble, over-turning dishes and bedclothes, and making spooky sounds at night.[7] Are these angels, demons, or something else? They have noble natures, and can behave nobly when in noble company, yet Cecco calls them demons and says that in some contexts they behave like what we would call poltergeists. They dwell in a northern part of the heavens, which is to say, neither heaven nor hell. Clearly Cecco was no adherent of a tidy two-type view of spirits.

When medieval magicians conjured demons, in many cases they were quite clear that they meant fallen angels, denizens of hell. But they might also sometimes call upon spirits like Floron or Oriens, who appear in texts of astral magic, and they might not distinguish rigor-ously between the demons of hell and the potentially ambiguous spirits of the heavens. We thus have an inherent ambiguity in this chapter, the reverse of what we faced in the last chapter: there we were dealing with angelic magic, but had to recognize that the "angels" might be of questionable nature and character, and here we are dealing with demonic magic, but find that some of the demons are less unambigu-ously evil than Thomas Aquinas or John Gerson would assume. Matters were clearer for those who adhered to a two-type conception of unfallen and fallen angels, but less so for those who held a multiple-type view and allowed for "angels" and "demons" that did not fit into the binary paradigm.

We have seen that angelic magic was prevalent in Jewish circles, and that works such as the *Book of Raziel* implied a multiple-type view of the spirits being invoked. Jewish magicians also had rituals for more unam-biguously demonic magic. The magician might stand inside a circle or square, burn incense, recite long verbal formulas, and display to the demons their own images and seals. Multiple demons could be assem-bled by these means and could be made to answer questions and carry out services. As in Christianity, such practices represented one end of a spectrum ranging from purely angelic to straightforwardly demonic magic.[8]

[7] Lynn Thorndike, *The Sphere of Sacrobosco and its Commentators* (University of Chicago Press, 1949), 486; Nicolas Weill-Parot, "Cecco d'Ascoli and Antonio da Montolmo: The building of a 'nigromantical' cosmology and the birth of the author-magician," in Page and Rider, *Routledge History*, 227.

[8] Bohak, "Jewish magic in the Middle Ages," 281.

The Making of a Clerical Underworld

Who were the necromancers? Both in legend and before the law it was clerics, above all others, who stood accused of conjuring demons. To speak of these magicians as clerics, however, is to speak with inevitable imprecision, since the term "cleric" could have many meanings. This was true of the Latin *clericus*, and equally of the English translations "cleric" and "clerk." Most broadly, the term could refer to anyone, even a boy still in adolescence, who had been tonsured as a mark of pious intent to be ordained. A bit more narrowly, it meant a person who had been ordained at least to lower orders: someone who had been ordained, for example, as a doorkeeper, a lector, or an acolyte. These offices had originally been connected with specific tasks, but in later medieval Europe they were merely steps that one took up the ladder toward the priesthood – steps that were available even for those who did not intend to climb all the way to the top of that ladder. One of the minor orders to which a cleric would be ordained was that of exorcist, and in the ordin-ation ceremony he would receive a book of exorcisms as a symbol of his theoretical function. He might never perform a real exorcism in his life, but if he went astray he might indeed have occasion to command demons. Students in medieval universities would be ordained to lower orders as a matter of course; anyone who went to a university would obtain ordination and thus qualify as a cleric. In other contexts, "clerk" referred to someone who had *not* been ordained at all, but helped the priest in various liturgical and practical functions.

Apart from this multiplicity of meanings, the identification of clerics was complicated by the informality of clerical training and the laxness of control over ordination. Aspirants to the priesthood in medieval Europe did not go to seminaries, where they might have received theological education linked with spiritual guidance. Seminaries were virtually unknown. Those who could afford to go to universities might do so, and from the thirteenth century onward bishops generally encouraged such a course of studies, but this would have been the exception, not the rule. The less affluent and less ambitious would still have been trained in a kind of apprenticeship. They would serve under a parish priest in a town or village, learn from him how to perform the rituals, and then present themselves to the bishop for ordination. They were expected to have at least a rudimentary knowledge of Latin, ritual, and doctrine, but the examinations were not uniformly strict, and reformers often pro-tested the numbers of unqualified candidates who slipped through. A visitation of the clergy in early fifteenth-century Bologna turned up clerics who could not read their breviaries, and the bishop who made this visitation felt obliged to repeat his predecessor's mandate that only an ordained priest could celebrate the mass.[9]

Many were ordained to lower orders and continued to claim the privileges of clergy, although they had no clerical employment; indeed they might be employed as merchants or artisans while still claiming to be clerics. Others, it seems, claimed falsely to be clerics to obtain the benefits of clergy, particularly immunity from secular jurisdiction when they got into trouble. In some places, these rogues came often before the law, on a variety of charges. In 1385, for example, a murderer and robber in Paris claimed to be a cleric, but during the trial he confessed that he had never gone to school and had merely had a barber shave his head to avoid the rigor of the law. In any case, these pseudoclerics differed little from those real ones who no longer functioned as such and had forgotten their learning and their prayers.[10]

Even a man who had been ordained as a priest might or might not have a regular position as curate or assistant in a parish. In the late Middle Ages, pious people often endowed positions for "chantry priests" to say mass for their souls after death and thus secure their speedy release from purgatory, and many clerics were, in effect, semi-employed in such positions. A chantry priest was expected to say the divine office each day as a minimum by way of private prayer, and was expected to say mass each morning according to the terms of the endowment. Once these duties were fulfilled, he would usually be free for the rest of the day. Having time on his hands, he might readily get into trouble. Conjuring demons was merely one of the forms this trouble might take: not the most common form, perhaps, but not the least interesting. Some of these priests might be assigned to teach Latin grammar to young boys of the parish, but anyone who thought such employment would keep clerics out of trouble might have done well to read John of Salisbury.

Monks could also enter into this clerical underworld. Since the high Middle Ages, most monks in the West had also been priests. In a monastery where discipline was strict and surveillance careful, monks

---

[9] Peter Heath, *The English Parish Clergy on the Eve of the Reformation* (London: Routledge, 1969); A. Hamilton Thompson, *The English Clergy and their Organization in the Later Middle Ages* (Oxford: Clarendon, 1947); Denys Hay, *The Church in Italy in the Fifteenth Century* (Cambridge University Press, 1977); Paul Adam, *La vie paroissiale en France* (Paris: Sirey, 1964). Recent work has largely focused on particular locations, but see John Shinners and William J. Dohar, eds., *Pastors and the Care of Souls in Medieval England* (Notre Dame, Ind.: University of Notre Dame Press, 1998); and David Lepine, "England: Church and clergy," in S. H. Rigby, ed., *A Companion to Britain in the Later Middle Ages* (Oxford: Blackwell, 2003), 359–80.

[10] Bronislaw Geremek, *The Margins of Society in Late Medieval Paris*, trans. Jean Birrell (Cambridge University Press, 1987), 135–66.

could be kept to their prayer and honest labor, but in a monastery that needed reform the monks might pursue less holy pastimes. One monk at Florence, named John of Vallombrosa (fourteenth century), was keenly interested in books during his early years in the monastery and spent day and night absorbed in them. Unfortunately, he developed an attachment to the wrong kind of books, learned the art of conjuration from them, and began to practice it in secret. Eventually, the other monks learned of his preoccupation; he denied it at first, but eventually was forced to admit his guilt. Several years in a dungeon left him broken in body and barely able to walk about, yet penitent and given to solitude as a spiritual discipline.[11]

If monks could engage in demonic magic, so too might friars. Alleged conjurers at the court of the antipope Benedict XIII (reg. 1394–1423) were supposedly in contact with an entire group of Franciscan magicians in southern France. One Franciscan theologian, Gilles Vanalatte, was charged with obtaining a book of magic from the Muslims. Benedict himself was accused of taking instruction in black magic and using a notorious book of magic called *The Death of the Soul*, and a book of such magic was ostensibly once found tucked away in his bed. Other figures in this alleged conspiracy include the prior general from an order of military monks and a young Benedictine monk.[12] There is little hard evidence against any of these people, and it is tempting to assume the charges were concocted, but there is nothing unlikely about people in these positions dabbling in magic of various kinds, sometimes demonic.

Doubtless there were some nonclerical conjurers as well. Conjurations sometimes appear in books otherwise devoted to medical material, which could indicate that they were used by clerics with an interest in medicine or by nonclerical physicians. For the most part, however, these magicians seem to have been clerics in one or another sense.

What do all these groups – diocesan priests, men and boys in minor orders, monks, and friars – have in common? What is most important for our purposes is that they all would have had at least a little learning, and for them this learning was a dangerous thing. Basic knowledge of the rites of exorcism, and perhaps an acquaintance with astrological images and other kinds of magic, might well lead them to experiment with conjuration. If they had access to the infamous books of demonic magic, and if they were curious enough to try them out, that was all they needed for

---

[11] *Acta sanctorum*, March, vol. 2 (Paris and Rome: Palmé, 1866), 49–50.
[12] Margaret Harvey, "Papal witchcraft: The charges against Benedict XIII," in Derek Baker, ed., *Sanctity and Secularity: The Church and the World* (Oxford: Blackwell, 1973), 109–16.

membership in this clerical underworld. The members of this company were no doubt linked by similar purpose more than by any formal or lasting bonds, and certainly there is no evidence that they were organized as a group.

The notion of a clerical underworld requires three main qualifications, however. First, there was no firm boundary between the lower and potentially renegade clergy and the higher clergy and established academics who also sometimes practiced magic, but rather a continuum. It may be that members of the lower and disengaged clergy, those who qualify as a clerical underworld, were more inclined toward overtly demonic magic, while those higher up the ladder tended more toward magic which at least ostensibly relied on angels or occult powers in nature, but we cannot assume a strict correlation. Second, laypeople surely took over some of the practices of the clergy, even if in simplified form, with less reliance on Latin and the apparatus of liturgy. Third, and perhaps most important, even those who we might think of as belonging to a clerical underworld did not necessarily think of themselves in those terms. They may have seen their magic as justified and, among other things, as a means for the upward mobility to which they were entitled.

The moral literature often represents demonic magic as a fascination of youth, which the practitioners outgrow and renounce as they become older, but which leaves its mark on their later lives. The Dominican reformer Johannes Nider (d. 1438) tells about a certain Benedict, whose life can be glimpsed from other sources as well as from Nider.[13] In his youth he was a notorious necromancer, minstrel, and mime, a man "of gigantic height and frightful appearance," who lived a dissolute life and followed his "demonic books of necromancy." Through the prayers of his sister, however, he was snatched from the demons' jaws. Penitent, he went about to various rigorous monasteries seeking admittance, but his appearance and notoriety gained him little sympathy. Finally, a monastery in Vienna took him in, and he gained fame for his holiness and preaching, but even so he found himself molested by demons through life. Whatever kernel of historical fact may underlie this story, in Nider's hands it becomes a kind of moral example with a dual thrust: it affirms the possibility that even a necromancer can find salvation, yet it warns of the lingering perils from a youth devoted to this iniquity.

---

[13] Richard Perger, "Schwarzkünstler und Ordensmann: Aus dem Leben des Schottenpriors und Seitenstettner Abtes Benedikt (+1441)," *Wiener Geschichtsblätter*, 32 (1977), 167–76; Georgine Ververka, "Der merkwürdige Fall 'Benedikt': Biographie oder Predigtmärlein?," *Wiener Geschichtsblätter*, 32 (1977), 177–80.

It is impossible to say in a particular case whether the legends and the legal records are grounded in fact. We do not know for sure that John of Vallombrosa was practicing demonic magic; his abbot may have put a bad face on study of more innocent astrology or some other occult knowledge. Benedict's necromancy, which Nider recounts with horror, may have amounted to little more than the tricks of performative magic. But instructions for authentic demonic magic do survive, and marginal comments in them make it clear that *someone* was engaged in these practices. Given the nature of these instructions, which presuppose a command of Latin and of ritual forms, the finger of suspicion points toward the clergy. The legends and the judicial accusations had verisimilitude, if not accuracy: they had the right sort of person in mind, if not the guilty individuals.

Formulas and Rituals for Conjuring Spirits

The Dominican inquisitor Nicholas Eymericus (1320–99) evidently had ample contact with necromancers. He reported in his *Directory for Inquisitors* that he had confiscated books such as the *Table of Solomon* and Honorius the Necromancer's *Treasury of Necromancy* from the magicians themselves, and after reading these books he had them burned in public. His knowledge of their contents was expanded by confessions the offenders made to him and other inquisitors. Their books recommended numerous forms of forbidden magic: baptizing images, fumigating the head of a dead person, adjuring one demon by the name of a higher demon, inscribing characters and signs, invoking unfamiliar names, mixing the names of demons with those of angels and saints to form perversions of prayer, fumigating with incense or aloes or other aromatics, burning the bodies of birds and animals, casting salt into fire, and much more. If some of these practices entailed implicit worship of the demons, others were more explicit: the practitioners genuflect and make prostrations in the demons' honor, promise them obedience and devote themselves to their service, sing chants in their honor, and offer not only animals but their own blood as a kind of sacrifice. They practice a kind of asceticism as well in their exercise of demonic magic. They fast, macerate themselves, and observe chastity with the perverse motive of honoring demons. Likewise out of reverence for the demons, they dress themselves in black or in white garments.

We cannot assume that Eymericus was simply inventing these charges. When he says he has read the necromancers' books, we have no reason to suspect he is lying. Other orthodox writers such as John Gerson, who seems also to have been familiar with the genre, corroborate much of what he had to say, and a writer like Cecco d'Ascoli (burned for his errors in 1327) gives extensive information on demonic magic even when professing to condemn it. For better or for worse, some of this material survives. The Munich handbook is a prime example of the sort of document Eymericus dealt with. It contains a wealth of magical operations, which, following standard usage of the era, it refers to as "experiments." Similar or identical material can be found in other manuscripts as well, at least in fragmentary form. Eymericus confiscated such materials in Spain, and there is evidence for parallels at least in Italy, Germany, France, and England. William of Auvergne claimed that when he was a student at Paris in the early thirteenth century, he saw books apparently of this sort. An inquisitor in Italy had a book with "diabolical figures" reduced to ashes "so that from it another copy can never be made."[14] In 1277 the archbishop of Paris condemned "books, rolls, or booklets containing necromancy or experiments of sorcery, invocations of demons, or conjurations hazardous for souls."

The uses of necromancy were legion. One conjuration in the Munich handbook, for example, is intended to summon a demon who will impart unsurpassed mastery of all the arts and sciences without any effort on the part of the practitioner. What we have here is a necromantic version of the *Ars notoria*. In general, however, the aims of this magic fall into three main categories. First, it is used to affect other people's minds and wills: to drive them mad, to inflame them to love or hatred, to gain their favor, or to constrain them to do or not do some deed. It is not only human beings who can be thus constrained, but spirits and animals as well. While demonic magic is not often used to work bodily harm, it can lead to discomfort that is physical as well as mental. A twelfth-century manuscript in Reims, for example, has a conjuration calling upon the demons to afflict some victim so that he cannot sleep, eat, drink, or do anything else.[15] In all likelihood, however, the ultimate goal here, as in similar cases, is to afflict the victim as a means toward some further goal: to keep him from sleeping, eating, and so forth, until he fulfills the conjurer's will.

Secondly, the conjurer can create illusions. He can create the semblance of a boat or a horse which will take him wherever he wishes to go. He can conjure forth an extravagant feast with banqueting and entertainment. (When writers of fiction said that such illusions might be accomplished "by craft or by necromancy," they were not necessarily joking.) Equally illusory is the use of demonic agency to raise the dead:

---

[14] Brucker, "Sorcery in early Renaissance Florence," 18–19 (with translation of quotation).
[15] Robert-Léon Wagner, *"Sorcier" et "magicien": Contribution à l'histoire du vocabulaire de la magie* (Paris: Droz, 1939), 49 n. 2.

a consecrated ring, placed on the hand or foot of a corpse, will suffice to summon six demons in turn, each of whom will animate the body for one day so that it can rise up and speak. The same ring, put on the finger of a living person, will make him appear dead until it is removed.

The third main purpose of conjuring demons is to discern secret things, whether past, present, or future. The Munich handbook gives detailed instructions for divinatory magic, corresponding closely to the account given by John of Salisbury. There are formulas for finding stolen goods, for identifying a thief or a murderer, for discerning whether a friend is sick or well, on the road or elsewhere, and in general for obtaining knowledge of anything that is uncertain. The desired information is to be provided by spirits, who will appear to a virgin boy (or, exceptionally, a girl) in a crystal, on a mirror, on the blade of a sword, on the greased shoulder blade of a ram, or on the boy's fingernail. Alternatively, if the purpose is to identify thieves, the thieves themselves may appear in the reflecting surface. In one procedure there are guidelines for what the boy should say when a spirit in the form of a king appears in his fingernail: he should invite the spirit to dismount from his horse and bring a throne to sit on; he should ask if the spirit is hungry, and if so he should suggest sending for a ram to eat; when the king has dined, the boy should have him remove his crown, put his right hand on his head, and swear to tell the truth. A medieval reader would perhaps have found nothing comic in the notion of a young boy holding such discourse with a shadowy image in his fingernail. The prospect might instead arouse horror, fascination, or both. In another case, a conjuration is intended to obtain visions of "angels" in sleep, so they may impart knowledge of past, present, and future things.

While the techniques for demon-conjuring can become complex, they reduce to a few main elements: magic circles, conjurations, and sacrifices are the most striking elements in this magic.

Circles are so important in demonic magic that the circle could be construed as the preeminent sign of Lucifer, as the cross was the sign of Christ.[16] Magic circles might be traced on the ground with a sword or a knife, or else inscribed on a piece of parchment or cloth. Sometimes they are simple geometrical forms, with perhaps a few words or characters inscribed about the circumference. More often, however, they are complex, with inscriptions and symbols of various kinds inside, positions for various magical objects, and a designated place for "the master,"

---

[16] Pietro Delcorno, "'We have made it for learning': The fifteenth-century Florentine religious play *Lazero ricco e Lazero povero* as a sermon in the form of theatre," in Maria Giuseppina Muzzarelli, ed., *From Words to Deeds: The Effectiveness of Preaching in the Late Middle Ages* (Turnhout: Brepols, 2014), 70–1.

meaning the conjurer. Both the material to write on and the fluid to use as ink may be specified. The Munich manual has the practitioner writing an inscription with the blood of a "mouser" on a piece of linen, which is then to be buried near the house of one's victim. Another inscription is to be written with the blood of a hoopoe. Yet another is to be written "in the Hebrew manner," presumably meaning from right to left, with the blood of a bat. John Gerson speaks of virgin parchment and the skin of a lion as used for invoking demons, apparently as materials for magic circles.

One particularly interesting circle from a fifteenth-century magical miscellany has the basic form of a single band with a triangular band inscribed within it (Fig. 19). In the center, various objects are depicted: a sword, a ring, a vessel for oil, a scepter, and a square tablet with the Tetragrammaton and four crosses on it. Inscriptions within the triangular band give various holy names separated by crosses. In and near the circular band are magical characters, crosses, and words, such as the common magical word "AGLA" (which in late medieval texts was taken as standing for *Ata Gibor L'olam Adonai*, Hebrew for "Thou art mighty forever, O Lord").[17] One inscription outside the triangular bands says that this "figure of friendship" should be made at the hour of Venus, while another such inscription says that it is a "figure for the making of bridges and [discovery of] treasures." This is, then, a multipurpose circle, with purposes that vary and with alternative inscriptions (given at the bottom of the page) to be used accordingly.

The term "circle" should not be construed as referring primarily to the actual circular border or band, which seems to have been less important to the conjurers than the signs and inscriptions with which it was filled. While there is ample evidence in medieval Europe for the importance of circles as foci of magical power, the demonic magicians evidently conceived them mainly as enclosures within which various signs and objects might be contained. The circular bands served as places to put inscriptions, which usually consisted of names for God or snippets from Christian liturgy. One magical circle has fully five concentric bands, with formulas such as *Salue crux digna* ("Hail, O noble cross"), and a complex of crosses, stars, and other signs in its center.[18] As we will see, legends about the necromancers interpreted these circles as protective devices within which the magicians were safe from demons, and in some cases demon-conjurers themselves viewed them in this way; but the primary function of circles for demonic magic, as for astral and angelic magic, was to serve as one of the means for achieving magical power. One experiment in the Munich handbook

[17] Mesler, "The Latin encounter with Hebrew magic," 88.
[18] British Library, MS Sloane 3556, fol. 1ᵛ.

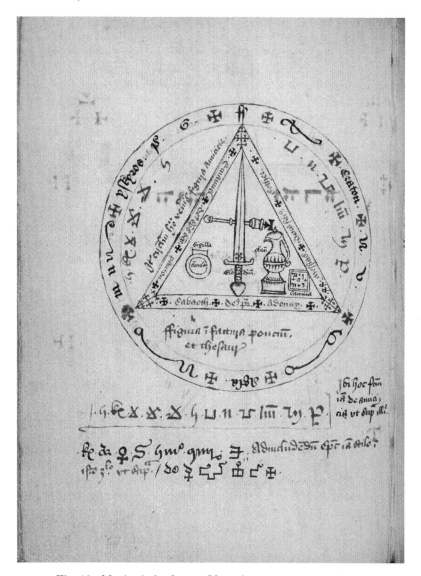

Fig. 19. Magic circle, from a fifteenth-century manuscript

expressly says that the demons will come, when invoked, *inside* the circle. In another case, in an experiment for love magic, the circle is a space within which the lovers can rendezvous, and the instruction says it is best if it has a wide circumference to allow them ample space. Apart from their conjuring and protective functions, magic circles may also be diagrams of the cosmos.[19] These various functions are not necessarily mutually exclusive: a circle can be a means for conjuring a spirit, for displaying symbols of the sacred powers by which the spirit is conjured, for indicating the structure of the cosmos from which the spirit is conjured, and at the same time for ensuring that the spirit comes in a nonthreatening form and manner.

If the circles given are inscribed on cloth or parchment, they may have powers other than conjuring demons. Thus, a circle intended primarily to summon a demon in the form of a horse may be used to protect its bearer from hostile horses, and if it is accompanied by the blood and tooth of a horse it will cause death to any horse that beholds it. A circle designed as part of a ceremony to resuscitate a dead person can be used for love magic, or for ascertaining whether a sick person will die, or for keeping dogs from barking. If they are traced on the ground, however, the circles are, so to speak, disposable. The Munich handbook is usually careful to instruct the practitioner when he should erase the circle, presumably so as to leave no evidence of his magic, though possibly also to prevent others from using it.

If the circle (taken as including both border and contents) is the main visual element in techniques for demonic magic, the conjuration is the key oral component. The conjuration usually revolves about one or another imperative verb for "command": the practitioner addresses the spirits with the order, "I adjure you" or "I conjure you" to appear and carry out some deed. Beyond this, the formula may be embellished in numerous ways. Standard Christian prayers are often mingled with conjurations to enhance their power: the Psalms, portions of the litany of the saints, and so forth. One experiment requires kneeling with folded hands, turning toward heaven, and confidently saying a "prayer" to "the most high and benign King of the East." The instructions sometimes say to repeat a conjuration three times, or seven times, or once in each of the four compass directions, or even four times in each of these directions.

Conjurations in the Munich handbook repeatedly instruct the spirits to appear in a pleasant, nonthreatening form. The accompanying text tells that when they do come it will be in the form of a king, a staff of servants, a band of sailors, a black man, or, above all, a knight. One fifteenth-century German manuscript now at Prague says that the Devil will come in the form of a black dog and will answer all questions.[20]

---

[19] Page, "Medieval magical figures," 442–51, discusses various forms of magical circle and related figures in ritual magic.

[20] Beckers, "Eine spätmittelalterliche deutsche Anleitung zur Teufelsbeschwörung mit Runenschriftverwendung."

Apart from the visual and oral elements in demonic magic, there were operative components: deeds that the magician performed, particularly sacrifices and sympathetic rituals. The Munich manual has the conjurer invoking the spirits at a crossroads with "the sacrifice of a white cock," which he beseeches them to accept. Another experiment requires taking a captive hoopoe along to the place of conjuration; at one stage in the proceedings the demons will ask for this bird, and when they have sworn to obey the magician he will give it to them. (Indeed, the Munich handbook says explicitly that the hoopoe "has great power for necromancers and invokers of demons" and is thus often used for their purposes. Albert the Great corroborates this testimony, reporting that the brain, tongue, and heart of the hoopoe are especially valuable for enchanters.) An early thirteenth-century conjuration in a manuscript now at Paris gives cryptic instructions which have been decoded and translated as, "Take a bat and sacrifice it with [your] right hand; with [your] left hand draw blood from [its] head."[21] It was widely believed that demons (like the ghosts of classical literature) can be enticed by blood, especially by human blood; thus, according to Michael Scot, necromancers often use water mixed with blood, or wine that resembles blood, "and they sacrifice with flesh or a living human being, such as a bit of their own flesh or of a corpse ... knowing that the consecration of a spirit in a ring or a bottle cannot be achieved except by the performance of many sacrifices."[22]

The sacrifice was thus usually of an animal, but sometimes other substances were offered to demons. The magician might be required to scatter milk and honey in the air, or to place ashes, flour, salt, and other items in jars which would be placed within the magic circle. The Prague manuscript tells the magician to offer coal, bread, cheese, three shoeing-nails, barley, and salt as "presents" for the demons.

When necromancy entails image magic it is usually sympathetic: the action carried out on the image is transferred to the person represented. Thus, love magic may involve writing the names of demons on an image of the intended person, so that these demons will afflict her until she submits to the practitioner's will. The demons symbolically represented on the image are to be really present in the woman. To gain favor from some dignitary, the magician carves an image of that person, bearing a crown if he is a king, or other symbols of power as the case demands.

[21] Marie-Thérèse d'Alverny, "Survivance de la magie antique," in Paul Wilpert, ed., *Antike und Orient im Mittelalter* (Berlin: de Gruyter, 1962), 159, 173.
[22] Thorndike, "Some medieval conceptions of magic," 123 (with translations of quotations).

Then he makes a second image to represent himself, and writes on these images the names of the persons represented. He binds a small iron chain to the neck of the potentate's image, places the other end of the chain in the hand of his own image, makes the image of the potentate bow before his own image, and so forth.

Often these sympathetic operations are accompanied by incantations explicating the gestures. If the conjurer is trying to arouse hatred between two friends he may heat two stones (representing the victims) over a fire, then cast them into frigid water, then strike them together. While so doing he will say, "I do not strike these stones, but I strike N. and N. whose names are written here." An experiment for love magic involves the formula, "as a hart longs for the fountain, so may N. long for my love, and as the raven longs for cadavers, so may she desire me, and as this wax melts before the fire, so may she desire my love."

Secrecy is vital to all these operations. The Munich handbook warns the practitioner at various points to keep the experiments secret because they have "great" or "ineffable power." Equally important is carrying out the experiments in a secret place, and guarding carefully the book "in which all power is contained." The *Book of Consecrations*, a text incorporated in the Munich handbook and found elsewhere as well, instructs its user to keep it carefully concealed so it does not fall into the hands of "the foolish."

If the magician wants to repeat an experiment, he may need to go through the original ceremony each time. In some cases, however, he may be able to make the demons swear the first time they appear that in the future they will come whenever called. He may have the demons "consecrate" some object, which will allow him to call them on subsequent occasions. A magic circle may itself be thus consecrated, or a bridle may be consecrated and then used to recall a spirit in the form of a horse.

The practitioner may also wish to undo the harm he has done, and this is easy enough if the original magic was accomplished through sympathetic operations that can be reversed. If stones have been buried to arouse hatred, friendship may be restored by digging up the stones, heating and crushing them, then casting the fragments into a river while saying, "May all enmity be removed ... by the mercy of the beneficent God, who does not respect the malice of sinners, amen." If a cloth with an inscription on it has been buried near a victim's house, the bewitchment may be undone by digging it up and burning it, then casting the ashes into a flowing stream. The effect may be guaranteed by reciting the formula, "Just as this fire consumes this cloth, so may all this work which I have done against N. be wholly consumed." The demons who have caused the damage may be released from this service, with words such as, "I, N., absolve you to go as you will."

One might well wonder what in fact happened when the conjurers of demons followed all these complicated instructions. Did the power of suggestion work upon their minds? Did demons appear? Did they try one or two experiments in vain and then give up? John of Salisbury's experience suggests a combination of results. Sometimes the magic would not work, in which case the magician or his assistant would simply abandon the effort, perhaps blaming the results on personal disqualification. At other times, the results would be persuasive enough to convince the believer that his belief was well-grounded. Most of the goals sought by this particular form of magic were in some way psychological and intangible, which would make it hard to prove that an experiment had utterly failed. If the magician tried to kill a person by magic and that person survived, the failure would be clear, but if the object was favor at court or enmity between friends, one could often point to apparent success, even if it was not dramatic.

The author of the Munich manual admits little possibility of failure and provides testimonials to the efficacy of his magic. He tells how an experiment for love magic was used by Solomon, who obtained any woman he desired by using it. After telling the various uses for a particular magic circle, he says that he has personally experienced all the effects he is describing, and he is leaving aside those he has not experienced. At another juncture he addresses a courtly reader, whether real or hypothetical: "You have often seen me carry out this work at your court." Stretching plausibility to breaking point, he tells how he once played a trick on the emperor and his nobles while they were out hunting. Summoning a band of demons, he had them attack the emperor as if they were human rebels, then erect an illusory castle in which the emperor could take refuge. The demons were in the process of besieging the castle when the time limit for this experiment ran out, whereupon rebels and castle all suddenly vanished, leaving the emperor and his men standing, perplexed, in a marsh.

In reading the necromancers' formulas, one may find oneself growing sympathetic toward the inquisitors who condemned all these works and pomp. The blasphemous use of ritual, the invocation of spirits for amoral or straightforwardly destructive purposes, the cruelty of their animal sacrifices, and the sheer megalomania of the conjurers can appear repulsive to modern as well as medieval eyes. These writings, however, do reveal certain things about the society that spawned them. The practitioners and the inquisitors alike believed in the awesome power of ritual. More specifically, they believed that by fulfilling certain outward and objective standards ritual could have automatic power. Inward disposition of the heart was not decisive; what counted most was the correct observance of outward forms. The host was effectively consecrated at mass, even if the priest was personally irreverent. So too, the necromancers believed, God could be effectively mocked and his power used for evil ends if the rituals of conjuration were correctly performed. Necromancy thus parodied the basic late medieval understanding of ritual.

The Sources for Demonic Magic

Necromancy is a blend of various practices, all incorporated into the framework of explicitly demonic magic. The sympathetic operations for sorcery, found in the common magical tradition without any overt appeal to demons, are here recast. Animals which appear elsewhere in magical lore, such as cats and hoopoes, here became sacrificial offerings to the demons. Divination using reflective surfaces (catoptromancy) becomes a means for conjuring evil spirits. Essentially, however, necromancy is a merger of astral magic and exorcism. The former is a foreign import, derived from Islamic culture; the latter is essentially a domestic product, long established within Christendom, though there is reason to suspect the influence of Jewish tradition in the development of this component. Even in early Christianity, forms for exorcism seem to have been molded according to Jewish practice; later Jewish influence shows especially in the reliance on holy names as forces to use against the demons.

The influence of astral magic shows quite clearly in the Munich handbook. The author comments after one experiment that all the Spanish, Arabic, Hebrew, Chaldean, Greek, and Latin "necromancers and astrologers" are agreed on its efficacy, and he cites books, evidently dealing with astral magic, from which it is taken. Experiments recommended in this manual are to be performed at fixed times: on a Saturday before sunrise and under a waning Moon, on a Thursday under a waxing Moon, at the first hour of a Wednesday under a waxing Moon, under a new Moon, and so forth. Most importantly, the boundary between astral and elemental spirits on the one hand and fallen angels on the other becomes confused, and necromancers appeal at times to one sort of spirit, at times to another. Michael Scot says that astrological images can serve to conjure not only the powers that rule the planetary orbits and demons associated with the Moon, but also the damned spirits present in the wind. There is much justice, therefore, to John Gerson's complaint that astrology, a handmaid of theology and "a noble and wonderful science, revealed to Adam," has been "disfigured by vain observances, impious errors, sacrilegious superstitions."

The practice of fumigation, common in astral magic, was taken over into demonic magic. The ceremonies often require fumigating an image with the fumes of myrrh and saffron, fumigating a circle with the marrow of a dead man, fumigating a circle with frankincense and myrrh, or fumigating a divinatory mirror with aloes, ambergris, myrrh, and frankincense. One list of fumigations in the Munich handbook gives a special formula for each day of the week, correlated with some particular purpose. On Thursday, for example, one burns frankincense or saffron to bring concord between enemies. Also perhaps borrowed from the tradition of astral magic is the practice of burying images. An experiment to gain favor with a potentate calls for carrying his image secretly throughout town, and if possible going into his very presence with the image secretly on one's person; then one should bury the image, "and you will see wonders." The details of this operation parallel closely those found, for example, in *Picatrix*.[23] So, too, one can find precedent in astral magic even for animal sacrifices to spirits.

It would be wrong to conclude, however, that necromancy is simply an extension of astral magic, with the demonic element in this magic made overt rather than merely implicit. Equally important is the other side of demonic magic, its link with exorcism. We saw in Chapter 4 that the adjurations of the common magical tradition are difficult to distinguish from exorcisms. Ordinarily, however, the healer or exorcist is trying to dispel the demons or the diseases they cause. The healer or exorcist conquers the demons, calling upon all the supernatural aid he can muster, and reminding the evil spirits that God's power is greater than theirs and is now being used against them. Necromancers use the same formulas with very different intent. Orthodox exorcists and those conjuring demons both use the terms "exorcise," "conjure," and "adjure" interchangeably. The Munich handbook, for example, regularly uses the formulas, "I exorcise and conjure you," or "I invoke and conjure and exorcise and constrain you." The *Book of Consecrations* explicitly speaks of the necromancer as an exorcist. The difference, of course, is that while the orthodox exorcist is struggling to dispel demons, the necromancer is trying to allure and use them for his ends. One lengthy conjuration contained

---

[23] *Picatrix* (discussed in Chapter 6) even refers to its magic several times as "necromancy," though most of it falls more clearly into the closely related area of astral magic; the distinction may work better for Latin than for Arabic texts.

in the Munich handbook is clearly adapted from an exorcism; this provenance shows, for example, in the following passage:

I command you, O most wicked dragon, by the power of the Lord, [and] I adjure you in the name of the Lamb without blemish who walks on the asp and the basilisk, and who has trampled the lion and the dragon; may you carry out quickly whatever I command. Tremble and fear when the name of God is invoked, the God whom hell fears and to whom the virtues of heaven, the powers, dominations, and other virtues are subject and whom they fear and adore, and whom cherubim and seraphim praise with untiring voices. The Word made flesh commands you. He who was born of a virgin commands you. Jesus of Nazareth, who created you, commands you, to fulfill at once all that I ask of you, or all that I wish to have or to know. For the longer you delay in doing what I command or order, the more your punishment will increase from day to day. I exorcise you, O accursed and lying spirit, by the words of truth.

The vocabulary of exorcism is all familiar, though the formula is obviously altered: instead of commanding the evil spirit to depart, the necromancer calls on him to serve.

Like the exorcist, the demonic magician routinely commands the demons by the power of holy persons, names, events, and objects. The early thirteenth-century conjuration mentioned above includes the formula: "I conjure you by the Father and the Son and the Holy Spirit, by Mary the mother of the Lord, by Mary Magdalene, and Mary [the mother] of James, and Salome" (Mark 16:1). Elsewhere the demons are adjured by the Trinity (perhaps the most common source of power), by God in his capacity as creator, by Christ as the Word by whom God created, or by Christ in his function as judge on the last day. The power of the saints in heaven and the Church militant of Earth can be called into service. Even the hierarchy of demonic spirits in hell can be called upon to constrain the demons whose presence is desired. "Tetragrammaton," a term for the unspoken name of God, appears routinely as if it were itself one of his names. The formulas may cite the ineffable names of the creator "at which all things in heaven, on Earth, and beneath the Earth tremble." Various names of Christ are used, including Ely, Sother, Adonay, Sabaoth, Alpha and Omega. And names of spirits may be used to constrain other spirits: one conjuration lists thirty-three names of "angels who are powerful in the air." Events of the Old and New Testaments are often included; one conjuration gives a precis of the Old Testament that runs to one and a half folios. Demons are made to quake by being reminded of the coming of Christ and the sentence they will hear at the Last Judgment. Among the objects whose power gets co-opted are the Sun and Moon; the heavens and Earth; all animals, creeping things, and flying things, whether bipeds, tripeds(!), or quadrupeds;

the wounds of Christ and the crown of thorns; all the characters of Solomon and the magical experiments of Virgil(!). In short, the demons are told that they have marshaled against them "all things which have power to terrify and constrain you." In all of this, the conjurations are following the spirit – and often the letter – of orthodox exorcism.

The stance of the conjurer, like that of the exorcist, is at the same time both coercive and petitionary: he commands the demons, but only by such power as is granted to him by God. In one fictional account a magician boasts that he has divine power and can summon the Devil "by a single word of command," but he is reminded that it is not by his own power, but by "the power with which God has imbued the words" that he is able to conjure.[24] The necromancers clearly did see themselves as constraining the demons by their commands. This claim provoked writers such as Arnold of Villanova and John of Frankfurt to retort that demons could not be coerced, and that if they came at all when summoned they came voluntarily, though they might persuade the magicians that they were constrained so as to ensnare them more effectively. What these writers could not accept was the notion that God would aid the necromancers in this process. The magicians' own stance vis-à-vis God was, in any case, different from their stance toward demons. This is quite clear in the *Book of Consecrations*, where the "exorcist" presents himself as a humble and unworthy supplicant before God, beseeching divine aid to attain power over demons. The same mentality is at least implied elsewhere, since the conjurer constantly uses orthodox prayers, both on the magic circles and in the conjurations themselves, in an effort to co-opt the divine power for his own ends.

Why God should consent to this use of his power is obscure. One possibility is that the necromancers held an amoral conception of God, as a being who could be influenced (if not coerced) by prayer to bestow his aid in all sorts of dubious enterprises. Alternatively, the conjurers may have persuaded themselves that their causes were in fact holy: that if they were destroying their enemies, they were righteous in so doing; that if they sought hidden treasures, they would use them only for noble purposes; and that if they won the love of married women, God would at least wink at their misconduct, even if he did not smile.[25]

---

[24] Nigel Bryant, trans., *Perceforest: The Prehistory of King Arthur's Britain* (Woodbridge: Brewer, 2011), 21, 339.

[25] See now Frank Klaassen, *The Magic of Rogues: Necromancers in Early Tudor Magic* (University Park: Pennsylvania State University Press, 2021), for a case of necromantic treasure-hunting.

Like manuals of orthodox exorcism, the books of demonic magic insist on ascetic preparation and ritual purity (if not moral integrity) as prerequisites for commanding the demons. The experiments call upon the magician to fast, to be bathed and shaven, to be dressed in white, and so forth. The conjurer is sometimes instructed to abstain from sexual contact for a certain number of days before performing an experiment; although orthodox exorcists were supposed to be celibate clerics, committed to permanent rather than temporary chastity, late medieval books of exorcism sometimes impose precisely the same restriction.[26] These ascetic procedures may be intended not simply to entice demons, but also, and perhaps more importantly, to protect the magician from the demons. Cecco d'Ascoli remarks that these conjurations require prayer and fasting precisely because of their "great peril." It would be naive, of course, to expect orthodox writers to approve of these practices. According to Gerson, the practitioners of these arts only compound their guilt by performing actions that are in themselves holy: their deeds are all the worse because they thus debase these observances.

More often than not, conjurers were quite unambiguous about the kind of spirits they were invoking. The Munich manual speaks of constraining "malign spirits," "airy powers and infernal princes," or simply "demons." The Reims conjuration says explicitly, "I conjure you, O devils who fell from heaven ... I conjure you, who in hell adore Beelzebut as your worthy prince." The Munich handbook and the Paris manuscript, too, invoke Satan, Beelzebub, and Lucifer, and other spirits of unmistakable identity, such as the demon Berich. The Prague manuscript gives a relatively simple formula: the magician should go out into the fields at night and cry out, "Diabolo diaboliczo, Satana sathaniczo, come here to me, I wish to speak to you, and take the presents that I have brought you." The use of ordinary names for the Devil, along with the general simplicity of the instructions, has prompted the editor of this text to suggest that it reflects folklore rather than learned tradition. Even when it is more clearly learned and clerical, however, demonic magic often incorporates elements of common folklore.

If necromancy is essentially a blend of astral magic and exorcism, however, it is not surprising to find occasional ambiguity about the spirits who are invoked. Some sources speak of neutral spirits, whether astral (associated with the heavenly bodies) or elemental (connected with natural powers on Earth). The Munich handbook says at one point that the spirits who come as sailors and transport the magician in an illusory

---

[26] Adolph Franz, *Die kirchlichen Benediktionen im Mittelalter*, vol. 2 (Freiburg im Breisgau: Herder, 1909), 567 n. 4.

boat are "between good and evil, neither in hell nor in paradise." Cecco d'Ascoli gives Oriens, Amaymon, Paymon, and Egim as the names of spirits who rule over the four compass directions and have legions of subordinate spirits at their service. One passage in the Munich manual suggests that good spirits should be invoked for good purposes, and evil spirits for wicked ones, but things are not always so simple: both kinds of spirit are invoked for purposes that are moral, immoral, or simply amoral.

Did genuinely benign spirits appear, or were they evil demons posing as angels of light? One orthodox test for the status of an angel was whether its name was traditional. The only good angels with names officially recognized are Gabriel, Michael, and Raphael. As early as the eighth century, when a priest supplicated the angels Uriel, Raguel, Tubuel, Adin, Tubuas, Sabaok, and Simiel, the bishops of his region condemned his prayer because the names were unfamiliar, which suggested to them, as to even earlier authorities, that these angels were in fact fallen.[27]

Attitudes toward even explicitly evil spirits might vary. The Munich manual tells the practitioner at one point that when the demons come he should greet them with a pious wish: "May the Lord in his mercy restore you to your former state," presumably meaning their condition as unfallen angels. Even a writer on the border of orthodoxy, however, would normally be cautious. Cecco d'Ascoli tells that Floron was from among the Cherubim, that he knew numerous secrets of nature, that he had been captivated within a mirror, but had deceived many by his ambiguous oracles. "So beware of these demons, because their ultimate intention is to deceive Christians to the discredit of our Lord Jesus Christ."[28]

Among the writings of the necromancers are catalogues of spirits with their forms, powers, and attributes. One fifteenth-century French manuscript, for example, lists Bulfas, a great prince whose function is to arouse discord and battles; Gemer, a great king who teaches people the virtues of herbs and all sciences, and both heals and inflicts diseases; Machin, who teaches the virtues of herbs and of gems, and transports the "master" from one region to another; and other spirits.[29] In the light of this material, it is not surprising that critics of magic should see even herbal lore as something taught by demons: the magicians themselves held this view.

[27] Aron Gurevich, *Medieval Popular Culture: Problems of Belief and Perception*, trans. János M. Bak and Paul A. Hollingsworth (Cambridge University Press, 1988), 66–7.

[28] Thorndike, "Some medieval conceptions of magic," 125.

[29] Trinity College, Cambridge, MS 0.8.29, fols. 179ᵛ–182ᵛ.

Further wrinkles in the complex mentality of the necromancers are suggested by a fifteenth-century manuscript that gives instructions for love magic. The heading reads, "Experiments which King Solomon devised for the love and courting of a certain noble queen, and they are experiments of nature." What follows is a list of magic tricks; presumably Solomon is supposed to have used these to entertain his beloved. He tells how to make a hollow ring leap and run through the house, how to carry fire in your shirt or hands, how to cause a person to strip, how to make a great flame explode in the face of a companion, and so forth. All these tricks are presumably meant as ways to a woman's heart. At the very end, however, the "experiments" abruptly change their tone and character; if up to this point they have been "experiments of nature," the last of them hardly qualifies for this description. It tells how to make a lead ring on the day and at the hour when Venus is dominant. After making the ring, one should fast through the day, then go out at night and offer sacrifice with the blood of a dove. Writing with this blood on the skin of a hare, one should inscribe the name and sign of the "angel" Abamixtra. After this ceremony has been carried out, one should approach the desired woman with ring in hand, and she will obey one's every wish. Certain key words in the instruction are given in cipher, but not enough to obscure the sense.[30]

The most perplexing feature of this text is its mixture of apparently playful tricks and seemingly serious necromancy. Was the author in fact a serious proponent of demonic magic, trying to disguise his mischief under a cloak of levity? Or was he rather a mere prankster using a necromantic formula as the mysterious climax to an essentially playful collection? The most plausible answer, perhaps, is a combination of the two: the same man could have different moods, and his magic could have different modes. It is not unlikely that people attracted to one form of magic would at least dabble in others as well.

Demonic Magic in the *Exempla*

The Pilgrimage of the Life of Man, an allegorical poem by Guillaume de Deguilleville (d. after 1358) translated into Middle English by John Lydgate (ca. 1370–1449), contains an episode in which the Pilgrim encounters a messenger of Necromancy. The messenger tells how his mistress, Necromancy, runs a school for scholars such as himself. Only

---

[30] British Library, MS Sloane 121, fols. 90ᵛ–93ᵛ. The words in cipher are *mxlkerem* and *xolkntbtem*, for *mulierem* and *volintatem* (*sic*). The name of the angel may be "Abanuxtra," but "Abamixtra" seems the more likely reading.

Fig. 20. The Pilgrim encountering a student of Necromancy, from Lydgate, *The Pilgrimage of the Life of Man*

those sent by Covetousness enter that school. What the scholars learn is how to invoke spirits and make them answer questions and obey commands. This power comes ultimately from the great King, namely God. The messenger demonstrates by tracing a circle on the ground, with characters and figures (Fig. 20). Previous scholars in this academy, he says, include many luminaries: Solomon, Virgil, Cyprian, and Abelard. The Pilgrim protests: surely Solomon and Cyprian repented before death! And surely these arts are diabolical and damnable. The messenger, however, remains unpersuaded, and the Pilgrim is lucky to escape without being destroyed by Necromancy herself.

The identity of the messenger in this story is unclear. While he is not explicitly spoken of in the text as a cleric, he is essentially a scholar, and what he gains from his mistress is a kind of learning. Necromancy herself, as a schoolmistress, carries a book entitled *The Death of the Soul*; this is not simply an allegorical motif, but the actual title of a medieval book of necromancy. Yet the image of the messenger probably comes rather from the tradition of sermon *exempla* than from any other source.

Preachers struggling to dissuade their congregations from sin often made their argument by telling edifying *exempla* or anecdotes, and among these stories are certain influential legends about magicians. The prototype of these tales is the legend of Theophilus, who is supposed to have learned from a Jewish sorcerer how to make a pact with the Devil by renouncing Christ and giving a written document to the Evil One. Later he regretted this deed, but was unable to recover his pact until he prayed to the Virgin and secured her intercession. The original version of this legend comes from sixth-century Asia Minor, and in Latin it was retold in numerous variations, which served much later as a basis for the story of Faust.[31]

Caesarius of Heisterbach (ca. 1180–1240), a Cistercian monk, gave several pertinent *exempla* in his *Dialogue on Miracles*. In one of these, a knight who does not believe in demons nonetheless challenges a cleric "famous for his skill in necromancy" to conjure some fiends and thus overcome his disbelief. After some protestation, the cleric takes the knight to a crossroads, traces a circle in the dirt, and warns that to protect himself from the demons the knight must stand inside the circle. When the demons come, they try to terrify the knight with howling wind, grunting swine, and other means. Finally, the Devil himself comes as a terrifying phantom, towering over the trees, cloaked in a dark robe. The Fiend represents himself as a useful servant of his friends, including the cleric who has summoned him. He accurately recounts the knight's sins, thus proving that no evil is hidden from him. Repeatedly he makes requests, all of which the knight refuses. Finally, he stretches out his arm as if to snatch the knight and haul him away. Terrified, the knight cries out, and the cleric comes rushing to his aid, whereupon the Devil vanishes. For the rest of his life, the knight has a deathly pale complexion and is scrupulously moral.[32]

This tale contains three motifs that are common in these necromantic *exempla*. First, the circle is clearly seen as a protective enclosure. Caesarius elsewhere tells of a priest who steps outside the circle and is attacked so viciously by the Devil that he soon dies, and in yet another *exemplum*, a magician's client rushes from the circle in pursuit of a

---

[31] Jerry Root, *The Theophilus Legend in Medieval Text and Image* (Cambridge: Brewer, 2017).

[32] Caesarius of Heisterbach, *The Dialogue on Miracles*, trans. H. von E. Scott and C. C. Swinton Bland, vol. 1 (London: Routledge, 1929), 315–17 and see 317–20.

beautiful woman, only to have his neck wrung like that of a hen being slaughtered.[33] This recurrent motif may be, at least in part, a way of dramatizing the precarious situation of those who dabble in necromancy: a way of saying, in effect, that one step in any wrong direction will lead to imminent perdition.

Secondly, the Fiend himself is shown as a lying and untrustworthy servant. This theme is nicely reflected in an *exemplum* told by John of Frankfurt about a bishop who gave himself over to a demon in exchange for honors, but who made many enemies. One day, these foes were attacking his castle and he consulted his demon to see if he should flee. The demon told him, "Don't! Stay put! Your enemies will come forth meekly and will be subject to you." Inspired to false confidence, the bishop stayed, his castle was captured, and he was burned for his offenses. Before he expired, however, the demon explained that his Latin could be differently construed as, "Don't stay put! Your enemies will come thrice in strength and will set fire beneath you."[34] Could the demon help it if the bishop had misunderstood? Another demon told a man he would discover treasure that he could keep until his death, but when the man found the treasure in a cavern, it collapsed and crushed him to death.[35] The moral could apply to necromancers and ordinary folk alike: he who trusts a demon deserves the consequences.

The third theme is the possibility of repentance. All good preachers know the principle of first arousing fear and then proffering hope. In another of his *exempla*, Caesarius tells of a student who does homage to the Devil merely by holding onto a stone that the Fiend gave him, in return for academic eminence. Fearing for his soul, however, the student throws away the stone and loses all his ill-gotten knowledge, but does save his soul. In yet another case, set in Toledo, a necromancer's pupil even gets dragged down into hell, and the master has to retrieve him through subtle negotiation with the Devil. Restored to life, the pupil leaves Toledo and atones for his sins as a Cistercian monk.

These tales must have been effective propaganda and must have done much to arouse fear of demonic magic in the preachers' congregations. But the question must surely have occurred, "What does all this have to do with us?" Most of the evidence suggests that the legends were right in showing the necromancers as clerics: few laypeople would have had the

---

[33] D. L. d'Avray, *The Preaching of the Friars: Sermons Diffused from Paris before 1300* (Oxford: Clarendon, 1985), 198–202.

[34] The first version is *Non, sta secure, venient inimici tui suaviter et subdentur tibi*; the second is *Non sta secure, venient inimici tui sua vi ter, et subdent ur tibi*. Hansen, *Quellen und Untersuchungen*, 79.

[35] Weill-Parot, "Cecco Ascoli and Antonio da Montolmo," 227.

command of Latin and of ritual necessary to work the "experiments" contained in the Munich handbook and other such sources. When they heard and repeated these stories, however, laypeople must have wondered whether other magicians as well were engaged in explicitly demonic magic. If even clerics could be guilty of such transgression, what of the old woman or the village leech who used odd herbal remedies and superstitious charms? Perhaps they, too, were practicing necromancy? The historian may venture a cautious negative answer to this question, but contemporaries were not always so generous.

9 Prohibition, Condemnation, and Prosecution

There were many reasons for opposing magic. Those who practiced it were in danger of physical and spiritual assault from the wily demons they sought to master. Even in its apparently innocent and entertaining forms it was, at best, frivolous and vain. It could involve presumptuous encroachment on the mysteries and creative powers of God. It involved erroneous assumptions about the demons, their power, and their dignity. All these arguments occur in medieval discussion of magic. In legislation, the central concern was fairly simple: magic can do grievous harm to other people. In moral and theological condemnations there were two further grounds for opposing magic: it may rely on demons even when it seems to use natural forces, and it makes sacrilegious use of holy objects or blasphemously mingles holy with unholy words. These anxieties may seem difficult to share in an age that widely professes disbelief in both religion and magic, but simply to understand the historical record we must be able to grasp what a threat magic represented in an age when its power was almost universally taken for granted.

It is perhaps misleading to distinguish between moral and theological condemnation on the one hand and legal prosecution on the other. When moralists condemned magic, they often cited legal enactments to show that it was immoral, and legislation always presupposed a moral stance. This interpenetration of the moral and the legal is effectively suggested by a German woodcut of 1487 warning against sorcery (Fig. 21). A witch in the center has demons around her and a bottle, presumably filled with a potion, in her hand. In separate circles are various authorities who had condemned magic, or whose words or experience served to warn against it: King Saul, the Apostle Paul, Isaiah, Pope John XXII, an emperor, St. Augustine, and the theologians of Paris; the circle on the bottom has a picture of the Devil himself, with an open book. The text below gives pertinent quotations from or about

Fig. 21. Fifteenth-century woodcut: warning against sorcery

each of these figures.[1] Legal prohibitions and moral condemnations are mixed at random in this effort to show that all authorities are united against sorcery.

While the two approaches thus go hand in hand, it may be useful to deal first with the legal prohibitions, which were developed early and then endlessly repeated, and which were relatively simple and straightforward in their contents. Then we can turn to the more elaborate statements of moral condemnation, for which more of our evidence comes from the later Middle Ages.[2]

Legal Prohibition

In principle, there were two kinds of legislation against magic: that of the secular authorities, such as emperors, kings, and town governments; and that of the Church, which continued through the Middle Ages to enact canons binding on clergy and laity.[3] Secular law could prescribe any of various penalties, including execution, for the crime of magic, but it was usually more concerned with the harm worked by magic than with the magical ceremonies themselves. The Church could require penance for the sin of magic or could excommunicate the offender, and was usually concerned with the offense against God as much as with any harm done to human victims. Yet this distinction, helpful as an index to general trends, breaks down at various points. Many secular rulers in the Middle Ages were under the influence of churchmen and issued laws clearly reflecting clerical concerns. Indeed, there were times when ecclesiastical legislation was taken over into secular codes. The distinction is thus real, but not absolute.

Early medieval law codes of the various Germanic peoples typically included strictures against harmful magic. A sixth-century code of the Visigoths, for example, refers to sorcerers who travel about and get paid by peasants for putting curses on their enemies' crops and animals. The same law code refers to sorcerers who arouse destructive tempests.

---

[1] See Paul Kristeller, ed., *Holzschnitte im Königl. Kupferstichkabinett zu Berlin*, ser. 2 (Berlin: Cassirer, 1915), 36–7. The quotations are from 1 Chronicles 10:13, 1 Corinthians 10:20, Isaiah 47:11–12, John XXII's *Super illius specula*, an imperial statute, the writings of Augustine, the condemnation of magic issued in 1398 by the theologians at the University of Paris, and Ecclesiasticus 13.

[2] For anti-magical writings generally, see Alan Charles Kors and Edward Peters, eds., *Witchcraft in Europe, 400–1700: A Documentary History*, 2nd edn (Philadelphia: University of Pennsylvania Press, 2001), 41–229.

[3] For this and following sections, Joseph Hansen, *Zauberwahn, Inquisition und Hexenprozess im Mittelalter, und die Entstehung der grossen Hexenverfolgung* (Munich: Oldenbourg, 1900), is still useful.

It seems to have made little difference whether the harm was done by magic or purely natural means; some of the codes deal with poisoning and harmful magic in close association with each other, as if there were little difference. Lawgivers under clerical influence sometimes showed religious concerns: the Ostrogothic king Theodoric (reg. 493–526), for instance, threatened death for conjurers because they were dealing with pagan gods, and the sixth-century Visigothic code proclaimed that sorcery could not bring about a person's death if it did not involve idolatry. In effect, the authors of these codes were (like many churchmen) assimilating natural magic to demonic magic.

Some of the strongest secular legislation against magic in early medieval Europe was that of Charles the Great. In a capitulary for the newly conquered Saxons, he declared that all those found guilty of sorcery or divination should be turned over to the Church as slaves, while those who sacrificed to the Devil (i.e. to Germanic gods) should be killed. In his *General Admonition* for his kingdom in 789, Charles included provisions against enchanters and other magicians; these measures were taken over from the early church canons sent to him for his enforcement by Pope Hadrian. Here Charles appealed explicitly to the strict prohibition of Moses against sorcery.

Later rulers could build on these early prohibitions, but they seldom did much to develop them. King Roger II of Sicily (reg. 1112–54) prescribed execution for anyone using poisons, presumably whether natural or magical, and indicated in vague terms that love magic should be punished even if no one was hurt: an indication that magic was evil in itself, apart from its potential harm to others. More often, however, the concern of secular rulers was with the actual damage rather than with the means for inflicting it.

Within the ecclesiastical tradition it is difficult to distinguish sharply between legal and penitential practice. The penitentials, which we have already discussed, were handbooks for priests to use in confession. The penances prescribed might be harsh: one such manual requires three years of fasting on bread and water, then four years of lighter penance, for using magic to kill a person or to raise storms. In principle, the system was voluntary. The penitent submitted to the priest and willingly accepted the penance. Yet some penitentials include synodal canons amid their guidelines, which suggests that there was no rigid distinction between legislation and penitential norms.

Specific procedures would vary from one jurisdiction to another, but the general outlines of ecclesiastical hearings are clear from instructions issued in 800 at a synod in Freising. This document specifies that when people have been charged with incantation, divination, weather magic, or other sorcery and have been captured, the archpriest of the diocese should subject them to thorough examination in the hope of eliciting a confession. If necessary they should be tortured, though not to the point of jeopardizing their lives; they should be kept in prison until they resolve to do penance for their sins. By no means should they be released merely after paying compensation, without a formal inquiry.[4]

It might have occurred to churchmen and secular authorities alike that all their legislation was doing little to curb the exercise of magic. One senses more than slight frustration in the complaint of the bishops at a Synod of Pavia in 850 that the magical arts still flourished, that sorcerers were still arousing passionate love and hatred by magical means, and that they even killed people by magic. These evildoers were subject to the strictest penance and should be readmitted to the Church only on their deathbeds. The exasperation only increased in later medieval centuries, when university-educated clergy sought to reform popular practice and impose their conception of pure religion on what they saw as the superstitious mass of uneducated Christendom.

Apart from legislation proper, in high and late medieval Europe there were legal commentaries and consultations that further developed the concepts of magic. The legal profession gained new sophistication when universities began teaching law in the high Middle Ages, and one result was detailed reflection on the principles underlying prosecution for magic. The jurist Oldradus de Ponte gave a legal opinion around 1325 about a man who had been condemned as a heretic for giving a woman a love potion. Drawing on canon law, Roman law, and theology, Oldradus argues that it does savor of heresy when a person conjures demons, offers sacrifice to them, and seeks to learn about the future from them, because God alone knows the future. But it is the Devil's nature to be a tempter, so calling on him to tempt a woman may be a serious sin, but it is not heresy. It is also relevant whether the magician simply commands a demon to give assistance (which is not heresy) or pays adoration to him to obtain that service (which is).[5] The significance of Oldradus' opinion for our purposes is that it shows a sense of caution about legal norms and the grounds for legal action. As trials for magic increased in the later Middle Ages, there was little real change in the laws

---

[4] See now Hubert Mordek and Michael Glatthaar, "Von Wahrsagerinnen und Zauberern: Ein Beitrag zur Religionspolitik Karls des Großen," *Archiv für Kulturgeschichte*, 75 (1993), 33–64, especially 41–3.

[5] Hansen, *Quellen und Untersuchungen*, 55–9. The name "de Ponte" is now standard in the literature.

against magic, but a great deal of development in these guidelines for prosecution.

Moral and Theological Condemnation

A story was told about a bishop who preached against the folly of using charms. To give an idea of what he had in mind, he recited a simple charm, saying it was as worthless as others of its kind. But an old woman in the congregation, hearing the charm, began using it and gained a reputation for her healing practice. The bishop found out about that woman and cited her as a heretic and corrupter of the faith, but she replied that she knew only one charm, and it was the one he himself had taught.[6] The problem was familiar to moralists: if you are too clear about what you are condemning, you are likely to give people ideas.

Preachers and other moralists had condemned magic in late antiquity, and they still found it necessary to do so even in the late Middle Ages.[7] The problem was perennial, and so was the campaign against it. When Franciscan and Dominican friars emerged as popular preachers in the thirteenth century, condemnation of magic was one of the staple topics in their sermons. The Franciscan preacher Bernardino of Siena (d. 1444) found a moral wasteland all around him: people used incantations to cure disease and divination to explore the future, they deceived their fellow mortals with magical illusions, and in short they devoted themselves more to superstitious than to pious observance. In their campaign against such things, Bernardino and other preachers were perhaps no more and no less successful than in their war against drunkenness, adultery, and gambling.[8]

While preachers would usually restrict themselves to preaching, they might, on occasion, take direct action. Bernardino's biographer tells how he gathered and burned a great heap of magical paraphernalia, including medicaments over which magical incantations had been sung, and writings with signs and characters evidently referring to demons. On another occasion, Bernardino attacked yet another form of popular "idolatry." He discovered that people in one location were taking their children out to a spring for purification, "like a new kind of baptism," and with these and other rites they paid veneration to the Devil.

---

[6] Hilka, "Altfranzösische Zaubersprüche," 460–1.

[7] See now Rider, *Magic and Religion*; and Kathleen Kamerick, "Pastoral literature and preaching," in Page and Rider, *Routledge History*, 475–86.

[8] See now Franco Mormando, *The Preacher's Demons: Bernardino of Siena and the Social Underworld of Early Renaissance Italy* (University of Chicago Press, 1999).

He aroused his congregation's fury over this custom, and they joined him, with crosses in hand, as he marched out to this place and destroyed a shelter that had been erected there.

Preachers and authors like Bernardino seldom made fine distinctions; they were more inclined to conflate subjects that we might consider quite distinct. An author might begin by condemning astrology and divination, then proceed to the folly of those women who believed they rode about at night with Diana, then attack the practice of singing the requiem mass to cause someone to die faster, then move on to a general diatribe against the Egyptian days and other superstitious observances, charms and inscriptions to enhance the power of herbs, and so forth, all in a discussion of "constellations."[9] So, too, in *The Pilgrimage of the Life of Man*, the allegorical figure Sorcery carries magical writings and images, herbs gathered under specific constellations, ointments, a hand (representing chiromancy), and assorted other appurtenances. All such things were patently the Devil's work.

The central underlying concern of the moralists was, in any case, the possibility that magic might be demonic even when it seemed innocent. It was easy enough for most Christians to agree that demonic magic was immoral; the difficulty was in telling whether a particular practice did or did not involve appeal to demons. One of the most common tests was whether it contained unintelligible words that might in fact be invocations of demons in some unknown tongue, or strange names that might be names for demons. The *Malleus maleficarum*, the most famous of late medieval treatises on witchcraft, conveys this widely shared fear when it warns that charms must not contain explicit or implicit invocation of demons, such as reference to "unknown names."

Later medieval writers with any theological savvy tried to puzzle out precisely which forms of magic *could* be natural, and which *must* be demonic.[10] They endeavored to work out the boundaries between natural and demonic magic. What is noteworthy is how much power they were willing to concede to the occult powers in nature, without positing demonic intervention. Certain thirteenth-century and later writers recognized that the evil eye (or "fascination") might work in natural ways. Some, relying on Arabic sources, explained this phenomenon by arguing that the human soul can in many ways affect other persons: the soul is superior to the body, and has power over its own body and other people's

---

[9] Jacobus, *Omne bonum*, British Library, MS Royal 6.E.VI, fols. 396ᵛ–397ᵛ; cf. British Library, MS Harley 275, fols. 149ʳ–153ʳ.

[10] See now David J. Collins, "Scholastic and high medieval opposition to magic," in Page and Rider, *Routledge History*, 461–74.

as well. Indeed, some held that the soul even has power to change inanimate matter, to cause fire, and so forth. Roger Bacon, appealing to the authority of ancient Greek writers, told how "a menstruous woman looking in a mirror infects it and causes a cloud of blood to appear in it," and how certain women with double pupils can kill men with a glance. So, too, individuals with infirm bodies and souls corrupted with sin can cause evil by their mere thought, if they have a vehement desire to harm others. Bacon even speculated that "infectious emanations" might be projected mechanically, as when Alexander the Great, instructed by Aristotle, managed to catapult the infection of a basilisk over the walls of a city he was besieging.

Powerful, awesome, and mysterious as nature might be, however, the theologians and philosophers were not willing to see all magic as natural. Even in granting the possibilities of natural effect, they often tended (like Augustine) to suspect that demons were somehow involved. Thomas Aquinas dealt with these matters at some length in his *Summa Against the Gentiles*. He did not deny that some magic works through the powers of heavenly bodies, but denied that all of it works thus. Magicians may note the positions of the stars, and may prepare their herbs to receive astral influences, thus giving the impression that they rely on these alone. But some of the things they do involve consultation of rational beings, such as ascertaining the presence of stolen property. Magicians sometimes even summon apparitions and speak with them, and these figures divulge information surpassing normal knowledge. The heavenly bodies cannot do these things. Nor can they unlock doors, make people invisible, or cause inanimate things to move or speak. When magicians use invocations and adjurations, and write characters and figures, they are clearly addressing intelligent beings. Since the magicians often use these arts for evil purposes, one can scarcely believe that these beings are anything but demons.[11] For the moralists, it was these cautionary words that were relevant, more than any speculation about how magic might be worked through natural processes.

From the early centuries of Christianity, churchmen warned about the dangers of deliberately or inadvertently invoking demons. Toward the end of the Middle Ages, when fear of magic grew all the more intense, the warnings multiplied. Women who place magical objects beneath the threshold of a house to work their bewitchment, or who utter some curse over an apple, are making offerings and paying homage to the demons who carry out mischief on their behalf. Women and men who perform

---

[11] Thomas Aquinas, *Summa contra gentiles*, iii.104–7.

rituals at wells or over ponds to produce hailstorms are, in fact, conjuring demons whether they know it or not. Even women who administer healing herbs are not beyond suspicion. Demons who know the medicinal uses of herbs may teach these uses to their friends.

Much ink was spilled in discussing whether demons – and thus, by extension, magicians – can in fact do the things ascribed to them. The challenge was to find a balance between conceding them too much power and acknowledging too little. If they had too much power they would infringe the prerogatives of God; thus, for example, it would be blasphemous to the creator to suggest that demons can create new creatures or change existing ones from one substance to another. If demons seem to change people into asses or other animals, the effect is only an illusion. Some writers made much the same argument about changes in the weather, but by the thirteenth century theologians were arguing that demons could arouse destructive storms, as Exodus 9 and Job 1 seemed to attest. Could they cause sexual impotence? Yes, Thomas Aquinas and other authorities concluded. As a lawyer in the late fifteenth century, Ulrich Molitoris encountered many cases in which women charged their husbands with impotence, but physicians testified that there was no natural cause, and thus they must be bewitched. Could demons foretell the future? Following Augustine, most authors argued that they could do so only through subtle conjecture, not through genuine foreknowledge, which God alone has. Even if magic worked wholesome ends, and even if divination sometimes proved true, this was only because demons sometimes do people favors to win more followers. To that end, the demons might even be able to take on bodies, which they fashioned out of physical elements gathered from the air, but serious doubt remained about whether these humanoid demons could perform genuine bodily functions such as digestion and sexual intercourse. The central concern of the theologians, in any case, was to explain how magic might be demonic, and this question required as much ingenuity as explaining how it might be natural.

The results of all this mental effort were two main conclusions: first, that many types of magic might be natural; but secondly, that virtually all types might be demonic. Even if magic involved some feat beyond the power of demons, it could still be carried out through demonic cunning and illusion. To some extent, the second conclusion canceled out the first. It made little difference that much magic could be explained in natural terms if the suspicion of demonic intervention remained. Like moralists generally, late medieval moralists tended to fear the worst, and it was all too easy to find confirmation that demons were at work.

The danger of demonic magic was not, however, the theologians' and moralists' only concern. Even if popular customs did not entail demonic magic, they might involve false claims about the power of words, objects, and gestures, and this is the essence of what later medieval writers meant by "superstition," a charge closely related to that of magic.[12] The term "superstition" had earlier applied to remnants of pagan tradition, and the word never lost this meaning altogether. In the later Middle Ages, however, when paganism as an integral system of beliefs and practices was a distant memory in most parts of Europe, the term often referred to misuse of religion: use of holy things for power beyond what they in fact held, imputation of power to unauthorized observances, and use of authorized observances without the proper intention. If a moralist presumed to judge a person's intention defective, he was more likely to charge that person with superstition than with magic. By either definition, superstition might overlap with magic, but they were not the same thing in principle.

It was, essentially, as superstition that many writers condemned charms. The authors of the *Malleus maleficarum* protested that some of these formulas contain falsification of the Bible, by which they presumably meant apocryphal stories. When passages from the Bible are written out, the authors insist that no vain hope be placed in the manner of their inscription or any other external factor, which would imply that power resides in the words themselves; all attention must be directed to the meaning of the texts rather than the manner of their inscription, and the results must be entrusted to God's will. Other authors, such as John of Frankfurt, were even more cautious about charms, and argued that they have no inherent power (unlike herbs and gems) and are not established by God (unlike the sacraments). They are not found in the Bible and do not have the sanction of the saints or of the Church, and thus must be either demonic or merely human. The sheer diversity of these formulas makes them suspect: different people use different words, each thinking that the precise formulas have special power. John Bromyard (fourteenth century) raised similar concerns about a popular charm that ran, "Holy Mary enchanted her Son from the bite of elves and the bite of men, and joined mouth to mouth, blood to blood and joint to joint, and so the child recovered." Bromyard asked, with evident exasperation:

---

[12] Dieter Harmening, *Superstitio: Überlieferungs- und theoriegeschichtliche Untersuchungen zur kirchlich-theologischen Aberglaubensliteratur des Mittelalters* (Berlin: Schmidt, 1979). See now Michael D. Bailey, *Fearful Spirits, Reasoned Follies: The Boundaries of Superstition in Late Medieval Europe* (Ithaca, New York: Cornell University Press, 2013), and Bailey, "Superstition and sorcery," in Page and Rider, *Routledge History*, 487–501.

What Christian would not call those words false and contrary to the Catholic faith! For never did such infidelity occur to the Mother of God. How could they have power to save man or beast?[13]

If prayers have efficacy, he insisted, it is only because of the moral value of the person who prays them. Linking prayers with apocryphal stories and magical formulas debases them and adds nothing to their power.

Even if superstition does not involve appeal to demons, it may, of course, still be inspired by them. All sin is, in that sense, demonic: it is the result of the demons' temptation. This is presumably what John of Frankfurt has in mind in refuting an argument sometimes made for superstitious charms: people claim they are using holy words, and thus their practice is not diabolical, but this claim itself is a diabolical fraud.

The muddle that could ensue from this complex of conceptions and definitions is well-illustrated by the trial of Werner of Friedberg in 1405.[14] Werner was tried not for magic, but for holding certain beliefs about magic and related subjects: that blessings are licit; that if they were not, the Church would not bless ashes, palms, and so forth; that the names of the magi may be used to prevent epileptic seizures; and that the Latin for "The Word was made flesh" may be carried to avert diabolical deception. Someone told the authorities that Werner had preached such notions, and an episcopal judge summoned him for interrogation. The judge asked at one point if he knew any *superstitious* blessings, and he said he did know just one: "Christ was born, Christ was lost, Christ was found again; may he bless these wounds, in the name of the Father and of the Son and of the Holy Spirit." Indeed, he had used this blessing himself, and found that it worked. The interrogator went on to ask what he told people in confession when he heard they had used blessings. He said he permitted them unless they contained invocation of evil spirits.

Werner evidently shared one concern with others of his age: there were numerous blessings that contained apparently meaningless words, and these might well be names of demons. While articulating that concern, however, he seems to have missed his judge's further concern about superstitious observances. When asked if he knew any superstitious blessings, he gave an example that did not really qualify – and then admitted using it himself! When asked about his counsel in confession he again showed himself inattentive to the whole question of superstition.

---

[13] Owst, "*Sortilegium*," 294–5.

[14] I am indebted to Robert E. Lerner for information on this case. For the document and a somewhat different interpretation, see Lerner, "Werner di Friedberg intrappolato dalla legge," in Jean-Claude Maire Vigneur and Agostino Paravicini Bagliani, eds., *La parola all' accusato* (Palermo: Sellerio, 1991), 268–81.

If he could not instruct his flock properly about these matters, he was failing in his duties.

Werner's judge, like Bernardino, was essentially a reformer. Many in the later Middle Ages were eager to reform the Church "in head and members," from the papacy downward. By attacking superstitious beliefs and practices, and by holding popular devotion to higher standards than had usually been maintained or demanded, they were doing their part to reform Christendom. They might be heavy-handed in doing so. They might have little understanding, let alone sympathy, for the popular customs they sought to uproot. Yet they were moved by a zeal to purge Christian society of false beliefs and observances. Many of their contemporaries were addressing the same problems by preaching, by instruction in the confessional, and by writing manuals for priests so as to raise the standards of clerical learning. This program of reform overlapped with that of the sixteenth-century Reformers, though Luther and Calvin had very different notions about how and where to aim the reforming axe. We miss the historical significance of these activities unless we see them as part of a broad effort at reform.

Ultimately, reform of this sort raises the question how zeal relates to zealotry. The zealous reformer becomes a zealot not simply by having more intense commitment, or by allowing fears and enthusiasms to impair critical judgment, or by erroneous perception in matters of fact, but by a fusion of all these factors. The zealot's intense commitment to principle is so charged with unrealistic fears or expectations that uncritical judgment cannot be corrected by contact with reality.

The program of reform might be not only heavy-handed, but also misogynist. Moralists often saw women, especially, as prone to magic and superstition because of their supposed moral and intellectual weakness. Ulrich Molitoris, after writing at length on the powers of demons, closed his treatise with an apparently gratuitous warning specifically to women, urging them in particular to be on guard against the Devil's wiles. Reforming passion linked to this sort of bias was enormously dangerous, and, as we will see, it led to extreme fanaticism. Even if the zeal of the reformers went astray, however, it was grounded in an urge that sober Christians of the late Middle Ages would have taken as good and holy.

Patterns of Prosecution

Most of the known trials for magic in the early Middle Ages, and a surprising proportion even from later centuries, involved important political figures as defendants, accusers, or victims. The reasons, however, are not hard to find. These sensational, high-society trials were the ones most likely to be recorded by chroniclers and other writers, and thus we are more likely to know about them than about trials involving ordinary townspeople and villagers. Gregory of Tours (ca. 540–94) told in his *History of the Franks* about accusations of magic at the royal court of sixth-century Gaul. Queen Fredegund, for example, widely suspected of sorcery, was accused of poisoning and bewitching the swords that killed an enemy king. So, too, in 899, when the emperor Arnulf died of a stroke, two people were executed for having bewitched him. The story was similar when William of Aquitaine fell mortally ill in 1028 and clay images were brought forth as evidence of a woman's sorcery. We have already discussed cases from the ninth and twelfth centuries involving royal marriage impeded by magic (Chapter 4). The heyday of these sensational trials came in the early fourteenth century, when several people were charged with using magic against Pope John XXII and against the king of France. The trial of the Templars in 1307–14 was a classic instance of prosecution for complex political and religious reasons and surely did much to enhance concern about magic. In the course of the trial, which was orchestrated by the royal court of France, the members of this military religious order were charged with venerating a magic head and a cat, among many other offenses.[15] In late medieval England, women at court could become suspected of plotting against rulers, sometimes because they were said to have used love-magic to gain their affection, or had horoscopes drawn up to determine their life span.[16] While the graph of such politically charged cases would show peaks and troughs, however, the phenomenon seems to have been a more or less constant factor in the history of medieval magic.

We know much less about prosecution at lower levels on the social scale, but we get some glimpses from cases of vigilante action. Thus, the citizens of Cologne in 1075 hurled a woman from the town walls because she had supposedly been bewitching men with her magical arts. In 1128 the people of Ghent eviscerated an "enchantress" and paraded her stomach about town. The role of popular outrage is especially clear in a case at Votting from 1090, at a time when local political rivalries left the area without effective government. Three women fell suspect as sorceresses and spoilers of people's crops. They underwent the ordeal

---

[15] Malcolm Barber, *The Trial of the Templars* (Cambridge University Press, 1978); Peter Partner, *Murdered Magicians: The Templars and their Myth* (Oxford University Press, 1982).

[16] Gemma Hollman, *Royal Witches: Witchcraft and the Nobility in Fifteenth-Century England* (New York and London: Pegasus Books, 2020).

by water as a test of their innocence, and though they were successful, the populace remained unconvinced. They were whipped to make them confess, but they refused to do so. Nonetheless, the people burned them alive.

Manorial courts in the villages and municipal courts in the towns might in the end inflict the same punishment, but their proceedings were usually less arbitrary. We know little about the involvement of manorial courts in these matters. In the late tenth century, an English widow and her son were convicted for driving iron stakes into a man's image, whereupon the woman was drowned and her son, who fled, was outlawed, but this information comes from a record of ensuing land exchange, and we do not even know what court was involved.[17]

It is difficult to know for sure when municipal governments became involved in prosecution for sorcery, but the gradual growth of towns in the twelfth and following centuries led to autonomy in government, including criminal justice, and it is likely that sorcery was, from the outset, among the crimes that could be heard in city courts. Caesarius of Heisterbach tells of a young cleric in the German town Soest, around 1200, who had refused a woman's amorous advances. When she then accused him of having bewitched her, it was the municipal court that burned him as a sorcerer. Until the late Middle Ages, however, municipal courts retained what is known as "accusatory" procedure: a trial would begin only when an aggrieved party pressed charges in court and took responsibility for proving them; if the accusers did not prove the allegations, they would typically be liable to the same punishment that the accused would otherwise have suffered. In other words, if a man took a woman neighbor to court and accused her of bewitching his cattle, she might be executed if he could prove the allegation, but if he could not do so, *he* would be executed. This was clearly an effective way to discourage prosecution, especially for a crime such as sorcery, for which tangible evidence was rare.

In the high and late Middle Ages, prosecution of magicians increasingly fell to inquisitors. In the early thirteenth century, Pope Gregory IX (reg. 1227–41) began the practice of appointing inquisitors to search out heretics. This task had previously been left to local bishops, but as the threat of heresy grew more intense the pope found it necessary to supplement (not replace) the episcopal courts with the aid of these special itinerant judges. Their procedure was "inquisitorial" rather than accusatory, which is to say that they undertook prosecution on their own

---

[17] Jane Crawford, "Evidences for witchcraft in Anglo-Saxon England," *Medium Aevum*, 32 (1963), 113.

initiative, without waiting for an aggrieved party to lodge an accusation and take responsibility for proving the charges. The judge could use intimidation, and torture if necessary, to secure a confession. (These methods were adopted by secular courts as well in the late Middle Ages, largely in imitation of ecclesiastical procedure.) The possibilities for securing conviction were greatly enhanced. Theoretically there were various legal safeguards to ensure that the use of torture would not result in condemnation of the innocent, but in the late Middle Ages these restrictions were widely disregarded. Thus equipped with considerable power, Franciscan and Dominican friars serving as inquisitors went through towns and villages scrutinizing popular religious life more carefully and systematically than it had ever before been examined.

A thirteenth-century guide to inquisitorial interrogation lists numerous forms of magic that the inquisitors might raise in questioning suspects: experiments with reflecting surfaces, invocation of demons, use of magic circles, sacrifices to obtain responses from demons, use of human heads or other bodily parts to obtain love or hatred, observation of the allegedly inauspicious "Egyptian days" and other superstitions, use of charms over herbs, baptism of images, use of the Eucharist or chrism or baptismal water for any magical experiment, and so forth.[18] This interrogatory suggests how suspicion on one count might lead to suspicion on others as well: once the inquisitor got started, it would be only natural for him to continue down the list and see just how many crimes the suspect had committed.

Not long after inquisitors were first appointed, they encountered occasional reports of sorcery. An inquisitor at Le Mas Saintes-Puelles had a woman brought before him in 1245 as a "diviner." Her neighbors had paid her to put magical charms on their clothes, perhaps as a form of love magic, and she had used magic to work cures as well. Yet she managed to persuade the inquisitor that she was not heretical; in the course of the trial she confessed that she did not even believe her own magic had any effect.

Cases of this sort, however, could easily have absorbed the inquisitors' energies and distracted them from other business. Thus, in 1258 and 1260, Pope Alexander IV declared that they should not dissipate their efforts by prosecuting people for magic unless their magic savored of heresy. Nonheretical magic should be left to the purview of local authorities. Inquisitors who wanted to deal with such cases thus had to argue that all magic implies heresy, and the usual way to make this point was to

---

[18] C. Douais, "Les hérétiques du Midi au treizième siècle: Cinq pièces inédites," *Annales du Midi*, 3 (1891), 377–9.

reduce natural magic to demonic magic, then to show that alliance with demons in itself entails false belief about these evil spirits. It was easy enough for Nicholas Eymericus and others to show that *necromancy* involved a false belief that demons were worthy of veneration, but magic of the common tradition as well could be represented as demonic and heretical. Apart from formally articulated theoretical heresy, there was such a thing as practical heresy implicit in a person's actions. Such reasoning led John XXII, following counsel from several theologians, to direct the papal inquisitors against necromancers and other magicians.[19]

Some of the trials in the later Middle Ages seem to have been directed against genuine necromancers. A case before an ecclesiastical court south of Paris in 1323 involved a group of monks, canons, and laymen, who were plotting to invoke the demon Berich from inside a circle made from strips of cat skin. An inquisitor in Florence condemned one Niccolo Consigli to the stake in 1384 for various kinds of magic, including conjurations, exorcisms, and a frustrated attempt at murder by sympathetic magic and invocation of Lucifer, Satan, and Beelzebub. Consigli possessed books of necromancy, which the inquisitor, following standard procedure, had burned.[20] There is no reason to doubt that the defendants in these cases were in fact necromancers. Indeed, a great many of the trials in the late Middle Ages, especially in the fourteenth century, seem to have been directed against clerics engaged in necromancy.

Yet matters were not always so simple. Inquisitors and other judges, aware that necromancy was a problem in certain quarters, sometimes confused even natural magic with this much more serious offense. An episcopal court at Sleaford in 1417 tried a man named John Smith for "the art of necromancy and sorcery and illicit and prohibited conjurations and invocation of malign spirits," which sounds very much as if he had been using something like the Munich handbook. In fact, however, he had merely been using divination with bread to detect a thief who had broken into the local church. He had used this procedure only once, but defended it as legitimate, and even claimed that Saints Peter and Paul had engaged in such practice, though it is not clear what basis he had for this notion.[21] An inquisitor at Florence in the 1340s found that various people were saying charms over plants to use them for cures and other

---

[19] Anneliese Maier, "Eine Verfugung Johanns XXII. über die Zuständigkeit der Inquisition für Zaubereiprozesse," *Archivum Fratrum Praedicatorum*, 22 (1952), 226–46.

[20] G. G. Coulton, trans., *Life in the Middle Ages*, vol. 1 (Cambridge University Press, 1928), 160–3; Gene A. Brucker, ed., *The Society of Renaissance Florence* (New York: Harper & Row, 1971), 361–6.

[21] Margaret Archer, ed., *The Register of Bishop Philip Repingdon, 1405–1419*, vol. 3 (Lincoln Record Society, 1982), 194–6 (reading *vnica ... vice* for *vinca ... vite*).

innocent magic. Several people – a widow, a monk, the rector of a church, and others – had to pay fines for engaging in these practices. When the inquisitor charged that a physician had bought a book of herbal remedies containing elements of "necromancy," however, the physician did not submit meekly, but insisted that the book contained nothing of the sort.[22] Since the terminology for magic was ill-defined and highly connotative, its more reckless opponents would naturally incline to use the strongest language possible.

Even if a person was practicing illicit magic, however, it might be possible to do so with impunity until someone decided to make an issue of the matter. The factors that could precipitate such a development would be altogether unpredictable. The safest generalization is that fingers would point most quickly at someone who had established a reputation for being a bad, disagreeable neighbor. Dorothea Hindremstein, tried by a municipal court at Lucerne in 1454, is a perfect example.[23] Some time earlier, her mother had been burned for sorcery in Uri, and if Dorothea had not fled she would have been burned as well; in the meantime, she had been made to swear that she would not return to Uri. Her neighbors, and even her husband at Lucerne, eventually concluded that she had inherited her mother's power to lay curses on people. One female neighbor told the court how her child had gotten into a fight and shoved Dorothea's child into the mud. Dorothea came out and angrily threatened that the witness's child would never forget this offense. Within twelve hours the offending child began to grow ill, and he lay sick for three weeks. Who could doubt that Dorothea's curse had taken effect? Another neighbor told how he had been careful not to antagonize Dorothea because of her ill repute. Yet he told how other people had quarreled with her and had soon suffered the consequences: illness of half a year's duration, death of a fine cow, or blood instead of milk from a cow. How had Dorothea done all this? The man could not explain – indeed, the witnesses were generally unconcerned about the precise mechanism of the supposed sorcery – but he feared that if she and her family were allowed to live they would inflict still more damage. Then he said no more, fearing that he might be ill repaid for his testimony.

In many ways, Dorothea fits the stereotype of the "old hag." Many of the women prosecuted for sorcery seem to have been old women who had no family to support them, or who received no support from the family they did have. Doubtless they tended, like Dorothea, to be

[22] Mariano da Alatri, "L'inquisizione a Firenze negli anni 1344/46 da un'istruttoria contro Pietro da l'Aquila," in Isidorus a Villapadierna, ed., *Miscellanea Mechior de Pobladura* (Rome: Institutum Historicum O.F.M. Cap., 1964), 233–5.

[23] Hansen, *Quellen und Untersuchungen*, 561–5.

ill-natured sorts, who bore resentment toward those about them and inspired resentment in return.

Recent scholarship has centered on the extreme case of a link between magic and approved religion: the apparent parallel between the witch and the saint. As much a theme in the history of magic as in that of witchcraft, this parallel calls to our attention the role of stereotyping, positive or negative, in attitudes toward wonder-workers.[24] The stereotypical roles of witch and saint tell us at least as much about society's needs and expectations as about any actual individuals distinguished for either sainthood or magic.

There seems to have been a rise in the frequency of trials for magic in the later fourteenth century, with great numbers of trials, especially in Switzerland and Italy. The increase may be, in part, a kind of optical illusion: in the fourteenth and fifteenth centuries, parchment was gradually replaced by the cheaper medium of paper, which meant that more information was written down and preserved, which in turn means that from this era we have more documents of various kinds and more information about numerous aspects of European life and culture. Yet this is surely not the full story; in all likelihood there was a real and not merely an apparent increase. The gradual shift from accusatory to inquisitorial procedure in the secular courts made this development possible. Once it became easier to secure a conviction for sorcery, and once it became clear that an informant did not have to take on the responsibilities of a formal accuser, charges would eventually become more frequent.

The increase in frequency at this point, however, was not so pronounced as to suggest any single, momentous upheaval in European social relations as an underlying cause. One might think that the Black Death and other adversities of the late Middle Ages aroused frustration, suspicion, and hostility among the survivors and that these emotions found indirect outlet in trials for sorcery. There was no direct connection, however, with these calamities: sorcery trials did not typically involve accusations that people had caused the Black Death. They began, rather, with allegations that people had inflicted illness on children, caused cows to stop giving milk, seduced their neighbors, and worked other forms of mischief that could occur in any era.

---

[24] See Peter Dinzelbacher, *Heilige oder Hexen? Schicksale auffälliger Frauen in Mittelalter und Frühneuzeit* (Zurich: Artemis, 1995), and Gábor Klaniczay, "*Miraculum* und *maleficium*: Einige Überlegungen zu den weiblichen Heiligen des Mittelalters in Mitteleuropa," *wissenschaftskolleg Jarhbuch*, 1990/1, 220–48. I have raised qualifications in my article, Richard Kieckhefer, "The holy and the unholy: Sainthood, witchcraft, and magic in late medieval Europe," *Journal of Medieval and Renaissance Studies*, 24 (1994), 355–85, published also in Scott L. Waugh and Peter D. Diehl, eds., *Christendom and its Discontents: Exclusion, Persecution, and Rebellion, 1000–1500* (Cambridge University Press, 1996), 310–37.

Fig. 22. Wall-painting in a Danish church showing a milk-stealing witch accompanied by a demon

These trials would be of interest in themselves, but they are of even greater concern because they paved the way for more dramatic prosecution to come.

The Rise of the Witch Trials

There had already been an increase in sorcery trials in the fourteenth century, but a much more dramatic upswing in prosecution occurred in the second and third quarters of the fifteenth century, especially in France, Germany, and Switzerland. Not only were the trials more frequent: they were different in kind from most of the preceding cases. Far more often they now developed into catch-all prosecution. Rather than merely dealing with a single suspect, inquisitors and other judges would urge the people of a town or village to seek out as many suspects as possible. The ruling passion now was not simply to secure justice against the specific offender, but to purge the community of transgressors. Furthermore, the nature of the charges shifted. No longer satisfied to show that the sorcerer had worked image magic or used potions, judges now sought evidence that they had participated in anti-Christian, diabolical rituals. No longer content with accusations of sorcery, or even with the suggestion that sorcery inherently entailed demonic magic, judges now wanted to portray the magicians as linked in a demonic conspiracy against the Christian faith and Christian society. The sorcerer, intent only on specific acts of malice against particular enemies, gave way before the company of witches committed to the destruction of Christendom. The term "witchcraft" is used in various ways, sometimes including sorcery or other forms of magic, but by the late Middle Ages the witch was someone who went beyond mere sorcery, someone who performed ritual acts of veneration to the Devil in league with other witches.[25]

How cases of simple and apparently harmless magic might lead to fanatical prosecution for witchcraft is clear from a sermon preached in 1427 by Bernardino of Siena. The friar spoke against various sins of pride, one of which was the use of charms and divination. When people use such things, he said, they are renouncing God and worshiping the Devil. Even countermagic is evil: anyone who knows how to break the force of charms knows also how to work them. When such people say they only wish to cure the sick, one should cry out, "To the flames! To the flames!"

---

[25] Martine Ostorero, "Witchcraft," in Page and Rider, *Routledge History*, 502–22, serves now as a review of the topic and of the extensive relevant literature.

Bernardino then held up as an example what happened in Rome when he preached there against the use of charms. At first, people thought he was raving, but then he warned that if they failed to report the culprits, they shared in their guilt. Soon, a great many women were accused. One of them confessed even without torture that she had murdered some thirty children by sucking blood from them; another sixty she had let loose, though for doing so she had to propitiate the Devil with sacrifices. She had killed many other people, even her own son, with a magical powder. When she gave specific names and dates for these murders they corresponded to known deaths. Among other materials that she used were herbs gathered on the feast of St. John and on the Ascension. She also had foul-smelling unguents. She and her ilk would anoint themselves, and though they appeared unchanged to others, they thought themselves transformed into cats. Bernardino reported with satisfaction that this woman had been burned as a witch. All others should be burned likewise, he maintained. Anyone who knew of such witches and failed to report them to an inquisitor would be responsible on the Day of Judgment for this omission.[26]

The Franciscan preacher Bernardino was one of the most important of the Dominican and Franciscan friars in Italy who, acting as inquisitors and preachers, played a major role in developing ideas about witchcraft.[27] They were familiar with themes from classical literature, such as the monstrous blood-sucking bird called the *strix* that attacks infants in their cradles. They knew of the beautiful Lamia, mistress of Zeus, whom Hera changed into a child-devouring monster. In the writings of Horace and Lucan they read about horrific old hags such as Canidia and Erichtho. They knew Homer's story about the crew of Ulysses, changed into animals by the witch Circe, and Apuleius' tale about the man changed into an ass. They also knew folklore about beneficent, fairy-like figures, or "good women," who provided festivals and bounty for those who associated with them at an assembly often called a "game." Some writers conflated this folklore with the notions condemned in the early medieval canon *Episcopi* about women who flew by night in the

---

[26] St. Bernardino of Siena, *Sermons*, ed. Nazareno Orlandi, trans. Helen Josephine Robins (Siena: Tipografia Sociale, 1920), 163–76. See Richard Kieckhefer, *European Witch Trials: Their Foundations in Popular and Learned Culture, 1300–1500* (London: Routledge, 1976), 121–2.

[27] Fabrizio Conti, *Witchcraft, Superstition, and Observant Franciscan Preachers: Pastoral Approach and Intellectual Debate in Renaissance Italy* (Turnhout: Brepols, 2015); Fabrizio Conti, 'Notes on the nature of beliefs in witchcraft: Folklore and classical culture in fifteenth-century mendicant traditions,' *Religions*, 10 (2019), 576; Marina Montesano, *Classical Culture and Witchcraft in Medieval and Renaissance Italy* (Cham: Palgrave Macmillan, 2018).

company of the goddesses Diana and Herodias.[28] The boundaries between fiction, folklore, and fact could seem fluid. There were writers who returned to the skeptical stance of the canon *Episcopi*, and there was a group of Italian Franciscans who challenged the mythology of the *strix* (now construed in Italian as the *strega* or witch), and, in particular, the idea of women transformed into animals. In many quarters, however, these strands of tradition were taken seriously and reinforced each other.[29]

The intertwining of literary and folkloric traditions could produce more than one composite image. The tendency in parts of Italy was to focus on small clusters of witches who violated the sanctity of the home: they changed into animal shape, flew to people's homes at night, and sucked the blood from babies in their cradles. In regions around the western Alps, the emphasis was on violation of what the Church presented as sacred: on a conspiracy of witches who flew to an assembly that came to be called the Sabbath, where they openly associated with the Devil, renounced their faith, desecrated crucifixes and consecrated hosts, ate the flesh of infants, had orgiastic sex, and were given magical powders and other means for bewitchment.[30]

Witch trials inspired more witch trials, because the report of action in one place would stimulate passions elsewhere. Oral report alone might have sufficed for this effect, but it was supplemented by inflammatory written accounts. In the mid-fifteenth century, for example, an anonymous author in or near Savoy wrote a treatise on *The Errors of the Gazarii*.[31] ("Gazarii" was a local term for witches.) The author was probably an inquisitor, and in any case he had access to inquisitorial records. For him, witchcraft was a "sect" whose members assembled regularly at "synagogues" or assemblies to satisfy their anger, gluttony, and lust. Once a person has been seduced into the sect, his seducer brings him to the synagogue and presents him to the Devil. While presiding at this assembly, the Devil assumes the form of a black cat, or sometimes a human being with some deformity. He interrogates the initiate and

---

[28] The canon is translated in P. G. Maxwell-Stuart, *Witch Beliefs and Witch Trials in the Middle Ages: Documents and Readings* (London: Continuum, 2011), 47–8, and in Kors and Peters, *Witchcraft in Europe*, 60–3. The title of the canon is *Episcopi*; referring to it as the *Canon Episcopi*, a common error, is like citing the *Novel Crime and Punishment*.

[29] On this interaction, see also Gábor Klaniczay, 'Learned systems and popular narratives of vision and bewitchment,' in *Demons, Spirits, Witches*, vol. 3: *Witchcraft Mythologies and Persecutions*, ed. Gábor Klaniczay and Éva Pócs (Budapest: Central European University Press, 2008), 50–82.

[30] Richard Kieckhefer, "Mythologies of witchcraft in the fifteenth century," *Magic, Ritual, and Witchcraft*, 1 (2006), 79–107.

[31] Hansen, *Quellen und Untersuchungen*, 118–22.

requires him to swear that he will be faithful to the sect and its master, that he will seduce others into it, that he will keep its secrets, that he will strangle as many children as he can and bring their bodies to the synagogue, that he will come at once whenever called to the synagogue, that he will disrupt as many marriages as possible by using witchcraft to cause impotence, and that he will avenge all harm done to the sect and its members. The initiate then kisses the Devil on the posterior as a sign of homage. Then all members of the sect hold a feast (in which the flesh of children is the *pièce de résistance*), followed by dancing, indiscriminate sexual intercourse, more feasting, and a parody of the Eucharist.

Members of the sect have powders and unguents for working harm. To destroy crops, they fill the skin of a cat with various kinds of vegetable matter, put it in a spring for three days, then dry and pulverize the concoction. On a windy day, they go up a mountain and scatter the powder across the land as a sacrifice to the Devil, who, in return for their offering, will destroy the crops. By touching people with an unguent (made from the fat of strangled children and the venom of toads and other animals), they can cause agonizing deaths. To procure the meat and fat of infants, they strangle them at night, pretend to lament their demise, then exhume their bodies. Certain witches have confessed that they killed and ate their own children and grandchildren. Yet to conceal their conduct they pretend to be faithful Catholics, going to mass, confession, and communion often.

This treatise is one of the earliest to spell out the details of the pact with the Devil, which held a prominent place in the mythology of witchcraft:

> when a person is initiated into the sect, after he has sworn his fidelity and given homage, the Devil takes a certain instrument and draws blood from the left hand of the one being led astray. The Devil then writes out a certain document with this blood, which he keeps for himself.[32]

Other trials inspired further literature. A sensational trial at Arras in 1459–60 led to the arrest of thirty-four people and the burning of twelve as witches. The inquisitor responsible for these proceedings extracted detailed confessions about the witches' sabbaths, and while there were many who feared that the prosecution had gotten out of hand, there were others who joined the inquisitor in this zealous effort to rid the town of such pestiferous company. An anonymous treatise lamented that this sect of witches was an unprecedented threat to Christendom, more loathsome than all paganism. The case inspired another treatise, by the theologian Johannes Tinctoris; a manuscript of this work contains an

---

[32] Hansen, *Quellen und Untersuchungen*, 121.

early depiction of the sabbath, with witches venerating the Devil in the form of a goat, and others flying through the air on extravagant woolly monsters.[33] The famed culmination of this literary tradition was the *Malleus maleficarum*, written in 1486 by the inquisitors Jacob Sprenger and Henry Kramer, partly on the basis of trials that Kramer had conducted.[34] Nor was it only inquisitors and theologians who wrote sensational accounts of witch trials: as early as the 1430s, a secular judge in the Dauphiné added his own contribution to the genre.[35]

The stereotype of the witch was complex, and its sources were various. Certain elements came from the exercise of sorcery in the common tradition of magic: the idea that magical potions can be lethal, or can cause impotence or other afflictions. Other details seem to have come from the manuals of necromancy. The idea of scattering powder as a sacrifice to the Devil could well have come from this source. More specific notions were taken over as well. The Munich handbook, for example, instructs the necromancer not to make the sign of the cross when flying on a horse provided by necromancy, since the horse is in fact a demon and will flee the blessing. The same manual, in describing the illusory banquet that the necromancer can conjure forth, says that there may be a thousand kinds of food, all extraordinarily delicious, but the more one eats, the hungrier one will become, because the food does not really exist. Both these notions are echoed in accounts of witchcraft.

Themes from much earlier tradition became woven into the witch stereotype. The notion of a pact with the Devil was grounded in the early medieval legend of Theophilus, and in the theological notion (held by Thomas Aquinas and others) that magic could work by an arrangement or "pact" between the magician and the demons, specifying the symbolic intent of various magical acts. The notion of a nocturnal orgy in the presence of a demon was a standard charge against heretics in the high Middle Ages – in fact, similar charges had been made much earlier against Christians in the Roman Empire – though calling this assembly a "synagogue" (and, from the late fifteenth century on, a "sabbath") was a sign of anti-Semitism. Witches were often thought of as flying through the air, a notion that could have come from various sources in folklore or from the necromancers' manuals. When theologians wanted to prove

---

[33] Hansen, *Quellen und Untersuchungen*, 183–8. The depiction of the sabbath is reproduced in Norman Cohn, *Europe's Inner Demons: An Enquiry Inspired by the Great Witch-Hunt* (New York: Basic, 1975), pl. 1.

[34] *Malleus maleficarum*, trans. Christopher Mackay (Cambridge University Press, 2006).

[35] Pierrette Paravy, "A propos de la genèse médiévale des chasses aux sorcières: Le traité de Claude Tholosan, juge dauphinois (vers 1436)," *Mélanges de l'école française de Rome. Moyen Âge–Temps modernes*, 912 (1979), 333–79.

that such flight was possible, they argued on biblical grounds: an angel carried the prophet Habakkuk through the air (Daniel 13–14), and demons, being merely fallen angels, retain this power. The concept of sexual intercourse with demons (called incubi if they took the form of men, succubi if they appeared as women) could also have come from many sources. Merlin's father was a demon, and when the Bible spoke of relations between the sons of God and daughters of men (Genesis 6:1), later medieval exegetes took this to refer to intercourse with incubi.

Theologians around the thirteenth century, including Thomas Aquinas, had refined and rationalized many of these notions. They had shown, for example, how it is possible for intercourse with an incubus to produce offspring: the demon appears first to a man as a succubus, obtains semen, then immediately takes the form of an incubus and transmits it to a woman. Other refinements occurred at roughly the same time: the pact with the Devil, for instance, was now seen as a formal act analogous to feudal homage.

A particularly important element in the stereotype of the witch was the centrality of women. The classic case of the misogynist witchcraft treatise is the *Malleus maleficarum*; earlier literature had seldom singled women out as specifically inclined toward witchcraft, but the *Malleus* and later texts routinely did so. In the courts, too, there was an increasing tendency to single out women for prosecution. In the fourteenth and fifteenth centuries, women outnumbered men by about two to one as defendants in witch trials; in the later fifteenth century the difference seems to have become more pronounced, and in following centuries it was greater still. This bias may owe something to the role of women as popular healers with herbs and charms, but there is no reason to think that women had a monopoly on these or other forms of magic. The association of women with witchcraft certainly cannot be explained as an outgrowth of the later medieval occult sciences and necromancy, since these were overwhelmingly the property of male clerics, both in fact and in legend.

Ultimately, the vulnerability of women in this context must be seen as a corollary to the precarious position women held in late medieval society (and, for that matter, in almost every society through history). The general culture portrayed women as having weak intellect and will. When institutions were set against them, women would have less power than men to resist. If the specific issue was witchcraft, it would be hard for anyone, woman or man, to disprove the charges, since tangible evidence was not expected and confessions could easily be obtained through intimidation, false promises of mercy, or torture. But if women were, in general, less trusted and more feared, these means for coercion would be directed against them more than against men. General misogynist stereotypes would encourage prosecution, which would then encourage further development of stereotypes. The stereotypes, however, do not by themselves cause prosecution. They may give it direction and aid in arousing passion, but when this happens they are called into service to justify and encourage prosecution motivated by other factors.

The provocation to judicial action might be personal, even idiosyncratic. An old woman might quarrel with her neighbors. A man might attempt to excuse a love affair, claiming that he had been bewitched. A midwife might be lured into a cockeyed scheme for curing leprosy with the fat of a miscarried fetus. Any of these situations might spark accusations of witchcraft. If the accused implicated other suspects, perhaps in revenge, prosecution might escalate. Impassioned townspeople, having dispatched one alleged witch, might decide to purge their society of all her associates.

Thus massive trials occurred, especially in the second and third quarters of the fifteenth century. Secular judges in the Valais condemned large numbers of witches in 1428 and again in 1447. In the first case, more than a hundred people are said to have been burned for killing people, destroying the crops, and working other harm through magic. This trial is especially important as the first for which we have firm evidence of the fully developed stereotype of the witch, complete with flight through the air and transformation of human beings into animals, along with more traditional notions, such as eating of babies and veneration of the Devil.[36] In judicial records from the Dauphiné, there are relatively few cases of witchcraft up to the early fifteenth century, and no gender imbalance, but in the years 1424 to 1445 there is an explosion of cases in which women outnumber men 175 to 83.[37] Mass prosecution occurred elsewhere, usually under secular judges, though in 1485 it was the papal inquisitor Henry Kramer who apprehended forty-eight women and two men at Innsbruck.

While some cases may have started with apprehension of a single suspect and then proceeded to others, a trial might also *begin* with accusation of a large group. One wonders in such cases whether the judge came upon a group of heretics and applied to them the traditional stereotypes of devil-worship, or whether he perhaps stumbled upon some

---

[36] Carlo Ginzburg, "The witches' sabbat: Popular cult or inquisitorial stereotype?," in Steven L. Kaplan, ed., *Understanding Popular Culture: Europe from the Middle Ages to the Nineteenth Century* (Berlin: Mouton, 1984), 39–51.
[37] Pierrette Paravy, *De la chrétienté romaine à la Réforme en Dauphiné: Évêques, fidèles et déviants (vers 1340–vers 1530)* (Rome: École française de Rome, 1993), 783.

agrarian ritual that he little understood and misinterpreted as witchcraft. These are always possibilities, though there is little reason to think that such mechanisms underlay more than a small proportion of the witch trials. When we can see the background of a trial at all clearly, or even glimpse it faintly, what seems to lie behind the stereotypes is some form of magic.

Why, then, was there such an increase in the frequency and fervor of prosecution in the mid-fifteenth century, and why did trials begin to become sweeping witch-hunts rather than focusing on individual suspects? Certain factors were important as necessary conditions for this development: widespread adoption of inquisitorial procedure, by secular as well as ecclesiastical courts; unrestricted use of torture; development of the witch stereotype, complete with the notion of a conspiratorial sect; and most important, suspicion (fed by stories of the necromancers) that apparently innocent magic might turn out to be demonic. But if these were the necessary conditions, what was the cause? The relationship between a condition and a cause is difficult to define. By way of analogy: when a long dry spell leaves a forest or a town vulnerable to fire, a spark may suffice to begin a conflagration, which will spread of its own accord. When all the conditions are set for the judicial hysteria of witch-hunts, the precipitating incidents may be less important than this conjunction of prior conditions, and for a time the sensation may sustain itself.

If we need to locate a spark, however, at least one source is clear: the vigorous drive for reform of the Church, in head and members, found throughout Western Christendom in the wake of the Council of Constance (1414–18). Reformist sentiment pointed toward useful reform of the Church, but, as we have already seen in the case of Bernardino, it was not free of fanaticism. A reforming theologian like John Gerson might direct his efforts mainly against genuine necromancers, and a reformer such as Nicholas of Cusa (1401–64) might find that women who confessed to the rites of witchcraft were merely mad, but even they were not immune to the fears of their age, and less discriminating minds would be less cautious.[38]

It was not only ecclesiastical courts that took up the cause of moral reform. Municipal courts were beginning to join in this cause, prosecuting behaviors such as blasphemy, sodomy, and sorcery in an effort to

---

[38] Françoise Bonney, "Autour de Jean Gerson: Opinions de théologiens sur les superstitions et la sorcellerie au début du XVᵉ siècle," *Moyen Âge*, 71 (1971), 85–98; Carl Binz, "Zur Charakteristik des Cusanus," *Archiv für Kulturgeschichte*, 7 (1909), 145–53.

cleanse the community of moral impurity.[39] Municipal authorities might at times achieve their goal by banishing the offenders so they could corrupt some other community, which was a solution that churchmen more rarely embraced. In either case, moral issues were increasingly seen as cause not just for penance, but for prosecution. The prosecutors were zealots, and like most zealots they were inspired by holy enthusiasm mixed with skewed perceptions. How their perceptions became skewed is a long story, and telling that story has been the point of this book.

Conclusion

If magic is a crossroads in medieval culture, it is one with numerous paths radiating from it. We have explored some of these paths at greater length than others. What should be particularly clear is the intersection of natural and demonic magic, and thus of the scientific and religious elements in the culture of medieval Europe. Distinguishing between natural and demonic forms of magic was not easy; agreement on the distinction was not to be expected. The history of medieval magic is essentially one of conflicting perceptions on just this issue. The tendency of the uneducated seems to have been to see magic as natural, while intellectuals were torn between three conceptions. Following early Christian writers, they might see all magic (even that of the common tradition) as relying at least implicitly on demons; with the transmission of Islamic scholarship in the twelfth century, intellectuals increasingly acknowledged (whether enthusiastically or grudgingly) that a great deal of magic was natural; yet the real and express invocation of demons by necromancers renewed old apprehensions and made educated people all the more suspicious that magic was really demonic, even if it appeared natural.

Special confusion emerged from special contexts. Early medieval missionaries in their conflict with Germanic and Celtic religion might preach against magic, yet in making accommodations to Germanic and Celtic cultures they allowed practices which, by late medieval definitions, would count as magical and perhaps demonic. No doubt the confusion was heightened by the importation of different kinds of magic from Arabic culture: the arrival of the occult sciences, grounded in metaphysics and cosmology, lent new respectability to nondemonic magic, but along the same route of cultural transmission came key elements in necromancy, and thus new disrepute for magic. The magical arts now stood both in

---

[39] Laura Patricia Stokes, *Demons of Urban Reform: Early European Witch Trials and Criminal Justice, 1430–1530* (New York: Palgrave Macmillan, 2011).

higher respectability and in deeper notoriety than before, forcing intellectually respectable astrologers and magicians to distance themselves as clearly as possible from their disreputable cousins the necromancers.

The real victims of this tension were those who continued to employ the natural magic of the common tradition, but were now thickly tarred with the brush of demonic magic. Those who prosecuted and condemned them were, after all, men with some education, who would naturally tend to see popular magic in terms of what other educated people were doing. Recognizing the threat of demonic magic in the clerical underworld, they would spontaneously project that model onto humbler magicians. To justify and promote their repression of popular magic, they imagined not only a demonic element in this magic, but a conspiracy of demon-worshipers. Between the magicians and their opponents lay a wide perceptual chasm.

It has been proposed that "The greatest magician would be the one who would cast over himself a spell so complete that he would take up his own phantasmagorias as autonomous appearances."[40] By this definition, paradoxically, it was the theologians, preachers, lawyers, inquisitors, and other judges who themselves became the greatest of magicians.

---

[40] Novalis, *Schriften*, vol. 2, ed. Richard Samuel (Stuttgart: Kohlhammer, 1960), 612, Fragment 88, as translated in Jorge Luis Borges, *Labyrinths: Selected Stories and Other Writings*, ed. Donald A. Yates and James E. Irby (New York: New Directions, 1962), 208.

Further Reading

General

Bailey, Michael D., "The age of magicians: Periodization in the history of European magic," *Magic, Ritual, and Witchcraft*, 3 (2008), 3–28.

    Magic and Superstition in Europe: A Concise History from Antiquity to the Present (Lanham, Md.: Rowman & Littlefield, 2007).

    "The meanings of magic," *Magic, Ritual, and Witchcraft*, 1 (2006), 1–23.

    "Was magic a religious movement?," in David J. Collins, S.J., ed., *The Sacred and the Sinister: Studies in Medieval Religion and Magic* (University Park: Pennsylvania State University Press, 2019), 143–62.

Cardini, Franco, *Magia, stregoneria, superstizioni nell'Occidente medievale* (Florence: La Nuova Italia, 1979).

Carroll, David, *The Magic Makers: Magic and Sorcery Through the Ages* (New York: Arbor House, 1974).

Cavendish, Richard, *A History of Magic* (New York: Taplinger, 1977).

Copenhaver, Brian, ed. and trans., *The Book of Magic: From Antiquity to the Enlightenment* (London: Penguin, 2017).

Flint, Valerie I. J., *The Rise of Magic in Early Medieval Europe* (Princeton University Press, 1991).

Jolly, Karen, Catharine Raudvere, and Edward Peters, *Witchcraft and Magic in Europe: The Middle Ages*, ed. Bengt Ankarloo and Stuart Clark (Philadelphia: University of Pennsylvania Press, 2001).

Kieckhefer, Richard, "The specific rationality of medieval magic," *American Historical Review*, 99 (1994), 813–36.

King, Frances, *Magic: The Western Tradition* (London: Thames & Hudson, 1975).

Klaassen, Frank, *The Transformations of Magic: Illicit Learned Magic in the Later Middle Ages and Renaissance* (University Park: Pennsylvania State University Press, 2013).

Lawrence-Mathers, Anne, and Carolina Escobar-Vargas, *Magic and Medieval Society* (London and New York: Routledge, 2014).

Levack, Brian P., ed., *Articles on Witchcraft, Magic, and Demonology: A Twelve-Volume Anthology of Scholarly Articles* (New York: Garland, 1992).

Otto, Bernd-Christian, and Michael Stausberg, eds., *Defining Magic: A Reader* (Sheffield: Equinox, 2013).

Rider, Catherine, *Magic and Religion in Medieval England* (London: Reaktion, 2012).

Thorndike, Lynn, *A History of Magic and Experimental Science*, 8 vols. (New York and London: Columbia University Press and Macmillan, 1923–58).

"Some medieval conceptions of magic," *The Monist*, 25 (1915), 107–39.

Wagner, Robert-Léon, *"Sorcier" et "magicien": Contribution à l'histoire de la magie* (Paris: Droz, 1939).

Watkins, C. S., *History and the Supernatural in Medieval England* (Cambridge University Press, 2007).

Wilson, Stephen W., *Magical Universe: Everyday Ritual and Magic in Pre-Modern Europe* (London: Hambledon, 2001).

Antiquity

Greek and Roman Magic

Asirvatham, Sulochana R., Corinne Ondine Pache, and John Watrous, eds., *Between Magic and Religion: Interdisciplinary Studies in Ancient Mediterranean Religion and Society* (Lanham, Md.: Rowman & Littlefield, 2001).

Betz, Hans Dieter, ed., *The Greek Magical Papyri in Translation, Including the Demotic Spells*, 2nd edn (University of Chicago Press, 1992).

Faraone, Christopher A., and Dirk Obbink, eds., *Magika Hiera: Ancient Greek Magic and Religion* (New York: Oxford University Press, 1990).

Frankfurter, David, ed., *Guide to the Study of Ancient Magic* (Leiden: Brill, 2019).

Gordon, Richard L., and Francisco Marco Simón, eds., *Magical Practice in the Latin West* (Leiden: Brill, 2010).

Graf, Fritz, *Magic in the Ancient World*, trans. Franklin Philip (Cambridge, Mass.: Harvard University Press, 1997).

Luck, Georg, trans., *Arcana mundi: Magic and the Occult in the Greek and Roman Worlds: A Collection of Ancient Texts* (Baltimore: Johns Hopkins University Press, 1985).

Meyer, Marvin W., and Paul Mirecki, eds., *Ancient Magic and Ritual Power* (Leiden: Brill, 1995).

Mirecki, Paul, and Marvin Meyer, eds., *Magic and Ritual in the Ancient World* (Leiden: Brill, 2001).

Noegel, Scott, ed., *Prayer, Magic and the Stars in Antiquity* (University Park: Pennsylvania State University Press, 2003).

Pliny, *Natural History*, trans. H. Rackham et al. (Cambridge, Mass.: Harvard University Press; London: Heinemann, 1938–63); esp. vols. 8–10 (books 28–37).

Ptolemy [Claudius Ptolemaeus], *Tetrabiblos*, ed. and trans. F. E. Robbins (Cambridge, Mass.: Harvard University Press, 1940).

Scott, Walter, ed. and trans., *Hermetica: The Ancient Greek and Latin Writings which Contain Religious or Philosophic Teachings Ascribed to Hermes Trismegistus* (Oxford: Clarendon, 1924–36).

Magic and Christianity

Augustine, Saint, *Concerning the City of God, against the Pagans*, trans. Henry Bettenson, new edn (Harmondsworth: Penguin, 1984), especially sections from books 8–10.

"The divination of demons," in Roy J. Deferrari, ed., *Saint Augustine: Treatises on Marriage and Other Subjects* (New York: Fathers of the Church, 1955), 415–40.

Barb, A. A., "The survival of the magic arts," in Arnaldo Momigliano, ed., *The Conflict Between Paganism and Christianity in the Fourth Century* (Oxford: Clarendon, 1963), 110–25.

Benko, Stephen, "Early Christian magical practices," *Society of Biblical Literature: Seminar Papers*, 21 (1982), 9–14.

Brown, Peter, "Sorcery, demons and the rise of Christianity: From late Antiquity into the Middle Ages," in Mary Douglas, ed., *Witchcraft Confessions and Accusations* (London: Tavistock, 1970), 17–45; reprinted in P. A. Brown, *Religion and Society in the Age of St. Augustine* (London: Faber & Faber, 1972), 119–46.

Janowitz, Naomi, *Magic in the Roman World: Pagans, Jews and Christians* (New York: Routledge, 2001).

Jenkins, Claude, "Saint Augustine and magic," in E. Ashworthy Underwood, ed., *Science, Medicine and History: Essays on the Evolution of Scientific Thought and Medical Practice Written in Honour of Charles Singer*, vol. 1 (London: Oxford University Press, 1953), 131–40.

Kee, Howard Clark, *Medicine, Miracle and Magic in New Testament Times* (Cambridge University Press, 1986).

Martin, Dale B., *Inventing Superstition: From the Hippocratics to the Christians* (Cambridge, Mass.: Harvard University Press, 2004).

Meyer, Marvin, and Richard Smith, eds., *Ancient Christian Magic: Coptic Texts of Ritual Power* (San Francisco: HarperCollins, 1994).

Remus, Harold E., "'Magic or miracle': Some second-century instances," *Second Century*, 2 (1982), 127–56.

Pagan–Christian Conflict Over Miracle in the Second Century (Cambridge, Mass.: Philadelphia Patristic Foundation, 1983).

Schoedel, William R., and Malina, Bruce J., "Miracle or magic?," *Religious Studies Review*, 12 (1986), 31–9.

Stratton, Kimberly B., with Dayna S. Kalleres, eds., *Daughters of Hecate: Women and Magic in the Ancient World* (New York: Oxford University Press, 2014).

Thee, Francis C. R., *Julius Africanus and the Early Christian View of Magic* (Tübingen: Mohr, 1984).

Ward, John O., "Witchcraft and sorcery in the later Roman Empire and the early Middle Ages: An anthropological comment," *Prudentia*, 12 (1980), 93–108.

"Women, witchcraft and social patterning in the later Roman lawcodes," *Prudentia*, 13 (1981), 99–118.

Germanic and Celtic Magic

Pagan Survivals

Chaney, William A., "Paganism to Christianity in Anglo-Saxon England," *Harvard Theological Review*, 53 (1960), 197–217.

Crawford, Jane, "Evidences for witchcraft in Anglo-Saxon England," *Medium Aevum*, 32 (1963), 99–116.

McNeill, John T., and Gamer, Helena M., eds., *Medieval Handbooks of Penance* (New York: Columbia University Press, 1938).

Vogel, Cyrille, "Pratiques superstitieuses au debut du XIe siècle d'après le Corrector sive medicus de Burchard évêque de Worms (965–1025)," in *Études de civilisation médiévale (IXe–XIIe siècles): Mélanges offerts à Edmond-René Labande* (Poitiers: Centre d'études supérieures de civilisation médiévale, 1974), 751–61.

Norse Magic

Bayerschmidt, Carl F., "The element of the supernatural in the sagas of Icelanders," in Carl F. Bayerschmidt and Erik J. Friis, eds., *Scandinavian Studies: Festschrift for Henry Goddard Leach* (Seattle: University of Washington Press, 1965), 39–53.

Davidson, H. R. Ellis, "Hostile magic in the Icelandic sagas," in Venetia Newall, ed., *The Witch Figure* (London: Routledge, 1973), 20–41.

Elliott, Ralph W. V., *Runes: An Introduction* (Manchester University Press, 1959).

"Runes, yews, and magic," *Speculum*, 32 (1957), 250–61.

Hastrup, Kirsten, "Iceland: Sorcerers and paganism," in Bengt Ankarloo and Gustav Henningsen, eds., *Early Modern European Witchcraft: Centres and Peripheries* (Oxford: Clarendon, 1990), 383–401.

Jarausch, Konrad, "Der Zauber in den Isländersagas," *Zeitschrift für Volkskunde*, n.s., 1 (1929–30), 237–68.

Lid, Nils, "The paganism of the Norsemen," in W. Edson Richmond, ed., *Studies in Folklore* (Bloomington: Indiana University Press, 1957), 230–51.

Meylan, Nicolas, *Magic and Kingship in Medieval Iceland: The Construction of a Discourse of Political Resistance* (Turnhout: Brepols, 2014).

Mitchell, Stephen A., *Witchcraft and Magic in the Nordic Middle Ages* (Philadelphia: University of Pennsylvania Press, 2010).

Morris, Katherine, *Sorceress or Witch? The Image of Gender in Medieval Iceland and Northern Europe* (Lanham, Md.: University Press of America, 1991).

Scott, F. S., "The woman who knows: Female characters of *Eyrbyggja Saga*," *Parergon*, n.s., 3 (1985), 73–91.

Simpson, Jacqueline, "Olaf Tryggvason versus the powers of darkness," in Venetia Newall, ed., *The Witch Figure* (London: Routledge, 1973), 165–87.

Celtic Magic

Borsje, Jacqueline, "Celtic spells and counterspells," in Katja Ritari and Alexandra Bergholm, eds., *Understanding Celtic Religion: Revisiting the Pagan Past* (Cardiff: University of Wales Press, 2015), 9–50.

Ford, Patrick K., *Celtic Folklore and Christianity* (Santa Barbara: McNally & Loftin; Los Angeles: Center for the Study of Comparative Folklore & Mythology, 1983).

Gantz, Jeffrey, trans., *Early Irish Myths and Sagas* (Harmondsworth: Penguin, 1981).

Henderson, George, *Survivals in Belief among the Celts* (Glasgow: Maclehose, 1911).

Loomis, C. Grant, *White Magic: An Introduction to the Folklore of Christian Legend* (Cambridge, Mass.: Mediaeval Academy of America, 1948).

Loomis, Roger Sherman, *Celtic Myth and Arthurian Romance* (New York: Columbia University Press, 1926).

MacCana, Proinsias, *Celtic Mythology* (London: Hamlyn, 1970).

Plummer, Charles, ed. and trans., *Bethada náem nÉrenn: Lives of Irish Saints* (Oxford: Clarendon, 1922).

Tuomi, Ilona, John Carey, Barbara Hillers, and Ciarán Ó. Gealbháin, eds., *Charms, Charmers and Charming in Ireland, from the Medieval to the Modern* (Cardiff: University of Wales Press, 2019).

The Common Tradition of Magic

Medical and Protective Magic

Albert the Great, *Man and the Beasts: De animalibus* (Books 22–26), trans. James J. Scanlan (Binghamton, New York: Medieval and Renaissance Texts and Studies, 1987).

Barb, A. A., "Birds and medical magic," *Journal of the Warburg and Courtauld Institutes*, 13 (1950), 316–22.

Bonser, Wilfred, *The Medical Background of Anglo-Saxon England: A Study in History, Psychology, and Folklore* (London: Wellcome Historical Medical Library, 1963).

Bozóky, Edina, *Charmes et prières apotropaïques* (Turnhout: Brepols, 2003).

Brévart, Francis B., "Between medicine, magic, and religion: Wonder drugs in German medico-pharmaceutical treatises of the thirteenth to sixteenth centuries," *Speculum*, 83 (2008), 1–57.

Browe, Peter, "Die Eucharistie als Zaubermittel im Mittelalter," *Archiv für Kulturgeschichte*, 20 (1930), 134–54.

Bühler, Curt F., "Prayers and charms in certain Middle English scrolls," *Speculum*, 39 (1964), 270–8.

Cameron, M. L., "Bald's *Leechbook*: Its sources and their use in its compilation," *Anglo-Saxon England*, 12 (1983), 153–82.

Dawson, Warren R., ed. and trans., *A Leechbook or Collection of Medical Recipes of the Fifteenth Century* (London: Macmillan, 1934).

Geier, Manfred, "Die magische Kraft der Poesie: Zur Geschichte, Struktur und Funktion des Zauberspruchs," *Deutsche Vierteljahrsschrift für Literaturwissenschaft und Geistesgeschichte*, 56 (1982), 359–85.

Grendon, Felix, "The Anglo-Saxon charms," *Journal of American Folk-Lore*, 22 (1909), 105–237.

Hälsig, Friedrich, *Der Zauberspruch bei den Germanen bis um die Mitte des XVI. Jahrhunderts* (Leipzig: Seele, 1910).

Hampp, Irmgard, *Beschwörung, Segen, Gebet: Untersuchungen zum Zauberspruch aus dem Bereich der Volksheilkunde* (Stuttgart: Silberburg, 1961).

Hunt, Tony, *Popular Medicine in Thirteenth-Century England: Introduction and Texts* (Woodbridge: Brewer, 1990).

Jolly, Karen, "Prayers from the field: Practical protection and demonic defense in Anglo-Saxon England," *Traditio*, 61(2006), 95–147.

Jolly, Karen Louise, "Anglo-Saxon charms in the context of a Christian world view," *Journal of Medieval History*, 11 (1985), 279–93.

Jones, Peter Murray, "Amulets: Prescriptions and surviving objects from late medieval England," *Beyond Pilgrim Souvenirs and Secular Badges: Essays in Honour of Brian Spencer*, ed. Sarah Blick (Oxford: Oxbow, 2007), 92–107.

Jones, Peter Murray, and Lea T. Olsan, "Middleham Jewel: Ritual, power, and devotion," *Viator*, 31 (2000), 249–90.

Kapaló, James Alexander, *The Power of Words: Studies on Charms and Charming in Europe* (Budapest: Central European University Press, 2013).

Klapper, Joseph, "Das Gebet im Zauberglauben des Mittelalters," *Mitteilungen der schlesischen Gesellschaft für Volkskunde*, 18 (1907), 5–41.

MacKinney, Loren C., "An unpublished treatise on medicine and magic from the age of Charlemagne," *Speculum*, 18 (1943), 494–6.

Olsan, Lea T., "Charms and prayers in medieval medical theory and practice," *Social History of Medicine*, 16 (2003), 343–66.

Pinto, Lucille B., "Medical science and superstition: A report on a unique medical scroll of the eleventh–twelfth century," *Manuscripta*, 17 (1973), 12–21.

Poulin, Jean-Claude, "Entre magie et religion: Recherches sur les utilisations marginales de l'écrit dans la culture populaire du haut Moyen-Age," in Pierre Boglioni, ed., *La culture populaire au Moyen-Age* (Montreal: Editions Universitaires, 1979), 121–43.

Radimersky, George, "Magic in the works of Hildegard von Bingen," *Monatshefte für deutschen Unterricht*, 49 (1957), 353–60.

Remly, Lynn L., "Magic, myth, and medicine: The veterinary art in the Middle Ages (9th–15th centuries)," in Guy R. Mermier and Edelgard E. DuBrock, eds., *Fifteenth-Century Studies*, 2 (1979), 203–9.

Sheldon, Sue Eastman, "The eagle: Bird of magic and medicine in a Middle English translation of the *Kyranides*," *Tulane Studies in English*, 22 (1977), 1–20.

Skemer, Don C., *Binding Worlds: Textual Amulets in the Middle Ages* (University Park: Pennsylvania State University Press, 2006).

Stannard, Jerry, "Greco-Roman materia medica in medieval Germany," *Bulletin of the History of Medicine*, 46 (1972),455–68.

Herbs and Herbalism in the Middle Ages and Renaissance, ed. Katherine E. Stannard and Richard Kay (Aldershot: Variorum, 1999).

"Magiferous plants and magic in medieval medical botany," *Maryland Historian*, 8(2) (1977), 33–46.

"Marcellus of Bordeaux and the beginning of medieval materia medica," *Pharmacy in History*, 15 (1973), 47–53.

Storms, G[odfrid], ed., *Anglo-Saxon Magic* (The Hague: Nijhoff, 1948).

Stuart, H., "Utterance instructions in the Anglo-Saxon charms," *Parergon*, n.s., 3 (1985), 31–7.

Tomíček, David, "Magic and ritual in late-medieval and early-modern popular medicine," in Albrecht Classen, ed., *Magic and Magicians in the Middle Ages and the Early Modern Time: The Occult in Pre-Modern Sciences, Medicine, Literature, Religion, and Astrology* (Berlin: De Gruyter, 2017), 591–608.

Vaughan-Sterling, Judith A., "The Anglo-Saxon *Metrical Charms*: Poetry as ritual," *Journal of English and Germanic Philology*, 82 (1983), 186–200.

Sorcery

Blöcker, Monica, "Wetterzauber: Zu einem Glaubenskomplex des frühen Mittelalters," *Francia*, 9 (1981), 117–31.

Crawford, Jane, "Evidences for witchcraft in Anglo-Saxon England," *Medium Aevum*, 32 (1963), 99–116.

Forbes, Thomas Rogers, *The Midwife and the Witch* (New Haven: Yale University Press, 1966).

Kieckhefer, Richard, *European Witch Trials: Their Foundations in Popular and Learned Culture, 1300–1500* (London: Routledge, 1976).

Siller, Max, "Zauberspruch und Hexenprozess: Die Rolle des Zauberspruchs in den Zauber- und Hexenprozessen Tirols," in Werner M. Bauer et al., eds., *Tradition und Entwicklung: Festschrift Eugen Thurnher* (Innsbruck: Institut für Germanistik der Universitat Innsbruck, 1982), 127–54.

Tucker, Elizabeth, "Antecedents of contemporary witchcraft in the Middle Ages," *Journal of Popular Culture*, 14 (1980), 70–8.

Divination

Braekman, W. L., "Fortune-telling by the casting of dice: A Middle English poem and its background," *Studia Neophilologica*, 52 (1980), 3–29.

Braswell, L., "Popular lunar astrology in the late Middle Ages," *University of Ottawa Quarterly*, 48 (1978), 187–94.

John of Salisbury, *Frivolities of Courtiers and Footprints of Philosophers*, trans. Joseph B. Pike (Minneapolis: University of Minnesota Press; London: Oxford University Press, 1938). (A substantial portion of this book, i.9–ii.28, is essentially a catalogue and condemnation of divinatory practices.)

Matheson, Lister M., ed., *Popular and Practical Science of Medieval England* (East Lansing, Mich.: Colleagues, 1994). (Includes works on astrology, geomancy, and palmistry in Middle English.)

Metham, John, *The Works of John Metham*, ed. Hardin Craig (Early English Text Society, Original Ser., 132) (London: K. Paul, 1916). (Includes a collection of late medieval divinatory treatises in the English language.)

Owst, G. R., "*Sortilegium* in English homiletic literature of the fourteenth century," in J. Conway Davies, ed., *Studies Presented to Sir Hilary Jenkinson* (London: Oxford University Press, 1957).

Pack, Roger A., "A treatise on prognostications by Venancius of Moerbeke," *Archives d'Histoire Doctrinale et Littéraire du Moyen Âge*, 43 (1976), 311–22.

Schmitt, Wolfram, "Das Traumbuch des Hans Lobenzweig," *Archiv für Kulturgeschichte*, 48 (1966), 181–218.

Thorndike, Lynn, "Chiromancy in medieval Latin manuscripts," *Speculum*, 40 (1965), 674–706.

Magical Trickery

Roy, Bruno, "The household encyclopedia as magic kit: Medieval popular interest in pranks and illusions," *Journal of Popular Culture*, 14 (1980), 60–9.

Volkmann, Kurt, *The Oldest Deception: Cups and Balls in the 15th and 16th Centuries*, trans. Barrows Mussey (Minneapolis: Jones, 1956).

Magic in Courtly Culture

Magicians at Court

Hartung, Wolfgang, *Die Spielleute: Eine Randgruppe in der Gesellschaft des Mittelalters* (Wiesbaden: Steiner, 1982), especially 9–20.

Kyeser, Conrad, *Bellifortis*, ed. and trans. Götz Quarg (Düsseldorf: VDI, 1967).

Lindsay, Jack, *The Troubadours and their World of the Twelfth and Thirteenth Centuries* (London: Muller, 1986).

Loomis, Laura H., "Secular dramatics in the royal palace, Paris, 1378, 1389, and Chaucer's 'tregetoures'," *Speculum*, 33 (1958), 242–55.

Ogilvy, J. D. A., "*Mimi, scurrae, histriones*: Entertainers of the early Middle Ages," *Speculum*, 38 (1963), 603–19.

Véronèse, Julien, "Contre la divination et la magie à la cour: Trois traités addressés à des grands aux XIVe et XVe siècles," in *I saperi nelle corti / Knowledge at the Courts* (Micrologus, 16) (2008), 405–31.

Magical Gems and Devices

Ball, Sydney H., "Luminous gems, mythical and real," *Scientific Monthly*, 47 (1938), 496–505.

Eamon, W., "Technology as magic in the late Middle Ages and Renaissance," *Janus*, 70 (1983), 171–212.

Evans, Joan, *Magic Jewels of the Middle Ages and Renaissance* (Oxford: Clarendon, 1922).

Kitson, Peter, "Lapidary traditions in Anglo-Saxon England," *Anglo-Saxon England*, 12 (1983), 73–123.

Marbode of Rennes, *De lapidibus*, ed. John M. Riddle, trans. C. W. King (Wiesbaden: Steiner, 1977).

Owings, Marvin Alpheus, "The supernatural," in Owings, *The Arts in the Middle English Romances* (New York: Bookman, 1952), 138–64.

Thorndike, Lynn, "De lapidibus," *Ambix*, 8 (1960), 6–23.

Truitt, E. R., *Medieval Robots: Mechanism, Magic, Nature, and Art* (Philadelphia: University of Pennsylvania Press, 2015).

Magic in Courtly Literature

Bachman, W. Bryant, Jr., "'To maken illusion': The philosophy of magic and the magic of philosophy in The Franklin's Tale," *Chaucer Review*, 12 (1977), 55–67.

Classen, Albrecht, ed., *Magic and Magicians in the Middle Ages and the Early Modern Time: The Occult in Pre-Modern Sciences, Medicine, Literature, Religion, and Astrology* (Berlin: De Gruyter, 2017), 291–74, 489–564.

Comparetti, Domenico, *Virgil in the Middle Ages*, trans. E. F. M. Benecke (London: Sonnenschein, 1895).

Cooper, Helen, "Magic that does not work," *Medievalia et Humanistica*, n.s., 7 (1976), 131–46.

Corry, Jennifer M., *Perceptions of Magic in Medieval Spanish Literature* (Bethlehem, Penn.: Lehigh University Press, 2005).

Doggett, Laine E., *Love Cures: Healing and Love Magic in Old French Romance* (University Park: Pennsylvania State University Press, 2009).

Green, R. B., "The fusion of magic and realism in two lays of Marie de France," *Neophilologus*, 59 (1975), 324–36.

Harf-Lancner, Laurence, *Les fées au Moyen Âge: Morgane et Melusine: La naissance des fées* (Geneva: Slatkine, 1984).

Hasty, Will, "On magic and its significance in the German Arthurian romances," *Nu lôn' ich iu der gâbe: Festschrift for Francis G. Gentry*, ed. Ersnt Ralf Hintz (Göppinger Arbeiten zur Germanistik, 693) (Göppingen: Kümmerle Verlag, 2003), 119–131.

Heng, Geraldine, *Empire of Magic: Medieval Romance and the Politics of Cultural Fantasy* (New York: Columbia University Press, 2003).

Goodrich, Peter, ed., *The Romance of Merlin: An Anthology* (New York: Garland, 1990).

Kelly, Henry Ansgar, "Canon law and Chaucer on licit and illicit magic," in Ruth Mazo Karras, Joel Kaye, and E. Ann Matter, eds., *Law and the Illicit in Medieval Europe* (Philadelphia: University of Pennsylvania Press, 2008), 211–24.

Kretzenbacher, Leopold, *Teufelsbündner und Faustgestalten im Abendlande* (Klagenfurt: Verlag des Geschichtsvereines fur Karnten, 1968).

Luengo, Anthony E., "Magic and illusion in the Franklin's Tale," *Journal of English and Germanic Philology*, 77 (1978), 1–16.

McAlindon, "Magic, fate and providence in medieval narrative and 'Sir Gawain and the Green Knight'," *Review of English Studies*, n.s., 16 (1965), 121–39.

Mauritz, Hans-Dieter, *Der Ritter im magischen Reich: Marchenelemente in französischen Abenteuerromanen des 12. und 13. Jahrhunderts* (Bern: Lang, 1974).

Ménard, Philippe, "Chrétien de Troyes et le Merveilleux," *Europe*, 60 (1982), 53–60.

Osborn, Marijane, *Nine Medieval Romances of Magic* (Peterborough, Ont.: Broadview, 2010).

Rollo, David, *Glamorous Sorcery: Magic and Literacy in the High Middle Ages* (Minneapolis: University of Minnesota Press, 2000).

Sherwood, M., "Magic and mechanics in medieval fiction," *Studies in Philology*, 44 (1947), 567–92.

Spargo, John Webster, *Virgil the Necromancer: Studies in Virgilian Legends* (Cambridge, Mass.: Harvard University Press, 1934).

Sweeney, Michelle, *Magic in Medieval Romance: From Chrétien de Troyes to Geoffrey Chaucer* (Dublin: Four Courts, 2000).

Tobienne, François, Jr., *The Position of Magic in Selected Medieval Spanish Texts* (Cambridge: Cambridge Scholars Publishing, 2008).

Whitaker, Muriel, *Arthur's Kingdom of Adventure: The World of Malory's Morte Darthur* (Woodbridge: Boydell, 1984).

Wilson, Anne D., "The critic and the use of magic in narrative," *Yearbook of English Studies*, 22 (1992), 81–94.

Wood, Juliette, "Virgil and Taliesin: The concept of the magician in medieval folklore," *Folklore*, 94 (1983), 91–104.

Arabic Learning and the Occult Sciences

General

Bartlett, Robert, *The Natural and the Supernatural in the Middle Ages* (Cambridge University Press, 2008).

Boudet, Jean-Patrice, and Julien Véronèse, "Le secret dans le magie rituelle médiévale," *Micrologus*, 14 (2006), 101–50.

Burnett, Charles, *Arabic into Latin in the Middle Ages: The Translators and their Intellectual and Social Context* (Farnham: Ashgate, 2009).

Collins, David J., "Albertus, *Magnus* or *Magus*? Magic, natural philosophy, and religious reform in the late Middle Ages," *Renaissance Quarterly*, 63 (2010), 1–44.

Collins, David J., S.J., "Scholastics, stars, and magi: Albert the Great on Matthew 2," in David J. Collins, S.J., ed., *The Sacred and the Sinister: Studies in Medieval Religion and Magic* (University Park: Pennsylvania State University Press, 2019), 257–76.

Hansen, Bert, "The complementarity of science and magic before the Scientific Revolution," *American Scientist*, 74 (1986), 128–36.

Nicole Oresme and the Marvels of Nature (Toronto: Pontifical Institute, 1985).

"Science and magic," in David C. Lindberg, ed., *Science in the Middle Ages* (University of Chicago Press, 1978), 483–503.

Kaye, Joel, "Law, magic, and science: Constructing a border between licit and illicit knowledge in the writings of Nicole Oresme," in Ruth Mazo Karras, Joel Kaye, and E. Ann Matter, eds., *Law and the Illicit in Medieval Europe* (Philadelphia: University of Pennsylvania Press, 2008), 225–37.

Kibre, Pearl, *Studies in Medieval Science: Alchemy, Astrology, Mathematics and Medicine* (London: Hambledon, 1984).

Láng, Benedek, *Unlocked Books: Manuscripts of Learned Magic in the Medieval Libraries of Central Europe* (University Park: Pennsylvania State University Press, 2008).

McAllister, Joseph Bernard, *The Letter of Saint Thomas Aquinas de occultis operibus naturae ad quemdam militem ultramontanum* (Washington, DC: Catholic University of America Press, 1939).

Marrone, Steven P., *A History of Science, Magic and Belief: From Medieval to Early Modern Europe* (New York: Palgrave Macmillan, 2015).

"William of Auvergne on magic in natural philosophy and theology," in Jan A. Aertsen and Andreas Speer, eds., *Was ist Philosophie im Mittelalter?* (Berlin: de Gruyter, 1998), 741–8.

Molland, A. G., "Roger Bacon as magician," *Traditio*, 30 (1974), 445–60.

Pingree, David, "Learned magic in the time of Frederick II," *Micrologus*, 2 (Sciences at the Court of Frederick II) (1994), 39–56.

Shumaker, Wayne, *The Occult Sciences in the Renaissance: A Study in Intellectual Patterns* (Berkeley: University of California Press, 1972).

Thorndike, Lynn, "The Latin pseudo-Aristotle and medieval occult science," *Journal of English and Germanic Philology*, 21 (1922), 229–58.

The Place of Magic in the Intellectual History of Europe (New York: Columbia University Press, 1905).

Astrology and Astral Magic

Abū-Maʿšar, *The Abbreviation of the Introduction to Astrology, together with the Medieval Latin Translation of Adelard of Bath*, ed. and trans. Charles Burnett, Keiji Yamamoto, and Michio Yano (Leiden: Brill, 1994).

Adamson, Peter, *Al-Kindi* (New York: Oxford University Press, 2006).

Alfonso X el Sabio, *Astromagia*, ed. A. D'Agostino (Naples: Liguori, 1992).

Boudet, Jean-Patrice, *Entre science et nigromance: Astrologie, divination et magie dans l'occident médiéval, XIIᵉ–XVᵉ siècle* (Paris: Publications de la Sorbonne, 2006).

Lire dans le ciel: La bibliothèque de Simon de Phares, astrologue du XV siècle (Brussels: Centre d'étude des manuscrits, 1994).

Brown, J. Wood, *An Enquiry into the Life and Legend of Michael Scot* (Edinburgh: Douglas, 1897).

Burnett, Charles, *Magic and Divination in the Middle Ages: Texts and Techniques in the Islamic and Christian Worlds* (Aldershot: Variorum, 1996).

Carey, Hilary M., *Courting Disaster: Astrology at the English Court and University in the Later Middle Ages* (New York: St. Martin's Press, 1992).

Clark, Charles, "The zodiac man in medieval medical astrology," *Journal of the Rocky Mountain Medieval and Renaissance Association*, 3 (1982), 13–38.

Coopland, G. W., *Nicole Oresme and the Astrologers: A Study of His Livre de Divinacions* (Cambridge, Mass.: Harvard University Press, 1952).

Curry, Patrick, ed., *Astrology, Science and Society: Historical Essays* (Woodbridge: Boydell, 1987).

d'Alverny, Marie-Thérèse, "Astrologues et théologiens au XIIe siècle," in *Mélanges offerts à M.-D. Chenu* (Paris: J. Vrin, 1967), 31–50.

Garin, Eugenio, *Astrology in the Renaissance: The Zodiac of Life*, trans. Carolyn Jackson and June Allen (London: Routledge, 1983).

Goldstein, Bernard R., and David Pingree, eds. and trans., *Levi ben Gerson's Prognostication for the Conjunction of 1345* (Philadelphia: American Philosophical Society, 1990).

Grant, Edward, *Planets, Stars, and Orbs: The Medieval Cosmos, 1200–1687* (Cambridge University Press, 1994).

Gregory, Tullio, "La nouvelle idée de nature et de savoir scientifique au XIIe siècle," in John Emery Murdoch and Edith Dudley Sylla, eds., *The Cultural Context of Medieval Learning: Proceedings of the First International Colloquium on Philosophy, Science, and Theology in the Middle Ages – September 1973* (Dordrecht: Reidel, 1975), 193–218.

Grévin, Benoît, and Julien Véronèse, "Les 'caractères' magiques au Moyen Âge (XIIe–XIVe siècle)," *Bibliothèque de l'école des Chartes*, 162(2) (2004), 305–379.

Grimm, Florence M., *Astrological Lore in Chaucer* (Lincoln: University of Nebraska, 1919).

Kennedy, Edward S., *Astronomy and Astrology in the Medieval Islamic World* (Aldershot and Brookfield, Vt.: Ashgate, 1998).

Mentgen, Gerd, *Astrologie und Öffentlichkeit im Mittelalter* (Stuttgart: Hiersemann, 2005).

Page, Sophie, *Astrology in Medieval Manuscripts* (University of Toronto Press, 2002).

Ryan, Michael A., *A Kingdom of Stargazers: Astrology and Authority in the Late Medieval Crown of Aragon* (Ithaca, New York: Cornell University Press, 2011).

Schwartz, Dov, *Studies on Astral Magic in Medieval Jewish Thought*, trans. David Louvish and Batya Stein (Leiden: Brill-Styx, 2004).

Shank, Michael H., "Academic consulting in fifteenth-century Vienna: The case of astrology," in Edith Sylla and Michael McVaugh, eds., *Texts and Contexts in Ancient and Medieval Science* (Leiden: Brill, 1997), 245–70.

Smoller, Laura Ackerman, *History, Prophecy, and the Stars: The Christian Astrology of Pierre d'Ailly, 1350–1420* (Princeton University Press, 1994).

Tester, S. J., *A History of Western Astrology* (Woodbridge: Boydell, 1987).

Thorndike, Lynn, *Michael Scot* (London: Nelson, 1965).

"Traditional medieval tracts concerning engraved astrological images," in *Mélanges Auguste Pelzer: Études d'histoire littéraire et doctrinale de la scolastique médiévale offertes à Monseigneur Auguste Pelzer* (Louvain: Bibliothèque de l'Université, 1947), 217–73.

Travaglia, Pinella, *Causality and Intentionality: The Doctrine of Rays in Al-Kindi* (Micrologus Library, 3) (Florence: Galluzzo, 1999).

Van der Lugt, M., "'Abominable mixtures': The *Liber vaccae* in the medieval West, or the dangers and attractions of natural magic," *Traditio*, 64 (2009), 229–77.

Wedel, Theodore Otto, *The Mediaeval Attitude Toward Astrology, Particularly in England* (New Haven: Yale University Press, 1920).

Weill-Parot, Nicolas, "Contriving classical references for talismanic magic in the Middle Ages and the early Renaissance," in Charles Burnett and W. F. Ryan, eds., *Magic and the Classical Tradition* (London: Warburg Institute; Turin: Nino Aragno, 2006), 163–76.

Les "images astrologiques" au moyen âge et à la renaissance: Spéculations intellectuelles et pratiques magiques (XIIe–XVe siècle) (Paris: Champion, 2002).

Wood, Chauncey, *Chaucer and the Country of the Stars: Poetic Uses of Astrological Imagery* (Princeton University Press, 1970).

Zambelli, Paola, "Albert le Grand et l'astrologie," *Recherches de Theologie Ancienne et Médiévale*, 49 (1982), 141–58.

Astrology and Magic from the Medieval Latin and Islamic World to Renaissance Europe: Theories and Approaches (Farnham: Ashgate, 2012).

Alchemy

Albertus Magnus, *Book of Minerals*, trans. Dorothy Wyckoff (Oxford: Clarendon, 1967).

Libellus de alchimia, Ascribed to Albertus Magnus, trans. Virginia Heines (Berkeley: University of California Press, 1958).

Constantine of Pisa, *The Book of the Secrets of Alchemy*, ed. and trans. Barbara Obrist (Leiden: Brill, 1990).

DeVun, Leah, *Prophecy, Alchemy, and the End of Time: John of Rupescissa in the Late Middle Ages* (New York: Columbia University Press, 2009).

Eis, Gerhard, "Von der Rede und dem Schweigen der Alchemisten," *Deutsche Vierteljahrsschrift für Literaturwissenschaft und Geistesgeschichte*, 25 (1951), 415–35.

Ganzenmüller, W., *Die Alchemie im Mittelalter* (Paderborn: Bonifacius, 1938).

Holmyard, E. J., *Alchemy* (Harmondsworth: Penguin, 1957).

Linden, Stanton J., ed., *The Alchemy Reader: From Hermes Trismegistus to Isaac Newton* (Cambridge University Press, 2005).

Multhauf, Robert P., "John of Rupescissa and the origin of medical chemistry," *Isis*, 45 (1954), 359–67.

Newman, W., "An introduction to alchemical apparatus in the late Middle Ages," *Technologia*, 6 (1983), 82–92.

Newman, William R., "An overview of Roger Bacon's alchemy," in Jeremiah Hackett, ed., *Roger Bacon and the Sciences: Commemorative Essays* (Leiden: Brill, 1997), 317–36.

ed. and trans., *The "Summa perfectionis" of Pseudo-Geber: A Critical Edition, Translation and Study* (Leiden: Brill, 1991).

Norton, Thomas, *The Ordinall of Alchimy by Thomas Norton of Bristoll, Being a facsimile reproduction from Theatrum chemicum britannicum* (London: Arnold, 1928).

Nummedal, Tara, *Alchemy and Authority in the Holy Roman Empire* (University of Chicago Press, 2007).

Obrist, Barbara, *Les débuts de l'imagerie alchimique (XIVe–XVe siècles)* (Paris: Le Sycamore, 1982).

Partington, J. R., "Albertus Magnus on alchemy," *Ambix*, 1 (1937), 3–20.

"Trithemius and alchemy," *Ambix*, 2 (1938), 53–9.

Plessner, M., "The place of the *Turba philosophorum* in the development of alchemy," *Isis*, 45 (1954), 331–8.

Principe, Lawrence M., *The Secrets of Alchemy* (University of Chicago Press, 2013).

Roberts, Gareth, *The Mirror of Alchemy: Alchemical Ideas and Images in Manuscripts and Books from Antiquity to the Seventeenth Century* (University of Toronto Press, 1994).

Waite, A. E., trans., *The Turba philosophorum or Assembly of the Sages, Called also the Book of Truth in the Art and the Third Pythagorical Synod: An Ancient Alchemical Treatise* (London: Redway, 1896; repr. New York: Samuel Weiser, 1976).

Books of Secrets

[pseudo-]Albertus Magnus, *The Book of Secrets of Albertus Magnus: Of the Virtues of Herbs, Stones and Certain Beasts*, ed. Michael R. Best and Frank H. Brightman (Oxford: Clarendon, 1973).

Eamonn, William, "Books of secrets in medieval and early modern science," *Sudhoffs Archiv*, 69 (1985), 26–49.

Manzalaoui, M., ed., "The pseudo-Aristotelian Kitab Sirr al-Asrar: Facts and problems," *Oriens*, 23(4) (1974), 147–257.

Secretum secretorum: Nine English Versions (Early English Text Society, Original Ser., 276) (Oxford University Press, 1977).

Ryan, William F., and Schmitt, Charles B., eds., *Pseudo-Aristotle, The Secret of Secrets: Sources and Influences* (London: Warburg Institute, 1982).

Schmitt, Wolfram, "Zur Literatur der Geheimwissenschaften im späten Mittelalter," in Gundulf Keil and Peter Assion, eds., *Fachprosaforschung: Acht Vorträge zur mittelalterlichen Artesliteratur* (Berlin: Schmidt, 1974), 167–82.

Williams, Steven J., *The Secret of Secrets: The Scholarly Career of a Pseudo-Aristotelian Text in the Latin Middle Ages* (Ann Arbor: University of Michigan Press, 2003).

The Renaissance Magus

Allen, Michael J. B., "Ficino's magical mousing cat: Knowing when to pounce," in Fabrizio Meroi and Elisabetta Scapparone, eds., *La magia nell'Europa moderna: Tra antica sapienza e filosofia naturale* (Florence: Olschki, 2007), 53–61.

Arnold, Klaus, *Johannes Trithemius (1462–1516)* (Würzburg: Schöningh, 1971).

Borchardt, Frank L., "The *magus* as Renaissance man," *Sixteenth-Century Journal*, 21 (1990), 57–76.

Brann, Noel L., *The Abbot Trithemius (1462–1516): The Renaissance of Monastic Humanism* (Leiden: Brill, 1981).

Copenhaver, Brian P., "Astrology and magic," in Charles B. Schmitt et al., eds., *The Cambridge History of Renaissance Philosophy* (Cambridge University Press, 1988), 264–300.

"Scholastic philosophy and Renaissance magic in the *De vita* of Marsilio Ficino," *Renaissance Quarterly*, 37 (1984), 523–54.

Couliano, Ioan P., *Eros and Magic in the Renaissance*, trans. Margaret Cook (University of Chicago Press, 1987).

Ficino, Marsilio, *Three Books on Life: A Critical Edition and Translation with Introduction and Notes*, ed. and trans. Carol V. Kaske and John R. Clark (Binghamton, New York: Medieval and Renaissance Texts and Studies, 1988).

Kieckhefer, Richard, "Did magic have a Renaissance? An historiographic question revisited," in Charles Burnett and W. F. Ryan, eds., *Magic and the Classical Tradition* (London: Warburg Institute; Turin: Nino Aragno, 2006), 199–212.

"Jacques Lefèvre d'Étaples and the conception of natural magic," in Fabrizio Meroi and Elisabetta Scapparone, eds., *La magia nell'Europa moderna: Tra antica sapienza e filosofia naturale* (Florence: Olschki, 2007), 63–77.

Levack, Brian P., ed., *Witchcraft, Magic and Demonology*, vol. 11: *Renaissance Magic* (Hamden, Conn.: Garland, 1992).

Rabin, Sheila J., "Pico on magic and astrology," *Pico della Mirandola: New Essays*, ed. M. V. Dougherty (Cambridge University Press, 2008), 152–78.

Shumaker, Wayne, "Johannes Trithemius and cryptography," in Shumaker, *Renaissance Curiosa* (Binghamton, New York: Center for Medieval and Early Renaissance Studies, 1982), 91–131.

Vickers, Brian, ed., *Occult and Scientific Mentalities in the Renaissance* (New York: Cambridge University Press, 1986).

Voss, Angela, "Marsilio Ficino, the second Orpheus," *Music as Medicine: The History of Music Therapy Since Antiquity*, ed. Peregrine Horden (Aldershot: Ashgate, 2000), 154–72.

Walker, D. P., *Spiritual and Demonic Magic, from Ficino to Campanella* (London: Warburg Institute, 1958; repr. University Park: Pennsylvania State University Press, 2000).

Yates, Frances A., *Giordano Bruno and the Hermetic Tradition* (London: Routledge; University of Chicago Press, 1964). (Chs. 1–6 deal with fifteenth-century subjects.)

Zika, Charles, "Reuchlin's *De verbo mirifico* and the magic debate of the late fifteenth century," *Journal of the Warburg and Courtauld Institutes*, 39 (1976), 104–38.

Invocation and Conjuration of Angels

Bresc, Henri, and Benoît Grévin, eds., "Les anges et la magie au Moyen Âge," *Mélanges de l'école française de Rome. Moyen Âge*, 114(1) (2002), 589–615.

Busch, Peter, "Solomon as a true exorcist: The Testament of Solomon in its cultural setting," in Joseph Verheyden, ed., *The Figure of Solomon in Jewish, Christian and Islamic Tradition* (Leiden: Brill, 2013), 183–96.

Fanger, Claire, ed., *Conjuring Spirits: Texts and Traditions of Medieval Ritual Magic* (Stroud: Sutton; University Park: Pennsylvania State University Press, 1998).

  Invoking Angels: Theurgic Ideas and Practices, Thirteenth to Sixteenth Centuries (University Park: Pennsylvania State University Press, 2012).

  Rewriting Magic: An Exegesis of the Visionary Autobiography of a Fourteenth-Century Monk (University Park: Pennsylvania State University Press, 2015).

Harari, Yuval, *The Sword of Moses: A Critical Edition and Study* (Jerusalem: Akademon, 1998).

Honorius, *Liber iuratus Honorii: A Critical Edition of the Latin Version of the Sworn Book of Honorius*, ed. Gösta Hedegård (Stockholm: Almqvist & Wiksell, 2002).

Johnston, Sarah Iles, "The *Testament of Solomon* from late antiquity to the Renaissance," in Jan N. Bremmer and Jan R. Veenstra, eds., *The Metamorphosis of Magic from Late Antiquity to the Early Modern Period* (Leuven: Peeters, 2002), 35–49.

Keck, D., *Angels and Angelology in the Middle Ages* (New York and Oxford: Oxford University Press, 1998).

Kieckhefer, Richard, "Angel magic and the cult of angels in the later Middle Ages," in Louise Nyholm Kallestrup and Raisa Maria Toivo, eds., *Contesting Orthodoxy in Medieval and Early Modern Europe: Heresy, Magic and Witchcraft* (New York: Palgrave, 2017), 71–110.

Láng, Benedek, "The art of memory and magic (the *ars memorativa* and the *ars notoria*)," in Rafel Wójcik, ed., *Culture of Memory in East Central Europe in the Late Middle Ages and the Early Modern Period* (Poznán: Biblioteka Uniwersytecka, 2008), 87–93.

Lesses, Rebecca Mary, *Ritual Practices to Gain Power: Angels, Incantations, and Revelation in Early Jewish Mysticism* (Harrisburg, Pa.: Trinity Press International, 1998).

Schäfer, Peter, "Jewish magic literature in Late Antiquity and Early Middle Ages," *Journal of Jewish Studies*, 41 (1990), 75–91.

Schwarz, Sarah L., "Reconsidering the Testament of Solomon," *Journal for the Study of the Pseudepigrapha*, 16 (2007), 203–37.

Swartz, Michael D., *Scholastic Magic: Ritual and Revelation in Early Jewish Mysticism* (Princeton University Press, 1996).

Veenstra, Jan R., "The Holy Almandal: Angels and the intellectual aims of magic," in Jan N. Bremmer and Jan R. Veenstra, eds., *The Metamorphosis of Magic from Late Antiquity to the Early Modern Period* (Leuven: Peeters, 2002), 189–229.

Véronèse, Julien, *L'Almandal et l'Almadel latins au Moyen Âge: Introduction et édition critique* (Florence: SISMEL, 2012).

L'Ars notoria au Moyen Âge: Introduction et édition critique (Florence: Sismel, 2007).

Conjuration of Demons

Boureau, Alain, *Satan the Heretic: The Birth of Demonology in the Medieval West*, trans. Teresa Lavender Fagan (University of Chicago Press, 2006).

Chave-Mahir, Florence, and Julien Véronèse, *Rituel d'exorcisme ou manuel de magie? Le manuscrit Clm 10085 de la Bayerische Staatsbibliothek de Munich (Début du XVᵉ siècle)* (Florence: Sismel / Edizioni del Galluzzo, 2015).

d'Alverny, Marie-Thérése, "Survivance de la magie antique," in Paul Wilpert, ed., *Antike und Orient im Mittelalter: Vorträge der Kölner Mediaevistentagungen 1956–1959* (Berlin: de Gruyter, 1962), 154–78.

Davies, Owen, *Grimoires: A History of Magic Books* (Oxford University Press, 2009).

Elliott, Dyan, "On angelic disembodiment and the incredible purity of demons," in Elliott, *Fallen Bodies: Pollution, Sexuality, and Demonology in the Middle Ages* (Philadelphia: University of Pennsylvania Press, 1999), 127–56.

Ibibarren, Isabel, "From black magic to heresy: A doctrinal leap in the pontificate of John XXII," *Church History*, 76 (2007), 32–60.

Kieckhefer, Richard, *Forbidden Rites: A Necromancer's Manual of the Fifteenth Century* (Stroud: Sutton, 1997; University Park: Pennsylvania State University Press, 1998).

"The holy and the unholy: Sainthood, witchcraft, and magic in late medieval Europe," *Journal of Medieval and Renaissance Studies*, 24 (1994), 355–85; and in Scott L. Waugh and Peter D. Diehl, eds., *Christendom and its Discontents: Exclusion, Persecution, and Rebellion, 1000–1500* (Cambridge University Press, 1996), 310–37.

"The necromancer as mountebank: Comic elements in a late medieval tragedy," in Richard Raiswell and Peter Dendle, eds., *The Devil in Society in Premodern Europe* (Toronto: Centre for Reformation and Renaissance Studies, 2012), 381–408.

Láng, Benedek, "The criminalization of possessing necromantic books in fifteenth-century Krakow," in Thomas Wünsch, ed., *Religion und Magie in Ostmitteleuropa: Spielräume theologischer Normierungsprozesse in Spätmittelalter und Früher Neuzeit* (Münster: Lit Verlag, 2007), 257–71.

Manitius, Karl, "Magie und Rhetorik bei Anselm von Besate," *Deutsches Archiv für Erforschung des Mittelalters*, 12 (1956), 52–72.

Marxreiter, Benedikt, ed., *Bern von Reichenau, "De nigromantia seu divinatione daemonum contemnenda": Edition und Untersuchung* (Wiesbaden: Harrassowitz, 2016).

Page, Sophie, "A late medieval demonic invasion of the heavens," in David J. Collins, S.J., ed., *The Sacred and the Sinister: Studies in Medieval Religion and Magic* (University Park: Pennsylvania State University Press, 2019), 235–56.

Rawcliffe, Carole, "The inventory of a fifteenth-century necromancer," *The Ricardian: Journal of the Richard III Society*, 13 (2003), 384–97.

Ruys, Juanita Feros, *Demons in the Middle Ages* (Kalamazoo, Mich.: ARC Humanities Press, 2017).

Thorndike, Lynn, "Imagination and magic: Force of imagination on the human body and of magic on the human mind," in *Mélanges Eugène Tisserant*, 7 (Vatican City: Biblioteca Vaticana, 1964), 353–8.

Waite, Arthur Edward, *The Book of Black Magic and of Pacts, Including the Rites and Mysteries of Goëtic Theurgy, Sorcery, and Infernal Necromancy* (London: Redway, 1898).

Prohibition, Condemnation, and Prosecution

General

Kieckhefer, Richard, *Hazards of the Dark Arts: Advice for Medieval Princes on Witchcraft and Magic* (Magic in History Sourcebooks) (University Park: Pennsylvania State University Press, 2017).

"Magic and its hazards in the late medieval West," in Brian P. Levack, ed., *The Oxford Handbook of Witchcraft in Early Modern Europe and Colonial America* (Oxford University Press, 2013), 13–31.

Owst, G. R., "*Sortilegium* in English homiletic literature of the fourteenth century," in J. Conway Davies, ed., *Studies Presented to Sir Hilary Jenkinson* (London: Oxford University Press, 1957), 272–303.

Peters, Edward, *The Magician, the Witch, and the Law* (Philadelphia: University of Pennsylvania Press, 1978).

Superstition

Bailey, Michael D., "The disenchantment of magic: Spells, charms and superstition in early European witchcraft literature," *American Historical Review*, 111 (2006), 383–404.

Fearful Spirits, Reasoned Follies: The Boundaries of Superstition in Late Medieval Europe (Ithaca, New York: Cornell University Press, 2013).

"A late-medieval crisis of superstition?," *Speculum*, 84 (2009), 633–61.

"Reformers on sorcery and superstition," in James D. Mixson, ed., *A Companion to Observant Reform in the Late Middle Ages and Beyond* (Leiden: Brill, 2015), 230–54.

"Witchcraft, superstition, and astrology in the late Middle Ages," in Martine Ostorero, Georg Modestin, and Kathrin Utz Tremp, eds., *Chasses aux sorcières et démonologie: Entre discours et pratiques (XIVe–XVIIe siècles)* (Florence: Sismel, 2010), 349–66.

Bracha, Krzysztof, "Magie und Aberglaubenskritik in den Predigten des Spätmittelalters in Polen," in Thomas Wünsch, ed., *Religion und Magie in Ostmitteleuropa: Spielräume theologischer Normierungsprozesse in Spätmittelalter und Früher Neuzeit* (Münster: Lit Verlag, 2007), 197–215.

Cameron, Euan, *Enchanted Europe: Superstition, Reason, and Religion 1250–1750* (New York: Oxford University Press, 2010).

Harmening, Dieter, *Superstitio: Überlieferungs- und theoriegeschichtliche Untersuchungen zur kirchlich-theologischen Aberglaubensliteratur des Mittelalters* (Berlin: Schmidt, 1979).

Kamerick, Kathleen, "Shaping superstition in late medieval England," *Magic, Ritual, and Witchcraft*, 3 (2008), 29–53.

Witchcraft and Witch Trials

Ankarloo, Bengt, and Stuart Clark, eds., *Witchcraft and Magic in Europe*, vols. 1–4: *Biblical and Pagan Societies, Ancient Greece and Rome, The Middle Ages, The Period of the Witch Craze* (Philadelphia: University of Pennsylvania Press, 1999–2002).

Bailey, Michael D., *Battling Demons: Witchcraft, Heresy, and Reform in the Late Middle Ages* (University Park: Pennsylvania State University Press, 2002).

Origins of the Witches' Sabbath (University Park: Pennsylvania State University Press, 2021).

"The feminization of magic and the emerging idea of the female witch in the late Middle Ages," *Essays in Medieval Studies*, 19 (2002), 120–34.

"From sorcery to witchcraft: Clerical conceptions of magic in the late Middle Ages," *Speculum*, 76 (2001), 960–90.

Barber, Malcolm, *The Trial of the Templars* (Cambridge University Press, 1978).

Ben-Yahuda, Nachman, "The European witch craze of the fourteenth to seventeenth centuries," *American Journal of Sociology*, 86 (1980), 1–31.

"Problems inherent in socio-historical approaches to the European witch craze," *Journal for the Scientific Study of Religion*, 20 (1981), 326–38.

Blöcker, Monica, "Frauenzauber – Zauberfrauen," *Zeitschrift für schweizerische Kirchengeschichte*, 76 (1982), 1–39.

"Ein Zauberprozess im Jahre 1028," *Schweizerische Zeitschrift für Geschichte*, 29 (1979), 533–55.

Broedel, Hans Peter, *The Malleus Maleficarum and the Construction of Witchcraft: Theology and Popular Belief* (Manchester University Press, 2003).

Brucker, Gene A., "Sorcery in early Renaissance Florence," *Studies in the Renaissance*, 10 (1963), 7–24.

Callan, Maeve Brigid, "The dawn of the Devil-worshipping witch" and "The churlish tramp from England: Richard de Ledrede tries the Alice Kyteler case," in Callan, *The Templars, the Witch, and the Wild Irish: Vengeance and Heresy in Medieval Ireland* (Ithaca, New York: Cornell University Press, 2015), 78–116, 117–48.

Camerlynck, Elaine, "Féminité et sorcellerie chez les théoriciens de la démonologie à la fin du Moyen Âge: Étude du *Malleus maleficatum*," *Renaissance and Reformation*, n.s., 7 (1983), 13–25.

Cohn, Norman, *Europe's Inner Demons: An Enquiry Inspired by the Great Witch-Hunt* (London: Chatto, 1975).

Conti, Fabrizio, *Witchcraft, Superstition, and Observant Franciscan Preachers: Pastoral Approach and Intellectual Debate in Renaissance Milan* (Turnhout: Brepols, 2015).

Ginzburg, Carlo, *Ecstasies: Deciphering the Witches' Sabbath*, trans. Raymond Rosenthal (New York: Pantheon, 1991).

"Présomptions sur le sabbat," *Annales*, 39 (1984), 341–54.

"The witches' sabbat: Popular cult or inquisitorial stereotype?," in Steven L. Kaplan, ed., *Understanding Popular Culture: Europe from the Middle Ages to the Nineteenth Century* (Berlin: Mouton, 1984), 39–51.

Golden, Richard M., *Encyclopedia of Witchcraft: The Western Tradition* (Santa Barbara: ABC-CLIO, 2006).

Hansen, Joseph, ed., *Quellen und Untersuchungen zur Geschichte des Hexenwahns und der Hexenverfolgung im Mittelalter* (Bonn: Georgi, 1901; repr. Hildesheim: Olms, 1963).

Zauberwahn, Inquisition und Hexenprozess im Mittelalter, und die Entstehung der grossen Hexenverfolgung (Munich: Oldenbourg, 1900; repr. Aalen: Scientia, 1964).

Harvey, Margaret, "Papal witchcraft: The charges against Benedict XIII," in Derek Baker, ed., *Sanctity and Secularity: The Church and the World*, Studies in Church History, 10 (Oxford: Blackwell, 1973), 109–16.

Hopkins, Charles Edward, *The Share of Thomas Aquinas in the Growth of the Witchcraft Delusion* (Philadelphia: University of Pennsylvania Press, 1940).

Hutton, Ronald, *The Witch: A History of Fear, from Ancient Times to the Present* (New Haven: Yale University Press, 2017).

Jones, William R., "Political uses of sorcery in medieval Europe," *The Historian*, 34 (1972), 670–87.

Kelly, H. A., "English kings and the fear of sorcery," *Mediaeval Studies*, 39 (1977), 206–38.

Kieckhefer, Richard, "Avenging the blood of children: Anxiety over child victims and the origins of the European witch trials," in Alberto Ferreiro, ed., *The Devil, Heresy and Witchcraft in the Middle Ages: Essays in Honor of Jeffrey B. Russell* (Leiden: Brill, 1998), 91–109.

European Witch Trials: Their Foundations in Popular and Learned Culture, 1300–1500 (London: Routledge & Kegan Paul; Berkeley: University of California Press, 1976; reissued London and New York: Routledge, 2011).

"The first wave of trials for diabolical witchcraft," in Brian P. Levack, ed., *The Oxford Handbook of Witchcraft in Early Modern Europe and Colonial America* (Oxford University Press, 2013), 159–78.

"Mythologies of witchcraft in the fifteenth century," *Magic, Ritual, and Witchcraft*, 1 (2006), 79–107.

"The role of secular authorities in the early witch-trials," in Johannes Dillinger, Jürgen Michael Schmidt, and Dieter R. Bauer, eds., *Hexenprozess und Staatsbildung / Witch-Trials and State-Building* (Bielefeld: Verlag für Regionalgeschichte, 2008), 25–39.

"Witchcraft, necromancy and sorcery as heresy," in Martine Ostorero, Georg Modestin, and Kathrin Utz Tremp, eds., *Chasses aux sorcières et démonologie: Entre discours et pratiques (XIVᵉ–XVIIᵉ siècles)* (Florence: Sismel, 2010), 133–53.

Kors, Alan Charles, and Edward Peters, eds., *Witchcraft in Europe, 400–1700: A Documentary History*, 2nd edn. (Philadelphia: University of Pennsylvania Press, 2001).

Lea, Henry Charles, *Materials Toward a History of Witchcraft*, ed. Arthur C. Howland (Philadelphia: University of Pennsylvania Press, 1939).

Levack, Brian P., *The Witch-Hunt in Early Modern Europe* (London: Longman, 1987).

Mackay, Christopher S., trans., *The Hammer of Witches: A Complete Translation of the "Malleus maleficarum"* (Cambridge University Press, 2009).

ed. and trans., *Malleus maleficarum* (Cambridge University Press, 2006).

Maier, Anneliese, "Eine Verfügung Johanns XXII. über die Zuständigkeit der Inquisition für Zaubereiprozesse," *Archivum Fratrum Praedicatorum*, 22 (1952), 226–46; reprinted in Anneliese Maier, *Ausgehendes Mittelalter: Gesammelte Aufsätze zur Geistesgeschichte des 14. Jahrhunderts* (Rome: Edizioni di Storia e Letteratura, 1967), 59–80.

Mitchell, Stephen, Neil Price, Ronald Hutton, et al., "Witchcraft and deep time – A debate at Harvard," *Antiquity*, 84 (2010), 864–79.

Murray, Alexander, "Medieval origins of the witch-hunt," *The Cambridge Quarterly*, 7 (1976), 63–74.

Nicholson, R. H., "The trial of Christ the sorcerer in the York Cycle," *Journal of Medieval and Renaissance Studies*, 16 (1986), 125–69.

Ostorero, Martine, "The concept of the witches' Sabbath in the Alpine region (1430–1440): Text and context," in Gábor Klaniczay and Éva Pócs, eds., with Eszter Csonka-Takács, *Witchcraft Mythologies and Persecutions* (Budapest and New York: Central European University Press, 2008), 19–22.

Le diable au sabbat: Littérature démonologique et sorcellerie (1440–1460) (Florence: Sismel, 2011).

Ostorero, Martine, and Julien Véronèse, eds., *Penser avec les démons: Démonologues et démonologies (XIIIᵉ–XVIIᵉ siècles)* (Florence: SISMEL, 2015).

Ostorero, Martine, Georg Modestin, and Kathrin Utz Tremp, eds., *Chasses aux sorcières et démonologie: Entre discours et pratiques (XIVᵉ–XVIIᵉ siècles)* (Florence: Sismel, 2010).

Ostorero, Martine, Agostino Paravicini Bagliani, and Kathrin Utz Tremp, eds., in collaboration with Catherine Chène, *L'imaginaire du sabbat: Édition critique des textes les plus anciens (1430 c.–1440 c.)* (Lausanne: Cahiers Lausannois d'Histoire Médiévales, 1999).

Peters, Edward, "The medieval Church and state on superstition, magic and witchcraft: From Augustine to the sixteenth century," in Bengt Ankarloo and Stuart Clark, eds., *Witchcraft and Magic in Europe: The Middle Ages* (Philadelphia: University of Pennsylvania Press, 2002), 173–245.

Quaife, G. R., *Godly Zeal and Furious Rage: The Witch in Early Modern Europe* (New York: St. Martin's Press, 1987).

Rob-Santer, Carmen, "Le *Malleus maleficarum* à la lumière de l'historiographie: Un *Kulturkampf?*," in Martine Ostorero and Etienne Anheim, eds., *Le diable en procès: Littérature démonologique et sorcellerie à la fin du Moyen Âge* (*Médiévales: Langue, textes, histoire*, 44) (Saint-Denis: Presses universitaires de Vincennes, 2003), 155–72.

Rose, Elliot, *A Razor for a Goat: A Discussion of Certain Problems in the History of Witchcraft and Diabolism* (University of Toronto Press, 1962).

Russell, Jeffrey Burton, *A History of Witchcraft: Sorcerers, Heretics, and Pagans* (London: Thames & Hudson, 1980).

    Witchcraft in the Middle Ages (Ithaca, New York: Cornell University Press, 1972).

Stephens, Walter, *Demon Lovers: Witchcraft, Sex, and the Crisis of Belief* (University of Chicago Press, 2001).

Stokes, Laura Patricia, *Demons of Urban Reform: Early European Witch Trials and Criminal Justice, 1430–1530* (New York: Palgrave Macmillan, 2011).

Thomas, Keith, *Religion and the Decline of Magic* (London: Weidenfeld & Nicolson, 1971).

Wright, Thomas, ed., *A Contemporary Narrative of the Proceedings against Dame Alice Kyteler, prosecuted for sorcery in 1324 by Richard de Ledrede, Bishop of Ossory* (London: Nichols, 1843).

Ziegeler, Wolfgang, *Möglichkeiten der Kritik am Hexen- und Zauberwesen im ausgehenden Mittelalter: Zeitgenössische Stimmen und ihre soziale Zugehörigkeit* (Cologne: Böhlau, 1973).

Index